IN YOUR FACE

IN YOUR FACE

The New Science of Human Attraction

David Perrett

palgrave
macmillan

© David Perrett 2010

First published 2010 by
PALGRAVE MACMILLAN

Palgrave Macmillan in the UK is an imprint of Macmillan Publishers Limited, registered in England, company number 785998, of Houndmills, Basingstoke, Hampshire RG21 6XS.

Palgrave Macmillan in the US is a division of St Martin's Press LLC, 175 Fifth Avenue, New York, NY 10010.

Palgrave Macmillan is the global academic imprint of the above companies and has companies and representatives throughout the world.

Palgrave® and Macmillan® are registered trademarks in the United States, the United Kingdom, Europe and other countries.

ISBN 978–0–230–20129–3

This book is printed on paper suitable for recycling and made from fully managed and sustained forest sources. Logging, pulping and manufacturing processes are expected to conform to the environmental regulations of the country of origin.

A catalogue record for this book is available from the British Library.

A catalog record for this book is available from the Library of Congress.

10 9 8 7 6 5 4 3 2 1
19 18 17 16 15 14 13 12 11 10

Printed in China

CONTENTS

11 Love potions
Transforming attraction to love

Epilogue

LIST OF FIGURES AND PLATES

Figures

Plates

ACKNOWLEDGEMENTS

I thank Louise Barrett, who shaped the entire work, who did so much with the first few drafts, and who was there for almost all of the adventure; Anne Perrett, who watched over each sentence and argument, and who has lived and breathed faces our whole life together; Tamsin Saxton, whose care clarified so much of the book; Monika Harvey, whose apt opinions improved the logic; Beatriz Martin-Andrade, who kept the storyline from being too wide of the mark; Jaime Marshall, my editor at Palgrave Macmillan, whose belief and coaxing sustained the project; Andrew Nash, whose thorough line editing transformed the text into a readable form; the many people, including Vinet Coetzee, Lisa DeBruine, Juan Carlos Gomez, Ben Jones, Ferenc Kocsor, Jennifer Lewis, Tony Little, David Milner, Marisa Parker, Daniel Re, Ian Stephen, and Ross Whitehead, who checked the text, giving praise when they felt it was merited, yet pointing also to places where the text was inadequate, flippant, patronizing, depressing, or soppy; Davis Buls, for some splendid artwork; Bernard Tiddeman, for the powerful computer graphics; and all those colleagues whose work in the Perception Lab at the University of St Andrews created the stuff to write about, including Lesley Ferrier who patiently organized us all.

DAVID PERRETT

FIGURE CREDITS

The Perception Lab is based at the School of Psychology, University of St Andrews, Scotland (http://perception.st-and.ac.uk/).

1.1 D. Buls (2009) Perception Lab (produced using Morphanalyser software developed by B. Tiddeman).

1.2 D. Buls (2009) Perception Lab.

1.3 D.I. Perrett, A.C. Little, B.P. Tiddeman & R.E. Cornwell (2009) Perception Lab (using Psychomoroph software developed by B. Tiddeman and others).

1.4 D. Buls (2009) Perception Lab.

1.5 D.I. Perrett (2009) Perception Lab.

1.6 D. Buls (2009) Perception Lab.

1.7 Cover picture for *Nature* 1998 (prepared at the Perception Lab).

1.8 *Left*: Leonardo da Vinci *Mona Lisa* (1503–1505). Musée de Louvre, Paris. http://commons.wikimedia.org/wiki/File:MonaLisa_sfumato. jpeg. Creative Commons [accessed 2010].
   Right: D.I. Perrett (2009) Charcoal and pencil drawing of Frida Kahlo based on her self-portraits.

1.9 Sadr, J., Jarudi, I. & Sinha, P. (2003) The role of eyebrows in face recognition. *Perception* 32: 285–293 (Figure 4). (Reprinted with permisson.)

2.1 Burt, D.M. & Perrett, D.I. (1997) Perceptual asymmetries in judgements of facial attractiveness, age, gender, speech and expression. *Neuropsychologia* 35: 685–693. (Reprinted with permission from Elsevier.)

2.2 Burt, D.M. & Perrett, D.I. (1997) Perceptual asymmetries in judgements of facial attractiveness, age, gender, speech and expression. *Neuropsychologia* 35: 685–693. (Reprinted with permission from Elsevier.)

2.3 D.I. Perrett (2009) Perception Lab.

2.4 Thompson, P. (1980) Margaret Thatcher: a new illusion. *Perception* 9: 483–484. (Reprinted with permission from Pion Limited, London.)

2.5 D.I. Perrett (2009) Perception Lab.

2.6 D.I. Perrett (2009) Perception Lab.

2.7 Young, A.W., Edward, H.F., De Haan, E.H.F., Newcombe, F. & Hay, D.C. (1990) Facial neglect. *Neuropsychologia* 28: 391–415. (Reprinted with permission from Elsevier.)

3.1 Reconstruction by D.I. Perrett of stimuli used by Goren, C., Sarty, M. & Wu, P. (1975) Visual following and pattern discrimination of face-like stimuli by newborn infants. *Pediatrics* 56: 544–549.

3.2 Farroni, T., Csibra, G., Simion, F., Johnson, M.H. (2002) Eye contact detection in humans from birth. *Proceedings of the National Academy of Sciences USA* 99: 9602–9605. (Copyright (2002) National Academy of Sciences, U.S.A.; reprinted with permission.)

3.3 Simion, F., Valenza, E., Macchi Cassia, V., Turati, C. & Umiltà, C. (2002) Newborns' preference for up-down asymmetrical configurations. *Developmental Science* 5: 427–434. (Reprinted with permission from Wiley-Blackwell Publishers.)

3.4 Pascalis, O., de Haan, M. & Nelson, C.A. (2002) Is face processing species-specific during the first year of life? *Science* 296: 1321–1323. (Reprinted with permission from the American Association for the Advancement of Science.)

3.5 Pascalis, O., Scott, L.S., Kelly, D.J., Shannon, R.W., Nicholson, E., Coleman, M. & Nelson C.A. (2005) Plasticity of face processing in infancy. *Proceedings of the National Academy of Science* 102: 5297–5300. (Copyright (2005) National Academy of Sciences, U.S.A.; reprinted with permission.)

3.6 Wikipedia: http://en.wikipedia.org/wiki/File:Gymnogyps_californianus1.jpg. Creative Commons [accessed 15/11/09].

3.7 Meltzoff, A.N. & Moore, M.K. (1977) Imitation of facial and manual gestures by human neonates. *Science* 198: 75–78. (Reprinted with permission from the American Association for the Advancement of Science.)

3.8 Ferrari, P.F., Visalberghi, E., Paukner, A., Fogassi, L., Ruggiero, A. & Suomi, S.J. (2006) Neonatal imitation in rhesus macaques. *Public Library of Science Biology* 4: 1501–1508. (Creative Commons Attribution License.)

3.9 Slater, A.M., Bremner, G., Johnson, S.P., Sherwood, P., Hayes, R. & Brown, E. (2000) Newborn infants' preference for attractive faces: the role of internal and external facial features. *Infancy* 1: 265–274. (Reprinted with permission from Taylor & Francis Group Publishers: http:/www.informaworld.com.)

3.10 Quinn, P.C., Kelly, D.J., Lee, K., Pascalis, O. & Slater, A.M. (2007). Preference for attractive faces in human infants extends beyond conspecifics. *Developmental Science* 11: 76–83. (Reprinted with permission from Wiley-Blackwell Publishers.)

4.1   *Top left*: Dr. Georg Buschan (1914). http://www.flickr.com/ photos/haabet/3736448826/in/set-72157622528353707/ [accessed 18/11/09]. Also published in: Jones, A. (2001) Dental anthropology: dental transfigurements in Borneo. *British Dental Journal* 191: 98–102. http://www.nature.com/bdj/journal/v191/n2/full/4801106a. html [accessed 01/09/09] (Reproduced with permission: Macmillan Publishers Ltd.)

    Top centre: Schijman E. (2005) Artificial cranial deformation in newborns in the pre-Columbian Andes. *Child's Nervous System* 21: 945–950. (Reproduced with permission from Springer-Verlag 2005.)

    Top right: Dr. Georg Buschan (c.1914). http://www.flickr.com/photos/ haabet/3735644729/. Creative Commons [accessed 18/11/09].

    Bottom left: Vitold de Golish (1958) *Au Pays Des Femmes Girafes*. Grenoble, Arthaud. http://www.flickr.com/photos/ haabet/3031018176/. Creative Commons [accessed 18/11/09].

    Bottom centre: Martin Hürlimann (c.1923) Taken in Chad. http:// www.flickr.com/photos/haabet/3516150860/. Creative Commons [accessed 18/11/09].

    Bottom right: Agência Brasil. http://commons.wikimedia.org/wiki/ File:Rikbaktsa.jpg. Creative Commons [accessed 18/11/09].

4.2   Cornwell, R.E., Law Smith, M.J., Boothroyd, L.G., Moore, F.R., Davis, H.P., Stirrat, M., Tiddeman, B.P. & Perrett, D.I. (2006) Reproductive strategy, sexual development and attraction to facial characteristics. *Philosophical Transactions of the Royal Society B-Biological Sciences* 361: 2143–2154. (Reprinted with permission from the Royal Society.)

4.3   Charcoal and pencil by D.I Perrett, based on image research by D. Buls (2009) Perception Lab.

4.4   Perrett, D.I., Burt, D.M., Penton-Voak, I.S., Lee, K.J., Rowland, D.A. & Edwards, R. (1999) Symmetry and human facial attractiveness. *Evolution and Human Behavior* 20: 295–307. (Reprinted with permission from Elsevier.)

4.5   Perrett, D.I., Burt, D.M., Penton-Voak, I.S., Lee, K.J., Rowland, D.A. & Edwards, R. (1999) Symmetry and human facial attractiveness. *Evolution and Human Behavior* 20: 295–307. (Reprinted with permission from Elsevier.)

4.6   D. Buls (2009) Perception Lab.

4.7   *Top left*: *Madonna of the Pomegranate* (c.1487). Galleria degli Uffizi, Florence, Italy. http://upload.wikimedia.org/wikipedia/commons/d/d2/ Botticelli_Madonna_of_the_Pomegranite.jpg [accessed 24/11/09].

Top right: Allegory of Spring La Primavera (c.1477). Galleria degli Uffizi, Florence, Italy. http://upload.wikimedia.org/wikipedia/commons/a/a4/Sandro_Botticelli_038.jpg. Creative Commons [accessed 24/11/09].

Right: Birth of Venus (c.1485) Galleria degli Uffizi, Florence, Italy. http://upload.wikimedia.org/wikipedia/commons/4/47/La_nascita_di_Venere_%28Botticelli%29.jpg. Creative Commons [accessed 24/11/09].

Bottom right: Allegory of Spring La Primavera (c.1477). Galleria degli Uffizi, Florence, Italy. http://upload.wikimedia.org/wikipedia/commons/a/a4/Sandro_Botticelli_038.jpg. Creative Commons [accessed 24/11/09].

Bottom left: Portrait of a Lady: Smeralda Brandini (c.1475). Victoria & Albert Museum. http://upload.wikimedia.org/wikipedia/commons/a/ab/Alessandro_Botticelli_Portrait_of_a_Lady_%28Smeralda_Brandini_.jpg [accessed 24/11/09].

Left: Madonna of the Sea (c.1477) Galleria dell'Accademia, Florence, Italy. http://www.lib-art.com/imgpainting/4/7/19074-madonna-of-the-sea-sandro-botticelli.jpg. Creative Commons [accessed 24/11/09].

Centre: D.I. Perrett (1996) Perception Lab.

4.8   Carbon, C.C. & Leder, H. (2006) The *Mona Lisa* effect: is 'our' Lisa fame or fake? *Perception* 35: 411–414. (Reproduced with permission from C.C. Carbon.)

4.9   DeBruine, L.M., Jones, B.C., Unger, L., Little, A.C. & Feinberg, D.R. (2007) Dissociating averageness and attractiveness: attractive faces are not always average. *Journal of Experimental Psychology: Human Perception and Performance* 33: 1420–1430. (Reproduced with permission.)

4.10 Perrett, D.I., May, K.A. & Yoshikawa, S. (1994) Facial shape and judgements of female attractiveness. *Nature* 368: 239–242.

4.11 L.K. Mackie, D.I. Perrett, and colleagues (1994) Perception Lab.

4.12 DeBruine, L.M., Jones, B.C., Unger, L., Little, A.C. & Feinberg, D.R. (2007) Dissociating averageness and attractiveness: attractive faces are not always average. *Journal of Experimental Psychology: Human Perception & Performance* 33: 1420–1430. (Reprinted with permission.)

5.1   *Ladies' Home Journal*, October 1900. commons.wikimedia.org/wiki/History_of_corsets [accessed 23/11/09].

5.2   D. Buls (2009) Perception Lab.

5.3   D.I. Perrett & I.S. Penton-Voak (1997–9) Perception Lab.

5.4   D.I. Perrett & D. Rowland (1996) Perception Lab.

5.5 Swaddle, J.P. & Reierson, G.W. (2002) Testosterone increases perceived dominance but not attractiveness in human males. *Proceedings of the Royal Society B* 269: 2285–89. (Reproduced with permission from the Royal Society.)

5.6 DeBruine, L.M., Jones, B.C. & Perrett, D.I. (2005) Women's attractiveness judgments of self-resembling faces change across the menstrual cycle. *Hormones and Behavior* 47: 379–383. (Reprinted with permission from Elsevier.)

5.7 Charcoal and pencil by D.I. Perrett, based on image research by D. Buls (2009) Perception Lab.

5.8 Cornwell, R.E., Law Smith, M.J., Boothroyd, L.G., Moore, F.R., Davis, H.P., Stirrat, M., Tiddeman, B. & Perrett, D.I. (2006) Reproductive strategy, sexual development and attraction to facial characteristics. *Philosophical Transactions of the Royal Society B* 361: 2143–2154. (Reproduced with permission from the Royal Society.)

6.1 Wikipedia: http://en.wikipedia.org/wiki/File:Veuve_de_Jackson.JPG. Creative Commons [accessed 20/10/09].

6.2 Wikipedia: http://upload.wikimedia.org/wikipedia/commons/thumb/1/1c/Moulay_Ismail.jpg/430px-Moulay_Ismail.jpg. Creative Commons [accessed 20/9/09].

6.3 Cornwell, R.E. & Perrett, D.I. (2008) Sexy sons and sexy daughters: the influence of parents' facial characteristics on offspring. *Animal Behaviour* 76: 1843–1853. (Reproduced with permission from Elsevier.)

6.4 Cornwell, R.E. & Perrett, D.I. (2008) Sexy sons and sexy daughters: the influence of parents' facial characteristics on offspring. *Animal Behaviour* 76: 1843–1853. (Reproduced with permission from Elsevier.)

7.1 Penton-Voak, I.S., Jones, B.C., Little, A.C., Baker, S.E., Tiddeman, B.P., Burt, D.M. & Perrett, D.I. (2001) Symmetry, sexual dimorphism in facial proportions, and male sexual attractiveness. *Proceedings of the Royal Society B* 268: 1617–1623. (Reproduced with permission from the Royal Society.)

8.1 J.S. Lobmaier (2008) Perception Lab.
8.2 D. Buls & R.E. Cornwell (2008) Perception Lab.
8.3 D. Buls & R.E. Cornwell (2008) Perception Lab.
8.4 M.L. Smith (2004) Perception Lab.
8.5 Hawkins, S.S., Perrett, D.I., Tiddemann, B.P., Burt, D.M., DeSantis, C., Meyers, C.L., Hoyberg, K., Wright, S.L. & Weinkauf, R.L. (2002) Novel approaches in texture measurement for cosmetic anti-ageing

evaluation. In *Proceedings of the 22nd IFSCC Conference*, pp. 317–323. Edinburgh, Scotland, September 2002. (Images courtesy of Unilever Research.)

8.6   D.I. Perrett (2008) Perception Lab.

9.1   Galton, F. (1883) *Inquiries into Human Faculty and its Development*. London: Macmillan.

9.2   Penton-Voak, I.S., Pound, N., Little, A.C. & Perrett, D.I. (2006) Personality judgments from natural and composite face images: more evidence for a 'kernel of truth'. *Social Cognition* 24: 490–524. (Reproduced with permission.)

9.3   Boothroyd, L.G., Jones, B.C., Burt, D.M., DeBruine, L.M. & Perrett, D.I. (2008) Facial correlates of sociosexuality. *Evolution and Human Behavior* 29: 211–218. (Reproduced with permission from Elsevier.)

9.4   Little, A.C., Burt, D.M. & Perrett, D.I. (2006) What is good is beautiful: face preference reflects desired personality. *Personality and Individual Differences* 41: 1107–1118. (Reproduced with permission from Elsevier.)

9.5   J. Engelmann & D.I. Perrett (2001) Perception Lab.

10.1 Bereczkei, T., Gyuris, P. & Weisfeld, G.E. (2004) Sexual imprinting in human mate choice. *Proceedings of the Royal Society* B 271: 1129–1134. (Reproduced with permission from the Royal Society.)

10.2 Jones, B.C., DeBruine, L.M., Little, A.C., Burriss, R.P. & Feinberg, D.R. (2007) Social transmission of face preferences among humans. *Proceedings of the Royal Society* B 274: 899–903. (Reproduced with permission from the Royal Society.)

11.1 Wikimedia: http://upload.wikimedia.org/wikipedia/commons/c/c4/ Der_kuss.jpg [accessed 10/12/09].

Colour plates

Plate I

A   P. Grogan & D.I. Perrett (1996) Perception Lab.
B   P. Grogan & D.I. Perrett (1996) Perception Lab.
C   *Left and right*: Perrett, D.I., Lee, K., Penton-Voak, I., Burt, D.M., Rowland, D., Yoshikawa, S., Henzi, S.P., Castles, D. & Akamatsu, S. (1998) Sexual dimorphism and facial attractiveness. *Nature* 394: 884–886. (Reproduced with permission.) *Centre*: D.I. Perrett and colleagues, Perception Lab.

Plate II

D   D.I. Perrett, R. Edwards & E. O'Loghlen (1998) Perception Lab.
E   D.I. Perrett and colleagues (2001) Perception Lab.

Plate III

F   Adapted from: Law Smith, M.J., Perrett, D.I., Jones, B.C., Cornwell, R.E., Moore, F.R., Feinberg, D.R., Boothroyd, L.G., Durrani, S.J., Stirrat, M.R., Whiten, S., Pitman, R.M. & Hillier, S.G. (2006) Facial appearance is a cue to oestrogen levels in women. *Proceedings of the Royal Society B* 273: 135–140. (Reproduced with permission from the Royal Society.)

G   V. Coetzee (2008) Perception Lab.

H   Jones, B.C., Little, A.C., Burt, D.M. & Perrett, D.I. (2004) When facial attractiveness is only skin deep. *Perception* 33: 569–576. (Reproduced with permission from Pion Limited, London.)

Plate IV

I   M. Stirrat, M.J. Law Smith & D.I. Perrett (2005) Perception Lab.

J   Stephen, I.D., Coetzee, V., Law Smith, M. & Perrett, D.I. (2009) Skin blood perfusion and oxygenation colour affect perceived human health. *Public Library of Science ONE* 4: e5083. (Creative Commons Attribution License.)

K   Burt, D.M. & Perrett, D.I. (1995) Perception of age in adult Caucasian male faces: computer graphic manipulation of shape and colour information. *Proceedings of the Royal Society B* 259:137–143. (Reproduced with permission from the Royal Society.)

Plate V

L   I.D. Stephen (2008) Perception Lab.

M   I.D. Stephen (2008) Perception Lab.

N   B. Wiffen (2007) Perception Lab.

O   B. Wiffen (2007) Perception Lab.

Plate VI

P   K. May, M. Burt & B.P. Tiddeman (1993–2001) Perception Lab.

Q   B.P. Tiddeman, Perception Lab. Reproduced in part from: Tiddeman, B.P., Perrett, D.I. & Burt, D.M. (2001) Prototyping and transforming facial textures for perception research. *IEEE Computer Graphics and Applications, Research* 21: 42–50. (Reprinted with permission © 2001 IEEE.)

Plate VII

R   I.D. Stephen (2009) Perception Lab.

S   D. Buls (2009) Perception Lab.

T   Jones, B.C., DeBruine, L.M., Little, A.C., Conway, C.A. & Feinberg, D.R. (2006). Integrating gaze direction and expression in preferences for attractive faces. *Psychological Science* 17(7): 588–591. (Reproduced with permission from John Wiley & Sons.)

Plate VIII

U   Penton-Voak, I.S., Perrett, D.I. & Pierce, J. (1999) Computer graphic studies of facial similarity and judgements of attractiveness. *Current Psychology* 18: 104–118. (Reproduced with permission of Springer Science and Business Media.)

V   Perrett, D.I., Penton-Voak, I.S., Little, A.C., Tiddeman, B.P., Burt, D.M., Schmidt, N., Oxley, R. & Barrett, L. (2002) Facial attractiveness judgements reflect learning of parental age characteristics. *Proceedings of the Royal Society B* 269: 873–880. (Reproduced with permission from the Royal Society.)

INTRODUCTION

This book is for anyone who is curious about beauty. Its purpose is to explain, from a scientific point of view, our attraction to faces – an attraction that has driven the evolution of our species for millions of years, but that has only recently begun to give up its secrets to scientific study.

While we can normally agree on who has an attractive face, one of my central motivations in writing this book was to bring together the scientific results that demonstrate the *diversity* in attraction, that is, the reasons why different people find different faces attractive. While the work in my lab at the University of St Andrews, in Scotland, has produced some general rules of attractive faces, it didn't take long for results to emerge that showed that not everyone plays by the same rules or focuses on the same cues when deciding who has an attractive face. Facial attraction is personal – and as we will see, it is heavily influenced by each of our unique upbringings, our experiences as well as our own appearance.

Perception is a well-established and widely taught branch of psychology and medical science that concerns how we make sense of the information coming at us through our senses. Visual perception is the most developed branch of this field. My interest in faces started as a student when I realized that the scientific methods for studying visual perception could be used to study more than just simple things like lines, distance, colour, and movement – they could be extended to more interesting aspects of our visual world. During the course of my doctoral training I became convinced that our brains have sections dedicated to helping us interpret faces. One night, sleepless with excitement, I knew that I would spend my whole career working with faces. I knew that it would be possible to answer many questions about how we see faces, but even then I knew that the subject would be so complex that there was not enough time in one life to address them all.

Once I began working on what makes faces attractive, the reactions my work received from fellow academics and others really surprised me: some people argued that human beauty *should* not be studied; most questioned whether it *could* be studied scientifically at all. I still fail to understand both of these convictions. Those that claimed that human attractiveness should not be studied were pointing to the wonderment and sense of magic alchemy surrounding beauty and attraction, which would be despoiled by scientific scrutiny. They argued that objectifying beauty, particularly female beauty, was dehumanizing and discriminatory, and turned individuals into statistics.

In my mind it was, and is, not at all demeaning to understand the origins of our feelings. An athlete is no less admirable because anatomy and sports science can pinpoint which muscles need to be developed to enhance performance. The colours of a butterfly wing or the smell of a lily are no less pleasurable when we know how these sensations are created by the physics of light and the chemistry of odours.

Other critics argue that beauty is subjective; it is in essence a personal feeling. This fact, it is argued, puts beauty beyond the methods of natural science, in the same way that the nature of conscious experience will always be just beyond the grasp of science. I believe that aesthetics, although subjective, *can* be studied using scientific methods, and it is my hope that many of my results will prove it to you.

My research into facial attraction comes from a strictly biological perspective. In this perspective, finding someone attractive is likely to reflect a purpose – not a *conscious* purpose but a biological function, much like finding food tasty helps us acquire the calories we need to power our life. In biology, the purpose of life is defined in terms of procreation, producing the next generation and the one after that. Not all attraction is related to sex and procreation, but a lot is. Consequently the book focuses on heterosexual attraction but all chapters also deal with face perception in a way that is independent of sexual preference. Ensuring offspring live long enough and well enough to produce their own offspring means that attraction has a more important role in human relations than simply influencing sexual allure.

Although I approach the subject as a scientist rather than a philosopher or poet, I cannot claim to have remained unmoved by many of our findings. Indeed, some of the results of our work have disturbed me for years. Our work on the influence of hormones on attraction, for instance, which I cover in the book, seems to imply that biology predisposes infidelity and will always threaten human relationships. Hormone influences are more subtle and interesting: they do not mean that cheating on a partner is predetermined, even if they imply Nature has some misgivings about long-term partnerships.

I have tried to write in a way that will allow the reader to 'dip in' and 'dip out'. I have also included images throughout, and if you are like me, the images should help you home in on a topic of interest, and reading about that topic should open up more of the material. The endnotes, numbered through each chapter and gathered together at the back of the book, present comments, details and enigmas for the curious reader. Those who wish to explore the field further may find the scholarly references to the research here.

Almost all the images were created with computer graphics developed in the laboratory by my colleagues and myself. These graphics have helped us to isolate particular facial cues and test their influence on the attractiveness of face images. Indeed, one reason why the science of attraction has developed so much is due to the recent advancement in technology. Before, psychologists could speculate about the role of colour, symmetry, and face shape on attraction, but they could not test their speculations easily. Now it is possible to change one characteristic of a face at a time and see if the difference matters.

The method I pursue is to take common judgements about faces (for example, 'these faces look attractive' or 'these faces look healthy') and assess to what extent people agree about which faces hold this quality. If there is sufficient agreement, the next step is to identify, in the laboratory, which cues trigger agreement. If we think we have found a cue, we alter it and test if we can shift the way people see images of faces. For example, we look at whether adding a suntan makes a face look more attractive or healthy. Readers can make their own judgements from the illustrations I have provided in the book, bearing in mind that their own judgements are no more or less valid than anyone else's. The reasons *why* some faces produce different impressions for different people is an interesting topic for future research.

Although the chapters do not lead towards a single conclusion, there is a central theme: while we may form some consensus on beauty, attraction is unavoidably personal, because while beauty and attraction both have their roots in evolution and in infancy, they are also shaped by family and friends, by our romances, and by our sexual experiences. Our individual experience of being attracted to someone, while it can often take us by surprise and seem overwhelming and irrational, nevertheless reflects the conscious and unconscious working of our own brains, and it is therefore amenable to systematic study.

We begin in Chapter 1 by considering a brief history of the face, exploring how each part of the modern face came about and how it is that our faces can communicate without words.

But why do we see one face as beautiful and another as just plain? To answer this question we need to know some facts about the brain. As Chapter 2 explains, attraction depends on links between the parts of the brain that help us to see faces and the parts that evoke pleasure or lust. Finding a person attractive depends on other factors, too: the ability to recognize a familiar face; to experience feelings of familiarity; to remember things about the person; and most importantly, to experience feelings of wanting and caring. As you discover how the brain recognizes faces, you will also read about brain cells that are so specific that some are exclusively dedicated to each person you love.

Right from the start of our lives, we are attracted to faces. The moment we open our eyes, faces grab our attention. Chapter 3 discusses the ways in which babies react to faces and how these reflect primitive brain machinery that is present even in frogs. This chapter also considers the extent to which babies and adults are attracted to the same faces.

Chapter 4 ponders beauty. It is often claimed that beauty lies in the proportions of the face, but which are the proportions that matter? The answer lies not in fancy geometry but in two basic relationships: whether the left side matches the right (symmetry), and whether the proportions match those with which we are most familiar (normality or 'averageness'). That beauty should lie in averageness is paradoxical, because we tend to think of 'average' as mundane. Sure, the most beautiful faces do *not* have average proportions, but nonetheless learning what is 'normal' for the faces around us is a powerful force in defining what for us is beautiful. While these two relationships are attractive the world over, not everyone attends to them equally; for some symmetry matters little, whereas for others it matters greatly. Even starting with a universally admired trait, we discover that the *level* of attraction to this trait can vary between observers.

If some facial traits can improve on 'average' proportions, then, which traits are those? One answer is that it is those traits that are shaped by sex hormones, either in the womb or at puberty. As Chapter 5 reveals, femininity in women's faces is universally admired. In contrast, masculinity in men's faces turns out to be a mixed blessing; while it signals desirable traits such as power and dominance, the very desirability of such traits can make high-testosterone men uncommitted to long-term relationships. Sex hormones can have an insidious control over attraction, dictating which facial cues we are attracted to, and when. As the levels of sex hormones wax and wane across the day, month, year and lifespan, changes in these levels modify the spectrum of facial traits to which each of us is attracted.

In the long run, though, what good is there in chasing after beautiful faces? Chapter 6 provides an answer: by winning a partner with an attractive face (and with luck being attractive ourselves), we improve the chance of a happy life and of leaving descendents on the planet. The quest for beauty is by no means just a matter of whim or of fashion. Nonetheless, successful relationships depend on heeding influences that personalize what we find beautiful.

Chapter 7 shows that good health is essential for beauty. In reality, most dimensions of facial attractiveness are signals to others of our health and our ability to shrug off disease. If we are the proud owners of genes that keep us strong and healthy, then we have excellent chances in the mating game – many others will be drawn to join us in spreading those genes.

By looking at a face one can see many health signals: some structural and stable, others subtle and changeable. The redness or yellowness of our skin, for example, indicates our circulatory, reproductive, and dietary health. In effect, therefore, our face provides a kind of health certificate – and we all check other people's certificates, both to ensure our own health and to choose genes for the next generation. There are exceptions, of course, such as 'heroin chic', but those have additional explanations related to culture and peer groups (see Chapter 10).

Chapter 8 explains how faces age along with the rest of our bodies and considers the impact of ageing on attractiveness. It charts the changes from birth, when we start to grow in attractiveness. But our beauty doesn't grow for long: we're at our cutest at about 8 months of age, and after that it's all downhill. That said, girls who are attractive as babies have an edge over their peers throughout their lives. For boys, though, ageing may see an ugly duckling turn into a swan, as initially unattractive traits turn to advantage later. As infants our faces may help persuade our parents to give us their loving care, but the reactions of adults to nuances in our infant faces may also have long-term implications for our developing personalities. Since adult attraction is intimately related to sex, the multiple signs of ageing may limit our shelf-life in the mating game – despite the cosmetic industry's best attempts to keep our faces looking young. It's not all bad news, for love can see past decades of deterioration.

Chapter 9 focuses on the fact that we don't all admire the same faces. You might think that the way we behave has nothing to do with the way that we look, but in fact the two are closely related. Firstly, the structure of our face determines how others react to us, and that in turn shapes our personality. In addition, our own behaviour affects others' impressions of our physical appearance and our attractiveness. One way or another then, we end up earning the face we have, through both our deeds and our predominant moods. And how we look is crucial: the influence of our faces in indicating our character cannot be overstated. *Looking* the part is as important as *playing* the part, in life as in love. As we vary individually in the personality we desire in a partner, so we vary also in the faces we admire.

Chapter 10 considers two further sources for the uniqueness of our attraction to others: our family and friends. Provided there is a loving bond between parents and children, usually a daughter will be attracted, unconsciously, to men whose faces resemble that of her own father, just as a son will be attracted to women whose faces resemble that of his mother. We also tend to follow our peers – the faces our friends fancy will bias the faces we ourselves admire or don't. In addition, the media focus on celebrity status and success provides a relentless pressure, not merely reinforcing natural desires but driving these to unhealthy levels. The chapter also explores how group membership can redefine the field of competition for mates.

Finally, Chapter 11 considers what facial attraction can lead to. Through arousal we convert interest to infatuation. As we share exciting experiences with another, the attraction we felt to begin with intensifies. Kissing and more intimate advances release a cocktail of pleasure chemicals and love potions in the brain, and these drugs link the particular facial characteristics of the partner to rewarding experiences. We get addicted. And what about falling in love? Love transforms attraction from general aesthetic appreciation for a kind of face to an intense desire for one face in particular. While it cannot guarantee fidelity, falling in love is the ultimate stage in individualizing facial attraction.

Chapter 1
FISH FACE

A brief tour of the face and its origins

Were someone to call you 'fish face', that would sound rude – yet it would also be more or less accurate. You *do* have a fish face: we all do. The human face, despite its sophisticated array of sense organs for seeing, smelling, and tasting the world, has rather humble evolutionary origins in the gills of our ancient fish-like ancestors.

The remnants of these gills are still observable during the development of human embryos. At about four weeks, when the embryo is barely bigger than the tip of a ballpoint pen, six round bumps form on each side near the front, and these bumps develop into pharyngeal arches – what would, in the fish, have been gill arches. As the embryo grows, the first arch later splits into structures that in turn develop into the upper and lower jaws and the chewing muscles. The second arch gives rise to other facial muscles; together with the remaining arches, it contributes to the structures in the inner ear, the voice-box, and the neck. The nerves and blood vessels also derive from these arches.

Just as our own faces reflect development from the jaws and faces of fish, so the faces of fish themselves resulted from the modification of the gill arches of even more primitive predecessors. These predecessors, which were kinds of jawless hagfish, had 'mouths' of simple round structures that allowed

Figure 1.1 Fish face to frog face – not yet human. To demonstrate our evolution, the image of a human face has been stretched over the heads of a primitive hagfish, a salmon, and a frog.

D. Buls (2009) Perception Lab.

them to filter food from the water or to rasp food off the sea-bed. If we use computer technology to stretch a human face over the head of a hagfish, the result shows just how far the human face has come (Figure 1.1).

Over the course of evolution, the first gill arch in some hagfish fused to the skull, and gradually through the generations of their offspring these transformed into mouthparts that could snap and bite (Figure 1.1, centre). The prehistoric seas offered multiple ways of making a living besides sifting gunk or feeding from the sea-bed; some fish, by random mutation, would have had slightly more mobile jaws, and these fish would have had an advantage in exploiting particular opportunities. These fish would be successful in leaving behind descendents; and in a few aeons of time, the selective advantage of having flexible mouths able to consume other sea creatures would have led to species evolving with more and more efficient snapping jaws. Even later, changes in the Earth's atmosphere gradually turned the land surface into an environment that supported newly evolving animals, animals that began to colonize the land. As these animals slowly adapted and began to breathe air, their gills were no longer needed to get oxygen from water and the gill arches could evolve into other structures. Different evolutionary lines led eventually to frogs (Figure 1.1, right), to lizards, and to mammals.

The distinctive appearance and character of each human face depend not merely on muscles and bones but also on other structures, including the eyes, the nose, and the mouth. These structures and their position on the front of our heads also reflect our fishy origins. Just as there is an advantage for fish in having the sensory organs located near the 'leading edge' of their bodies, where they first encounter food and hazards as they swim along, humans also benefit from having all the sense organs – eyes, ears,[1] nose, and mouth – up front so that we can detect what's in front of us and take action quickly. Not all animals have a front-end and a tail-end, and such animals do not have faces; think of mussels, starfish, and sea-urchins. In our own case, though, the gill changes and the aggregation of the sensors on the heads of our ancestors have suited us both to taking in information from the environment and to sending out signals to the world.

A face that sucks and chews

We have a much more flexible face than a fish, frog or lizard. This gives us and other mammals an advantage during development in being able to suckle from our mothers. The single sheet of muscle that covers the head of a fish simply isn't up to sucking from a nipple or, after weaning, to gripping solid food. As we compare the amphibian face with the rodent face (Figures 1.1

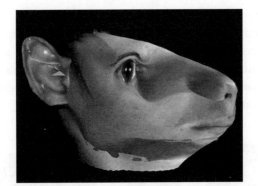

Figure 1.2 Rat face. A human face reshaped into a rat.
D. Buls (2009) Perception Lab.

and 1.2), we are observing the evolutionary development towards more flex-ible jaws, lips, and cheeks. All these features are advantageous for chewing and hence for digesting food. The rodent face is similar to that of the tree-shrew ancestors of primates, the division of mammals that includes lemurs, bush-babies, monkeys, apes, and humans.

The faces of modern humans, apes, and monkeys are more mobile and expressive than those of other mammals, such as dogs, cats, or rats. This partly reflects the fact that we have come to rely on vision rather than smell to navigate our way around the physical and social worlds; whereas an ani-mal that relies on smell must devote much of its facial apparatus to picking up scents, our own reliance on daytime seeing means that primates like us can use our faces to signal to one another. Dogs, in contrast, have upper lips that are fixed in position, split in the middle, and attached directly to wet nostrils. These features increase the effectiveness of the odour recep-tors in their noses, but they also constrain the number of expressions that dogs make. Lemurs and bush-babies, which are more primitive night-active primates, have snuffling features and fixed expressions; bush-babies are well-known for their 'caught in the headlights' goggle-eyed stare.

Animals that rely on smell must feel their way around with care. If you live in the dark, especially, you must take care to avoid damaging your delicate facial sensors. Whiskers are useful in this regard: they allow you to detect objects before you bash into them, but whiskers need nerves to send signals to the brain and muscles to twitch and direct them, and this apparatus limits the range of facial expressions.

The switch by early primates to daylight living can be traced to the demise of the dinosaurs, around 65 million years ago. Before then, mammals were small, mouse-like creatures confined to the dark; the fact that they were hot-blooded allowed them to be active at night, when the temperatures had dropped and they were not in competition with the dinosaurs. Once the dinosaurs had gone, though, new ways of making a living suddenly opened up, allowing smaller mammals including the primates to flourish and diversify, and eventually to develop into a wide variety of separate species (Figure 1.3).

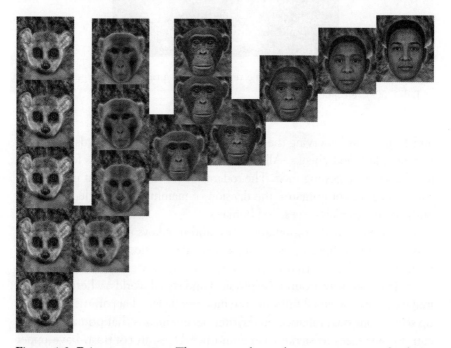

Figure 1.3 Primate ancestry. The top row shows the great variety in the forms of primate faces, including examples of average prosimian, macaque monkey, chimpanzee, and human faces. The human face shown is a blend of equal portions of African, European, west Asian, and east Asian male and female faces. Lower levels in the 'tree' represent ancestral forms that have been interpolated. Note that the top-line primates are equally evolved, in the sense of being equally specialized for current environments.
D.I. Perrett *et al.* (2009) Perception Lab.

For faces, the implications of these evolutionary developments were profound. Without the need for whisker control, facial muscles could be used to make expressions that reflected emotional states. Animals could influence one another in a more immediate way. Communication by scent-marking is a long-term process; a scent mark can stink for days. Facial expressions, in contrast, are fleeting: the communication of threat or of fear can be immediate and can change rapidly. This too played its part in evolution: as it became less important to pick up scents from one's neighbours, it also became less important to have such a large snout, and monkey and ape faces gradually became flatter than those of their scent-dependent nocturnal cousins (compare Figure 1.4 with Figure 1.2). Animals no longer needed a permanently wet nose and a fixed upper lip, and their faces could become mobile. Snouts didn't disappear altogether, however. Our closest living relatives, the chimpanzees (Figure 1.4), gorillas, and orang-utans, all have pronounced muzzles. Fossils from around three to four million years ago reveal similar facial profiles in the earliest apes to walk upright.

Another crucial change occurred during primate evolution: better vision favoured a face without a mask of fur, perhaps because such a face could give better signals using subtle muscular movements and variation in redness of skin.[2]

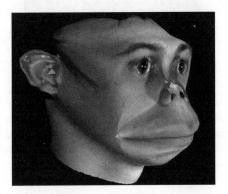

Figure 1.4 The human face of a chimp. The face of this chimpanzee, one of our closest living relatives, displays many of the characteristics of a human face.
D. Buls (2009) Perception Lab.

Despite their switch to walking on two legs, the ancestral human-apes remained chimp-like in most other characteristics, including their protruding jaws, their large teeth, and their relatively small brains (one-quarter the size of those in modern humans). The sexes differed dramatically both in the size of their canine teeth and in their body size, as is true of modern great apes. The males' large teeth and jaws were probably used as weapons (particularly in fights over females), and also helped them cope with the tough foods they were eating. One group relied on very hard, fibrous foods, such as sedge roots and tubers, to get them through periods when other more palatable foods were scarce; their diet is evident from the remains of their teeth and their skulls.[3] Back teeth of both sexes were astonishingly large – double the size of human teeth – and these human-apes had enormous chewing muscles which allowed them to grind hard foods to a pulp. The outsize molars and chewing muscles resulted in a face quite unlike that seen in any primate before or since: the cheekbones bulged forwards, accommodating all the chewing muscle underneath (Figure 1.5). The bones and the muscles of the face were bulky and sturdy, and thus robust, but otherwise these primates were really quite petite, standing only about a metre high.

Figure 1.5 The face of a 4-million-year-old fossil. *Paranthropus boisei* was one of several species evolving alongside ancestral humans. Its large cheekbones and jawbones gave it extraordinary chewing power and an unusual 'dished' face. D.I. Perrett (2009) Perception Lab.

The earliest human species appeared around two million years ago, and their arrival is accompanied by the first appearance in the fossil record of stone tools. The tools were probably used to butcher animals that had been scavenged or hunted. The ability to make and wield tools meant that teeth were no longer as important as weapons or for biting into tough carcasses. Meat provided another source of food, making it less necessary to be able to chew through tough plant food in order to survive dry, lean seasons. Early humans could get by with smaller and narrower teeth, and over time their cheekbones and their jawbones became less robust. Were we able to travel back two million years to meet those early humans, we would find ourselves looking into faces that were already beginning to lose their ape-like qualities, and we might feel a shiver of recognition.

The human face takes shape

At around the same time – two million years ago – the climate in Africa became variable, in part because the growth of the Himalayas was playing havoc with rainfall patterns. Such changes in the climate created new opportunities in the savannah and a number of different types of human-apes evolved there; as many as sixteen different species may have roamed the African plains at that stage.[4] This period of changeability also saw an increase in brain size. Bigger brains meant better problem-solving abilities and more flexible behaviour, and these gave an edge when the climate shifted and the habitat changed. The sides and the front of the skull expanded, reflecting growth in the parts of the brain that lie just beneath the bone – the temporal lobes on the side, which are critical for memory and for recognizing faces (see Chapter 2), and the frontal lobes, which are used in planning.[5]

Earlier human species had both low foreheads, which sloped back from the face, and heavy prominent brow-ridges. Big-brained[6] modern humans have high, rounded foreheads which sit atop our faces with almost no brow-ridges; our frontal lobes have evolved and increased in size, and at the same time the bones at the front of the skull have literally bulged out-wards. If you're a fan of science-fiction films, you'll have noticed that when film-makers want to indicate the presence of a superior intellect among aliens, they often use the same technique – a high, bulbous forehead is an obvious way to indicate the presence of a large brain. Advertisers too have recognized this; during the 1980s Tefal, makers of Teflon-coated (non-stick) frying pans and the like, ran a series of advertisements that featured the 'Tefal-heads': brilliant scientists blessed with huge foreheads and, by implication, enormous brains.

The development of the forehead is evident if we contrast the human with the chimp, and extrapolation of the same kind of development may indicate the possible appearance of a future human (Figure 1.6). The

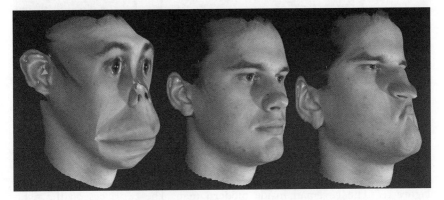

Figure 1.6 The face of things to come. A human face (*centre*) is contrasted with that of a chimp (*left*) to show how human faces might look in the future (*right*) if we continue to diverge from chimpanzees in the same way.
D. Buls (2009) Perception Lab.

forehead may become more prominent, as may the chin and the nose. (Despite the bigger brains, the expression in this 'flash-forward' suggests that the future for humankind may not be bright!)

In human evolution, both technology and culture have played a role in changing the anatomy of faces. While the invention of tools had already relieved some of the burden on the teeth and jaws for food-processing, the subsequent discovery of how to control fire and to cook food had an even greater effect. Crunching on a raw carrot requires more time and more jaw-power than devouring the delicately roasted version, and even a tough old oxtail will become tender if stewed for long enough. With less strain on their teeth and chewing muscles, thanks to fire, humans no longer needed such sturdy jawbones and, in comparison with our earlier human relatives, our faces are now much smaller, flatter, and more delicately featured – we are Nicole Kidman compared to their Arnold Schwarzenegger. Indeed there seems to have been an evolutionary selection for a reduction in robustness, and a decrease in the difference between male and female

Figure 1.7 The caveman inside modern man. The two faces on the right, each shown in full and partial profile, were made by increasing the way current-day European and Asian men's face shape (seen at left) differs from that of women.

Cover picture for *Nature* 1998 (Perception Lab).[7]

skull shapes. The human line has been evolving to a more gracile, refined feminine appearance, as you can see from Figure 1.7. (This trend is discussed further in Chapter 5.)

Modern humans had evolved by around 100,000 years ago, and skulls show the emergence of a facial feature that is unique to humans: a chin. Viewed in profile, the lower jawbones of apes and early human species slope backwards from the mouth, whereas human lower jaws have a bony protuberance that points forwards. (To see humans compared with chimpanzees, see Figure 1.6.) Why we should have developed a chin is an interesting question. It may be merely a by-product of the evolutionary change in the lower jaw and teeth,[8] a process that left a remnant knob of bone which, because it did no harm, remains to this day as the chin. If so, it is the facial equivalent of an appendix – another evolutionary leftover that serves no real purpose today. Alternatively, it may be that chins accommodate the long roots of the front teeth or support the lower jaw against the stresses of chewing.

Our prominent noses have also been a topic of debate. Again, some scientists favour a by-product explanation: perhaps the nose was left sticking out as the jaws moved back. Others argue that a nose that sticks out is very useful because it can warm and moisten air before the air gets into our lungs.[9] A third and rather delightful suggestion is that humans may have gone through an aquatic stage in evolution[10] during which a nose that stuck out provided a 'lid' over the nostrils, preventing water from shooting up the nose while diving. Sadly, though, the evidence for this 'aquatic ape' ancestry is not convincing.

The flexible nature of our faces allows us to communicate our feelings to the world, but as already noted that wasn't the reason why we developed this flexibility. Many of our facial muscles are primarily concerned with suckling, biting, and chewing. We have other muscles, too, such as muscles around the eyes and attached to the eyelids that allow us to wink flirtatiously or to widen our eyes in amazement; originally these eye muscles had other functions, such as preventing objects from getting stuck in the eye. Blinking – which we do about fifteen times a minute, usually without noticing – keeps the eye surface from drying out, something our fish-like forebears didn't need to worry about.

When we blink, we gather tears from glands located in the upper outer corner of the eye and sweep them down over the eye. (In slow motion one can see that the eyelid actually shuts from the outside in, more like a zip fastener than a final curtain dropping vertically over the eye.[11]) Any excess tears drain through the duct in the innermost corners of the eye – the small hole visible if you pull your lower eyelid down and look in the mirror. From there the tears drain into the nasal sinus, and this is why getting something in your eye and needing tears to flush it out can lead to major sniffles. In thinking about our eyes we naturally focus on the social function of winks, blinks, smiles, and other forms of facial signalling, but most of our facial muscles are in fact serving dual functions, supporting not just communication but also the everyday business of self-protection.

The whites of our eyes

While most of our face is important in helping us to communicate, it is our *eyes* that are the most crucial: our ability to 'read' faces – to interpret people's intentions or to sense they might be thinking – is largely a matter of observing what they do with their eyes. This is made easy by the fact that we have a large, highly distinctive white area in our eyes, the sclera, a feature shared with no other primate species.[12]

The adults of most primates have a brown sclera that blends with the colour of the iris, which is usually brown also. The large white area in human eyes makes it easy for us to monitor the direction of other people's gaze, and this helps us to recognize the focus of their attention and to anticipate how they are likely to act.[13] One suggestion is that the evolution of cooperative behaviour in our early human ancestors – behaviour such as hunting and scavenging – relied on members of the group being able to coordinate their actions with others. If so, this in turn may have favoured efficiency in communication: individuals whose gaze could be seen and followed more easily may have been understood better than those whose eyes were less revealing. Stealth and silence are often key elements of successful hunting, and silent communication that used gaze direction and eye movements to indicate one's own intentions[14] and to direct others may have made all the difference between getting meat for dinner or going hungry.

If this is true, it suggests that the reverse may be true for our primate cousins. In their case the dark sclera may have developed to disguise their gaze, thereby making it difficult for other animals to know where they were looking, particularly when the head was turned to one side, since gaze direction and head direction are usually matched. Among primate species for whom facing and staring at another animal constitutes a threat, this kind of 'eye camouflage' would be an advantage: if it is difficult to see where another animal is looking when the head is turned to the side, there is less chance of being caught looking and having that look interpreted as a threat. Eye camouflage is likely to be most useful at a distance: at very close quarters gaze direction can be detected more easily, even with dark sclerae.

Baboons provide an interesting case. In the social life of monkeys there is a delicate balance to be maintained between being able to detect another's gaze and making sure your own gazing isn't misconstrued, and the brown sclerae help to maintain this balance. Adult males can be very volatile; the degree to which they will tolerate another individual close to them, especially while they are feeding, is unpredictable. If young juvenile baboons have to walk past an adult male and put themselves in arm's reach, they monitor the eyes of the adult male closely and are careful not to let him catch them in the act in case their own gaze is interpreted as a challenge. The slightest flicker of a male's gaze towards them, even in the absence of any head movement, leads youngsters to jump right out of the adult's way. The same is true for macaque monkeys; at middle distances, low-ranking animals will turn their heads away from a dominant male, but will continue to monitor his attention out of the corners of their eyes. If the male's gaze strays towards them they may make a show of non-threatening gestures such as lip-smacking (an equivalent of human bowing or curtseying), which may help to appease the male.[15] With the head turned away, a juvenile may glance furtively towards the adult male: the adult will find it difficult to tell where the juvenile is looking because the iris and the sclera are similar in colour and because little of the juvenile's eyes will be visible. If the juvenile had white sclerae, this would give the game away – looking away would appear light, whereas direct eye contact would look dark. Interestingly, some baboons and chimpanzees do indeed possess white sclerae (the result either of genetic mutation or of eye disease[16]), and of course it is very easy for a human to detect where – at what or at whom – these animals are looking: as they shift their gaze, the flash of white is highly visible. If human onlookers can interpret this gaze, presumably monkeys and apes who might be watching them could do the same.

The part of the eye that contains the most light-sensitive cells or photoreceptors is called the fovea; it is in this part of the retina that the photoreceptors are most tightly packed together, so this is the part with the sharpest vision. In order to see things clearly, we adjust our view so that the image of what we're looking at falls directly onto the fovea. One way to make sure that an image falls on the fovea is to move the head; for bigger bodies, however, the energy needed to move the whole head is proportionately greater than that needed to move the eyes alone, and simply swivelling the eyeballs allows a very large primate, such as a human being, to save energy.

As well as having more noticeable white sclerae than other primates, humans also have the largest area of *exposed* sclera. This is because our eye sockets are more oval, which gives the eyes a wider space in which to move around, and because swivelling the eyeballs far enough round to see things at the sides also means exposing more of the whites of the eye.

While the mobility of our eyes reflects our body size, the specific shape of our eyes is thought to reflect our evolutionary history as a ground-living primate. Compared with those of tree-living species, our eye sockets are less round and more almond-shaped. Ground-living species need to keep scanning the surrounding environment, not least in watching out for potential predators; more almond-shaped eye sockets allow ground-living species to scan a wider distance without needing to move their heads. Although humans in the modern world no longer have the same pressing need to watch out for predators, our highly mobile eyes are instead put to very good use in social signalling – you will often have exchanged meaningful sidelong glances with someone else, for example; it's astonishing how much can be conveyed by a simple flick of the eyes.

Eyebrows

The signals we give out using our eyes are emphasized by another of our facial features: our eyebrows. Our 'false brow' of hair overlies the bony brow ridges but can easily be raised or lowered, thereby altering the apparent structure of the face. We can entirely change our expression simply by moving our eyebrows, without any other facial movements; when we also change other aspects of facial expression, the extra emphasis added by our eyebrows makes it more likely that the expression will be noticed by others.

This probably explains why removing the brows makes a person's face look really odd – compare Leonardo da Vinci's *Mona Lisa* (Figure 1.8, left), which lacks eyebrows and consequently looks enigmatic, with Frida Kahlo's self-portrait (Figure 1.8, right), which shows heavy eyebrows and consequently looks formidable. At the University of Lethbridge in Canada, a sponsored head-shaving event is organized each year to raise money for cancer research. One year the event organizer shaved off one eyebrow as well. The effect was startling: to the audience it appeared as though half of his face had become paralysed.

It is always disconcerting to watch an inexpressive face, and loss of expressiveness can be an unwanted side-effect of cosmetic treatment. A well-known example is 'Botox', which comprises paralysing toxins from *Clostridium botulinum* bacteria. Hoping to increase their facial beauty, many people pay for Botox to be injected into the muscles of the forehead. While this stops the brows being lifted and thus helps to keep forehead wrinkles at bay, it also results in a rather vacant look. It does seem ironic that many actors, whose trade relies on their being able to express emotions in a seemingly authentic way, undergo a treatment that makes their faces immobile.

Figure 1.8 Highbrow art. Leonardo da Vinci's *Mona Lisa* and Frida Kahlo's self-portrait. Eyebrows contribute to expressions: when they are not apparent, as with the *Mona Lisa*, the expression is difficult to read, while conversely their dominance in Frida's image makes her look stern.
Left: Leonardo da Vinci *Mona Lisa* (1503–1505).
Right: Frida Kahlo
Charcoal and pencil by D.I. Perrett (2009).

As well as their use in emphasizing emotions, our eyebrows are also useful for sending deliberate social signals. You may not have noticed yourself doing it, but frequently we use an 'eyebrow flash' when greeting someone – we briefly raise and lower our brows, sometimes accompanying this with a smile. This may form the prelude to a spoken greeting or a full-on conversation, but often it substitutes for any kind of verbal exchange. At a distance or in a noisy situation, an eyebrow flash can be more effective than speech – we can see and understand the flash, whereas we might mistake what someone is trying to say or miss it altogether.

Other primates too make use of the brow region in their social signals, and thus indicate a likely origin for our own eyebrow flash. Many monkeys have light-coloured eyelids that contrast with their dark facial skin and eyes; they can make a highly impressive flash and use this in threat displays as a way of saying 'Back off!' Raised brows can feature in friendly overtures, as well. Baboons, for example, offer one another grooming (a helpful tidying-up of fur, rewarded by the occasional tasty flea), and use a facial expression known as the 'come-hither' face when they see another animal they are keen to groom: they pull their ears very flat against their heads, raise their eyebrows, and smack their lips together rapidly. In truth, it might be more accurate to call this expression an 'I'm in a friendly mood' face, as baboons produce this expression involuntarily as a reflection of their own emotional state rather than as a deliberate means of trying to communicate with another individual; they produce the face even when other animals are too far away to see them clearly or have their backs turned. The same is true of us when the sight of a friend in the distance produces a smile on our own face.

Eyebrows are highly variable – some are naturally bushy, some thin, some meet in the middle (the so-called 'monobrow'). This variability is a great advantage in social situations as eyebrows provide handy cues for recognizing familiar faces. If people are shown photographs of a celebrity's face from which the eyebrows have been removed by digital manipulation, they often fail to recognize the person in the photo (Figure 1.9, left). Intriguingly, a picture of a face missing the eyebrows is much harder to recognize than a face missing the eyes but with eyebrows left intact (Figure 1.9, centre).[17] The distinctiveness we attribute to our eyes is really a tribute to the anatomy of our hairy brows.

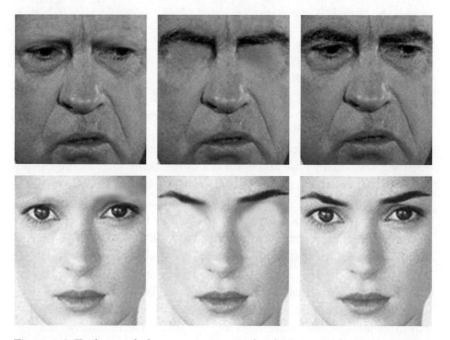

Figure 1.9 Eyebrows help recognition. Richard Nixon and actress Winona Ryder, along with modified versions lacking either eyebrows or eyes. Note that the absence of eyebrows disrupts recognition more than missing eyes.
J. Sadr *et al.* (2003).

Communicating without words

Humans have particularly rubbery faces, reflecting the particularly large and complicated array of facial muscles beneath the skin. Indeed, we have the most complex array of facial muscles of any mammal, with twenty-two separate muscles on each side of the face. This allows us to produce a very large repertoire of facial expressions, ranging from a subtle wry smile to a full-on expression of open-mouthed outrage. Like all the muscles in our bodies, our facial muscles are attached at one end to bone. The other end of each muscle is usually attached to bone also, but some facial muscles are attached directly to our skin. As a result, most of the feedback we receive from our faces (that is, our sense of what our faces are doing) results from the way in which our muscles pull and stretch the skin. This greater sensitivity to detecting our own facial expressions from the inside, along with the greater variety of expressions that humans are able to create, has long intrigued scientists.

One of the greatest scientists of them all was Charles Darwin. In 1872 he published a book called *The Expression of the Emotions in Man and Animals*, in which he pointed out the continuity that exists between our own array of facial expressions and the expressions found in other parts of the animal kingdom. This research formed part of Darwin's continuing effort to extend the evolutionary arguments that he had first put forward in 1859 in his most famous book, *The Origin of Species*. Darwin described facial expressions that he suggested were shared by all humans and represented our common evolutionary ancestry. He argued that these were recognized by people from diverse cultural and social backgrounds and that, because the same expressions were displayed even by individuals born deaf and blind who would have had no opportunity to learn them by copying others, these expressions were in some sense 'instinctive'. He also traced the similarity of human expressions to those of other species, suggesting a common origin of expressions in shared ancestral species. For example, in a section on 'pleasure, joy, affection', he describes how:

> If a young chimpanzee be tickled – and the armpits are particularly sensitive to tickling, as in the case of our children – a more decided chuckling or laughing sound is uttered; though the laughter is sometimes noiseless. The corners of the mouth are then drawn backwards; and this sometimes causes the lower eyelids to be slightly wrinkled. But this wrinkling, which is so characteristic of our own laughter, is more plainly seen in some other monkeys. The teeth in the upper jaw in the chimpanzee are not exposed when they utter their laughing noise, in which respect they differ from us.

Nowadays, we call the facial expression described a 'play face'; it is most frequently seen when two young chimps are cavorting together. One suggestion is that it functions as a signal to let the other chimpanzee know that, even if the play gets a bit rough, it is not real aggression. This may be one reason why the teeth remain covered by the lips as Darwin describes: it is then unlike the bared-teeth grin seen when animals express submission to a more dominant animal, or the exposed canines of an aggressor about to attack.

It seems likely that the play face in chimps is the expression most closely related to the human smile. In addition to being produced in comparable contexts, the play face involves the same muscle that is used when humans produce a smile, the *zygomaticus major*. In humans, genuine smiles involve a second set of muscles that circle around the eyes, the *orbicularis oculi*, whose contractions are what eventually lead us to get crows'-feet wrinkles. These muscles are very difficult to control voluntarily, a discovery made in 1862 by Guillaume Duchenne, a French neurologist who used electric shocks to stimulate facial muscles in a patient who felt no pain.

Only truly happy people can produce that crinkly-eyed look when they smile – fake smiles never reach the eyes. What is surprising, and it shows our social nature, is that genuine smiles (or 'Duchenne smiles', in his honour) can be contagious. When we see someone smiling, our own smiling muscles start to contract involuntarily, even though this may be so slight that no actual change in our expression may be noticed by an observer or felt by ourselves.[18] The more intense and genuine the smile we see, the more our *zygomaticus* and *orbicularis oculi* muscles contract, and the more pleasure we experience. Mimicry of this kind produces greater feelings of liking and comfort toward a person who shares our smile.

The telltale crinkly-eyed appearance allows us to pinpoint when babies begin to produce social smiles directed to particular people. Before the age of about two months, babies produce mouth-only smiles which are caused by spontaneous firing of the neurones in the brain stem, one of the most primitive parts of the brain. At around two months, another part of the brain gains importance. Groups of neurones called the basal ganglia become coated in a fatty substance that insulates them and improves the transmission of nerve impulses (on exactly the same principle as the plastic coating of electrical wires). By enabling information to be transmitted more effectively, this process of coating, called myelination, brings additional areas of the brain 'online'. It seems that once the functioning of the basal ganglia has improved in this way, babies begin to respond in a more obviously social manner, and their smiling eyes let us know when this has happened.[19]

Interestingly, even blind babies produce these kinds of social smiles in response to the mother's voice, suggesting that social smiling is a real human instinct, just as Darwin suggested – we don't need to learn how to do it, we just can, and social smiling happens naturally when we are happy. This doesn't mean that smiling isn't influenced by subsequent learning. Babies who can see begin to produce more elaborate and responsive smiling expressions as they get older, whereas blind babies' smiles do not change in this manner: they begin to smile less and they become generally less responsive in their facial expressions. Without the visual feedback of another smiling face looking at them, there is little reward or reinforcement for the non-verbal 'conversations' through which sighted humans convey happy feelings to one another.

Do we mean what our faces say?

While the English language offers thousands of words to describe emotions and expressions, many refer to the same general feeling. Much of our rich vocabulary can be boiled down to just six basic mood states: fear, anger, disgust, joy, sadness, and surprise. For each of these states there is a unique recognizable face. As Darwin argued, there is substantive agreement in how these basic emotions are expressed across diverse cultures – whether they live in Caracas, Kyoto, or Kansas, people are consistent in the face they make for the same emotional scenario: 'smiling' on an unexpected meeting with a good friend, or wrinkling the nose on coming across a decaying animal carcass. Even in the most isolated parts of Papua New Guinea, away from the pervasive influence of television, people still match photos of facial expressions to emotional situations in the same ways.[20]

Research shows that other more complex emotions, such as shame and pride, are expressed similarly by people of different nations, whether they are congenitally blind or sighted.[21] The full display of human shame includes tilting the head forward and covering the face, shaking it from side to side with the body slumped over, lowering the shoulders, and decreasing chest volume. The posture may derive from the cringing and submissive stance adopted by the losers of disputes throughout the animal kingdom, from salamanders to wolves. Pride provokes the opposite posture: the head is tilted up, raising the chin; the face smiles; and the arms are raised as the chest is expanded. At the 2008 Beijing Olympic Games, for example, contestants from all over the world gave similar displays of disappointment and pride on losing or winning competitions.

What did vary at the Olympics from culture to culture was how often such expressions were used. One factor is that cultures differ in the relative importance they place on the individual or the group; in general, America and Europe encourage individuality and self-assertion to a greater extent than Asian countries. On losing contests, competitors from individualistic societies showed less outward expression of shame than competitors from collectivist societies which emphasize the importance of the group. In the West, individuals who lose contests may learn to suppress the display of shame in order to protect their self-esteem. Of significance to researchers in detecting *instinctive* responses, therefore, is the behaviour of blind individuals: as they do not see others show or suppress emotional expressions, they may be less aware of cultural norms and how others regulate their emotional displays. Indeed, blind competitors at the Paralympics did not differ in expressing a sense of disappointment whether they were from Asia or America, whereas their sighted counterparts did express this differently according to the country they represented. Disappointment with oneself, or shame, is felt by everyone when expectations do not match achievements, however great or small these may be (and Paralympic athletic achievements are as great as any), but whether or not such emotions are shown in the face and body depends on experience.

Close observation of this sort, of particular individuals in particular situations, can yield insights about how humans in general behave. The fact that people tend to express their emotions with the same kinds of facial movements, however, does not imply that exactly the same things make people happy, sad, angry, or disgusted. That will vary culturally; indeed, it varies individually. If you've gone to a neighbour's house for dinner – if you've had any human contact at all! – you'll know that people vary enormously in what they find annoying, funny, and sad. What provokes pleasure or disgust varies, too: for instance, the very same food may produce retching or salivation. Sardinian Casu Marzu, for example, is rotten cheese which the locals say must be eaten with maggots still moving inside; and the traditional way of making Scandinavian gravlaks is to put fish directly into a hole in the ground, to cover it with birch bark, and to leave it for several months. Not everyone would enjoy the results equally as delicacies! While the basic expression of emotions may be shared, the frequency of these expressions and the factors that trigger them differ from person to person.

Can we control our faces?

Despite the pervasive influence of Darwin and our understanding of human evolutionary heritage, some people continue to deem humans superior to other animals, at least in part based on the belief that humans alone can control emotions and their expression – the implicit assumption being that emotional reaction is intrinsically inferior to reasoned action. After all, don't we have the ability to impose morality in decision making, keeping in check those base emotions that would otherwise threaten civilization?[22]. Does our education not allow us to control the 'animal impulses'? Yet brief considerations such as those presented here suggest that, on the contrary, we and other animals are not so different: we both have some control over our emotions and their expression, though none of us has *full* control.

To be sure, we adjust our expressions to some extent, depending on who is around. Other animals also vary their communication according to their audience: roosters are more likely to raise the alarm when they spot a fox if they have some hens to protect (or impress) than if they are on their own,[23] and chimps too adjust their calls of excitement on finding food depending on who is in the vicinity.[24] The moderation of emotional responses here may be contextual or strategic: we and other animals all benefit from displaying or withholding emotional outbursts in particular circumstances.

We produce certain facial expressions voluntarily to amplify or comment on spoken language. If a person arrives late for a meeting, for instance, we may add emphasis to the question '... And where have you been?' by raising our eyebrows, or allow a facial signal such as this to stand in completely for the spoken sentence. If the late colleague were to give some lame excuse we might communicate our disbelief by raising one eyebrow and twisting the mouth in an eloquent expression of scepticism, or by smiling benignly and giving a wink we might communicate 'Your secret's safe with me!' Such signals, or 'emblems' as they are called, are produced consciously and so conspicuously that people often respond to them as though the person had actually spoken: on seeing our facial expression, the tardy colleague may blurt out, 'It's true!' Winking, raising eyebrows, and blowing raspberries show that we can control facial muscles in communication, although these are not true expressions of emotion.

It may be a source of pride to us that we can control our feelings, but some expressions are not under voluntary control. Our forehead creases under severe pain, regardless of how hard we try to control ourselves,[25] and other reactions that are well-nigh impossible to control include those made in response to the tastes of an unripe lemon, bitter medicine, and rich hot chocolate (or any other sweet culinary vice). Each expression is distinct, and these facial responses are innate: one gets the same facial reactions in newborn infants to sour, bitter, and sweet liquids.[26]

Interestingly, our reactions to food and tastes are more apparent in the presence of others than when we are on our own.[27] At dinner parties, though, politeness calls for us to display pleasure – we feel that our face should not show that we find the wine undrinkable: rather than display disgust, it seems wiser to pass it to a less discerning partner, or if that fails, dump it into a flower pot. Eating food generously prepared by a host can require great self-control, yet despite the façade of civilization, taste reactions are not always possible to suppress. Perhaps you have witnessed the sudden departure of someone from the dining table who moments earlier had shown a flash of distress or disgust? Similarly, we know that enjoying someone's misfortune is socially inappropriate, yet it may be impossible to stifle a grin or a giggle.

Humans never lose the capacity for emotional reactions even if it seems like they grow 'less emotional' as they develop into adults. What actually happens is that the stimuli that engender emotional responses change, and adults also become more adept at using emotional displays strategically to engender desired responses in others.

While our emotions and their accompanying expressions (like the structure of our faces) have obvious animal origins, this fact does not detract from the value of these endowments or make us somehow 'less human'. In fact, recognizing and allowing emotional feelings to play a part in our decision making can make us even more successful in human affairs than we would be if we could banish emotions entirely. The value of being in touch with one's feelings is demonstrated by the finding that some decisions are aided by a 'hunch' – an emotional feeling – even when we can't say why following the hunch would be beneficial.[28] University education, for all its worth in enhancing intellectual skills, may actually impair our ability to be guided correctly by emotional hunches[29] when decisions are uncertain. Given these findings, it would seem the more we understand about our relation to other animals the more human we become.

Chapter 2
SEEING FACES

How we recognize faces and why we like them

In Chapter 1 we looked at how the structure of the human face evolved in a way that allows each one of us to communicate emotional expressions. But, like a tango, communication takes two: it requires a flexible face to send the signals, and a sophisticated mind to understand them. In this chapter we explore the specialized systems which have developed in the brain that enable our minds to understand what a face is telling us about its owner. And a face can tell us a lot – it provides not only answers to a basic questionnaire on sex, age, and ethnicity, but also clues to other aspects of what we really want to know about the person, such as the nuances of their mood, their health, and whether or not we are attracted to them. Our ability to derive a diversity of facts and impressions from the appearance of a face requires not only precise observation of subtle visual clues in faces but also some fancy detective work in making sense of those clues.

Our response to each person's face is rather like that of a detective at a crime scene, and our own investigations, whether conscious or unconscious, also rely on the skills of many different specialists – a graphic artist, as it were, to re-create the correct proportions in a likeness so that we can recognize the face next time; record keepers, so that we can check past form and note new misdemeanours; some clinical forensic scientists, who can painstakingly link details about voice, smell, and clothing that might prove irrelevant or perhaps crucial to the inquiry; and characters with hot-blooded feelings, whose intuitions seem to go beyond the evidence yet help to solve the case.

As we are used to many human experts working on an investigation, it should not surprise us that the brain, too, employs a variety of experts in its own inquiries, each specializing in a particular skill, be that in memory, feelings, or face reconstruction. By listening in to the smallest working components in the mental labour force, the brain cells, researchers have learned that these cells show many specializations. As we listen to an individual cell's activity or pulse, which beats faster when the cell says something to its neighbours, we hear it talk in a language that is easy to understand, and in the past forty years scientists have learned how to eavesdrop on cells talking to one another about faces and other matters.

The specialized cells are grouped together into departments – one with experts on how things move, another with specialists that talk about colour with great precision,[1] and other, more interesting, departments that focus on how bodies look[2] or that specialize in memories. Scientists can listen to the chatter of individual cells or, by using a scanner, measure the activity of an entire brain department. In effect the scanners represent activity in the brain, which of course we cannot see from outside the head, as images in which 'hot spots' – areas of electrical activity – can be displayed in colour to reveal the localized working of the brain. By monitoring the chatter of individual cells and the activity of whole departments, we can piece together the story of how normal brains identify, interpret, and catalogue faces.

Further insights into how the brain deals with faces come from the strange ways in which faces are processed in special circumstances: in instances of particular brain malfunctions, for example, faces may turn into fish-heads or aliens, they may get duplicated, or they may all become beautiful or entirely lose their appeal. Such anomalies occur when the expertise of particular departments of the brain becomes compromised or when departments lose touch with one another.

You are biased

All this specialization in the brain produces huge biases in the way we understand faces. Even you? Yes, if you are normal, that is to say, unimpaired by brain disorder, disease, or drugs, you too are biased in the way you look at faces, even in making the simplest of judgements about whether or not the owner of the face is male or handsome. Go on, try looking at Figures 2.1 and 2.2.

Just as the majority of humans are right-handed, so too most people are 'right-brained' when it comes to making judgements about faces. When asked to judge which of the two faces in Figure 2.1 is the more feminine, most people choose the lower image.[3] In reality each face is half man and half woman, the halves subtly blended across the midline so that you do not notice the join. You can confirm this by covering one side of the two faces: covering up the right-hand side of each face should make the top face look male and the bottom face female; covering up the left-hand side of the image pairs should do the opposite, making the top face female and the bottom face male. As the two faces are in fact the same except for being mirror reflections, one might expect that observers would find it difficult if not impossible to decide: one might forecast that in a group

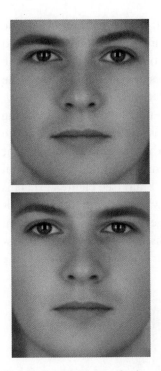

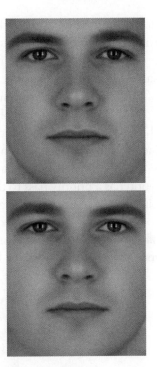

Figure 2.1 Which of these faces looks more feminine? Your choice can indicate a specialized face-processing system in your brain (see text).
D.M. Burt & D.I. Perrett (1997).

Figure 2.2 Which of these males looks more handsome? The image you choose can reveal how your brain analyses faces (see text).
D.M. Burt & D.I. Perrett (1997).

of observers, choices would be random, with 50 per cent of observers choosing the upper face as more feminine and 50 per cent choosing the lower. In fact, people do *not* find it difficult to make a choice, and most choose in the same way: in classroom demonstrations, up to 95 per cent of observers choose the lower image as more feminine. This demonstrates that when they make their choice most people are in fact attending preferentially to the left side of each image.

Figure 2.2 is a comparable test which shows that the perception of 'attractiveness' is equally biased. To take the test, simply decide which male you personally find looks more attractive. Now cover the left-hand side of both top and bottom images. If your opinion changes, you have just covered up the side of the face that you use when judging men's looks. To make this demonstration, researchers at the Perception Lab first manufactured two complete images of men's faces, selecting images that most people thought differed in attractiveness: we then cut the faces down the middle and stuck the different half-faces together. If it's true that in judging how handsome those faces are (Figure 2.2) you attend preferentially to the left side of the faces, your choices should be the same whether you evaluate the complete faces or cover up the right side of both faces so that you are looking at the left side only.

Why should most of us place more weight on the left side when judging the sex of a face or assessing how attractive it is – why does the left of the face grab our attention? The short answer is that for most of us the right side of the brain is better at face-processing, and the left half of the visual world has a priority pass to the right side of the brain (see Figure 2.3). This bias in where we concentrate our attention when judging faces extends to all kinds of decisions about sex, beauty, age, identity, and expression. These simple tests show that we have a specialist face-processing brain system, and that this is usually located on the right side of the brain.

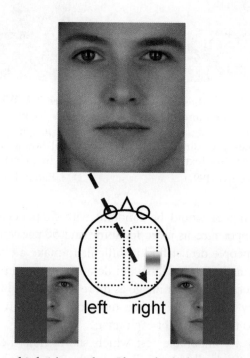

Figure 2.3 If you think it's a girl … If you think this is a girl, you're using the right side of your brain for face processing. When you (represented by the central schematic head) look at the middle of the complete face image (at the top), the *left* half of the face goes straight to the *right* side of your brain (dashed arrow). Brain activity in the dominant *right*-side face-processing system (grey patch) depends mostly on cues from the *left* side of the face (in this case the side that is feminine).

D.I. Perrett (2009) Perception Lab.

Not everyone has the right-brain bias in face-processing, just as not everyone is right-handed. In any case, face-processing is not done entirely by only one side of the brain; in reality, both sides of the brain get involved, just as both hands are used in everyday tasks, even by strongly right-handed individuals. As will become evident soon, when it comes to seeing faces, the brain doesn't just employ two hands; in reality it is more like the Hindu god Vishnu, with multiple arms or structures, each of which contributes by processing a specific aspect of the face.

Recognizing familiar faces

Recognizing a familiar face in a crowd is something we can all do with tremendous ease. It doesn't seem to require any effort at all; faces we know just pop out at us. But this ability, which we take for granted, is apparently so complex that despite many years devoted to the problem no one has yet been able to build a computer program or robot that can do the same with the same level of accuracy. What, then, is so difficult about recognizing familiar faces?

At a fundamental level, the face changes continually as our expression changes – it rarely looks the same from moment to moment, particularly in social situations. As we speak and gesticulate with animation, we contort our faces this way or that. Were humans unable to overlook all this variation and respond only to those underlying features of a face that are the cues to identity, our best friend when smiling at us would appear to be a completely different person when frowning at us. It is not just expressions that change, either; as light conditions change, strong shadows can make people's faces look very different, and we may also see a given person from a variety of different angles. If we couldn't compensate for these superficial differences, we would never be able to distinguish one face from another. Just such difficulties can result from brain damage: in such circumstances a changed facial expression may look like a different person, and changed shadows on the face or the same face turned through 45 degrees may also produce a face with a new identity.[4]

Consider the problem that confronts us when we see a face. First, we have to recognize that what we're looking at actually is a face, and not a teapot or a guitar. Second, we have to assess whether the face is one we know, one with particular memories linked to it. If it is, then seeing the face of someone we know should trigger the recollection of that person's name. When the problem is split into two tasks in this way, we can see that the initial task in recognition is one of vision and that the second task is one of memory.

Seeing a face as a face

The job of vision in working out the structure of a face independent of all changeable conditions is indeed a hard one, and this big task is accomplished as a series of smaller tasks. To begin at the beginning, first the brightness and colour at each point in the image are recorded by circuits at the back of the eye, rather like a digital camera. This mass of details is sent to the back of the brain, where it is analysed in several stages even before it reaches the brain regions that specialize in decoding faces.

The first stage sorts out the edges that are present in the image. Here there are billions and billions of brain cells, each dedicated to detecting the presence of one type of edge or one local element. Each cell sits in silence until the relevant edge is present at just the right angle and just the right point in space; when this happens the cell sends a signal to the next stage of processing, something like 'thick vertical edge, dead ahead', whereas another cell may signal 'thin, horizontal bar, slightly up and left of centre'. These cells define where all the image elements lie: their lengths, their angles, their contrast type, their colours, and their thicknesses. The next few brain stages take care of how edges align and extend in space, curving this way or that, and how they link at intersections or join together to form particular shapes. Further stages then combine the vocabulary of shapes with a vocabulary of textures and colours (round and red, spotty and triangular, and so on).

The shapes that the brain is analysing are only fragments or features of whole objects in the real world. As we look at something, what we want to know is whether we are looking at a pig or a Porsche, a face or a fruit-bowl. To answer this the brain cells need also to analyse how the parts or fragments are laid out in relation to one another. In building up an impression of a car, the brain, like a factory employing specialized mechanics, attaches components together two at a time (no more). In visual recognition, as in building the real car, the process centres on the biggest part: the chassis. Large components are bolted on first. Progressively smaller parts and fragments are added until the form of the overall car emerges. In a real car-production line a mechanic or a robot may link two pieces together without worrying about the overall construction scheme: the same is true in the brain, where individual cells specify how each pair of features fits together. The cells work independently, each doing its job and signalling when the right pair of features (or parts) is visible, but otherwise remaining inactive. The real car emerges at the end of the factory line when the activity of all the mechanics has resulted in all the parts having been attached; even if a few pieces were missing, the car would still be recognizable (though sales might suffer). So it is with sight – we see objects as combinations of parts laid out in a specific plan or configuration: even if only some of the features or some of the plan were evident, we could guess the rest.

Sight, then, is a process of working out what parts are evident and how they fit together. But parts of faces don't look like parts of words or parts of cars. This is not a problem for the brain, however, because the brain cells used in seeing faces are appropriately specialized. The brain has evolved to be *so* interested in faces, in fact, that it has a series of factory departments with nerve cells that specialize exclusively in putting together face parts. There may also be departments for other important visual items, such as text,[5] but faces must be really special because there are so many brain departments that process faces and because they are so specialized.

In the back half of the brain there are at least six of these departments dedicated to faces: three on the left side of the brain and three on the right.[6] Each face department is a small patch of brain tissue some 3–5 millimetres across – much less than the width of a fingernail, for example – and is packed with about ten million brain cells. The departments are found consistently in the same places in different people, though some individuals have additional departments, or departments that are extra large or extra small. This may explain why some of us are particularly good at face recognition, while others are unusually poor.

The activity of face-processing departments shows up in brain scans of humans or monkeys as they look at faces. The departments remain quiescent while other objects are viewed,[7] but kick into action when a face comes on the scene. The similarity of brain organization in face-processing in humans and monkeys points to a common ancestry and a common function.[8] The great surprise to brain scientists is just how specialized are the brain departments when it comes to face-processing. By listening in on the activity of individual brain cells within the face-processing departments of monkeys we can determine that virtually *all* of the constituent brain cells are dedicated to detecting faces and face features.[9] One cell will signal away with gusto when an eye is visible, but remain eerily silent when any other sort of object or pattern is viewed. Another will spring to life when an open mouth is on show, but keep entirely quiet otherwise. All of the cells come to life in response to one aspect or another of faces, and none respond to any other object or pattern at all.

In the manufacturer's blueprints for a new car, the designs will specify the car's appearance from a number of perspectives – a front elevation view, a plan view, a side view, and a rear view – and in addition there will be separate detailed plans for key components, such as the wheels, the dashboard, and even the engine. In the same way, the brain manages to recognize a variety of views, but the 'blueprints' it uses (the specialized cells) are far more numerous. For each familiar face, the brain keeps a variety of separate plans – plans of different perspective views,[10] and plans of how faces appear in different orientations, at different distances,[11] under different lighting, and even at different locations in the visual world. Once again, the dedication and specificity of the plans for faces is truly remarkable. The discoveries of how the brain handles faces have provided a major insight into how the brain handles *any* complex task.

As already explained, the brain's plans are embodied in groups of specialized cells. What this means is that when we see a person who is initially looking away from us and who then turns round to face us, different plans are brought into operation during the rotation: initially one set of cells, dedicated to the back view, is active; then another set becomes active, for the profile view; then another set, for the half profile; and finally yet another set, for the front view.[12] Taken together, these numerous plans for the different views allow recognition across the wide variety of circumstances in which faces are encountered in everyday life.

This multiplicity of plans doesn't seem very economical, but the brain contains so many cells (roughly 100,000,000,000) that it can easily afford to dedicate a few million to faces and hundreds of thousands to analysing a given view of any head. One priority shown by the brain, which may also represent an economy, is to keep the most plans and the most detailed specifications for the views that are commonly encountered. In practice we most often see faces upright, and that is the orientation for which most of our face-recognition hardware becomes specialized: we have lots of brain cells responsive to an upright face shape and lots of cells responsive to upright mouths, but we have only a few cells responsive to unusual orientations.[13]

This privileged processing of upright faces and face features is illustrated in the famous 'Thatcher illusion' (Figure 2.4), which appears in many psychology textbooks. If you look at the upper pair of upside-down images of Margaret Thatcher, the former British Prime Minister, you will see that they look pretty much the same. If you now look at the bottom pair of images, in which the inverted images have been turned upright, the effect is somewhat surprising: the face on the right now appears quite grotesque. This effect can be produced using any person's face; flipping the regions containing the eyes and mouth upside-down turns the smile into a bizarre grimace.[14] Our failure to notice that anything is wrong in the upside-down photograph is understandable given the way our brain cells are accustomed to specifying the shape of the mouth and eyes in the normal upright view. In this case, therefore, the mouth is analysed as a normal upright smile.

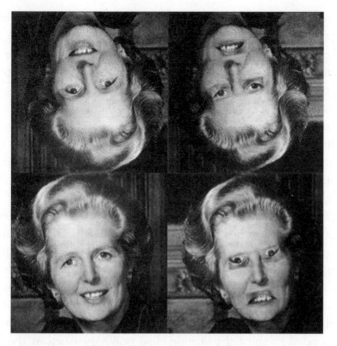

Figure 2.4 The Thatcher illusion. *Top row:* The upper pair of face images, both inverted, look fairly normal. *Bottom row:* It is only when the faces are turned the right way up that the features on the right look strange (see text for details).
P. Thompson (1980).

A Halle Berry brain cell?

In the stages just described, most of the cells respond to the general characteristics of faces for a wide range of species, so long as the faces are round and have a mouth and eyes. In addition, quite a few of the cells show specific influences from learning, and these appear to be dedicated to the visual cues present in faces that have acquired significance during the life of the brain's owner.[15]

The cells are akin to visual records of familiar faces, but the visual records are unlike photos in that a given photo represents only one instance of one person. The cells respond to many instances of faces. Some may respond specifically to many instances of one type of face; in monkeys, for example, there are cells which may respond preferentially to faces of monkeys and other cells that respond to human faces, or to particular familiar human faces. In the brains of sheep some visual cells are tuned to human or dog faces, and others to sheep faces.

Once we have started the recognition process and have a detailed visual description of a face and its features, associated memories can be activated in which the features of a familiar face are linked to other kinds of information we have stored about the person, such as her or his name and relationship to us. Recordings of brain activity have begun to yield clues about how a face and information about it are linked. In people undergoing surgical treatment for epilepsy, probes may be used to record activity in brain cells in an area at the side of the brain (the temporal lobe) associated with epilepsy. It may take several days before a seizure occurs and the surgeons can pinpoint the source of the epilepsy so that they can plan surgery to remove the abnormal brain tissue, and the long recordings made while waiting for a seizure may present an opportunity to examine what information is processed by individual cells in different parts of the conscious brain.

The patients who agree to these experiments are shown various photographs of celebrities, or of interesting scenes, animals, and food items. All the while, the activity of their brain cells is monitored.[16] Recordings over many test sessions in different patients showed that individual cells became active when the patient looked at particular faces; these cells remained silent when pictures of other people or scenes and objects were shown. Different brain cells responded when particular types of food were shown, just as other cells responded to the sight of individual buildings (such as the Leaning Tower of Pisa, the Sydney Opera House, or the World Trade Center), and yet other cells responded to particular animals. The particularity of these cell responses is surprising enough, but findings for cells activated by the sight of faces are even more remarkable. These proved to be extraordinarily selective; for example in one experiment one of these cells was sensitive *only* to the image of the actress Jennifer Aniston,[17] while another cell responded *only* to the sight of the actress Halle Berry. Other brain cells studied have responded only to images of famous people, such as President Clinton or Homer Simpson (so even cartoon characters are represented), or to particular members of the patient's family.[18] The link between the facial image of a person and the other information we store about them seems to be highly specific. Further probing of a brain cell that responded only to photographs of Halle Berry's face showed that this same cell also responded to a simple line drawing of her face, to images of her dressed as 'Catwoman' (in which guise she had a mask covering most of her face) and, most intriguingly of all, to the mere sight of her name spelled out in letters. This shows that the cell's response to Halle Berry was not due to a particular visual feature found in photographs of her face – the only thing common to an image of her face, letters spelling her name, and an image of a woman dressed in a cat suit is the *concept* of 'Halle Berry', the person and actress.

The fact that one cell responded to Jennifer Aniston while another responded to Halle Berry does not mean that within our brains we have one and only one specific cell dedicated to recognizing each person we know.[19] In fact, we give over thousands of visual cells and memory cells to coding those people who are important to us, be they family, loved ones, or favourite actors or actresses. In general, the more important any given skill is to us, the more brain cells we set aside for it. Since recognizing our partner is particularly important, we have lots of cells to do just this. Likewise we will have many cells dedicated to each familiar person: possibly hundreds for each of our favourite TV stars, hundreds for each work colleague, and thousands and thousands for our children. Each high-level cell handling a specific face depends on inputs from millions of other cells working in the earlier stages of vision to determine how all the edges and colours are arranged in the image and the particular shapes of facial features. There will also be many high-level cells working at the same time on the details of a familiar face. Overall, therefore, recognition always involves the activity of many millions of cells.

At this stage of the recognition process, all kinds of information (written words, knowledge of an actress's film roles, the sound of her name, and perhaps her voice[20]) becomes integrated with face-specific information so that a cell becomes programmed to respond to a wide variety of images and sounds that relate to that person. The brain contains multiple separate processing systems – one that investigates faces, one that investigates bodies, another that investigates text, and yet another that investigates the sound of voices. In the response of the cell in the memory system to Halle Berry's face, her cat-suit costume, and her written name, what we are seeing is the coming together of the results of three separate investigations, all pertaining to visual characteristics associated with Halle Berry.

When recognition fails

Faces are so important that several brain systems are dedicated to studying their features, notifying us about how appealing their owner is, and alerting us to what we know about him or her. The initial realization that the brain includes dedicated face-recognition systems came from strange symptoms described in medical journals over the past fifty years. For several centuries, indeed, the disturbing problems experienced by people in everyday life when they have suffered damage to a part of the brain have been the main source of understanding how the mind works when it is healthy. It is paradoxical that we can learn most about brain machinery when it is partly broken, but when it is well it runs so smoothly that we are unaware of the contribution of its various components. In the same way, an Olympic athlete will only realize how one of the body's thousands of muscles contributes to performance when that one muscle is injured.

Strokes can result in 'ignorance' or, to use the medical label, 'agnosia' (from the Greek word for 'not knowing'). People with agnosia fail to recognize objects even though they may still see colour and edges and retain the ability to resolve small details, such as being able to see two dots close together as separate rather than seeing them blurred together into one blob. For example, Oliver Sacks describes a patient, Dr P., who at the conclusion of a consultation 'reached out his hand and took hold of his wife's head, tried to lift it off, to put it on. He had apparently mistaken his wife for a hat!'[21]

Strokes may result in 'face ignorance', known medically as 'prosopagnosia' (derived from the Greek words for 'face', *prosopon*, and 'ignorance', *agnosia*). People with prosopagnosia, then, are literally ignorant of faces, despite the fact that their ability to recognize all other kinds of object remains intact. People who suffer in this way have to use specific cues, like the hairstyle or some item of clothing, to recognize friends and family. Dr P. could only recognize his brother by a chipped tooth. As you can imagine, relying on hairstyles or clothing that are liable to change makes recognizing any one person hopelessly unreliable. Voices, on the other hand, provide a more stable cue, and this was how Dr P. usually identified his wife.

About three hundred patients with such symptoms have been described in detail. Most of these are even more remarkable than Dr P. in that their recognition problem is specific to faces. Dr P. had difficulty recognizing a hat, but patients with prosopagnosia normally have difficulty only with faces – they can tell all other types of object apart without difficulty. Most patients were normal one day and then, following a brain injury (usually a stroke), suddenly changed so that they could no longer recognize their friends, their spouses, or their children, and sometimes not even themselves. The sudden loss of recognition would be both devastating and keenly felt. (If you had lived your whole life being unable to see the differences in faces, you might not realize that there was a problem – after all, people can usually be recognized by their voice, their manner, and the context – but sudden loss of a familiar skill is a different matter.) Actually, difficulties in recognizing faces may be as common as difficulties in reading. You may have experience of this in your own life: if you consistently recognize a person only to find her looking straight through you, it may be not that she is being aloof but that she is just poor at recognition. Difficulties in reading are spotted at school, but no one tests school kids' ability to recognize faces. Just as problems in reading words vary in severity, so do difficulties in reading faces; since the advent of the internet, people have become more likely to realize that they have had a problem in recognizing faces and that they have had this problem all their life.[22] Websites[23] have been set up for people to report their problems, and thousands are indeed reporting them. Current indications suggest that this condition may affect more than 2.5 per cent of Caucasian populations.[24]

The symptoms of changed recognition described by patients are surprisingly varied: to some, faces may appear distorted and ugly; to others, they may all look like dogs; and to yet others, a given face may be clearly recognizable but at the same time feel literally alien. Each symptom is as disturbing to the patient as it may be intriguing to the rest of us. How can such debilitating and varied conditions arise?

With just a few assumptions about brain systems, the aberrant symptoms concerning face recognition can give us insight into how we judge faces in terms of their familiarity and their beauty. Dr P., for example, had problems that affected the very earliest stages of face perception; faces simply made no sense to him, which is why they could be confused with other objects, such as hats. Other patients have problems linking faces to memory, but no problem with the early visual part; in looking at a face they can tell you about the features, the person's age and sex, and whether two pictures show the same or a different person, but from the face alone they can't tell you the person's name or whether or not they've ever met that person. Faces are recognized as faces, but they aren't seen as known individuals. For these patients, there is disruption to the brain pathways that connect visual analysis of faces to memory systems. Since there are alternative pathways to memory (from speech analysis, for example), such patients can still identify others (on the basis of their voices, for instance).

Forgotten faces

Interestingly, although people with prosopagnosia cannot conjure up a name or say anything about a person when shown his or her face, they do sometimes show a glimmer of an emotional response to familiar faces. These emotional flurries can be picked up with a sensitive 'lie detector' device which measures how sweaty the skin gets. Any time we are slightly aroused, our heart beats a little faster and our skin becomes a little sweatier, and a familiar face seems to be spotted by the patient's emotional system, even if what gets through to the memory is not sufficient to recall details about the face.[25]

Everyone may show this emotional flutter in response to familiar faces, even when memory seems to fail. Tapping into the emotional response is just a more sensitive way of finding out whether there is any residual face-memory left. One way of demonstrating residual memories is with photos that offer a 'blast from the past'. Imagine being shown a photo of all the kids with whom you went to school: if your school days were long ago and your school was quite large, there would be bound to be faces you could not remember. In this situation, you might show the same symptoms as a prosopagnosic patient: an individual face might give you a vague feeling of familiarity, even if you couldn't say to whom the face belonged, while for other faces you might have absolutely no recollection of who they were and might even deny that you ever knew anything about them. We could take such unrecognized faces and teach you to assign names to them. You (like many of the patients) would be quicker to learn *true* names for familiar but forgotten faces than to learn to call them by *false* names, however plausible. This difference would occur because for some faces there would be links to memory so weak they would be insufficient for any recollection, yet these weak connections could be strengthened by relearning a true name. For patients with strokes that have affected face recognition, the damage is not always complete; bits of the system can survive. A patient's residual ability to recognize faces, demonstrated by sensitive tests, is just that – a residual capacity in a partly damaged system.[26]

These different types of test highlight the importance of emotional feelings of familiarity, as well as more 'intellectual' recollections in face recognition: we recognize people on the basis of how they make us *feel*, and not only on the basis of what details their face allows us to recall. To recognize familiar individuals truly and accurately, both of these systems need to work for us in concert.

Aliens and impostors

The two ways of recognizing faces – through cold logical memory and through emotional feelings – are also suggested by another form of brain damage. People with Capgras syndrome have no difficulty at all in recog-nizing the faces of familiar individuals: the problem they do have is in insisting that the people they recognize are, in fact, impostors. Such feel-ings must be truly worrying for the patient. For example, one report details how a patient minutely examined his father's face before accusing him of being a criminal double who had taken his father's place.[27] Another report details a young man (DS) with Capgras syndrome who believed that his father and he himself had been duplicated. His existential doubt is poign-ant when he asks: 'Mother, if the real DS ever returns do you promise that you will still treat me as a friend and love me?'[28]

Capgras patients can recognize the identity of a face, but the sense of familiarity or *déjà vu* that should occur with a family face is missing, with the result that a known person may *look* right but not *feel* right. The delusions of Capgras patients are usually restricted to their family members. Close family are likely to evoke higher levels of emotional response and familiarity than your bank manager or Halle Berry, so the discrepancy between how familiar they look and how familiar they feel is sensed more acutely.

We appear to have two types of memory. One type of memory is for facts (names, occupations, and all the trivia we have on someone); a second type of memory gives the sense of familiarity but no facts. This second kind of memory registers everything experienced before with one tag: 'seen that'.[29] Without the tag, items appear novel. One explanation for the different symptoms in prosopagnosia and Capgras syndrome is that the bits of the brain concerned with seeing faces have distinct output connections to these two different sorts of memory. For Capgras patients, it is suggested, damage leaves the connections to factual memory intact, such that all the details *about* people can be recalled, but compromises the other set of connections to familiarity. The face of a family member will have all the distinguishing characteristics necessary to be recognized and to evoke the person's life details, yet at the same time the face will feel strangely unfamiliar. Capgras patients do not show the skin-sweatiness response that indicates differentiation between familiar and unfamiliar faces.[30]

When a Capgras patient says that a face belongs to an impostor or a double, the psychiatrist labels this 'delusional'. It is certainly a delusion, but we now have the beginnings of an explanation as to how the delusion may arise: the emotional reaction and distinct sense of familiarity that normally come with a highly familiar face both appear to be missing. As such delusions make clear, it is just as important to recall the appropriate *feelings* that should go with a familiar face as it is to recall mundane information such as the person's name.

Picasso's faces

For some stroke patients it's not the recognition that's the problem but the way the faces look. Everyone may appear as if they have fish heads or look like figures from a Picasso painting. Here the stroke victim is referring not to our evolutionary forebears or to the gill arches discussed in Chapter 1, but rather to the fact that the eyes and nose can appear misshapen and slightly out of place (Figure 2.5). At other times people may appear as chimaeras amalgamating different species: a human body but the head of a different animal. One woman reported that all the faces around her suddenly looked like dogs, while another girl described seeing faces as something like a Magritte painting with skin covering where the features should be. So how is it that such profound disturbances can happen to the appearance of faces?

Figure 2.5 Picasso faces. *Left:* Picasso's portraits of faces distorted the size, view, and configuration of facial features. Brain injury can produce distortions in a real face (*Centre*) such that the face looks as though it had been painted by Picasso (*right:* simulation). (See Chapter 4 for an account of the simulation of portrait styles.)

D.I. Perrett (2009) Perception Lab.

We can begin to account for each type of face strangeness by realizing three basic facts – facts that should be in a starter pack for anyone who is thinking of becoming a neurosurgeon. Fact One: brain regions are specialized for particular functions. Fact Two: there is a region of the brain that is dedicated to seeing faces. Fact Three: connections between brain systems sometimes get disrupted, for example by bursting blood vessels, by tumours, or by epileptic short-circuits. In considering each problem with faces, therefore, we need to work out which brain system is no longer properly connected to the brain centre for seeing faces. It may be that the relevant connection is broken or it may be that it is over-active.

Take the problem of seeing distorted faces. There is one brain system that helps us to appreciate the size of objects. On the right side of the brain, this system helps to judge the importance and the size of the left side of objects.[31] When this brain system is disrupted by a stroke, the left side of an object begins to look narrower than the right side. The contraction can be quite marked. All the features are still there: it's just that they are crammed together in half the space. If a brain injury occurs and disconnects the face-handling system from this part of the brain – the part that is responsible for appreciating the left side – the result will be a contraction of the left side of all faces (Figure 2.6), even though no other type of object will appear distorted. If *all* objects were contracted on the left side, the patient might not notice;[32] when the size distortion is restricted to faces, however, the patient may start to notice that the left side of every face is a bit squashed relative to the left side of the body.

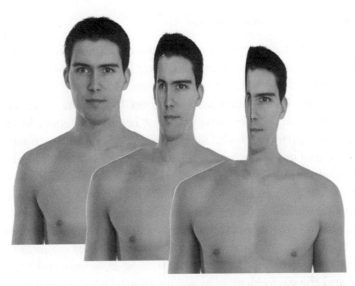

Figure 2.6 Distorted face perception. Damage on the right side of the brain can disrupt the appreciation of size on the left side of objects. Such distortions can be face-specific,[33] so the patient would notice that the faces were shrunk on the left side (or perhaps expanded on the right[34]) relative to the rest of the torso or other objects. This is illustrated here by the cascade of upper bodies. *Left:* The left and right sides of the face are normally proportioned. *Centre and right:* The left side of the face is progressively shrunk, while the left and right sides of the torso remain in balance.

D.I. Perrett (2009) Perception Lab.

Figure 2.7 shows constructions by a patient who could recognize faces but thought they looked odd. He described all faces as fish-like. When asked to arrange the features of a car and a face, he arranged the car features correctly, but the face that he constructed had all the left-hand features compressed together.

Figure 2.7 Fish faces: distorted face perception after a stroke. Arrangements of face and car features by a patient who reported that every face looked to him like a fish-head.

A.W. Young *et al.* (1990).

Changes in face attractiveness

Individuals with face-recognition problems may report that faces change subtly; with no change as dramatic as jumping species, as just described, faces may nevertheless alter in attractiveness. One young man[35] described how after a stroke his wife's face no longer looked the same. He sadly recalled her beautiful eyes, now that that beauty had gone. In fact, she was the same person with the same eyes, but for him the attraction and wonderment of her eyes was now missing – when he gazed at her face, the eyes were almost blanked out; they had no significance. This was for him one of the most devastating changes that had happened after his stroke.

Following a motorcycle accident, another man not only had problems in distinguishing the faces of family members, but also found that the faces of pretty girls were no longer visually arousing – they no longer turned him on.[36] Though he could still be aroused by touch and sound, the beauty and the excitement from seeing an attractive women had simply disappeared: they just seemed 'dull, all the same'.[37]

In circumstances you might have experienced yourself, the attractiveness of faces can get an upgrade over the space of a single evening. When we have an increased blood-alcohol level, the attractiveness of other people's faces increases. For young adults studied the effect occurs way before closing time, so this cannot just reflect the increasing desperation of any who were on the look-out for a partner – the longer the clock ticks without a successful move, the more likely it is that they will go home alone.[38]

We may explain the changes in the attractiveness of faces – whether for better or for worse – by thinking about the connections within the brain between the parts that allow us to see faces and the parts that give us pleasure. If these connections become completely broken, then the capacity to find any face attractive will be lost. If the connections are primed by alcohol[39] or pathologically over-stimulated through epilepsy, this might distort the attractiveness of faces, making them all beautiful for a while.

Pay-per-view for sexy faces

We know that people like looking at pretty faces. What is surprising is that in the lab we can get them to work for access to those faces. Researchers at Harvard Medical School paid heterosexual men to view faces. How long any one image remained on the screen was under the men's control: if they wanted to keep viewing a particular image, they could alternately press the 'N' and 'M' keys of a computer keyboard; if they did not, the image would change. The men worked hard (pressing 130 times a minute was not uncommon during the test, which they were told would last 40 minutes). Not all the images produced such furious manual responses. Female faces already rated as attractive by a control group of other participants turned out to be just those that the research subjects chose to view longer: the experiment therefore demonstrated that the men were prepared to work hard at pressing keys for the sole reward of seeing a pretty girl's face.

Men and women usually agree on which males are attractive and which males are not. If people are asked to assign ratings of 1–7 to pictures of faces on the basis of attractiveness – so that 7 means 'very attractive' (hot) and 1 means 'definitely not', with 4 meaning 'average' – then the scores of men and women are virtually identical. In the key-pressing task, by contrast, there are marked sex differences. Despite the starting agreement on *aesthetics*, attractive faces provide different *incentives* for men and women. For 'straight' men beauty counts, but only if it is *female* beauty. Female attractiveness alone is motivating; the men do not work any harder to see male faces, not even to see those that are judged by others or by themselves as attractive.[40] What is remarkable is that 'straight' women find the faces of both handsome men *and* beautiful women worth putting in extra effort to see:[41] they will work quite hard to see either. Perhaps this motivational effect explains the preponderance of female faces on the covers of women's magazines. Why straight women are so interested in the faces of pretty women is a bit of a mystery; my female colleagues suggest that it is to check out the competition. (This in turn is intriguing because of its mixture of possible motives – competitors might have fashion tips that could be copied, or they might have men worth taking note of! See Chapter 10.)

To understand why faces provide so strong an incentive, we need to look at the structures in the brain that control motivation. These are the structures where all addictive drugs (be they cocaine, cannabis, or coffee) have their effect. Animals will work to get this system stimulated, either through the natural rewards of sex and food or through artificial rewards of addictive drugs. Patients suffering from depression that is unresponsive to all normal treatments show benefits from direct electrical stimulation of this brain system: after stimulation the patients have a better mood and want to seek out pleasurable activities.[42] It is not surprising, then, that these brain structures are called 'pleasure centres' or 'reward systems'.

One can see how faces cause a surge of activity in the pleasure centres. When cells in one part of the brain are activated, those cells use up energy. To replace their energy, the body diverts blood to this part of the brain so that extra oxygen is available to utilize food stores: the brain part becomes literally flushed with blood. (In much the same way, if you lift weights repeatedly your muscles will get tired: they too will get pumped up when blood rushes to the muscles to allow the body to replenish the spent energy.) This response is the basis of most brain scans, which work not by measuring the brain activity itself but by spotting which parts of the brain are pumped up with blood – these parts are assumed to have been getting a good work-out from whatever the person was doing or thinking in the brain scanner. (Incidentally, there are also devices that measure blood flow to the genitals, and such devices might well reveal many men's motivation in viewing images of pretty women.[43]) For heterosexual men watching faces, it is clear that attractive women's faces produce heightened activity and a rush of blood to the pleasure centres. Handsome *male* faces just do not make the grade – they have little effect on the pleasure centres. So when straight men see attractive or unattractive male faces there is no change in activity in blood flow to their pleasure centres. Hence the brain activity is related not to beauty but to wanting (lusting), and to the effort men will make for access to female beauty.[44]

History records the lengths to which men will go when attracted to a female face, whether it be launching a thousand ships, writing a love poem, or, more difficult still, getting down on their knees and begging. The prosaic truth is that all such egregious or romantic acts of infatuation arise from the hero's desire to have a particular face before his eyes so that it will activate brain connections between his face-handling system and his pleasure centres.

Sexual orientation affects the brain responses to faces[45] in ways that largely match one's intuitive expectations. Lesbians react to female faces in the same way that heterosexual men respond to female faces: that is, there is more activity in the brain's reward systems when they are looking at attractive women's faces than when looking at men's faces. For gay men, the pattern of activity is opposite; for them, men's faces produce more activity than women's faces. Perhaps the biggest surprise, is the responses in the brains of heterosexual women, where the difference between the impact of male faces and of female faces is so slight. These women's brains are turned on by male faces, as one might expect, but even in straight women female faces too can produce almost the same level of activation in the pleasure centres.

In general, then, sexual orientation influences both the interest in faces and the brain's response to faces. There are interesting sex differences: whatever their sexual orientation, men seem to be more visually turned on than women;[46] they will work much harder than women to see faces that they regard as beautiful. Attractive faces seem to drive brain systems that provide 'pleasure' and that control 'wanting'[47], but *how* faces drive them differs between men and women.

Mirror, mirror

The concern with beauty can reflect an obsession with our own appearance, as was the case for the Wicked Witch in the fairy tale 'Snow White and the Seven Dwarves'. Mirrors tell the truth about our appearance, even if they do not speak out loud. And as we will see in the rest of the book, the witch had it wrong – whatever is true about our appearance in mirrors, this cannot tell us much about whether other individuals will or won't find us 'attractive'! Nonetheless, brain disease can make us doubt the truth of reflections.

Dementia[48] can induce some very unusual face-recognition problems. Imagine looking in the mirror and seeing not yourself but another person! This is the stuff of nightmares. Two patients in Sydney developed exactly this symptom with the onset of dementia. One was so disturbed by his reflection that he had to cover up all the mirrors and reflecting surfaces in his home, so that his other self did not spook him. He could still identify other people's reflections correctly; it was only his own reflection that gave him problems. He was unable to accept that it originated from himself, even if it 'looked somewhat like him'. He was able to describe his mirror-self correctly, noting the lack of hair – just like himself. During an interview, indeed, he demonstrated to a film crew the baldness of 'the man in the reflection' by tilting his own head forward in order to make the hairless crown more visible in the reflection. This seems strange: he retained knowledge of how to control his reflection, even while he did not believe that the reflection showed himself.

Even without dementia, experience with mirrors is not always comforting – not least because it reveals all those signs of ageing! Reflections can be very disturbing. For example, I recall an unnerving experience one night in an Edinburgh pub where I sat at a curved bar. Like many bars, this one had mirrors behind the bottles and one could gaze idly at the reflections. I could see the reflection of the guy sitting on my right, and when I turned to my left there was the reflection of the person on my left – but when I looked straight ahead, there was a blank. The mirror worked to reflect the real world, yet I was not there; 'mirror me' had slid out of the picture. Perhaps I wasn't really there? Or worse, was I like the undead of horror movies, without shadow or reflection? The truth was simpler: the reflections that I could see came from two mirrors angled in such a way that my own reflection was not bounced back in my direction.

The Dracula nightmare that denies *any* reflection is an extreme case, but the inability to see one's own reflection accurately is quite common in psychiatric disorders such as schizophrenia.[49]

One way in which we learn about our own reflection is by noticing the correlation between any movement we make and the movement taking place in the mirror.[50] We don't need to worry about our reflection: we are the puppet master, controlling the strings.

We make a clear distinction between the movements, noises, and touch that we cause, and can therefore expect, and all other unpredictable sensations. One brain system that picks up unexpected movement, noise, and touch lies right next to a region of the brain that analyses faces.[51] This proximity is probably not mere coincidence: ancient brain systems that alerted us to the presence of other animals could have expanded during evolution to provide an analysis of the facial expressions and social signals of our own species.

This discussion of our sense of agency and control is a digression with a purpose: we can use it to explain why mirror reflections are so intriguing to infants, and why the Australian patients had problems in recognizing their own facial reflections but not the reflections of others. Our own mirror reflection is odd for more reasons than just being the flip side of our real self, one being that other people's reflections behave differently from our own. When we see someone else's face and the reflected image of that face, the two move in perfect harmony. This is not true for ourselves – when we smile at the mirror, we cannot *see* our own lips moving and compare them with the lips in our reflection: we can *feel* them move, but we *see* them move only in the mirror. To recognize that the reflection in the mirror is our *own* reflection requires us to notice the synchrony between muscle contractions, skin tension, and the smiling in the mirror image. If there were a problem with the links between face-processing and the system for spotting self-generated sensations, that might well prevent us from recognizing our own mirror image, though it would not prevent us from recognizing other people's reflections. While my reflection and your reflection have much in common, I know my reflection is mine by matching the way my body feels during actions with the way I see my reflection moving. I cannot do this to work out whether *you* are the source of *your* reflection.

It should now be clear that the particular systems of the brain that help us understand faces can go wrong on their own, independent of other systems, creating peculiar effects. So we should not be surprised that, following brain damage or disorder, problems can arise in recognizing faces – problems that may be highly specific, weird, and extremely disturbing for the sufferers. One thing that we have *not* yet considered, though, is how the brain comes to have dedicated face-handling hardware and software in the first place. Are we born already able to see faces, as distinct from everything else? Are some faces intrinsically nice to look at, or does our early experience shape which faces we find attractive? To answer these issues, we need to learn about infants.

Chapter 3
A BABY'S BIAS

Born to be fascinated by faces

When we talk about 'attractiveness' in faces we are often referring to *sexual* attraction, but attraction comes in other, non-sexual forms, too, which at a fundamental level can be about a simple compulsion to look at this or that face. Infants, as you know if you have spent any time around them, seem to enjoy looking at faces. They stare at them and will smile cutely at mum, dad, sister or brother, or even at crude patterns in the shape of faces. Where do these reactions to faces come from? Are certain faces intrinsically pleasurable to look at, or do our first experiences shape which faces we grow up to like especially?

We spend nine months in the womb, floating in the dark and sheltered from the outside world. When we are born we are thrust into a bright, noisy confusion of people and objects, and we begin the task of learning about the world around us. That's a lot of stuff to get a grip on, but babies are exceptionally good at it. Their immense and obvious helplessness tends to obscure the fact that babies are better than even the most diligent university students at taking in information, learning new skills, and applying their knowledge to new problems.

But how do newborns react to faces in the way that they do when they have never seen them before? Adults have many parts of the brain dedicated to handling faces, but what about infants? Are we born with these parts switched on, so that we can already recognize faces as distinct from everything else? Although babies in the womb can learn something about the muffled sound of their mother's voice, what she likes to eat, and even the theme tune to her favourite soap opera, how could they recognize her face? Indeed how could they recognize any face at all, given their lack of experience?

There are two possibilities. The first is that babies are born with the ability to recognize faces; faces would be a special kind of feature of an infant's world to which they were tuned to respond 'instinctively'. The second option is that babies must learn how to recognize them starting from scratch, just like any other object.

Testing what babies do and don't know requires a little ingenuity, because they can't tell us. One thing we can do is measure how long they spend looking at a picture or an object. If we make the assumption that the length of time they spend looking at it is an indication of how interesting they find it, this simple test leads us to a stunning conclusion: babies as young as a minute old prefer looking at a schematic, cartoon-like face compared to a pattern that contains the same features jumbled up (Figure 3.1).[1] This reaction to face patterns is remarkable and indicates both the profound importance of faces and the extent to which the whole visual system and the brain are already organized at birth.

Figure 3.1 Born with an eye for faces. Even within the first minutes of life, schematic faces attract an infant's interest more than a scrambled pattern with the same features.

D.I. Perrett (based on C. Goren *et al.*, 1975).

In these studies, everyone in the delivery room wore masks so that the babies had no chance of seeing a human face before being tested. When the face-like pattern was moved, the babies turned their head and eyes to follow it. They followed the rearranged face-feature pattern less. As they have no experience at all of faces, this reaction of babies shows that they possess some kind of instinctive face-recognition mechanism. Or does it?

Fuzzy faces

Newborn babies' eyesight is, as you might guess, a little fuzzy. Because the world is pretty blurred, babies like looking at patterns with large features and lots of contrast – small details and subtle shades of grey are simply invisible. Fortunately, the face has some large and obvious features. The eye region stands out because it is generally darker than the rest of the face, particularly when the face is looking forward. Figure 3.2 shows how a face appears to a newborn infant when the face is about 40 cm away; this would be how a baby sees the mother's face when cradled in her arms. Visibility is pretty poor, but just about good enough for the

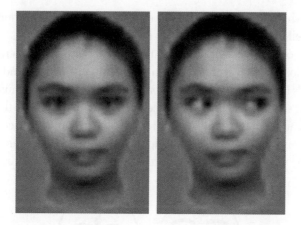

Figure 3.2 What newborn infants may see in a face. The images have been blurred to mimic how a face would appear to an infant when it is positioned about 40 cm (1 foot 4 inches) away.
T. Farroni *et al.* (2002).

infant to make out the main features and to differentiate eye contact from averted gaze.[2]

The brain is not wired up properly at birth. The insulation that wraps around brain cells and allows long-distance connections to work efficiently has yet to develop fully.[3] This means that information cannot pass easily between brain regions – any attempt to send signals across long distances is slow and error-prone because connections are likely to 'short-circuit'. Whatever is happening to faces in the newborn, therefore, must be based on blurred images that lack detail and on a brain that has started up with just the primitive parts working well.

Top heavy

Clearly, there is a puzzle here. Babies prefer faces to other patterns, yet they have poor eyesight and their brains are not well developed. Infants' reactions must therefore be guided by very basic cues that are easy to spot in any face. One difference between the normal and scrambled face patterns is that the real face has more features in the top half than in the bottom half: the scrambled image is more balanced in this respect. This top-heavy configuration seems to be the key to unlocking the interest of the babies. If babies are shown the patterns on the left side of Figure 3.3 they respond in the same way that they do to faces, even though the patterns are not particularly face-like. Bottom-heavy patterns, like those on the right of Figure 3.3, get less attention.[4]

Figure 3.3 The building blocks of a face. Infants prefer to look at top-heavy patterns (*left*) rather than bottom-heavy patterns (*right*).
F. Simion *et al.* (2002).

Top-heavy patterns can be made from either light or dark blobs, but in either case infant fascination is restricted to patterns in which the elements are darker in the upper half than in the lower half.[5] In real faces, the eyes within the confines of a face make a pattern that fits the bill. Humans, and virtually all animals with a backbone, have two eyes paired horizontally, and these usually lie in the upper half of the face above a smaller, central, and single mouth. In addition, the eyes of humans and of many mammals are darker than the surrounding face because the pupils and iris are dark,[6] and when the sunlight is brightest above the head (as it often is), shadows are cast in the eye sockets. Thus the inborn sensitivity matches many aspects of a face. One might think of the babies' sensitivity as curiously adapted to detecting weird patterns found only in psychologists' labs – or one might see the inborn visual preference as ideal in allowing the infant to pay attention to caregivers' faces.

Infant gibbons,[7] chimps,[8] and monkeys[9] born in captivity show an equivalent interest in face patterns soon after leaving the womb, and this inborn face interest may not be unique to primates – if the capacity in primates is innate and relies on primitive sections of the brain, then it may well be present in many mammals and perhaps in other life forms, be they crocodiles or birds,[10] or even fish or frogs. The reactions to faces exhibited by most animals new into the world have yet to be studied, so the attraction (or repulsion) may be much more widespread than is currently known.

We should not lose sight of the fact that the ready-made programming of primates to look at faces represents amazing engineering. Most of the human-made appliances we use today have a tedious set-up process. Imagine that on taking delivery of a baby you were also given a master disk to insert and instructions to install software and then to press 'restart'! Instead, infants are born with marvellous visual-detection programs preloaded and highly functional. Infants open their eyes and find faces interesting. How can this be? Where exactly does this bias to look at top-heavy 'facey' patterns come from?

One suggestion is that babies 'learn' it prior to birth. This may seem incredible, because there is nothing to see in the womb and therefore nothing visual to learn. As Groucho Marx quipped, 'Outside of a dog, a book is man's best friend. Inside of a dog, it's too dark to read.'[11] It's very dark inside your mother, but it is possible for the way we see patterns to be trained up even in the dark. We know that waves of electrical activity radiate across nerve cells in the eye before birth. These cells will sense light once the eyes open, but in fact they are already active during growth. Their electrical signals travel to the brain and wire it up to respond to particular patterns.[12] When a pebble is thrown into a pond, the edges of the radiating ripples link up neighbouring points on the water surface. In a similar manner, the radiating waves of electrical activity in the eye link up all the neighbouring light-detecting cells in the eye that lie on a straight (or slowly curving) line; this patterned electrical input produces brain cells that respond best to straight light–dark edges.

There are types of electrical brain waves which originate in the visual parts of the brain that are in evolutionary terms the most ancient. In adults, these waves are strongly linked to the vivid visual images we experience in dreams. It seems that the waves activate the brain just as though there were real visual signals coming into the eye. We know that the developing foetus spends a high proportion of its time dreaming: perhaps the waves and the dreams train the visual system and by the time the baby is born he or she has already developed a bias to be interested in certain kinds of visual patterns,[13] even though the baby has had no opportunity to see anything. Getting the visual system going before birth by dreams or other means is an amazing and mysterious feat.

Biased to learn mum's face

It seems reasonable to wonder why the infant brain isn't pre-programmed to respond only to the faces of its own species. Human babies would then like human faces more than any of the other patterns, including those in Figure 3.3. It is conceivable that such an innate program could be written into the connections of brain cells, but if it were it would be pretty useless. Consider what would have happened as the face changed during the course of evolution (see Figure 1.1): these facial changes would mean that the face-detection program would have been constantly out of date – while the facial appearance of adults would have progressed, each baby would be looking for a face representing a more ancestral 'throwback'. Think of the frantic development of personal computers – you would not like your brand-new computer to be stuck with an ancient operating system! Upgrades to software and hardware need to keep pace with one another. Likewise, any genes controlling infant reactions to faces would have to keep in step with the genes controlling the anatomy of the face, or the emerging newborn would be sadly disappointed with the appearance of Mum and Dad, and might prefer looking at the cat.

A simpler and more efficient strategy is one that uses a basic system to detect, and orientate towards, the basic characteristics of *all* faces. This approach, coupled with reward-based learning, is all that is needed. Any infant who receives lavish parental affection will have ample chance to learn what the face of its species looks like: Mum and Dad are perfect examples of that species.

Infants are remarkably quick learners – they manage to learn about their mum during day one. We know this because, given a choice between the mother's face and that of a stranger, infants even at the end of their first day are more likely to turn and gaze at their mother. Infants do this even when they are not being coaxed by the comfort from her smell or the sound of her cooing.[14] The cues that the baby uses to spot Mum's face seem to be contained in her hairdo, specifically the shape of the contours of her head and hairline rather than the shape of her mouth and other face parts (but see later). If she wears a head-scarf or puts on a wig, though, the baby shows no preference to look at her at all. Worrying, perhaps – mums would need to avoid bad-hair days to ensure their own babies recognize them. Fortunately, babies learn not just about the appearance of their mother but also about her smell and the way she sounds.[15] Indeed the mother's voice is recognized even before birth: despite all the gurgles and sighs that the baby is also hearing, a recording of Mum reading a poem will speed up the heartbeat of the foetus, whereas the sound of another woman reading the same poem will slow it down. The lilt of Mum's voice is familiar and exciting, while other voices are not.

The infant's ability to notice a change in Mum's hairstyle after just a few hours is pretty impressive; many partners take far longer. And as adults we have an excuse: in recognizing highly familiar people we rely heavily on the eyes, the nose, and the mouth, so it is not uncommon to confuse changes elsewhere on the face and head. We may notice that there is something different about a face but not know what it is: have they shaved off a beard, changed their glasses, or just had a haircut? How could we possibly confuse these? Yet some of us do. For an *unfamiliar* face we are more like an infant, swayed by features external to the face. As adults we learn just as much about details of the hairstyle of a new acquaintance as we do about the particular arrangement of their eyes, nose, and mouth.[16]

It seems to take infants three months of development before they learn to recognize the internal details of faces reliably. By that age, hair has lost its domination in recognition: babies prefer to look at their mother's face, even when she is wearing a scarf – a wig no longer makes her a new woman in the infant's eyes. The specific size and shape of face features acquire importance, as befits the sharpening of the baby's eyesight and the movement from a simple bias toward face-like patterns to a reaction to actual people.

Given that a human infant will inevitably encounter a human face within moments of birth, it is efficient to have a very basic face-pattern bias built in and then let all the faces in the environment do the work of refining face recognition. The simple bias mechanism allows human infants to lock on to the facial differences that are important, the individual and family traits, and also to the facial characteristics common to the local community, and indeed to all humans (see later). The combination of a simple bias developed before birth and learning after birth shows that the two options proposed at the outset of the chapter were misleading: the way in which we see faces need not be either entirely instinctive or entirely learned. Our superb ability to recognize faces comes both from an inborn bias *and* from the experiences to which we are inevitably exposed. Faces both are and are not special – when we are very tiny, any object with the right kind of top-heavy bias is equally fascinating to us: it's just that an object with paired dark horizontal blobs in its upper parts is likely to *be* a face. Moreover, this type of pattern occurs at the same place as the source of the interesting sounds and movements made by the parent talking to the infant. Our constant, intense, and rewarding exposure to faces means that faces acquire a prominence and a significance for us that no other object can match.

Open eyes

Without any experience of faces, human babies turn towards and prefer to look at face-like patterns, reacting with the same kinds of positive responses seen in our primate relatives. Eye gaze plays an important part in all this.

Newborns prefer to look at people who have open rather than closed eyes. This isn't too surprising, given their preference for contrasting top-heavy patterns: open eyes provide more contrast than closed eyes, because closed eyelids are the same skin colour as the rest of the face. When a person facing us looks sideways, the top half of their face lightens because more of the whites of the eyes become visible (Figure 3.2). Given that infants are attracted to dark top-heavy patterns, they prefer faces that are making eye contact to faces that are looking away.[17] This means that infants find people who are paying them attention more interesting than people who are distracted by other things going on in the world. It is a self-centred perspective that persists through life.

We know that in adults, too, the experience of gaze, whether direct or averted, has a profound impact on a host of brain systems. Recent technical innovations have allowed us to study the effects of gaze on these same brain systems in infants. By monitoring the brain activity, paediatricians can pick up abnormal brain responses to gaze. There is growing evidence that in children with autism the gaze signals are not handled normally in the brain,[18] and this may contribute to many of the symptoms of autism.[19] The ability to detect abnormal brain reactions to gaze early in life could help diagnosis and allow early training which could try to offset the profound later social difficulties that accompany autism.

When a brain system becomes active, it changes the blood in that region. The active nerve cells in effect suck oxygen from the blood in order to help generate the energy needed to produce nerve impulses, and this causes a change in colour: oxygenated blood is bright red, while blood low in oxygen is a darker bluish-red maroon colour. We can see this colour change by looking directly into the brain. If one shines a red (or near infra-red) light into a skull, the light goes straight through the skin and bones of the head. If there is actually anything between the ears, then less light comes back than went in: some of the light is absorbed by the brain, and some of it gets reflected back. Red oxygen-rich blood reflects light differently from maroon oxygen-depleted blood, so by measuring the light that is bounced back we can literally see whether there is any colour change in the blood, and from this we can tell how active the cells are in a particular region of the brain.[20] The technique works even better in infants than in adults because their skulls are thinner and allow more light to shine through. Using this method, activity has been detected in several brain areas during eye contact between babies and adults. Amazingly, the same brain regions that control adult reactions to eye gaze are fully operational at four months of age.

Light is not the only way to monitor the brain activity: we can also record electrical changes from the scalps of infants. When brain cells are working well, they 'hum' at a specific frequency related to their coordinated activity: a hum with a frequency of roughly ten cycles per second indicates that the brain is working well. If you were to place a stethoscope over a hollow tree containing a nest of bees, the hum of the bees would be louder the closer you were to the hidden nest. The same is true in picking up the signals from a baby's brain: a monitoring device placed on the scalp picks up the brain's hum best when the hum comes from the parts of the brain directly underneath the device. If we cover a head with an array of monitoring devices, we can construct a map of where the brain is humming most, and thereby identify when and where activity is occurring. Using this technique, we have learned that in the young infant the brain regions just above the ears start buzzing around one-third of a second after the baby sees a face that is making eye contact. A buzz of activity is seen later in the front of the brain. The initial activity relates to identification of the plain geometry of the eyes – something like 'forward-facing eyes' – while the front parts of the brain provide the meaning in terms of how this geometry affects the infant – something like 'looking at me'.

Gazing is good

The enjoyment we get from looking into another person's eyes is fundamental to encouraging our social interaction. It is often claimed that while we humans enjoy looking at one another, most other animals find direct gaze unpleasant.[21] In fact eye contact can be desirable for apes and monkeys too;[22] chimpanzees, for example, will seek eye contact when trying to make up after a fight.[23] It may be that *no* species likes prolonged eye contact, for indeed a long-lasting stare becomes unwelcome and unnerving for humans, too.[24]

Although newborn babies do not actually understand the social significance of being looked at, their preference for dark eye regions over light ones allows us to say that, in some sense, babies 'like' eye contact with other people. A baby's preference for eye contact is, in turn, rewarding for mothers and for any other people who interact with the baby. The way in which a baby looks at the mother's face and eyes leads the mother to respond in more intense and positive ways: making faces and cooing at the baby, playing games like peek-a-boo, and increasing the amount of affectionate touching and stroking.[25] Since these are all enjoyable, the baby will do what he or she can to get more of the same. The baby learns to associate looking at Mum with tickling, with amusing noises, and with great games, so she or he is likely to look at faces even more. Over time the baby will grow more and more attracted to faces in general and to the faces of family members in particular.

Attraction to one's own kind

Infants begin life attracted to face-like patterns. Very soon they start being attracted to one specific face: the face of their mother. What about *other* faces – do infants find the same ones attractive that we do as adults? For infants, we measure attraction in terms of *interest* – how much they like to ogle a particular face. If we make things equal for adults by measuring attraction in the same way, then we can find out whether or not our taste in faces changes as we grow up.

When pictures of human faces are shown to us as adults, any repeated picture soon gets boring – we cannot maintain the level of interest we feel in looking at the face of someone new. This is true when the faces are human, but it doesn't hold if the faces are those of monkeys (Figure 3.4); adults spend an equally short time looking at the new and the old monkey pictures. Nine-month-old infants behave in the same way: they are interested in looking at new faces of men and women, but they show an adult indifference to new monkey faces.[26] It seems that we only care in detail about our own species. This disposition is observable by our first birthday, but what about when we are first in the cradle? It is possible that our attraction to top-heavy patterns may fit the face of a monkey as well as that of a human, though it would probably not fit every animal; but it may be that our recognition of top-heavy patterns is not sufficiently precise to let us detect differences between two individuals of any species, not even humans.

Amazingly, younger infants are equally captivated by both species. Change faces from one human to another, or from one monkey to another, and a baby at six months is equally fascinated by the new face. It seems that we start life keen on the faces of humans and monkeys and are attentive to the subtle differences between individual humans and between individuals

Figure 3.4 Spot the difference? Adults and nine-month-old human infants look longer at novel human faces, but not at novel monkey faces. Six-month-old human infants look longer at novel faces of both species.
O. Pascalis *et al.* (2002).

of other primate species, but soon lose our *general* interest in faces and become more narrowly focused on the faces of our own kind.

This specialization could reflect upbringing, and a subtle experiment with infants' storybooks suggests that it does.[27] One group of parents was encouraged to show a monkey-face book to their infants at six months of age. These babies were shown six faces (Figure 3.5) for just one or two minutes each day for two weeks, and then less frequently thereafter. When tested at nine months, those 'trained' on this jungle book with the small troop of monkeys showed interest when a new monkey face was presented. Other babies with the normal reading diet – *Thomas the Tank Engine*, for example, and no monkey business – were unimpressed by the change in monkey faces. This experiment shows that our interest and attraction gets locked onto those faces we grow up seeing. We are not born liking only human faces, but by the time we approach our first birthday, our experience has narrowed down our world; it's now only human faces that we bother about. Monkey faces, although they are made up of the same building blocks (eyes, nostrils, mouth, ears) and were once as fascinating as human faces, no longer hold our interest.[28]

There is an equivalent case of 'use it or lose it' when it comes to hearing speech sounds.[29] For example, the sounds for the letters *l* and *r*[30] are

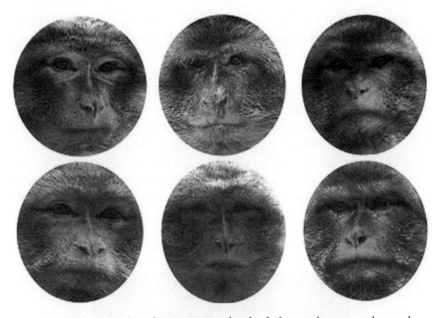

Figure 3.5 The monkey-face training book. Infants who were shown these faces for a few minutes each day kept alive their inborn interest in novel monkey faces.

O. Pascalis *et al.* (2005).

present in English but absent in some Asian languages; a Japanese speaker who doesn't hear the sounds of *l* and *r* early in life will grow up deaf to the difference. Similarly, Swedish speakers employ seventeen simple vowel sounds, while English speakers use fewer[31] and fail to appreciate some of the subtleties in Swedish pronunciation. Babies start with an all-hearing sound system, perfectly competent at hearing any of the sounds the human voice can produce, be they English consonants, Swedish vowels, or the clicks of African languages. As they grow older, though, they lose the ability to hear sounds that are missing from their own acoustic world. Unless the infant's voice-recognition system gets practice in listening to particular speech sounds, the adult later will be unable to hear them properly. The same thing happens with the infant's world of faces.

For monkeys the picture is much the same.[32] In early life they can be equally interested in human and monkey faces, but as adults they have a clear preference for looking at their own species. Monkeys can tell different monkey faces apart, but fail to distinguish between humans. Again, early experience of faces is important: monkeys reared by humans at the beginning of their lives like to look at the faces of humans rather than at the faces of their own kind. Similarly, they can recognize subtle differences between human faces, but do not show any interest in the subtle distinctions between one monkey's face and another.

It seems clear that early socialization with humans has long-lasting effects. Even after living with other monkeys for a year, those bottle-fed and nursed by humans continued to prefer looking at humans to looking at monkeys, and did not seem to detect the differences between monkeys.

It is possible, therefore, that biases in early face experience might be saving up trouble for later. With this in mind, when zookeepers intervene to rear infant animals rejected by their mothers, there is concern that being brought up by humans will lead to problems for the animal in later life. To avoid this, keepers go to extraordinary lengths to keep the upbringing as normal as possible. For example, chicks of the nearly extinct Californian condor were fed by an ugly but life-like puppet condor head[33] so that they would not get too keen on humans or too ignorant of condor looks (Figure 3.6).

Figure 3.6 Learning mum's appearance. A Californian condor chick is fed by a puppet condor in an attempt to make sure that in later life the bird will be more attracted to condors than to humans.
Wikipedia.

There is a great deal of evidence that such zookeeper worries are well founded and that early socialization does indeed leave a lasting impression, not only on preferences for face images in later life (which might not be a serious concern), but also on preferences for sexual partners.[34] For birds it has been recognized for decades that there are two types of 'imprinting'[35] or ways in which young lock onto their parents' looks and habits. In the first, chicks learn the characteristics of their mother and then, not surprisingly, follow her everywhere since she is often the source of food and or protection. In the second, the offspring learn about parental qualities, such as a particular song the parents keep singing or the colour of their feather coats. Then, as adults, they express sexual interest in individuals with just those characteristics. What is surprising is how open chicks are to imprinting on a range of foster species. If goslings are reared by a person, for instance, then the young geese are later prepared to follow that person everywhere: on land, on water, and even in the air – once they can fly, they are willing to follow a human foster parent who takes off in a slow-flying 'microlight' aircraft.

Imprinting occurs in mammals, too. You may have wondered about this when a male pet pays undue attention to human legs! Such imprinting is evident from cross-fostering of sheep and goats. A male lamb raised by a goat will grow up to treat goats rather than sheep as playmates, and as an adult it will be sexually attracted to its foster-mother species (goats) more than to its biological-mother species (sheep).[36] Adopted male animals can imprint on the foster mother's voice or smell, but it is clear that there is an imprinting on the foster mother's face: hold up two magazines, one with a cover picture of 'Dolly the sheep' and an equivalent with 'Jenny the goat', and the fostered ram will choose 'Jenny the goat' as his pin-up every time. You may be wondering what would happen if we humans were brought up by monkeys – or even by condors. Certainly we would grow up as a monkey-face or condor-face expert, but would there be other long-term effects? We'll return to this in Chapter 10, which discusses whether or not humans imprint on parents' faces in a way that determines preferences for sexual partners later in life.

Copycat!

Babies do much more than simply look at faces – they also make their own facial expressions in response. If, for example, you poke out your tongue at a tiny newborn baby, you will find that, quite remarkably, the baby will return your gesture, sticking his or her own tongue out at you. Babies will also imitate mouth-opening and pursing of the lips (Figure 3.7), and there are claims that they will return a hand wave – or at least open up their own hand, when shown the same gesture.[37] Babies do not always imitate facial expressions immediately, but the kinds of face they pull and how often they do so are closely tied to what the baby has recently seen. Though debate continues over just how many different gestures trigger mimicry, most developmental psychologists accept that babies copy tongue-poking[38] right from the very beginning of life.

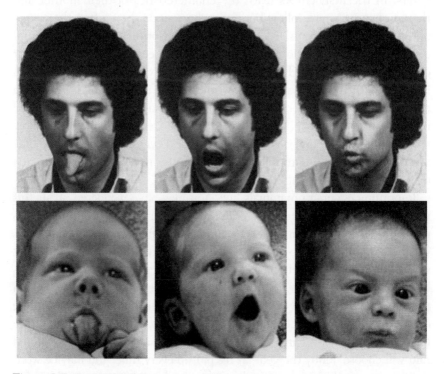

Figure 3.7 'I can do that too!' Imitation of face gestures by babies in the first days of life.
A.N. Meltzoff & M.K. Moore (1977).

Such behaviour is quite baffling since it's fairly unlikely that a baby who pokes out his tongue is intending to insult, simulate a feeling of disgust, or send a friendly greeting (the Tibetan meaning of the gesture)[39].

If a newborn baby recognizes its mother by her hairdo, it seems doubtful that the baby can see a protruding tongue very clearly, let alone recognize the nuances of the gesture. Perhaps the human infant is actually doing something far simpler and more like a toad. Toads turn towards slowly moving insects and worms and, via a reflex action, flick out their tongues to catch them. When toads are presented with just a dark spot or a horizontal bar, they show the same tongue-flicking response as to a real fly or worm.

The suggestion is both speculative and provocative, but we might consider the possibility that a baby's tongue-poking is akin to the toad's tongue-flicking reflex. The behaviour would then reflect the primitive origins and common amphibian ancestry shared by today's toads and toddlers. If this were the case, then we would expect that *other* tongue or worm shapes, such as the movement of a pencil pointed towards the infant, would also lead babies to poke out their tongues – an experiment that new parents can try at home. Indeed, a moving pen or ball *is* just as effective as the human tongue in getting six-week-old infants to stick our their tongues.[40]

Perhaps, then, we should not think that babies actually *copy* tongue gestures, but suppose rather that the baby sees a characteristic movement and that this stimulates a toad-brain reflex and out pops the baby's own tongue. In toads the worm-snapping reflex is controlled by a circuit running from the eye to a particular region of the brain, the optic tectum, and from there to muscles that control eye-turning and tongue-extension. All animals that have descended from amphibian ancestors, including ourselves, have the ancient optic tectum in their brain; and in all of the animals that have an optic tectum it continues to do many of the things it was doing long before the dinosaurs, such as controlling where we point our eyes and hence what we look at. In toads the connections that run from the outer side of the eye to the optic tectum are stronger than those that run from the inner side of the eye: this means that flies seen with the *outer* sections of the eye are more likely to trigger the reflex that turns the toad's head and launches the tongue. Similarly, for newborn babies the attraction to top-heavy face patterns is strongest when the face is seen by the outer side of the eye.[41] This bias fits the idea that the ancient tectum controls the newborn's gaze, as well as the way the baby's head turns towards to faces,[42] so the tongue-poking response to faces could be part and parcel of the same command-and-control system. The attraction of human infants to faces and their early reactions to faces could both owe a lot to humble toad ancestors.

As adults, we know how compelling faces are. When you notice someone you fancy, no matter how hard you try you find your eyes being drawn back to that person's face. It takes a considerable effort of will to stop our eyes from such wandering. If we are told to look away from an image when it appears, sure enough we can do this: when the appearing image is a face, though, we find it much harder to obey the instruction to look away, and our gaze often slips back to the face, despite our best efforts not to look.[43] In this situation, what is happening in the brain involves two competing systems: the control needed in looking away requires the front parts of the brain, which have evolved only recently; the natural response in looking at the face reflects much older systems, part of our species' evolutionary history for millennia and used so much early in our lives. Like infants, adults show a side bias; face patterns seen by the outer half of the eye are more effective in attracting our attention than face patterns falling on the inner, nose-side of the eye.[44] Again, this is the hallmark of the ancient visual operations. Despite all of the specialized face systems that have developed in the brain (see Chapter 2), our primeval brain pathways continue to work in us, in adulthood as in infancy, as a kind of 'face alert' system. Just as it has for millions of years, the tectum prompts us to notice whenever a face comes on the scene, and urges us to pay attention to it.

Friendly tongues

Even if it is produced by ancient brain pathways, the newborn baby's tongue-poking is a little more advanced than amphibian fly-snapping. The baby's tongue-play is more a social reflex, involving turn-taking and reciprocation between two parties, so this behaviour is likely to reflect our more recent primate ancestry. Several monkey species use repetitive mouth-opening and lip-smacking or teeth-chattering as a greeting or as a way to make amends to one another. These signals appear during bouts of excited grooming, and even more often during bouts of excited sex or courtship.[45] For several species with repetitive social mouth actions, the tongue pops out each time the jaw drops. Our own tongue-poking actions as babies are likely to derive from these friendly facial expressions common to primates. In its historical context, reciprocal tongue-wagging may have sweetened the interactions between infants and carers. Lip-smacking exchanges occur between mother and infant monkeys in the first few days of life. Infant chimpanzees just three days old open their mouths and poke out their tongue when human caregivers demonstrate these actions. For monkeys, even human mouth-opening produces tongue-poking or lip-smacking movements from infants on day one.[46] By day three, baby monkeys have begun to imitate human tongue-poking (Figure 3.8), and they copy lip-smacking accurately.

In imitating an adult's mouth movements, human babies could be using instinctive facial signals that in former times encouraged friendliness and bonding. Nowadays this reflex, like others, is residual and has lost its function. To give another example of an out-of-date reflex, infants come into the world with an unbelievably tenacious grip reflex. This would have been important to ancestral infants in gripping onto a hairy mum. Modern human infants still have the grip, but mums have lost most of the stuff they could hang onto. Both the grip and the tongue-protrusion[47] disappear as the baby grows and as reflexes are replaced by more sophisticated control.

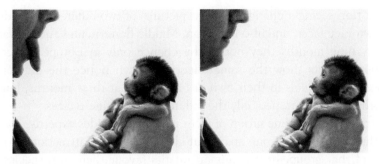

Figure 3.8 The same to you! A monkey imitating the experimenter poking his tongue out.

P.F. Ferrari *et al.* (2006).

Although the origins of facial imitation are being downplayed here and presented as a basic reflex, we should not discount the importance of imitation during infant and child development. Imitation has a powerful role in early socialization[48] and in the acquisition of many skills. We imitate unconsciously and deliberately both those we admire and those to whom we are attracted.

The universal and the culturally specific

The initial, biological bias toward top-heavy patterns that we show as newborns interacts with the learning that takes place in the baby's social world over the course of development, to produce the unique and varied blends of *universal* and *culturally specific* desires that characterize different human populations. The fact that we learn as we develop explains why people in different cultures have slightly different notions of beauty, and why different individuals within one culture show idiosyncratic face preferences. Our long-drawn-out development actively encourages this variability across individuals and populations.

Experience makes it easier to recognize new faces from our own ethnic group than new faces from other groups; this is known as the 'other-race effect'. This is likely to stem from the fact that as infants we see and interact most often with close relatives, who in many families will be people of the same ethnicity. As we have seen, we have an own-species effect whereby we find it easier to distinguish between human faces than between monkey faces. This develops in infancy between the ages of six and nine months, as a consequence of seeing humans but not monkeys. Similarly the other-race effect develops between three months and nine months. At three months white European infants react with renewed interest on seeing a change between pictures of two different individuals for own-race faces, and also for Asian, Middle Eastern, and African faces, but by nine months they notice the change only in European faces.[49] Chinese infants show the same effect: they can notice the differences between individuals in their own or other races at three months, but six months later they notice only the differences in Chinese faces.[50]

Experience with one group of faces not only provides expertise in telling the faces in that group apart, but also produces an attraction[51] to the faces of that group. Just as human infants favour their own species, by three months of age they favour their own race. They look more at faces of their own race than at others,[52] though racial bias was absent at birth. Likewise, most infants grow up seeing women's faces more often than men's, and this woman-dominated world produces both a preference for female faces and a better memory for female faces than for male faces. The opposite is true for babies brought up mainly by men, who prefer to look at male faces.[53]

Infants and attractive faces

All of this makes it abundantly clear that the species, the race, the gender, and the particular identity of faces a given infant sees determines the faces that the child later finds interesting and attractive. What about faces that infants have not seen before – do infants show spontaneous preferences for attractiveness in these faces? Here we can only use adult judgements as our guide, so we must reformulate the question: do infants show an adult-like sense of aesthetics?

There have been several indications that they do: by adult standards, infants look more towards attractive than towards unattractive faces. This is true whether the faces are of their own or other ethnic groups, and whether the faces are adult or infant.[54] Infants, of course, are not swayed by what adults say or write about celebrities' faces, so in this sense they are not taught by the media (or at least not taught verbally) which faces to admire and which to ignore. Nonetheless, even three to six months of experience does affect infants' reactions to faces, so any critical test must measure the impact of attractiveness close to birth – at only one or two days old, say, while experience is still restricted to just a handful of faces.

What would you expect of naïve observers, just a day or two old – would they discriminate according to facial beauty? Surprisingly, the answer is that they would. When shown a pair of faces, newborn infants do indeed prefer to look at the more attractive face.[55] Incredibly, their selection of attractiveness is dependent on the main facial features (the mouth, nose, and eyes); we know this because when the hair is constant and only the main face parts differ (see Figure 3.9), infants once again prefer the faces that adults, too, consider more attractive.[56] If the main face parts are constant but the hair changes, then the infants show no difference in which faces they prefer to look at. Very young babies must therefore be sensitive to the main parts of faces, not just to the hairline as reactions to their mum's face had suggested.

Figure 3.9 A test of infants' perception of attractiveness. Which of these pairs of faces do you find most attractive? For each horizontal pair, the hair is the same, so any difference in attractiveness relates to the facial features. Would newborn infants agree with you? See the text ...
A.M. Slater *et al.* (2000).

This preference is present at the remarkably early age of just two days old. It could be that the ability derives from the fact that attractive faces more closely match a template that is inborn, or it is just about possible that the infant, after as little as one day's exposure to different faces, has already learned some general rule about their proportions.

The tiger and the pussy cat

The extent of the alignment between babies and adults on their tastes for faces is quite remarkable. Some recent work even found that when four-month-old infants were presented with pairs of cat faces (see one example in Figure 3.10, top row), they looked longest at the same cats that adults too found more attractive. Good-looking cats are good-looking even to the youngest of judges.

How can this be? Perhaps babies are eyeing up the cat pictures using a general sense of what looks good in a human face. Cats have been pets since the early Egyptian pharaohs; maybe in those 4,000 years of selective breeding humans have changed cats' facial form to suit our inbuilt notion of aesthetics. If so, this might add to the attraction of cats in general, but would not really explain why infants as well as adults are attracted to some more than to others. In any case, such an issue of domestication should not apply to tigers, as tigers are not bred as pets, yet infants turn out to be just as discerning about tiger faces (Figure 3.10, bottom row) – they look longer at the faces that adults, too, prefer.[57]

Tigress beauty, it turns out, can even affect infant memory. To show this we can start with the facts that infants like both novelty and alluring faces. If these two interests combine and if beauty controls infant powers of recollection, then switching from an ugly tiger to an attractive new tiger face should get all of the infant's interest, whereas switching the other way, from an attractive tiger face to a new but less attractive tiger face, should temper the infant's novelty drive. This is exactly what was found: infants not only *like* attractive tigers better, but also *remember* them better than unattractive tigers!

Figure 3.10 Which cat and which tiger do you find more attractive? Probably the faces on the left – and the chances are that an infant of four months old will share your preferences.
P.C. Quinn *et al.* (2007).

Given there is not much evolutionary value in liking tigers, why should an infant have this fascination with good-looking tiger faces? What might be going on is that attractive faces of any species may conform to the same set of geometric rules. Some of the rules could be built into the dark top-heavy detector (perhaps this is also a 'fearful symmetry' detector?[58]) with which infants start life.[59] This would work for the faces of humans and monkeys, and perhaps even for a furry, feline face. Other rules for face attractiveness might be based in experience, even experience as limited as that of a newborn. Newborns do appear able to learn unbelievably quickly about the common trends present in different faces:[60] attractive pussycats and tigers may just have faces similar to something the infant has already learned from the human faces she or he has seen so far. What these rules for facial attractiveness might be is a topic for the next chapter.

Chapter 4
BEAUTY IN BALANCE

The proportions that really are universally attractive

When we look around the world, we see an enormous diversity in facial appearance. If we scan the writings of anthropologists and explorers, we find an equally mesmerizing array of facial augmentations, making it clear that different cultures can have different standards of beauty. Why else would moustaches be tattooed on Ainu women in Northern Japan,[1] scars from deliberate blows to the head be accentuated by Yanomamö men in Venezuela,[2] or teeth be blackened by peoples of Borneo,[3] filed by Bogobo women in the Philippines, or chipped down to the gums by the Moi of Vietnam?[4] And yet these seem like minor modifications when compared to designer skulls, whereby infants' heads are bound in order to produce flat or cone-head shapes. You might suppose that such practices were restricted to skulls in Egypt some four thousand years ago, but not at all – the practice spanned the globe, being favoured by peoples in Australia, Africa, North and South America, and the Pacific islands, and surviving in parts of France until just over a hundred years ago.

Any part of the face that *can* be modified *has* been modified, in one culture or another, with effects that make contemporary teenage lip- or nose-piercing look quite restrained (see Figure 4.1). The necks of Karen-Padaung women in Thailand are lengthened using neck rings, for example; the lips of Kayapo men of Brazil and the Mursi women of Ethiopia are enlarged with plates made of pottery or wood; and the earlobes of Kikuyu men in Kenya and the Rikhaksta men in Brazil are elongated by means of weights. To a Western eye these variations may seem extreme, yet within their cultures they are considered elegant, and possessing them signals that you are regarded as an adult and are eligible to marry.

With such extraordinary variety in different cultures, it may seem absurd to search for facial attributes that *everyone* finds beautiful – given such cultural diversity, how could there be faces that are universally thought attractive? Nevertheless, this is the quest of this chapter and the next: to explore whether there is a common key to beauty – some aspect of face shape

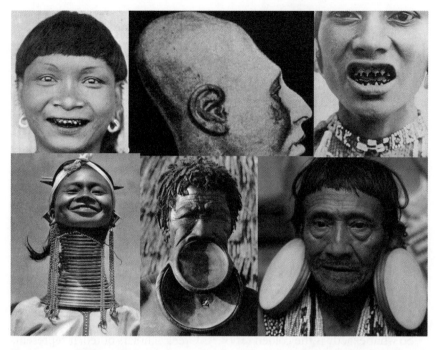

Figure 4.1 Elaboration of faces in the name of beauty. *Top left:* Dayak woman with blackened teeth, Indonesia. *Top centre:* Skull reshaping reconstruction (University of Buenos Aires Ethnographic Museum). *Top right:* Bogobo woman with filed teeth, Mindanao, Philippines. *Bottom left:* Padaung woman with neck rings, Thailand. *Bottom centre:* Sara woman with lip plates, Chad. *Bottom right:* Rikhaksta man with earlobe extensions, Mato Grosso, Brazil.

Top left: Dr G. Buschan (1914); A. Jones (2001). *Top centre:* E. Schijman (2005). *Top right:* Dr G. Buschan (c. 1914). *Bottom left:* V. de Golish (1958). *Bottom centre:* M. Hürlimann (c.1923). *Bottom right:* Agência Brasil.

that can win admiration from everyone, no matter who they are or where they come from. If there are indeed such universals, it would seem that a fortunate few have a head start and the majority little hope.

Reading feminist literature, one could be forgiven for suspecting that beauty in Western society is entirely a construction of the cosmetic, dieting, and plastic-surgery industries[5] (a topic we return to in Chapter 10). If indeed it were solely a media construction, you would expect to find differences in opinion among people, reflecting upbringing and exposure to the media. In fact, the opposite is true: studies of attractiveness find remarkable agreement on which faces are attractive and which are not. Further, there is consistency between men and women in their opinions when assessing the same faces, and there is agreement between people in different countries.[6] If the populations of two countries each ran a beauty competition with the same contestants, all of whom were from a single ethnic background, the votes from the two countries would be likely to be about 90 per cent similar.[7] This is an amazing level of agreement. You might think that culture at least explains the remaining 10 per cent of differences in opinion, but this is not the case; instead, any two groups of judges, whether from the same culture or not, are as likely to agree by the same amount. Clearly, therefore, people are agreeing on what constitutes beauty … but what are they agreeing on?

A golden mean

The secret of facial or bodily beauty is often said to lie in its proportions, but what proportions matter? There is one proportion, the golden ratio or golden mean, that features heavily in aesthetics and might be relevant to beauty, too. The golden mean has engaged the minds of the greatest of mathematicians, Pythagoras and Euclid, as well as the minds of artists and architects. Its august and almost mystical background has ensured that many have looked to the golden mean as a proportion that might explain human facial attractiveness.[8]

So what exactly is the golden ratio? As Greek scholars noted, it represents the proportions of a rectangle whose longer side is 1.618 times the length of its shorter side. Mathematically, such a rectangle has this fascinating property: that the ratio of the *smaller side* to the *longer side* is exactly the same as the ratio of the *longer side* to the *longer and shorter sides* put together (see Figure 4.2). But this is not just a mathematical curiosity; as it turns out, a rectangle with these proportions is the most aesthetically pleasing, appearing neither too thin nor too broad. So if you were a Greek builder knocking up a rectangular building – the Parthenon on the Acropolis, say – you would make sure that your building met this aesthetic length-to-width standard. A modern-day TV comes close to this shape, but is about 10 per cent too wide.

Interesting, perhaps, but faces are not rectangular: how is this relevant to beauty? Hunters of the golden mean are subtle; they divide the face up into parts and work out the relative proportions of the two parts. For example, if the lower face is about five-eighths of the whole face (the lower and the upper face combined), then the proportions of the lower to the upper face are close to the golden ratio.[9] This is just one pair of measurements; perhaps if other features also bore this relationship one to another, then the face would be that of a Greek hero – perfection.

So does attractiveness conform to the golden ratio? If only it were that simple! Despite the claims, in peer-reviewed scientific journals there is no evidence to show that the golden ratio is more prevalent in beautiful faces than in unattractive faces. If someone tells you that attractive

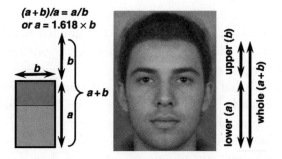

Figure 4.2 Perfect proportions: a rule of attractiveness or a quack claim? If the length of the lower half of the face is 1.618 times that of the upper face, the proportion conforms to the golden ratio. *Left*: A rectangle in the proportions of the golden ratio. *Right*: The lower face shows roughly the same proportion to the whole face that the upper face shows to the lower face.
R.E. Cornwell *et al.* (2006).

faces have the proportions of the golden mean, ask them to provide some proof – particularly if surgery is to be planned on the basis of this claim!

If you calculate the ratio between any two features of a face, you will discover two things. First, you will find that an awful lot of ratios are possible. And secondly, you will find that some by chance come close to the golden mean. Some do, but many do not; the ratio of the distance between the nostril centres to the length of the lower face, for example, is nowhere near the golden mean. This fact should not be ignored. Hunting for the golden ratio will indeed throw up examples of what is being looked for, but in regarding such examples as evidence that the golden mean ratio underlies beauty without noting the multitude of other proportions, one would be guilty of wishful thinking rather than scientific insight.[10]

Many claims are made about good looks. Some seem plausible and one can be bamboozled by fancy geometry. That said, there are also two candidate keys to beauty for which there is more persuasive evidence: facial symmetry and 'averageness'. These too can be seen as aspects of harmonious proportions; with *symmetry* the left side matches up exactly with the right side, and with '*averageness*' the overall shape conforms precisely to our notion of normality.

The plan for a perfect body

Humans are largely symmetrical. If you were folded in half lengthways, each side of your body would match up neatly with the other half. Your arms, legs, hands, ears, and eyes are matched in size. Not all animals show this symmetrical and balanced body plan; male fiddler crabs, for example, have one small feeding claw and one enormous claw, which they wave at females to entice them to mate. Symmetry isn't inevitable, and animals also show examples of systematic or design asymmetry; humans have only one heart, for example, which is located on the left in almost everyone, and we also have one spleen on the left side, and one liver which lies to the right side of the midline.

It is also true that not even symmetrical animals are perfectly symmetrical. There can be small discrepancies in the sizes of the ears on each side of the body, or in the lengths of the limbs, and, in the case of birds, in the lengths of tail feathers. Even single structures can be asymmetrical; human mouths may curl up on one side more than the other, and the position of the mouth may be slightly off-centre. The same is true of our noses; and our nostrils can be surprisingly different in size and shape (you may not have paid a great deal of attention to nostrils hitherto, but when you do, you will find that the variability is evident). The left–right differences in face and body structures are usually very small – only a matter of millimetres – so they are not glaringly obvious; as we'll see, though, others can apparently detect them. In some species, the *level* of these small random asymmetries[11] is related to success in the mating department. For instance, male barn swallows with more symmetrical tail feathers mate earlier in the breeding season, and raise more offspring per year, than asymmetrical males.[12] Why should this be? And what does the asymmetry signal?

Natural bodily and facial asymmetry reflect disruptions that occurred during development, both before and after birth. Disease, exposure to toxins, and high levels of stress can all lead to variations in the growth and differentiation of cells on each side of the body, with the result that the body parts fail to match exactly. While it is easy to see how a physical blow to one side of the body could lead to slowed, abnormal growth on that side, it is less easy to understand why indirect stresses such as the mother getting an infection during pregnancy, say, or the child getting coughs and colds – could lead to slightly wonky patterns of growth, but they can.

It might be helpful here to think of the developing body as a large and complex construction site. If there is a serious outbreak of flu, for example, many construction workers will be too sick to report for duty or, if they do show up, they may not be able to work well. One part of the site may be able to muster a sufficient crew of bricklayers and building will continue unimpeded; another part of the site may have no bricklayers at all and work will have to stop. As a result, building work will be inconsistent, with some parts shooting up rapidly while other parts lag behind. There may also be problems with the supply of building materials. If the construction company is hit by cash-flow problems, deliveries will be erratic and there will be an uneven supply of materials. What's worse, the materials themselves may change in quality; bricks may differ slightly in colour or size. The changes in the supply and quality of building materials, combined with the varied capacities of the construction workers, will leave a legacy in the completed building; the finish may be uneven, and there may be irregularities in shape and size.

A baby growing inside its mother is equally susceptible to variations in the quality and quantity of materials available. A lack of folate (a B vitamin), for example, can slow or even halt DNA production, which seriously disrupts development. Worse, folate deficiency can cause change in the actual DNA code itself when it gets copied for each new cell.[13] Tinkering with the DNA master plan has a cascade of consequences and will cause a general failure to deliver sufficient 'building materials' to the right place at the right time. Similarly, a shortage of food will result in a lack of the supplies needed in building a baby, and may cause the baby to have a small body size overall, as well as greater asymmetry. The same is true once babies are born. If their food supply is low in quality, or if they become severely infected and sick, these events can further disrupt growth and development. Asymmetry in male barn swallows, it turns out, can be traced to a parasite that attacks nestlings, and the females who choose symmetrical males are picking those who were able either to avoid infection or to fight it more effectively so that it did not disrupt their growth. If this parasite-resisting ability has a genetic basis, the females who pick symmetrical males are in fact picking fathers who will pass on their 'good genes' to their own offspring.

Are symmetrical men better in bed?

A similar argument has been made for humans. Symmetry is suggested to be a signal of good-quality genes for all sorts of traits, not just disease resistance. Indeed, the claims made for symmetry in the scientific literature grow ever more dramatic. Men with symmetrical bodies apparently have a higher IQ, they run faster,[14] dance better,[15] sing better,[16] are less depressed, smell sexier, sound nicer, and produce more and faster-swimming sperm than their asymmetrical counterparts.[17] As if that's not enough, women with symmetrical partners apparently experience more orgasms than women with asymmetrical partners.[18] Symmetrical men, it seems, really are better-quality mates. This all sounds too good to be true; are symmetrical men really superhuman?

Let's consider the question of symmetrical men being better lovers. Although the relationship clearly exists and is statistically valid, it does not mean that symmetry itself is what makes these men better in bed – there may be other factors. One could posit that symmetrical men may become sexually active at an earlier age, for example, and that it is their extra experience that makes them better at bringing women to orgasm. We should also consider the female side of the equation. If symmetry is seen as attractive, then we would expect more women to be more attracted to the symmetrical men, and so those men will have a wider array of potential mates to choose from. If symmetrical men are free to choose exactly the kind of woman they would like to go to bed with, they may be more considerate and better motivated to perform well sexually. Equally, while most men may like to hear cries of passion, it might be that the popular, symmetrical men are better able to entice those women who find it easy to achieve orgasm[19] back to bed as long-term lovers. At the moment, it is not clear what exactly is responsible for the link between male symmetry and women's sexual pleasure, so we mustn't be hasty in assuming that symmetrical men are displaying inherently better quality through greater sexual prowess.

What about faces in all of this – does facial symmetry influence our perceptions of attractiveness? And does the precise degree of symmetry really matter that much to us?

Does symmetry equal beauty?

Given the greater advantages shown by more symmetrical men in all sorts of areas, we would predict that symmetry would be regarded as attractive in a potential mate. Despite this, most of the evidence up to the late 1990s supported the claim that it was *asymmetry* that made a face beautiful. Whether it was adults or infants who were tested, an asymmetrical face was generally preferred over a symmetrical one. A number of plausible explanations were put forward as to why asymmetry looked best. First, there is good psychological evidence to show that the more 'normal' a face is (that is, the more average and symmetrical), the more forgettable it is.[20] The face of the French actor Gérard Depardieu (Figure 4.3) is very asymmetrical, but this makes him stand out from the crowd and creates a more lasting impression. It is difficult to fancy someone if we keep forgetting who they are.

A second point is that highly symmetrical smiles, and other facial expressions, can strike us as false. The fixed grins displayed by politicians as they work a crowd are usually symmetrical, but these are not true smiles and they never quite reach the eyes. Genuine smiles tend to be asymmetrical – just like Depardieu's. It is not only our facial expressions that are naturally one-sided, either; speech control is usually located in the left side of the brain, and this side of the brain controls the motor nerves that move the muscles of the mouth and the tongue on the right side of the body. During speech, most

Figure 4.3 The young Gérard Depardieu: asymmetrical but charismatic.
Depardieu's face has asymmetry both in his transient smiling expression and in
his facial structure: his nose appears to deflect slightly to the left. Despite this he
has been regarded by many as attractive, particularly in his youth.
Charcoal and pencil by D.I. Perrett (with D. Buls) (2009) Perception Lab.

people (76 per cent) move the right side of their mouth to a greater extent
than the left side;[21] the discrepancy between left and right is often noticeable when watching presenters read the news. Over time, this asymmetrical
use of the face may produce lasting changes in the muscles and skin creases
that we can pick up on. Perhaps this leads us to view less symmetrical faces
as more attractive because they appear more natural, and so more sincere.

Many early studies of symmetry[22] were flawed in the way that they
presented the stimuli, and this may account for why the participants in
the studies didn't actually find symmetry attractive.[23] Early studies created
symmetrical faces by splitting a facial image in half and reflecting one
half of the face onto the other side, creating a face made from either two
right sides or two left sides (see Figure 4.4, rows 2 and 3). Although this
produces images in which both sides of the face are identical and perfectly
symmetrical, it also produces some pretty weird face shapes. For example,
if someone's mouth is a little off-centre, and displaced to the right of the
midline (Figure 4.4, row 1, left), then when the face is reflected to produce
the symmetrical version, the mouth will look too wide in one image and
too narrow in the other (Figure 4.4, rows 2 and 3). Facial images generated
in this way, although completely symmetrical, look very odd.

The take-home message here, then, is that any improvements to the
symmetry of a face image must be done carefully so as not to distort

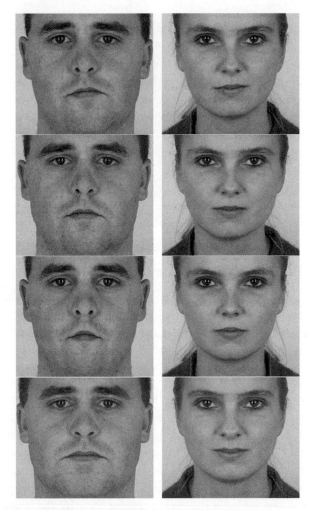

Figure 4.4 Manipulations of facial symmetry. *Row 1*: The top row shows two original faces. *Row 2*: The faces have been made symmetrical by mirroring: each image comprises the right half of the original face, together with a mirror image of the same right half. *Row 3*: This shows similarly symmetrical faces, this time made from the left half face and its mirror image. Rows 2 and 3 are symmetrical, but mirroring introduces unnatural feature shapes and may not enhance attractiveness. *Row 4*: This shows the two original faces, but with increased symmetry. Here the original faces have been reshaped so that the left and right sides are more even, but the original skin textures, including any asymmetries in pigmentation or spots, remain unaltered.

D.I. Perrett *et al.* (1999).

a person's face away from a natural condition. The advent of modern computer 'morphing' techniques does allow us to make the *shapes* of the left and right sides of the face symmetrical, even while keeping skin and features natural-looking.[24] When we increase symmetry in this way, around 60–70 per cent of people find the resulting faces more attractive than the less symmetrical original faces (compare the top and bottom rows in Figure 4.4).[25] The change is pretty subtle, but it works. This kind of manipulation of the outline shape of features doesn't make faces perfectly symmetrical, because the natural skin textures on the left and right sides of the face are still different. [26]

We can see the role of symmetry more clearly if we work with faces that start with perfectly smooth skin texture (see Figure 4.5). If these faces are made symmetrical in shape, we find a more dramatic increase in ratings of attractiveness. Virtually all face shapes (96 per cent) look nicer when snapped into perfect symmetry, so symmetry in faces is indeed more attractive after all.

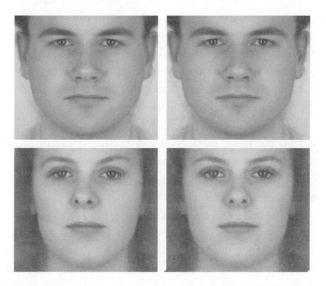

Figure 4.5 Perfect symmetry. *Left*: Naturally asymmetrical face shapes, each with a perfectly smooth skin texture. *Right*: Completely symmetrical face images, made by averaging the shapes on the left and right sides of the smooth-skinned faces.
D.I. Perrett *et al.* (1999).

What is remarkable is that few people who take part in such experiments have any idea that they're responding to symmetry. When asked why they chose one of a pair of faces rather than another, people comment that they were more attracted to the eyes (for instance, looking kind or not), or the mouth, or the overall expression (for example, looking grumpy or angry), but hardly anyone at all comments on the degree of symmetry. What's more surprising still is that even if the researcher tells people that the symmetry has been changed, most will deny that this had any effect on their judgement, even though they clearly preferred a symmetrical face to an asymmetrical one.

Symmetry, it seems, does have an allure after all. But we mustn't get too carried away; after all, Gerard Depardieu *is* still attractive to many despite his face being lopsided, and quite a few people in each of the relevant studies actually did *not* seem to care about symmetry. That 74 per cent of people prefer perfect symmetry[27] is more than one would expect by chance (50 per cent), but it is by no means the unanimous preference that one would expect if symmetry were a 'human universal' of attractiveness.

Given that preferences for symmetry are quite variable, then, it becomes interesting to ask why it matters to some people and not to others. At least part of the answer is that people's preferences seem to reflect how confident they feel about their own appearance. People are quite willing to rate themselves for attractiveness and, amusingly, the results reveal a degree of wishful thinking, particularly on the part of men. Most people rate themselves 'above average' in attractiveness, and there is often a sex difference, with men rating themselves higher than women rate themselves. In studies with large numbers of participants, we would expect the same number of men and women to be 'below average' as are 'above average' for attractiveness – it is impossible for a clear majority to be 'above average' – yet studies of ratings show us that people think more highly of themselves than others do. You might think we know ourselves better than anyone else, but we don't. Unrealistic positive thinking preserves our self-esteem,[28] and this is generally higher in men than in women.

Women who think they are good-looking are especially attentive to symmetry, and consistently choose a more symmetrical male face as more attractive. Women who rate themselves as either 'average' or 'below average' in looks are much less discriminating, they prefer symmetry, but aren't as picky as women who think they are 'above average'.[29] When women were asked to rate the female faces that varied in symmetry, none of these effects was found: those who considered themselves attractive and those that didn't were equally discriminating amongst female faces. Clearly, the symmetry preference shown by attractive women is linked to attraction to the opposite sex. One can reason that good-looking women (and perhaps those confident in their appearance) receive more attention from the opposite sex and, with more men on offer, they are able to be much choosier.[30]

The important point here is that we can already see how a supposedly universal rule of beauty is not so universal after all. Not everyone cares about symmetry, and this suggests that in judging prospective mates we must also be using some other means of assessing the faces we see around us. Perhaps it's another 'universal' measure: perhaps it's 'averageness'.

Attractive faces are only average – or are they?

Two centuries ago, Francis Galton used photography techniques to blend together the faces of different individuals. His quest was to find out whether or not criminal ways were written in the face (a topic explored in Chapter 9, on personality). To his immense surprise he found that the more faces he put into the mix, the more handsome the resultant face appeared. No matter that the faces he was blending together were the faces of hardened criminals: the composite face was still much more attractive than any of the individual faces that went into it. A hundred years later, Galton's blending experiments were repeated, this time with law-abiding citizens and more systematically. As two, four, eight, or sixteen faces were blended together, so the image produced became progressively more and more attractive. This was true for both male and female faces.[31] It seems, therefore, that the most attractive faces are those that are most average. Yet such a claim flies in the face of experience – attractive faces are attention-grabbing and striking, surely; how can they be just ordinary, even mediocre?

Well, as it turns out, you'd be right to have a few doubts about the claim that beauty is simply a manifestation of averageness. First, there are technical reasons why blending faces makes them appear more attractive. One is that blended faces differ from real faces in more than just their averageness. In the earliest studies claiming that beauty was averageness, all the faces combined in the blends were lined up with each other using just the eyes. This meant that *other* regions of the face were not aligned with one another; as a result, the more faces that were put into the blend, the more blurred became the features. You might suppose that this blurriness would detract from beauty, but consider what happens to the skin in such an image: as more faces are blended together, all the idiosyncratic lines, wrinkles, spots, and blemishes seen on the individual faces become averaged out (see Figure 4.6, bottom right). Every model, actor, and photographer knows the advantages of soft focus: a dab of Vaseline on a camera lens similarly blurs an image and works wonders for the model; it softens features and makes wrinkles less evident, even if it doesn't do the lens any good. These days, no model who appears on the front cover of a fashion magazine is likely to have escaped retouching to eradicate skin blemishes. This used to be possible using just airbrushing techniques; with the rise of digital photography and software packages such as Photoshop, the camera can now not only lie but reinvent reality completely.

As more and more faces are added to a digital blend, so the skin of the resultant image gets smoother and smoother. The final image in Figure 4.6

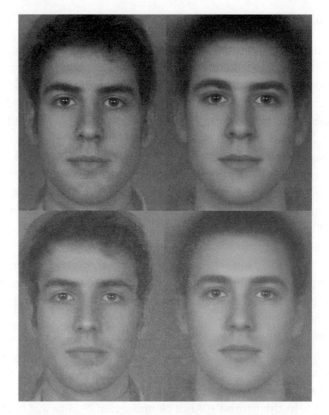

Figure 4.6 Making a face more average. *Top left*: A real man's true face. *Bottom right*: An image created by blending the same face with many other male faces. Note that both the shape and the texture differ, and that the 'average' skin texture is smoother than those of real-life faces. *Bottom left*: An image created by keeping the true texture but reshaping the face to give it more average facial proportions. *Top right*: An image created by keeping the true proportions but smoothing the skin texture. The disappearance of skin blemishes can account for the better looks in both right-hand images.

D. Buls (2009) Perception Lab.

(bottom right) is the average of many different young men's faces. It is spared the reality of puberty, and there's no spot or blemish to be found anywhere. This skin-smoothing effect alone can explain why average faces are perceived as more attractive.[32] Averaged skin texture always looks nicer than the original skin texture, even when the shape of the face is held constant (compare the top left and top right images in Figure 4.6). These results suggest that it's perfect skin, rather than perfect features, that matters for beauty.

If we want to show that averageness is the secret of beauty, we need to keep the *skin* the same but perform computer-graphic surgery on the image of a given face to give it exactly average proportions. This too has been done in Figure 4.6: the top left image is the original photograph; the bottom-left image is the same image stretched and compressed in different regions to give it the proportions of an average male face. (The bottom-right image, as noted already, shows the shape *and* texture of the average male.) Because averageness is achieved by reshaping a single face to fit the average rather than by blending different faces together, the skin texture is the same in both the original face and the modified face: this means that any change in attractiveness cannot be explained by airbrushing. Using this more reliable technique, it turns out that for the majority of faces the average face shape does prove to be more attractive than each person's *original* face shape.[33]

Counter to intuition, therefore, we learn that there is something good about looking average! There are two ways to explain these surprising results. First, a preference for more average and hence more 'normal' faces can also be reinterpreted as a dislike of highly unusual faces. By shunning weird faces we might, in effect, be avoiding harmful genetic mutations; after all, many congenital disorders that lead to physical and mental deficits are associated with distinctive and unusual facial features:[34] preferring the average in the population might thus be a way of playing safe when choosing a mate. This suggestion, then, is a functional or long-term evolutionary reason for why preferring the average matters: it may help to increase the survival and reproductive success of our offspring.

A second explanation of our liking of averageness is more psychological and concerns the reasons that lead us to make any particular choice in the here and now. The two types of explanation – long-term functional or evolutionary reasons, and short-term psychological reasons – apply to *all* of our likes and dislikes. For example, the long-term function of liking ice cream is that it helps rebuild our bones, brains, and brawn after they get worn down by simply living; the psychological reasons include knowing that the cool, creamy texture will give us a feel-good calorie hit. These two types of explanation, while they may seem quite separate, are in fact two sides of the same coin: what we perceive as long-term evolutionary trends are simply the accumulated effect of biological motivations acting in individual animals over many generations. For example, the reason why an individual beaver builds a dam is not because it 'knows' that its entrance needs protecting, but from some instinct – perhaps it is 'programmed' to respond to the sound of running water by piling mud and twigs around the source of the sound. Whatever the basis of beavers' behaviour, the outcome is that because they build dams they also surround their lodges with water and a beaver-friendly pond, which hides the entrances and makes them safe from predators. In the longer term, this behaviour incidentally increases their chances of surviving and reproducing. In the same way, a consequence of preferring average faces may be that we are less likely to pass on harmful mutations to our children. If so, that won't be because we know anything about genetics or are thinking about our descendents: the immediate cause will be something quite different, with a more immediate benefit. It seems that our general preference for averageness may simply reflect the way in which our visual system works.

We are quickest at recognizing things when they are typical of their group. Birds, for example, come in lots of different shapes and sizes, but we will be especially quick to recognize a bird if it has the typical characteristics of a bird – two wings that can be used for flying (not something unusual, such as the flippers of a penguin), a typical neck length (not unusually long, like that of a swan), a typical body (not unusually big, like that of an ostrich, or small, like that of a hummingbird), and a typical leg length (not unusually long, like those of a flamingo, or short, like those of a swallow). There are many birds with this typical kind of shape – robins, sparrows, starlings, blackbirds – and that is exactly the point: this bird shape is *common*. Precisely because it is common, we see it all the time and come to find it 'average' or 'prototypical'. We take longer to realize that an unusual species – such as an ostrich, a hummingbird, or a flamingo – actually is a bird. To use a language-based metaphor, we are more 'fluent' in normal bird shapes than in unusual ones.

The fluency we accumulate from seeing average examples of a given category is what gives those average examples an advantage in the attractiveness stakes: we can recognize them easily, they feel familiar, and this makes them more attractive. And this applies not only to faces: average-looking wristwatches, spectacles, handguns, birds, dogs, monkeys, horses, and Chinese ideographs are also judged more attractive than unusual-looking examples.[35] We might think that our own unusual watch is stylish and fashionable, but most people would find a standard watch face more attractive.

When we see a typical object with average properties, we quickly recognize what it is. We can do this even though we would be quite unable to recite a list of the properties common to that type of object. Recognition works without our consciously using logic and knowledge, and we are rarely able to describe in words *how* we recognize something. What is it exactly that tells us a portrait was indeed painted by Botticelli? And yet we know that it was. Most of us would probably mumble something about 'style', but without really knowing what we meant. So it is too with attractiveness; when people are asked what it is *exactly* that makes a face attractive, they are often at a loss for words – they may say something about the eyes, but in general their answers will be vague.

Of art and art historians

Let's use Botticelli's portraits of female faces to consider in more detail our ability to recognize general, or typical, characteristics. A short journey into the art world has a second purpose, as it provides an opportunity to introduce some computer-based graphic techniques that are used in studying faces generally and beauty in particular.

Botticelli painted only a few portraits of women, and many of those women appear to be in a state of religious ecstasy. His Madonnas, in particular, possess other-worldliness; their heavy-lidded eyes suggest not only attention to the infant Jesus but also contemplation of something more profound. By taking the six original paintings and isolating the faces portrayed, we can make an 'average' portrait that is a mathematical blend of the separate portraits (Figure 4.7). The six original faces painted

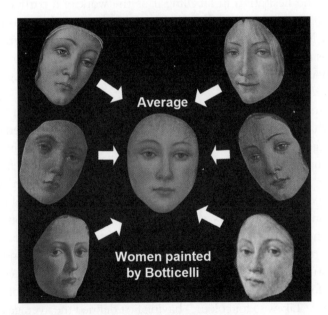

Figure 4.7 Botticelli's style of woman. The central image is a computer blend of the six paintings of women arranged around it, all by Botticelli.

Top left: Madonna of the Pomegranate (c.1487). *Top right: Allegory of Spring La Primavera* (c.1477). *Right: Birth of Venus* (c.1485). *Bottom right: A second face from Allegory of Spring La Primavera* (c.1477). *Bottom left: Portrait of a Lady: Smeralda Brandini* (c.1475). *Left: Madonna of the Sea* (c.1477). *Centre: D.I. Perrett* (2009) Perception Lab.

by Botticelli lie around the outside; the central face, which blends them together, should thus contain the characteristics that are common to Botticelli's paintings without being recognizable as any individual painting. As you can see, this works: the average portrait *does* capture some of Botticelli's stylistic traits – the eyelids are droopy, for example; there is a far-away stare; and the head is inclined at an angle, just as it is in many of the originals.

Most painters have characteristic styles of painting; with experience, we can become very adept at spotting a particular artist's style. Each of the eight faces shown in Figure A (Plate I) is a composite of images from an individual artist – can you guess who the artist is in each case? (The answers are given in the endnotes.[36]) At the centre of the figure is a blend of all eight portraits; this represents no single particular style, therefore, but is in essence an 'average' artist's portrait.

Confronted either with a computer composite made from several different paintings by the same artist or with an original painting, art history experts are equally accurate in naming the painter.[37] Even though the experts cannot have seen the computer composite portrait before, they have no hesitation in labelling it as the work of a particular artist. In terms of their recognizability, the computer 'forgeries' pass as plausible originals. Moreover, they illustrate that what the experts were picking up on was not the specific details of a known portrait, but the overall *style* of a particular artist's portraits – how else could they have recognized the composite?

Caricature artists pick out features that are unique to a particular face – the features that are emblematic to its recognizability and distinctiveness – and then exaggerate these features. Computer graphics can be used in a similar way to amplify the distinctive shapes and colours of particular faces. The caricature artist's formula can be applied in a computer program. To produce a caricature one need only measure how the position of the tip of the nose in a *particular* face – the 'target face' – differs in position from the tip of the nose in the *average* face and then amplify this difference.[38] In such a caricature, the tip of a long nose will grow like Pinocchio's, and that for a short, stubby nose will become even stubbier. The same process can be repeated for every facial feature, creating an overall caricature of the total face shape.[39] Likewise for colour – having first defined the average colour of faces, one can measure, for each point on the target face, whether the skin is redder, greener, or bluer than the average. Each colour difference can then be amplified to caricature the colouring of the target face.[40]

This process is illustrated in Figure B (Plate I). As well as the composites and original portraits, our art history experts were also given caricatures of the work of eight different artists to identify. In assigning an artist to each caricature portrait, they performed more accurately than they had done with either the originals or the composite images: while 62 per cent of the originals and 63 per cent of the composites were recognized accurately, 74 per cent of the caricatures were correctly assigned to an artist. This again shows that it is the recognition of the pattern of an artist's *style* that is important, rather than a detailed knowledge of specific portraits. Exaggeration of relevant cues therefore aids recognition.

The computer techniques can be extended to demonstrate recognition of the general style of faces in another way, too. The difference in shape and colour between a particular artist's style and that of the 'average' artist's style (Figure D, left: Plate II) can be added to any real person's face image. The resulting image is that person portrayed 'in the style of' that artist (Figure D, right). Computer transformations allow this, even though the genuine artist might be unable to oblige with a personal sitting because of being too busy, too expensive, or unable to travel through time. The art transformations maintain the identity of the person – one can see who is painted in the portrait. With art transformations such as these we find that the majority of art styles can be recognized by art history students.[41] These transformations reveal how, with training – and training we do not necessarily realize that we're getting! – we are able to learn the general characteristics or genre of a class of faces.

This consideration of art style exemplifies the way in which we can become familiar with a particular type of face, learning to recognize the characteristics that epitomize how that facial type differs from others. Many readers will recognize the typical style of a famous artist, whether depicted as an 'average' portrait or mimicked using computer software to render any new face in the painter's style. The experience we have with a class of objects or faces allows us to recognize the average characteristics of that class. Deviations from this central tendency look strange and relatively unattractive, while average proportions by contrast appear familiar. Feeling comfortable with the average proportions for that type of face, we also find them relatively attractive.

Figure 4.8 shows a highly distorted version of Leonardo da Vinci's *Mona Lisa*. No way is *this* a masterpiece! Such obvious deviations from normal make the image look grotesque. After looking at the long-nosed version for thirty seconds, however, long noses will have become more familiar to us and thus more average in our minds, and we will no longer be able to tell whether *Mona Lisa* with a slightly longer nose is the real thing or a fake.[42]

As we become highly familiar with one type of face, we start to see that type as more normal-looking;[43] this is going on with even thirty seconds

Figure 4.8 Distorted experience alters our sense of aesthetics. Looking at the distorted *Mona Lisa* for thirty seconds leaves us less certain about which of the two lower images is a fake.
C.C. Carbon & H. Leder (2006).

of inspecting the long nose of the distorted *Mona Lisa*. Should we see that face more often, the effects will become more durable.[44] As discussed in Chapter 3, infants tune into the face type of their own species, their own race, and their own mother; seeing such faces frequently makes them more recognizable and more attractive – in effect, familiarity breeds content. The same thing happens to us as adults. We may see the face of our spouse, lover, or best friend so much that this may become the norm, and the faces of quite a few other people may begin to look a just a little weird by comparison!

The average of what?

Averageness is attractive because it captures and epitomizes the overall 'style' of the human faces to which we have been repeatedly exposed, and this style has acquired extra resonance for our pattern-recognizing visual system. But surely we can't be talking about the average of all the faces we encounter, can we? Men's and women's faces differ markedly; for example, men tend to have larger chins, larger jaws, and heavier brows than women. If our pattern recognition for facial beauty simply relied on detecting averageness, then the most beautiful people of all would be those who somehow managed to combine both masculine and feminine looks in the same face – an androgynous form, neither man nor woman but a blend of the two. This doesn't seem to ring true: we recognize beauty amongst women's faces, and this is something different from beauty in men's faces. Equally, the people we see on a regular basis vary widely in age, so our 'average' face pattern should combine elements from both young and old faces. Yet if that were true, we should be showing an increasing preference for older-looking faces among models, actors, TV presenters, and newsreaders, because with a progressively ageing population, our 'average' pattern, and so our attraction to faces, would be being biased by the greater number of older faces we see around us. It's clear that this isn't the case, either; we're probably more youth-obsessed now than at any other time in history.

In defining what is attractive, then, we are not referring to an average of *all* people's faces, independent of their sex or age. No, we have separate ideas of what is attractive for different categories of faces;[45] what we find attractive in women, in men, and in babies, is distinct for each category.

Exceptions to the averageness rule

Changing facial proportions toward the average does increase attractiveness for most people's faces, but not all. In particular, it failed to work on those faces that started out attractive. For those faces, forcing them into average proportions *destroyed* their allure and made them *less* appealing. This observation guides the quest for cues to beauty in a new direction – if there are faces that are naturally better than average, they must have something extra, and it should be possible to find out what that something is.

To see whether beauty relates to some particular better-than-average quality, our research group blended together the European faces deemed *high* in attractiveness at the start and then, separately, blended together the faces that had been judged as *low* in attractiveness at the start. This gave us two face shapes, which we can call the 'High' shape and the 'Low' shape to denote the attractiveness of the faces from which they were derived. Thirdly, we also blended *all* the faces together to make an 'Overall' average composite face. If the attractive subset is systematically different in shape from the rest, then the differences should be visible. As you can see from Figure 4.9, which shows the 'High' and 'Overall' shapes, the shape of the High subset of faces *is* distinctively different from the Overall shape and – surprisingly for the 'beauty is average' theory – people judge it to be more attractive. By contrast, the Low shape is judged to be less attractive than the Overall shape. Both of these results directly contradict the averageness hypothesis, because by that logic it should be the *Overall* average that is most attractive, and it's not. It is, in fact, just 'average': it sits right in the middle, between the High and Low faces.[46] The relationship between beauty and averageness is not as simple as it seems.

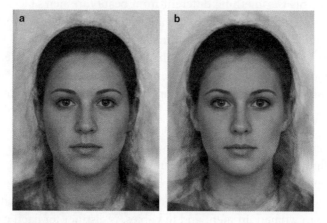

Figure 4.9 Doing better than average? (*a*) The 'Overall' average shape of the population studied. (*b*) The 'High' average shape of the most attractive sub-group of the population studied.

L.M. DeBruine *et al.* (2007).

Let's look more closely at the attractive faces and see whether we can identify exactly what makes them distinctive. We can amplify any difference between the shape of attractive faces and the shape of the overall population's faces. This amounts to caricaturing the difference between the High and the Overall shapes, in the same way as we did for Botticelli's style (Figure B, Plate I). Caricaturing Botticelli's style improved recognition by art historians, so caricaturing the High shape might make it easier for us to recognize its attractive attributes, which might amount to making it more good-looking. Indeed, this is what we found: caricaturing the High face *does* make it even more attractive (Figure 4.10). Likewise, when we considered the Low faces, we found that we could make this shape even *less* attractive by amplifying its difference from the Overall average.

It is important to reflect on what has been done here. We have captured the essence of beauty or attractiveness from a group of faces and augmented it using scientific principles and democratic opinions. We simply asked people which faces they found attractive, and amplified the features consistently present in those that the majority found attractive. Although the process might seem straightforward in retrospect, there were sceptics

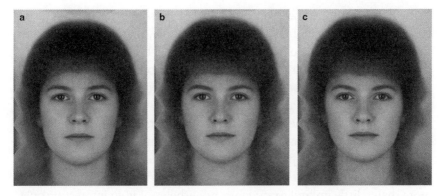

Figure 4.10 Caricaturing attractiveness (*a*) The Overall shape of a population of young European women. (*b*) The High shape of the most attractive sub-group. (*c*) A 50 per cent exaggeration of how the High shape differs from the Overall shape.

D.I. Perrett *et al.* (1994).

who claimed that beauty would not give up its secrets to academic study, while others argued that beauty *should* not be studied scientifically at all, since objectifying beauty is demeaning to people.

Having identified attractive aspects in European faces, we wanted to test whether or not the same aspects were matched in other cultures' notions of beauty. We therefore needed to repeat the tests with faces and evaluators from another country.[47] If attractive faces have a little something extra, and if the something extra has a biological basis, then this something extra should be present in attractive faces from all parts of the globe. In fact the results were indeed consistent, independent of whether we conducted our computer-graphic beauty pageant in Osaka, Japan, or in St Andrews, Scotland. Japanese and UK judges gave their highest ratings to the caricatured Japanese High face and their lowest ratings to the caricatured Japanese Low shape. Reciprocally, UK and Japanese judges gave their highest ratings to the caricatured UK High face and their lowest ratings to the caricatured UK Low shape. An attractive Japanese face is attractive in the same way as an attractive European face, even though the two shapes are distinctively different. Attractive cues depart from average for both types of faces and judgements of attractiveness are concordant across cultures. In other words, the 'style' of an attractive face is the same across different cultures – and this style is distinctively different from that of the *average* face.

This deduction is borne out by asking people to make a different type of judgement about the faces in Figure 4.10, or a whole series of faces in which the shape has been pushed very far in the direction of the High shape and very far in the direction of the Low shape. If instead of assessing attractiveness people are asked to say how 'normal-looking' the faces are, then most viewers agree that the Overall average looks more *normal*. Yet the High faces are still the most *attractive*.[48] In other words, 'average' is considered normal, but it is not considered the most attractive or the most beautiful. *Beautiful* faces are unusual.

Most studies on facial attractiveness employ faces of university students. Some critics of the work argue that students are not representative; they might have faces that are actually a bit odd in some systematic way in comparison with the population as a whole.[49] Such a view is tantamount to claiming that this section of the population looks abnormal, which is more than a little unkind to students; nonetheless it is an interesting question as to whether the same effects occur for the faces of models. People selected to work as models are being paid for being better-looking than the rest of us; if we consider *their* faces, can we define attractive characteristics unique to the top models? If we used only the best-looking people, we could perform a more stringent test of the 'beauty is unusual' finding.

Work with photographs of sixty-two professional models and those who profited from their appearance in the fashion industry produced results similar to those based on student populations.[50] While all the models' faces were good-looking, the High-shaped face derived from the twenty most attractive female faces beat the Overall shape from the whole set of faces, which in turn beat the Low shape from the twenty least attractive models (see Figure 4.11). A highly attractive face really does have a little *je ne sais quoi* that averageness alone cannot explain.

Low   Overall   High

Figure 4.11 The best of the best: top models. *Left*: The Low shape: the average shape derived from the faces of the twenty models who were judged least attractive among sixty-two female models. *Centre*: The Overall shape: the average shape derived from the faces of all sixty-two models. *Right*: The High shape: the average shape for the twenty models who received the highest ratings for attractiveness.

L.K. Mackie *et al.* (1994) Perception Lab.

Super-attractive or bug-eyed monster?

It is clear, therefore, that the shape of *attractive* faces is different from that of the *average* face. As always, though, we must be careful not to take this too far. At a certain point, amplifying the features of attractive faces creates a face so exaggerated that it falls outside the range of faces we experience on a daily basis. Although large eyes are attractive, we wouldn't expect that by creating faces with ever larger eyes we would be able to increase the attractiveness of a face indefinitely – at some point, we would create a bug-eyed monster, or a strange creature reminiscent of a bush-baby, which we would no longer see as human, let alone attractive. Figure 4.12 shows faces that have been pushed to the extremes of attractiveness. In the unattractive direction, exaggeration makes the face shape more heavy-set. It is no surprise that with exaggeration in this direction, face shape does not improve but gets steadily less attractive. What is more interesting, though, is that things don't get ever better in the other direction, either, towards greater attractiveness. When you look at this series, it is clear that there is a natural limit beyond which the facial configurations no longer appear super-attractive: on the contrary, they begin to look odd. The wide eyes and ears get larger, the nose longer, the mouth wider, and the chin begins to vanish. The face becomes less human and more elf-like.

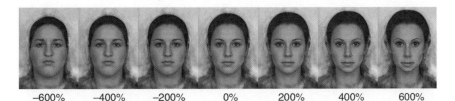

| −600% | −400% | −200% | 0% | 200% | 400% | 600% |

Figure 4.12 Things can only get better – up to a point. 0 per cent represents the population average. 100 per cent represents the average shape of the attractive sub-group of the population studied. Amplifying the difference to 200 per cent produces a very attractive face shape, but with further amplification, to +400 per cent or +600 per cent, the shape no longer gets progressively more beautiful – instead, the eyes begin to look out of proportion and the face loses its chin.
L.M. DeBruine *et al.* (2007).

Respect for averageness

Considerable space has been devoted to challenging the notion that 'beauty is only average'. This doesn't mean that averageness has no role to play in judgements of attractiveness. Average faces are indeed attractive, although the *most* attractive faces are more than simply average. The idea that our perceptions of attractiveness are linked to the range of faces we experience naturally is an interesting and a powerful way of explaining many aspects of attractiveness. This is because the averages of different populations will tend to be similar in key properties; for example, any average will be highly symmetrical. A face that deviates substantially from the average in one population is likely to be highly unusual in other populations as well. The same idea can account for why people come to have subtle differences in cultural tastes: the faces we see and learn about will be different from those seen by someone else in a different culture. The idea can also explain our negative emotional reactions to disfigurement, since disfigurement changes faces away from the average we normally encounter. Averageness can explain how differences between the various faces to which we are frequently exposed can bias our personal notions of attractiveness in distinct ways. Such influences from experience can also help to explain why we find a family resemblance to be attractive under certain circumstances (see Chapter 10), and why we grow to love the face of a long-term partner (see Chapter 11). Averageness is not to be overlooked or underestimated.

Even so, it's now clear that highly attractive faces are different from those that are attractively average, though in this chapter we haven't yet identified the particular facial traits that give some faces the edge over the rest. One facial attribute still to be explored concerns the differences between men and women that make it easy for us to distinguish people's sex by looking at their facial features. As we'll see, while the facts unfold easily for female faces, when it comes to male facial attractiveness, controversy remains.

Chapter 5
HIS AND HERS

How sex hormones influence our looks and our attraction to others

In Chapter 4 we concluded that highly attractive faces have the edge on those that are average in shape for the population. This is hardly unlocking the secrets of beauty; other than symmetry, we haven't yet defined the characteristics that give some faces this edge. Likely candidates are those aspects of face shape that allow us to tell men and women apart. After all, we want to find a mate of the desired sex. The degree of femininity or masculinity in a face is an excellent cue to a person's sex, and it makes sense that we should find such cues attractive.

Girls will be girls: femininity

If the biological function of attraction is procreation (see Chapter 6) then one would expect that men might be attracted to the characteristics of a woman that indicate her capacity to have lots of children.[1] We will briefly consider what makes bodies beautiful; and because most men are preoccupied with women's bodies, these provide clear lessons for beauty in faces.

Women's body shape differs from that of men for two obvious reasons: wider hips for giving birth and larger breasts for producing milk. Simply because of these anatomical facts, women's bodies curve at the waist more than men's, and that curve is related to fertility. Women with curvier figures have higher levels of the female reproductive hormones,[2] and these increase the likelihood of getting pregnant. Would-be fathers should therefore prefer women with the waistline that is associated with high fertility: the most attractive female body shape should be one in which the waist curves in an hour-glass fashion, rather than one that goes straight up and down.[3] While preferences for the degree of curviness do vary across the globe,[4] it is true that in general people everywhere prefer women to have more of an hourglass shape than men.

There are limits to how curvy a body can be. The Victorian corset pushed the envelope here (Figure 5.1, left), and in some cases produced 15-inch (38 cm) waists. The considerable pressure from whalebone and tight lacing generated a figure that exaggerated a feminine body shape. Edwardian corsets changed posture and bustles added to the effect by enhancing the size of the hips and the bottom (Figure 5.1, right). The constriction of extreme corsets was not exactly healthy, and since the curves that resulted from padding here and squeezing there were artificial,

Figure 5.1 Augmented body shapes. *Left*: The corset-narrowed waist. *Right*: The bustle-enlarged backside.
Ladies' Home Journal, October 1900.

this fashion made it a bit tricky to judge a woman's fertility and general health from her apparent body shape.

Apart from the effect of clothes, waist size may be important, since very fine judgements about curviness may not be needed. In fact, decisions about women related to the desirability of youth and hence fertility may be made at a much cruder level – and they often are. A slender waist relative to broad hips and breasts may be favoured simply because their shape is a good indicator of a person's sex, irrespective of what they say about her fertility. Exaggerating female curves makes more sense when we think in these terms; it presents most men with a 'super-normal' version of what they are looking for.[5]

What about the face? Does it show the same kinds of obvious differences between the sexes as body shape shows? As Figure 5.2 demonstrates, the answer is very clearly yes. As we pass through puberty, our bone structure is heavily influenced by sex hormones. Elongation of the arm and leg bones makes boys suddenly shoot up. Bone changes begin to show in the face, too, courtesy of the flood of testosterone. As boys turn to men, their eyebrow ridges grow more prominent, and their jawbones enlarge rapidly. Maleness is also clear from the width of the upper face (that's the width across the cheeks compared to the distance between the eyebrows and the mouth).[6] This measure of relative width is greater for men than for women, and the difference emerges as males pass through puberty.

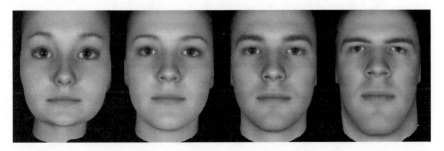

Figure 5.2 Exaggerated sex differences. *Centre left and centre right*: A pair of heads, average for 21-year-old male and female Europeans. *Left*: The female head shape has been adjusted away from the male, amplifying female face traits. *Right*: The masculine facial proportions of the male head have been amplified in the same way.

D. Buls (2009) Perception Lab.

Sex differences in faces can be traced to our primate ancestry. Thanks to competition over access to mates, adult male primates are more powerfully built and more strongly muscled than females, and they have larger teeth and jaws. This allows them to see off rivals, thereby ensuring that they are the ones who get to father offspring. To a lesser extent the same remains true for human males.

Although women also get an increase in testosterone at puberty, they have much higher levels of the sex hormone oestrogen, which prevents the bone growth we see in men. The net result is that while men's head shape changes a lot, women's head shape stays as it is and retains more child-like proportions. Female faces are 'neotenous' (from the Greek meaning 'extended youth'), with less prominent brows and jaws, thicker lips, a smaller nose, a smaller head size, and large eyes relative to the rest of the face. All these differences are evident in Figure 5.2, particularly when sex differences have been enhanced. In effect, computer graphics have done for a female face what the corset does to a woman's body.

Since making women's bodies more feminine goes down well with men,[7] it seems a good idea to test the same effect on facial shape. If we feminize

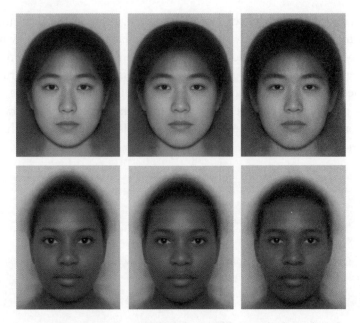

Figure 5.3 Femininity and women of the world. Female faces from Japan and Jamaica: feminized (*left*), average (*centre*), and masculinized (*right*).

D.I. Perrett & I.S. Penton-Voak (1997–1999) Perception Lab.

adult female faces by moving their shape a little further away from that of the typical male face (see Figure C, Plate I), we mimic how the face would grow with higher levels of female hormones and lower levels of male hormones. This feminization should increase the face's attractiveness, because the result represents the face of a superwoman whose sex should now be unmistakably female, and whose attributes signal super-charged hormones which in turn should indicate definite fertility.

In our laboratory, we gave people the chance to evaluate beauty in a range of female head shapes by allowing them to control face shape interactively using a computer. Moving the computer mouse in one direction made the displayed face progressively more masculine; moving it in the opposite direction made the face increasingly feminine. In these experiments, we ensured that change was restricted to face shape: no skin-tone changes accompanied the adjustments, as we didn't want the female faces to develop a five-o'clock shadow as they became more masculinized.

Presenting faces in this way gives people control over what they see. There is no right or wrong answer; instead, we simply ask participants, acting as evaluators, to adjust the face until it is as attractive as possible within the range available (the left and right images in Figure C, Plate I show the limits). In these interactive studies, an astonishing 95 per cent of men and women decided that feminization of women's faces made them more attractive. Our evaluators often exaggerated the feminine shape by the maximum level allowed – in their quest for ideal beauty, they would have cranked up the femininity levels further had we let them. We found exactly the same results for faces of European, African, and Asian descent (Figure 5.3[8]). And it didn't seem to matter who was adjusting the face: we got the same results from Japanese[9] and from black South Africans.[10] Femininity was definitely attractive. This explains why attractive faces are not average: a highly attractive female face is more feminine than the average.

The use of cosmetics shows intriguing parallels. Women often alter their facial features: eyebrows are plucked out and then pencilled in both thinner and more arched; lipstick is applied to make lips fuller. Our studies indicate that one reason why make-up increases attractiveness is because it makes the eyebrow and lip shapes appear more feminine. In the same way that our evaluators used the computer mouse to push faces toward the feminine end of the shape spectrum, women in daily life use cosmetics to push their face shape further away from that of men.

Different preferences

Femininity in female face shape seems universally preferred across cultures, but this doesn't mean that there is no variation at all in the preferences shown for femininity. Indeed, we found that a few men actively preferred more masculine-looking women. Maybe they are the ones who end up with a spouse who looks domineering. (Hen-pecked husbands are discussed in Chapter 9.)

Men and women from Japan, the UK, and South Africa all preferred a feminized shape for all female faces, and in all cases this preference was strongest for faces from their own culture. One possibility is that people may learn what is attractive in a female face first and foremost by working out how female faces differ from male faces. The differences learned in one culture will apply to other cultures, too, because sex hormones act in a similar way across all human populations. We can therefore expect there to be broad cross-cultural agreement about which female faces are beautiful and which are not. Faces do vary slightly from population to population, of course, and our particular upbringing will attune us to the specific male–female differences most prevalent in our own population.

Some cultural differences can be identified. In rural Jamaica, for example, men prefer higher levels of masculinity in women's faces.[11] One possible explanation for this could lie in the fact that disease is both more prevalent and more life-threatening among these people than in any of our other study populations. A higher degree of masculinization may be a signal of greater resistance to disease (see below), in which case a more masculine female face might be viewed as more attractive because it has become linked to greater health.[12]

Masculinity in men

As already noted, testosterone increases both bone growth and muscle bulk. Some scientists have argued that men with facial features that indicate high testosterone might, in some sense, be 'showing off' the quality of their immune system,[13] in the same way that stags show off their large antlers or male birds their elaborate and colourful plumage.[14] The argument is as follows: one of testosterone's effects is to *weaken* the immune system, so only top-quality males – those with strong immune systems and a resilient body – will be able to grow the impressive ornaments that depend on testosterone while still being able to resist disease. A poor-quality male whose body pumped out testosterone would not cope with the problems it caused for his immune system: he would be vulnerable to infections, which would leave him in a sorry state. Likewise, the ornaments he was growing might develop unevenly, with the result that he would be unable to fight off rivals or display to potential mates. In short, he would be in a worse state than had he not grown such big ornaments. In other words, the traits associated with testosterone represent a 'handicap' – if males can display the handicap *and* stay fit, then they are clearly top-notch chaps.

If this logic applies to humans, women should prefer masculine-looking males. Using the same interactive techniques our group had earlier used to look at preferences for femininity, we explored whether more masculine faces were generally considered to be attractive (see Figure 5.4). To our surprise, we found that increasing masculinity makes male faces *less* attractive to women and men. Even more surprisingly, we found that people preferred male faces with a slightly *feminized* shape, and this preference was consistent across Japanese, UK, and South African populations.

It seems that humans are different from other species, in which elaboration of male traits increases a male's attractiveness and breeding success.[15] Why should this be? One idea is that male facial characteristics may not be a 'handicap' or an 'ornament' in the way that has been supposed. Masculinity in a man's face does not relate clearly to his current health or immunity.[16] Given that masculinity in male faces appears to be actively *disliked*, could it be that in humans masculinity is associated with negative, rather than positive, traits?

Men behaving badly

One clue that this might be the case came from remarks people made on seeing the artificially masculinized faces: our evaluators said they looked 'less kind'. Altering just this one dimension of masculinity–femininity seems to lead to a changed perception of the man's personality (see Figure 5.4). When we specifically asked people to attribute personality traits to masculinized faces, we found that the remarks made earlier were borne out by the results: these faces were judged by the majority to be less emotional, colder, less honest, less co-operative, and less likely to be a good parent. Feminization of male face shape had the opposite effect, making the faces look warmer, more emotional, more honest, more co-operative, and potentially a better parent.[17]

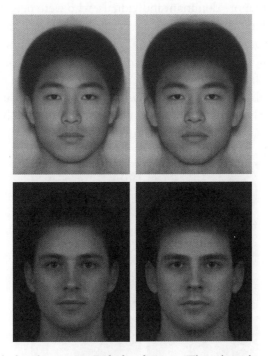

Figure 5.4 A dark side to men. *Right-hand images*: These have been masculinized in face shape, moving them away from female faces. *Left-hand images*: These have been reshaped in the opposite way, in effect feminizing them. Such changes affect the way in which viewers perceive personality. Look at each pair. Which of the two do you think looks warmer, more honest, or more likely to be a better father?

D.I. Perrett & D. Rowland (1996) Perception Lab.

Such judgements seem stereotypic, yet they may have at least some basis in actual behaviour. In real life it seems that men with more masculine faces do, in fact, show more aggressive[18] and more uncooperative behaviour. Men with masculine face proportions commit more fouls in ice-hockey games and end up with a greater number of time-out penalties than men with more feminine facial proportions. Off the pitch, in an experimental set-up in which players can gain resources, defend them, and steal from others, men with masculine facial proportions choose to retaliate aggressively when other players steal from them and then to steal right back. In contrast, men with feminine facial proportions are more likely to build defences against further infringement. Furthermore, men with high testosterone (that is, those likely to have a masculine facial appearance[19]) have more troubled relationships, and show increased rates of infidelity, violence, and divorce.[20] Masculine males, it seems, are more likely to behave like cads than be good dads.

It wasn't all bad news, though; masculinized faces were judged to belong to stronger and more dominant individuals, who were perceived as no less intelligent. This fits with other research in which male faces have been made more masculine by amplifying the specific structural changes that develop during puberty, as a boy turns into a man.[21] These changes, too, make a male's face look more dominant (Figure 5.5). Men with dominant faces do actually turn out to be physically strong,[22] so you can tell from a man's face whether he could give you a bone-crushing handshake and whether he would be a formidable adversary.

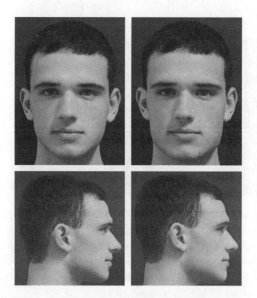

Figure 5.5 How puberty changes male face shape. Enhancing the structural changes in the face that mark the passage from boyhood (*left*) to manhood (*right*) enhances masculinity and apparent dominance, but does not enhance attractiveness.

J.P. Swaddle & G.W. Reierson (2002).

Attraction to masculinity in men's faces is intriguing. Preferences for masculinity are neither dramatic nor consistent, unlike the preferences for femininity in women's faces. Many studies either find no preference or find that masculinity in men's faces is actually off-putting. Some studies find a preference for a slight degree of masculinity, but no one has found an overall preference for a high degree of facial masculinity.[23] It therefore becomes important to try to identify the reasons why preferences for masculinity are so variable between different women: this could give insights into attraction. One possible reason why preferences might vary relates to cyclical shifts in female hormone levels.

Sex and the cycle

From a biological perspective, the most significant consequence of attraction is the possibility of making babies. Will attraction lead to sex? And will sex lead to pregnancy? It therefore makes perfect sense to look at likes and dislikes in relation to fertility. Sex can, and does, happen at any time of the day or month, but even if it is pleasurable on every occasion, it will not result in pregnancy unless it occurs within a quite narrow time window. How does this window affect attraction?

To answer this we need to know when fertility is high and low, so here's a brief sex-education course focused on when women can get pregnant. A normal female menstrual cycle in humans takes around twenty-eight days. During the first two weeks, one egg matures, generating ever more oestrogen. Around day fourteen of the cycle, the mature egg is released from the ovary (ovulation), and travels through the fallopian tubes, taking about three or four days to reach the womb. If it encounters a sperm loitering in the tubes, it may be fertilized. Many people do not realize that sperm live inside a woman for up to six days after sexual intercourse; all this time they swim around in search of their quarry. An egg that doesn't meet up with a sperm dies within a single day. The lifespan of sperm after the man's moment of pleasure means that a woman can get pregnant *only* if she has sex on the day of ovulation or on one of the five days before. In other words, there are just six days a month that are good for making babies.[24]

As soon as ovulation happens, the cells that have nurtured the egg in the ovary begin making progesterone, the pregnancy hormone, and continue to do so for the next fortnight or so. Progesterone causes marked changes in both body and mind. It helps the lining of the womb to thicken and become ready to host the fertilized egg that will grow into a baby. If the egg is fertilized and becomes embedded in the womb, it sends a message to keep the pregnancy preparations going; if not, the ovary stops producing progesterone after a couple of weeks. The fall in progesterone signals that the womb lining is not needed, and this lining is discarded in the period of menstrual bleeding. The six fertile days during which there is a green light for getting pregnant therefore coincide with high oestrogen[25] and low progesterone levels.

In the late 1990s, our research team started looking at facial attraction across the cycle. Working with a UK magazine, we published five images of men who ranged in masculinity. Women wrote to us telling us which male they fancied most, and details of their own menstrual cycle.[26] We excluded women who were using hormone contraception, because they have no change in fertility and because natural changes in hormone levels are altered or masked by the artificial contraceptive hormones. For each of the remaining women, we estimated where she was likely to be in her cycle, and split the data into the days when the women might get pregnant after sex and the other days when this was unlikely. To our amazement, we found an increase in the level of masculinity preferred during the most fertile period of the cycle.[27] These findings were not restricted to faces: at their most fertile, women prefer men who display more masculine, dominant behaviour; have deeper, more masculine voices;[28] and have a more masculine body shape, with broad shoulders.[29]

Bearing in mind the earlier supposition that masculinity may signal to potential mates a great immune system and an ability to fend off rivals, these shifts in preferences seem to imply that, at times of high fertility, a woman's interests become tuned to a male's quality as a stud. She will, in essence, become especially attracted to men who are likely to produce strong healthy kids. If she is choosing a partner for a short-term sexual encounter, then without successful contraception she will be favouring[30] pregnancy by a man who can give her offspring a strong immune system. In strictly biological terms, such a man (and his genes) comes with a kind of 'highly-approved' quality rating. The preference in the non-fertile phase for more feminine-looking men can be seen as a drive to get a friendly, helpful husband who will be faithful and supportive. Indeed, when women are asked to choose the face of someone as a long-term partner, they are likely to choose a feminine-looking guy; whereas if they are asked to choose a man for a short-term sexual relationship only, they are more likely to pick a masculine guy.[31]

As you may have noticed, there is a conflict of interests taking shape. One would expect men to be interested in propagating their own genes, and therefore in supporting their own flesh and blood. The shift in a woman's preferences however, may imply a shift in the men with whom she prefers to get intimate: the 'nice guy' with whom she chooses to settle down and bring up a child might not be the same man with whom she chose to have sex to produce the child in the first place. There certainly are cases when Dad turns out not to be the biological father of a child he believed was his. Such cases cause debate both inside the courtroom and in academic journals. Currently the best estimates we have of such 'extra-pair paternity' suggest that the rate is about 3 per cent;[32] that is, about one in thirty men is bringing up a child to whom he is not related, without being aware of it. This need not always imply cuckoldry, because the 'nice guy' may have been chosen after conception. (It is not unheard of for the mother to be unsure as to who got her pregnant as in the film *Mamma Mia!*) In any case, since the 'nice guy' who believes himself the father of the extra-pair child is likely to make other babies with the woman, maybe everything is okay in the long run for him?

Worryingly, if one asks couples about their happiness and their commitment to one another, certain patterns emerge.[33] Although women are equally happy with a long-term romantic partner throughout their menstrual cycle, the level of *commitment* they feel to their partner goes up and down with the level of their progesterone. Women feel most committed in the last two weeks of the cycle, when progesterone is high and when they might be pregnant. The flip side of the coin is that the same women feel *least* committed when they are at their most fertile – at exactly the time when they find masculine faces, bodies, and behaviour most appealing. During the first two weeks of the cycle, therefore, the fluctuating levels of hormones may incline some women to stray from their partner for a dalliance with a man who appears more masculine.

When questioned, women admit that most of their sexual fantasies about men who are not their primary partner occur during the time of their peak fertility, and that their fantasies about sex with other men depend on the body symmetry of their long-term partner.[34] Those with an asymmetrical partner are more likely to fantasize about other men. Since asymmetrical partners do not have the best genes – for resisting disease and growing evenly in the face of life stresses (see Chapter 4) – reduced feelings of commitment and more frequent wandering sexual thoughts might encourage women to go elsewhere to collect better-quality genes. Being attracted to other men of higher quality (as it were), while this may be considered immoral, could thus make biological sense – sometimes the attraction will lead to sex and conception. Although this might not be good for the long-term partnership, the woman's personal sense of guilt, or the risk of divorce, it might nevertheless benefit the woman[35] by mixing her genes with a set that will better help her children resist disease. Of course, the stakes are high: divorce could lose her support in rearing children.

While the scenario here is speculative, the conflict of interests is quite acute and we might expect men to adjust their behaviour accordingly. In this situation, a man should pay attention to his partner when she is most fertile, to guard against the unwelcome attentions of marauding opportunists. As noted earlier, progesterone levels are lowest and oestrogen levels highest at the most fertile part of a woman's cycle. This unique state of reproductive hormones is the probable cause of a long list of changes that make women more attractive to men. Close to ovulation, a woman's face is prettier, her voice sounds sexier, her body has a more desirable odour, her breasts, ears, and fingers are more symmetric, and she is also likely to behave more flirtatiously, wearing clothes designed to be attractive.[36] Indeed women at this time, with or without a partner, feel the greatest urge to go out to places (such as dance clubs and parties) where they might meet men. Male partners have quite an incentive to respond! And indeed they *are* more attentive, even to the extent of expressing more feelings of love, and they show a greater tendency to 'guard' their mates.[37] They get more jealous in their perceptions of other men and more possessive of their partner when she is most fertile. Protectiveness is most marked in men who don't think themselves very sexy.

All of this makes up the spice of life and provides good soap opera material. It implies that there is a special kind of struggle between men and women: each woman is unconsciously[38] pursuing the best male genes for her children's strength and health, even if they come from outside the partnership; and each man is unconsciously trying to make sure that it his genes alone that combine with his partner's.

Do shifts in attraction imply cheating?

Changes in women's level of attraction to masculinity across the menstrual cycle seem to have two unsettling implications: that women are slaves to their hormones and – worse – that hormones predispose women to cheat on their partners.

The first conclusion is unfair because it implies that only women are slaves to their hormones. Not so. It is now clear that hormonal influences are just as prevalent in men. Testosterone levels in men change profoundly in daily cycles; levels are highest in the morning on waking and can drop by 40 per cent by midday. Changing levels of testosterone are linked to changes in a man's attraction to feminine faces,[39] with the strongest attraction to femininity occurring when the testosterone level is highest. Testosterone changes may also be at the root of the annual cycle that men show in attraction to female faces and bodies:[40] the testosterone level is higher in winter than in summer months, and in winter men are even more attracted to women's bodies than in summer. So men are subject to the vagaries of hormones, just as much as women.

Indeed men may be even more strongly governed by their gonads than women, precisely because testosterone is so changeable. In a competition, a man's testosterone can shoot up if he wins and down if he loses.[41] For his testosterone to change he need not even compete himself; it is enough that the team he supports triumphs or is defeated.[42] The hormone swings depend on what he believes caused his success; if he puts the win down to luck, then there's little change.[43] The mere anticipation of a challenge or a big game causes testosterone to rocket.[44] In general, testosterone in men is all over the place, so hormonal drives in attraction and self-control may challenge men more than women.

The second implication of changes in attraction to masculinity across the menstrual cycle – that hormones predispose women to cheat on their partners – is perhaps a real cause for concern. Note the sexism in the way the implication is phrased here: men are not presumed to succumb to temptations to cheat on partners when their testosterone levels fluctuate, despite the fact that such changes are linked to face preference. Now that a few years have passed since the original results of our group's studies, we have several reasons to think that changes during the menstrual cycle *don't* in fact instigate cheating. It's time to air some of these and set the record straight.

Let's consider first the role of a woman's relationship with her father. Women whose fathers have been absent during the first five years of their life (typically through divorce or separation) tend to have a distinct growth and reproductive profile. First, the absence of the father early in life speeds up sexual maturation: puberty comes six months earlier than in those whose fathers were present during childhood.[45] Reproduction itself starts early too, with first pregnancies occurring at a younger age.[46] One explanation for the link between the father's absence and fast-track baby production is that in evolutionary terms it may make sense when life is tough and uncertain to have lots of kids and to have them quickly: that way there is a greater chance that some of them may live long enough to reproduce themselves and so pass on the family genes.

Childhood experience sets up expectations for adult life and the family set-up. For example, growing up without a father can lead women to anticipate that men will not stick around or provide fatherly support. If a man can be relied upon only to make a sperm donation, then one might expect preferences for masculinity to be heightened in women growing up without a father. The choice of masculinity could be a choice for physical strength, dominance, and immunity, since these are the characteristics the child will need, especially if no father is around to help. And so it proves: we find that in women who had a poor-quality relationship with their father during childhood, there is a much greater tendency for the menstrual cycle to affect their masculinity preferences than in women who grew up with their fathers present.[47] In other words, cyclic shifts in masculinity preferences were most prevalent in a particular small sub-group of women.

Women's preferences for a particular relationship type can also influence the degree to which they prefer masculinity.[48] Those who wanted a stable, long-term relationship showed little or no cyclic shift: their liking for masculinity was the same whether they were fertile or not. Those who wanted their relationships to be short-term only did show pronounced cyclic shifts and were most impressed with masculinity in the middle of their cycle. None of these women were likely to be tempted to cuckoldry, therefore – those who wanted long-term partners did not shift in their preferences, and those who only wanted short-term partners can't be accused of being tempted to cheat because they didn't want a committed relationship!

Most studies of cyclic shifts in women have dealt with young adults, often students. Many of the participants will have steady boyfriends, presumably, but such relationships may differ from relationships between committed partners who plan to have families soon. Cyclic shifts in preferences may certainly lead young women to change partners, but change could be 'trading up' to get a better model within the confines of an exclusive (though not necessarily permanent) relationship. Studies need to consider the stability, duration, and quality of relationships. Rather than being a disruptive force, menstrual-cycle shifts might be cohesive, tending to bring partners closer together, for example if the woman is drawn to her partner's characteristics more strongly at times of high fertility.[49]

Although sex outside marriage or other 'committed' partnerships does inevitably happen, society cannot countenance it happening too frequently. Some behaviour must remain rare or it may induce dramatic changes to our whole social structure. Consider a trading analogy. Imagine a society in which there two types of people. One type, the 'doves', thrive by cooperating; the second type, the 'hawks', thrive by reneging on deals and exploiting the doves. Both types of person can coexist, but only so long as there is balance. With too many hawks there would no longer be any safe basis for cooperation, and as the doves would invariably get ripped off, they would eventually stop behaving as doves. When cooperation stopped, hawks could not function either – there would be no offers from doves that the hawks could exploit. The lesson is this: deceit can operate only if it is relatively rare. When it comes to sexual infidelity, there is a very high price to pay if the deceit is discovered – a woman found to be unfaithful, or suspected of being unfaithful, risks desertion or worse. Being single can place a huge burden on a parent, and children's health care and education can suffer.[50]

If 'extra-pair' paternity becomes too frequent, then family support structures may need to change. In societies in which fatherhood is uncertain, wealth is often passed from a man to his *sister's* son rather than to his 'own' son.[51] A man can be certain that he shares half his genes with his mother and his sister, so he must share a quarter of his genes with each of his sister's children. That's better odds than giving the family heirlooms to a child who might be unrelated and have zero genes in common. Infidelity can happen, but it is unlikely to become so commonplace that a man is only rarely the biological father of the children of his partner who are born during their partnership.

Trading machismo for family values

Earlier we saw that preferences for symmetrical faces depended on people's assessments of their own attractiveness. We found a similar effect in women's preferences for masculinity: women who think themselves attractive tend to like men with masculine faces, whereas women who perceive themselves as unattractive like more feminine-looking males.[52] This difference in tastes is partly related to a woman's physical qualities.[53] If her body is curvaceous or her face is seen by others as good-looking, then she sets more store on masculinity. But physical appearance is only half the story – what matters just as much is self-confidence.

Young women were shown collections of face photos that had been collected from the website 'Hot or Not?' (This is a site[54] where people can upload photographs of themselves; website users then decide whether the person is 'hot', and give ego-boosting marks, or 'not', and award crushingly low ratings. Subtle, it isn't.) Some participants were shown collections of photos that were biased to include pretty women already rated as 'hot'. Other participants saw photos biased to include less attractive women (already rated as 'not'). Exposure to a collection of 'hotties' depressed women's self-esteem and evaluation of their own of attractiveness, whereas exposure to 'plain Janes' did the opposite and boosted self-confidence. So far, not very surprising – who *doesn't* feel a little less adequate after watching beautiful young actors and actresses, for example? What was interesting was that this manipulation of esteem was enough to swing a woman's opinion about the type of man she desired. Women with boosted confidence were more eager for men with masculine faces, whereas women made insecure about their looks shied away from such men.[55]

This study shows the interplay between the objective, stable side of beauty that can be verified with a tape measure or the votes of an independent panel, and the subjective, changeable side of beauty – the erratic faith in one's own looks. Self-confidence makes all the difference: with confidence you can carry off ludicrous chat-up lines and you can dress in clothes suited to someone who's 'worth it'. The confidence to take an initiative and the flamboyant clothes both increase allure. We compete for the attentions of others, and our perception of our own 'market value' dictates the compromises we make. If the most beautiful people do not appeal to us because we lack confidence, then we may just stop trying to win partners with those attributes. One student showed particular insight; when shown an unfamiliar male face, she told me: 'He is attractive, so he will be conceited and I won't like him.' If we can't get the most beautiful, perhaps we can get the most considerate, the funniest, the smartest, or the kindest – in the end, the best for us.

Attraction does not have to be guided by rational thought: repeated frustration and desertion can mould our desires. If those responsible for our failed relationships share a consistent face type, we can tune into this and know without thinking whom to avoid. Conversely, the rewards of success in romantic conquests can attune us to different dimensions of people. In short, the type of person to whom we are attracted is honed by experience (a theme we return to in Chapter 11). Even if we all *start* by liking the same type of guy or girl, each of us may soon learn that another type of guy or girl is actually more fun to be with, less heartache, and – for us – more of a heartthrob.

A girl's best friend

A woman's attraction to enhanced male masculinity during peak fertility is countered by her attraction to feminine characteristics during non-fertile times. The latter, it is supposed, may predispose her to secure a partner to help during pregnancy and to share in raising children. Yet such help could come from many quarters, and indeed female friends are likely to be roped in to provide help in some capacity, whether as a birth partner or a babysitter. If it is really a need for support that drives the menstrual shifts in preferences, then we should see changes in attraction to women's faces as well.

During the early studies in our laboratory, we did find that preferences for masculinity in both female and male faces peaked in the fertile phase of the cycle. We did not regard this shift as having a function, so we did not talk to fellow scientists or the media about it. With hindsight, though, the change is important. Femininity, in both men and women's faces, is associated with a warmer, more caring personality. During the potentially pregnant phase of the cycle, a shift towards preferring women who look caring makes sense.[56] Such findings do not require an explanation in which attraction to masculinity is designed to inspire the collection of good genes for the next generation, and cuckoldry to boot.

There are other indications, too, that women are more man-orientated or more woman-orientated at different stages of the cycle. Attraction to masculinity in faces is linked to attraction to a male odour[57] – women who like highly masculine faces also like the smell of a possible male sex-pheromone[58] (a chemical that is closely related to testosterone and that may act as an airborne signal affecting sexual attitudes and behaviour). During the fertile phase of their cycle, women show an increased attraction to the smell of the same male sex-pheromone, whereas the odour of this 'manly' substance becomes less pleasant in the last two weeks of the cycle. Actually most women think it stinks all the time (often like a urinal), it's just that at mid-cycle the smell becomes more bearable. By contrast, the odour of an oestrogen-derived compound and possible female sex-pheromone becomes more attractive exactly at the point at which the testosterone-related odour becomes less popular.[59] (As an aside, opinion varies as to the smell of this female sex-pheromone; one man said it was like his 'girlfriend in the morning' and another that it reminded him of 'a fridge that needs clean-ing'. Men who are attracted to very feminine female faces are the ones who are keenest on the female sex-pheromone odour.[60])

During high fertility, then, women are drawn more to an odour associ-ated with men, and during the two weeks preparing for pregnancy, women are drawn more to an odour associated with their own sex. A swing in preference does not mean a change from a heterosexual to a homosexual orientation each month, but it might imply a greater affiliation with women at a time when this is likely to be of practical benefit.

Blood is thicker than water

A woman's family and relatives are some of the people most likely to pro-vide support because blood relatives share genes; to help one's kin (even kin in the womb) is to help one's own genes.[61] We might therefore expect cyclic changes in attraction to family faces.

To investigate this, we can take the distinctive shape of one person's face and transpose it into another face – much as we did when portray-ing faces in the styles of different artists (Chapter 4). This process creates 'family look-alike' faces; for example, Figure 5.6 shows two women's faces together with teenage and middle-aged female and male faces that share a resemblance. These manufactured faces might look like the faces of a potential younger sister, aunt, younger brother, and uncle. Remarkably, research shows that a woman's attitude to such faces *does* change through her cycle: she is attracted to self-resembling faces only during the last two weeks of her menstrual cycle, when the body is preparing for pregnancy,[62] while in her fertile phase she has no particular attraction to family faces. More specifically, this cyclic change in facial attractiveness was found only for women's faces, not men's. When progesterone is high, women are being drawn towards their female relatives (sisters, cousins, mother, or aunts), so it looks as though cyclic fluctuations enhance women's affiliation with their female kin, who might provide most support. Once again, cyclic change is part of a bigger story – this is not about duping husbands, but about garnering support.[63]

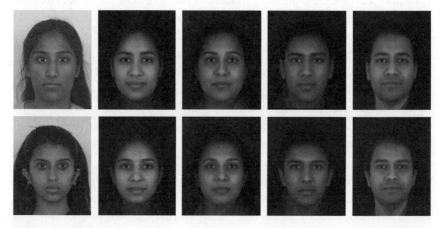

Figure 5.6 Keeping it in the family. *Left*: The two left-most images depict the faces of two real women. *Upper row*: The faces of a young woman, a middle-aged woman, a young man, and a middle-aged man have all been shaped to take on a 'family' resemblance to the face on the left. The younger faces could be those of a sibling or cousin, for example, while the older faces could be those of an aunt or uncle. *Lower row*: The same process has been repeated for the second face on the left.

L.M. DeBruine *et al.* (2005).

Are men one-dimensional?

It should be clear by now that masculine and feminine facial characteristics on their own do not automatically make for attractive male faces. Arnold Schwarzenegger's face is ruggedly masculine, but not everyone thinks he is good looking. By contrast, George Clooney's face is also very masculine, and he has twice been voted the 'sexiest man alive'.[64] We could speculate that part of the difference lies is in the facial expressions they're famous for: Clooney with his charming if faintly mischievous smile, and Arnie with his glowering 'Terminator' look (see Figure 5.7).

Figure 5.7 Images epitomizing different types of masculinity. *Left*: Arnold Schwarzenegger – tough, but with the cold emotion of a machine. *Right*: George Clooney – masculine, but with a hint of humour that makes his misdemeanours (for example in O *Brother, Where Art Thou?*) mostly forgivable.
Charcoal and pencil by D.I. Perrett (with D. Buls) (2009) Perception Lab.

Taking a person's photograph is a special interaction; the sitter will find it hard not to develop some kind of personal, albeit transient, attitude to the photographer. Even when they were asked to keep a neutral expression, most women are subsequently judged more attractive in shots taken by a male photographer than in shots taken by a female photographer.[65] Maybe there is a little flirtation from both parties – many men will not be satisfied until they have won a smile from a female. Men are not immune to friendly females, either; even a brief conversation with a woman can make their testosterone soar.[66] In photographs taken after five minutes' chat with a sociable female, men looked significantly happier; they were also voted more attractive as a long-term partner than they were in photos that had been taken after they'd spent five minutes waiting alone.[67]

Cameras don't lie – maybe not, but they don't tell the whole truth either. Being told to hold a smile is not conducive to a natural positive emotion. Women may differ from men more generally in their tendency to put on a socially positive, engaging face – men are more often prepared to look disinterested and dour. Perhaps the aversion to masculinity seen in many experiments is actually a result of this sex difference in the expressions made while being photographed in an ostensibly neutral pose. When masculinity is amplified, the expression on the face is amplified as well, and men end up looking increasingly grim – more Arnie than

George. People may find masculinity unattractive because computer graphic manipulations have been unwittingly masculinizing mood as well as anatomy.

A better way of getting positive emotion is to film people's faces while they talk about enjoyable events, such as a night out or a holiday. The attractiveness of men in film with natural expressions of this kind does not tie up that well with their attractiveness in still photos, whether with or without a smile.[68] A picture isn't always worth a thousand words; engaging him in conversation is what allows a man's true character to come over.

Humour plays a vital role in the mating game; witness how often the acronym GSOH ('Good Sense of Humour') is sought in personal ads. Humour is often used to flirt and is attractive.[69] Women like men to be fun, and men like women to respond their jokes, particularly those with sexual innuendos. Animation in faces is attractive when the movement is made in response to social interaction, such as nodding or smiling back after a comment.[70] So it's not just looks and facial expressiveness that are attractive: on a date, attention and interaction are vital in making a positive impression, since they indicate generosity as well as other aspects of the overall personality.

One important quality to which we would expect women to be sensitive is men's attitude to children and how broody the men are. After all, a man who wants to be a dad is a better bet for making a family than one who doesn't, and it is quite clear that men vary in how interested they are in babies. This broody side is not linked to testosterone (although testosterone levels do drop when men get married and have a baby born into their life[71]). What is particularly interesting is that women can pick up on this broodiness trait from men's faces alone.[72] So it seems that there are two dimensions which women can detect in men's faces: their dominance levels (which are related to testosterone and masculinity) and their family friendliness (which isn't). And what facial characteristic do you think suggests to women that a guy is good with kids? Too easy ... it's a smile. If the guy looks warm and positive – if he smiles – then he is rated as kid-friendly. Presumably he is also rated as people-friendly and partner-friendly too. The power of a smile!

Sexual maturation and attraction to faces

So far we have focused on how sex hormones affect face growth and how hormone fluctuations affect attraction. One major difference between people is when their hormones kick into action: this affects both face development and the onset of sexual activity. Adolescents grow up at surprisingly different rates (see Chapter 9). Some boys will start shaving and dating a long time before others, just as girls vary in the age at which their breasts develop and their periods start.

Such differences in the rate of development seem to have an influence over which faces are found attractive to young adults at 21 years of age.[73] Young men who say they went through puberty faster than their peers and were sexually active at a relatively early age (before 17 years old) show the strongest attraction to feminine cues in women's faces (Figure 5.8). The same thing happens for young women: those who have been sexually active at an early age also have the strongest attraction to masculinity in men's faces[74] (Figure 5.8[75]).

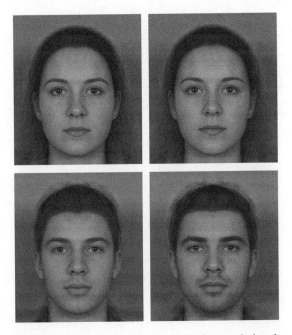

Figure 5.8 Matching preference to the speed of sexual development. *Upper row:* Men who reported faster sexual development than their peers were more attracted to the right-hand image. *Lower row:* Both male images were attractive to women, though those who had relatively fast development in their sexual experience were more attracted to the right-hand, masculinized image. Women whose development had been slower were more attracted to the left-hand, feminized image.

R.E. Cornwell *et al.* (2006).

These findings link the teen years to the twenties and provide yet another basis for postulating why different people are attracted to different faces. Teenagers who are speeding to adulthood in growth and sexual behaviour are likely to get on well with peers who are developing at the same fast pace.[76] They and their fast-growing peers are going to look mature for their age, and hanging out or sleeping with these people will tend to enhance attraction to sexually differentiated faces. Those who go through adolescence late are likely to be spurned by the fast-maturing crowd: their friends and lovers will be biased towards having less sexually developed faces. Experiences at a formative time of life have surprisingly durable effects on attraction to faces (see Chapters 10 and 11).

So we now know a lot about the mechanics of attraction and how attraction develops. But *why* does it develop – why does attractiveness matter, and what qualities should we be attracted to? In short, what's the point of beauty?

Chapter 6
THE POINT OF BEAUTY

The face you get and the face you leave

In our discussion of attraction so far we have not yet addressed its *point*. In the long run, is there any purpose in chasing after a beautiful face?

There are, depending on one's perspective and the choices available in one's life, many possible qualities to consider when selecting a partner and most people who are in a position to be choosy try to achieve some kind of balance. To some, a sense of humour is paramount. Others might prioritise wealth or future earning potential or fame. A high intelligence might be important. But whatever the set of attributes that matter consciously or unconsciously to us, it turns out that most of the ways we assess a potential lover are actually good for working out who is most suited to producing children and grandchildren.[1] For example, humour helps keep bonds between partners tight so that any kids that are produced can be supported over time, high intelligence makes for clever offspring who are more likely to prosper and reproduce, fame generally implies some earning power, and money pays the bills and indicates an ability to support lots of children.[2]

Sex and choice

Of course we may not be consciously thinking in terms of children, let alone grandchildren, when we fall for Mr Right or Ms Perfect, but then neither is any other animal who selects a mate. We need to look at how members of other species select their mates, and why, to see whether the same principles apply to humans.

According to her species, the female varies in what she requires from a male before sex. A female chimpanzee may only require interest, and will parade outrageously in front of the male she chooses. In some species of bird, the female requires a long courtship ritual with her betrothed, in which they swoop and tumble through the sky like practised acrobats, or dive in synchrony for nest material. A female bird of paradise will sit back, pull out the score card, and require a male to get a perfect ten on the dance floor with moves he has practised for years.[3] A female widowbird rates males' tails as the males jump and parade on circular tracks especially cleared around grass tufts (Figure 6.1). A female deer, on the other hand, may get little say in the matter – she may *want* the best-quality grass, but that may come with the territory of the rut champion and being part of a harem.

Figure 6.1 A male widowbird, whose tail defines his beauty. The success of the widowbird in producing offspring depends largely on the length of his tail. Wikipedia.

In any of these species, the act of consummation is indeed the culmination of a long process. If we wind the clock back a bit, we will find that for quite a while the male has been working hard to be 'the one'. He may have spent many hours of many days parading his dandy colours and ornaments; he may have been persistent in courting, singing, or chirping; he may have struggled to beat off rivals in epic battles. The selected males have not been idle: in many ways their whole lives have been geared up to being selected by the female, or at least to winning her over for the few seconds spent copulating.

So how does all this female choosiness and male competitiveness and wooing affect success? From a biological perspective, the main reason for any animal getting together with an attractive partner is to make babies which can grow and make more babies. Success from the biological perspective is measured by how many grandchildren and great-grandchildren we leave behind. *Fostering* a lot of children doesn't count; nor does marrying into a family that already has a lot of children or grandchildren. To count, the kids have to be our own flesh and blood: they must share our genetic material. Moulay Ismaïl Ibn Sharif, Sultan of Morocco (Figure 6.2), was unusually successful by these standards – it is claimed that he fathered 888 children.[4] So humans can vary hugely in the number of their descendents, and we will need to see whether this relates to beauty and not just royal birth.

Figure 6.2 'Ismaïl the bloodthirsty' (1672–1727). With his 600-strong harem, Ismaïl is claimed to have fathered 888 children.

Wikipedia.

The long tail

To get the most children, an ideal arrangement for a man is to have many wives, like Ismaïl. An alternative is to go around playing fast and loose with lots of different women, though to each he could give nothing more than sperm. This is the life of the male widowbird, the stag, and the drone bee. All the males do is impregnate the female; after that, she's on her own, and she alone will take care of the young. In other species, males contribute a lot more. A male seahorse takes on board fertilized eggs and nurtures them in his brood pouch until the baby seahorses can look after themselves – in essence, he becomes pregnant and gives birth. A male stickleback fish builds the family nest and looks after the kids as a single parent. A male Emperor penguin sits on the family egg in minus 50 degrees Celsius throughout the cold dark Antarctic winter. He meets his wife again in the spring, when she returns to vomit up some fish for the newly hatched infant. In these cases the males contribute to the upbringing in an obvious way, and the range of care offered by males and male choosiness are themes we will explore later.

On what basis should the discerning female widowbird choose her mate or the queen bee her drones? For a widowbird there's one obvious thing she can judge: she can just choose the male with the longest tail. Such a choice may seem shallow and superficial, based as it is on outward appearance. Nevertheless, the tail may be a good guide in the long run, for two reasons. When she chooses great tail, the female widowbird also buys into what is in effect a kind of multi-generation endowment mortgage. So long as she invests time in incubating the eggs, she gets long-term advantages when they hatch. Her chosen mate's sperm come with the best set of genes in the population. These genes may guarantee immunity against the current bugs (and since the chicks can't rely on antibiotics, they are really going to need the immunity). The male widowbird showing off his fantastic tail is also boasting about the power of his immune system: because he grew up without getting sick, he could put all his energy into growing a superb tail.

For male widowbirds, tails are everything – an astonishing 50 per cent of success in breeding is down to natural tail length.[5] If an inquisitive experimenter trims the widowbird's tail slightly shorter, then the bird's manhood is trimmed too: he misses out on visits from females, so he misses out on copulation.[6] Even for animals that have no choice in mating because of male coercion, selection is still occurring as males compete with one another. For deer and their overlord, the battles that have gone on between the stags have ensured that only the biggest and most powerful stag, the one who was able to fight off all pretenders to the throne, will mate with the does. For the queen bee flying off on her maiden flight, it is only the males with Olympian speed and aerodynamic skill who will get sex on the wing.

This strategy – of selecting the male with the greatest physical prowess or some other sign of fantastic growth – will only work if whatever qualities the females are selecting remain similar across the generations. Females need to be hooked on the same thing year on year. If fashion came and went, it would spell disaster. Consider the female widowbird, for example: if she paired up with the guy with the long tail, she would have thought she had done well; but if styles changed in the new season and the next generation of widowbirds ignored the tail feathers and admired instead long male foot spurs, she would in fact have squandered all her eggs by producing the wrong sort of male chicks. Sure, her kids might be healthy and they might develop wonderful tails – but if big tails are no longer seen as desireable, she might still end up with no grandchildren. Human fashion, with its ultra-fast turnover, is fickle; what's in vogue for other animals is much more durable. The plumage, song types, and courtship dances that are all the rage one year are still going to be hot for a long time to come.

Could it be that male qualities aren't really good in and of themselves and that they just need to look good in the eyes of the females?[7] Could these qualities be hollow advertisements? The most remarkable advertisements, after all, are those that effectively persuade us that we really need to have something that has no real use to us at all.

Sexual selection can indeed operate like that. In the end, having a long tail may not actually need to demonstrate the toughness of the male's immune system – perhaps a long tail is just what lady widowbirds *like*. If the females are addicted to tail characteristics, males with the best tails will produce sons with the best tails, and those sons are going to grow up popular with the females. This is an important concept: that sexy dads will produce sons who will be seen as sexy to tomorrow's choosy females.[8] Two conditions are necessary: that tail characteristics carry down through genes, and that female desire for tails is stable over generations.

This idea of 'sexy sons' has become widespread in evolutionary biology. We can now turn back to humans and ask whether or not the idea applies to us, too. If it does, attractive men should have attractive sons, and we should be able to test this by asking a panel of women to pick the sexiest out of a group of fathers who have sons, and we should then find that those men produce sons who also get the sexiest ratings in *their* generation.

Evolutionary biology may be guilty of a sex bias here, since selection is usually couched in terms of male-trait inheritance. We should not forget that forming a human partnership is a two-way process – girl chooses boy, but boy chooses girl too. And with good reason. Compared to widowbirds, most men will make a far greater investment in their children, so they will want a good return on their investment. They too need to find a partner with great genes for making babies and grandchildren. Men will choose the most attractive of the women who are available and attainable. It was argued earlier that feminine faces and bodies are attractive because they indicate a capacity to produce lots of kids. Men who choose feminine women may benefit in the first generation when they may get lots of kids, but will the female offspring be attractive when they grow up? Is there a 'sexy daughters' phenomenon? We can test whether this notion has any real-life validity in humans: all we have to do is find out whether mums and their daughters are similar in attractiveness.

After four years of collecting face images of students at St Andrews, and images of their parents also, a colleague and I were ready to find out what facial traits were common between offspring and biological parents.[9] Did attractiveness run in families – did it pass from father to son, or from mother to daughter, or both?

What we found was a clear relationship between the attractiveness of the daughters and their parents. If you inspect Figure 6.3, you should be able to match parents and offspring through their average appearances.

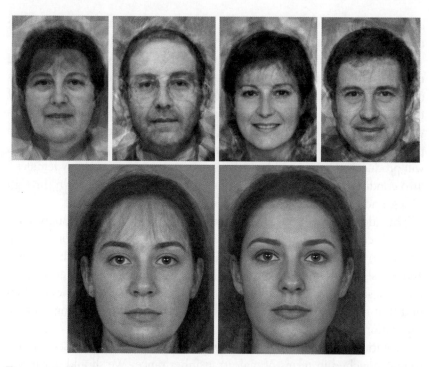

Figure 6.3 Do sexy parents beget sexy daughters? Each image contains fifteen faces blended together. *Upper row*: From a photograph collection, the fathers and mothers from the most and the least attractive couples were blended together. *Lower row*: The daughters of each set of parents were likewise blended into two composite images. If attractiveness runs in families, then attractiveness of the images of the daughters should follow those of the parents. Which of the two younger women do you think looks more attractive?

R.E. Cornwell & D.I. Perrett (2008).

Note that each face depicts not one person but a composite of fifteen people. To make these images, we sorted families according to the parents' attractiveness. We then identified the fifteen families in the collection in which the mums and dads scored highest in their *combined* attractiveness rating, and blended them to give composite images: one of the fifteen mums from the attractive couples, the other of the fifteen dads. Similarly we made composites from fifteen less attractive couples. As you may have guessed, mum and dad tended to be similar in attractiveness – as argued in Chapter 4, competition for partners leads to matching in attractiveness. From the four composite parent faces, therefore, you should be able to choose which blend of dads is married to which blend of mums – one blended dad and one blended mum are better-looking than their counterparts. (The right couple represent the partners in the couples whom our judges decided were better-looking. Do you agree with them?) Interesting as this exercise may be, all it tells us is that attractive women marry attractive men.

Next we pulled out the images of the fifteen daughters from the fifteen most attractive parents and distilled them into one combined image. Separately we took the fifteen daughters of the fifteen least attractive parents and melded those together. If beauty of mums and daughters is related, then the two blended images of the daughters should look different – and they do. Also, the daughters of the better-looking parents should be more attractive than the daughters of the less good-looking parents. This is what judges decided with the original photos of each person, and it is also apparent in the composite faces in Figure 6.3 (in which the daughters are vertically beneath their parents).[10]

Attractiveness definitely passes down the generations: mums and daughters were similar in attractiveness. As you can see from the illustrations, so too were dads and daughters. Men able to marry pretty wives are doing well from several perspectives. They may get biological benefits in terms of increased probability of children, because pretty women have high fertility, but their union may have a longer-term success as well: any daughters produced are going to be pretty too, and so will be able to choose high-quality lovers from their many suitors. From a biological perspective, the whole point of choosing an attractive partner seems justified – attractive partners produce attractive daughters, who presumably will go on to produce attractive granddaughters. The process can repeat indefinitely.

Sexy sons?

When we tried the same tests with photos of dads and sons, we got a big surprise. We found no relationship between the attractiveness of father and son or between the attractiveness of mother and son. A good-looking son could come from any dad, whether the dad was good-looking or not!

Our study did find some evidence that facial characteristics pass from father to son; masculinity does pass down the male line. Figure 6.4 is constructed in the same way as the composite images of parents and daughters. In this case we had all the fathers rated for masculinity, and separately we had all the sons rated for masculinity. We found that the most masculine dads had the most masculine sons, as should be evident in Figure 6.4.

Can we reconcile these findings – that masculinity but not attractiveness passes down the male line? We can, given what we know about masculinity and attraction. First, we saw in Chapter 5 that women differ in their opinion as to the attractiveness of masculine faces. Consequently, looking

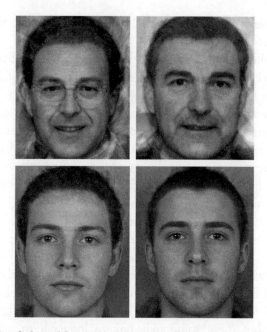

Figure 6.4 Like father, like son? Can you tell which father produces which son? If masculinity in facial appearance is inherited, then the sons should follow their fathers. Each image is a composite of fifteen male faces from a photograph collection. *Upper row*: A blend of the fathers who looked least masculine, together with a blend of the fathers who looked most masculine. *Lower row*: A blend of the sons of the least masculine fathers, together with a blend of the sons of the most masculine fathers. If masculinity in facial appearance is inherited, then the sons should follow their fathers.

R.E. Cornwell & D.I. Perrett (2008).

more or less masculine will not necessarily imply that a man is perceived to be more or less attractive – there may be differences of opinion as to which dads are most attractive, just as there may be differences of opinion about the attractiveness of their sons. In this situation, there will be no clear pattern in the inheritance of men's attractiveness.[11]

By contrast, with females there is more agreement. Since most people think that feminine traits in women's faces are beautiful, both femininity and attractiveness can pass together from mother to daughter.

Here, then, we find one aim of the quest for beauty fulfilled. People who try their hardest to get the most beautiful spouse attainable do succeed in producing the most attractive offspring they can – well, at least the most attractive daughters. What we don't know is whether beauty in offspring translates into a multitude of grandchildren.

Beauty succeeds

'Live long and prosper.' Although *Star Trek*'s Mr Spock was from the planet Vulcan, his salutation reflects the human side of him. If key criteria for success are longevity and prosperity, facial attractiveness could see you all right. For example, a study of faces in school photographs from the 1920s revealed that their attractiveness was an effective predictor of how long their owners would live – more attractive people clock up more years on their gravestone.[12] And yes, it's official; having an attractive face promotes a higher income and means that you'll be less stressed out by money prob-lems.[13] How does beauty give rise to a dollar halo? There are two factors. First, those with good looks have higher evaluations of themselves. It doesn't matter whether the feelings of high self-worth in attractive people are justified by real abilities; simply thinking highly of themselves leads to greater earning potential. Secondly, and unexpectedly, good looks result in people staying in education longer. Teachers, like parents, are not immune to beauty, and as they may respond more supportively to attractive pupils, their encouragement will help those pupils to find school rewarding. Later, the greater number of years attractive people have spent in learning gives them access to higher salaries. Beauty really does lead to prosperity.

These side-effects of attractiveness count for little from a biological perspective; a longer life and riches mean nothing unless they go hand in hand with a big family. With this in mind, we need to turn to reproduc-tion to find out whether facial attractiveness provides more than equal opportunities here. If it does, qualities that can be seen in photographs of faces should predict sexual behaviour. And yes – they do. Facially attractive men and women report more short-term sexual partners than do their peers.[14] Having a feminine and symmetrical-looking face means that a woman is more likely to be active sexually at an early age. Neither of these behaviours (sexual activity at an early age and frequent sexual partnerships) necessarily result in more children or grandchildren, since both may detract from family stability and long-term nurture. Moreover beauty is only one factor that predisposes early sexual relationships; other factors include deprivation and poverty. Dundee in Scotland, for example, has high levels of privation, and while the people of Dundee are no more or less beautiful than people elsewhere in the UK, Dundee tops the UK teenage pregnancy charts with one in ten girls aged 13–15 giving birth.[15] Such statistics are alarming and illustrate the point that although early sexual activity is not a direct measure of reproduction, it *is* related to the possibility of pregnancy.

There are other, more unusual, indices that are relevant to reproduction. One comes from getting women to rate images of males for attractiveness in a long-term partnership: compiling this index is straightforward. Getting the same men to give a sample of semen takes a little tact and more privacy, but the result makes possible some interesting comparisons between faces and fertility. By assessing the number of sperm, their shape, and how well they can swim, it becomes possible to relate facial attractiveness to sperm quality.[16] In these sperm championships, facial attractiveness doesn't relate to the *number* of sperm, but men with attractive faces do produce sperm that can swim faster and are in better shape (literally – more will have one straight tail rather than a crooked tail or a double tail). Such a relationship is important and needs confirmation[17] because in fertility treatment semen from men with mostly normal-shaped sperm is more likely to result in pregnancy than semen from men with a large proportion of abnormally shaped sperm.[18] In choosing an attractive man, therefore, a woman is choosing someone more likely to get her pregnant. Attractiveness is thus an indicator for the chance of pregnancy, but is it an indicator for children?

It is in the harsh places on the planet, where life expectancy is low, that one can expect to find the clearest relationship between attractiveness and procreation. Belize, in Central America, is one such place; life is tough, and for men it involves hunting and slash-and-burn farming. With such a hard life, you might be surprised to learn that most 40-year-old Belize men father around eight children[19] – this sounds a lot until you realize that half die as infants. What is more significant to the discussion here is that men in Belize with symmetrical hands, elbows, and ears live longer and father more offspring than asymmetrical men. Symmetrical men also report having had more sex partners in their lifetime than their less symmetrical brethren. So in a pre-industrialized society, symmetry, which we know to be attractive, *does* predict success in reproducing. To relate this back to sperm quality, the body symmetry of men is linked to the speed and number of their sperm,[20] so symmetrical men are the least likely to shoot blanks. Symmetry is partly inherited,[21] so when a Belizian woman chooses an attractive symmetrical guy to father her children, her choice is also rational from a biological perspective – although she is unlikely to be aware of it, a symmetrical man is likely to increase her chance of producing symmetrical offspring, who in turn will produce more grandchildren than children conceived with an asymmetrical guy.

Very little work has been done to evaluate the prediction that the most beautiful people leave behind the most descendents, so we should pay attention to the answers produced by these sparse studies. The topic is not easy to study, as family planning may mean that there is no longer any relationship to be found between looks and the number of descendants. In today's hunter-gatherer societies – similar to those we presume existed during early human evolution – attractive women are likely to have more children than unattractive women.[22] In industrialized nations these days, all families, whether conceived by attractive or unattractive parents, are likely to include a similarly small number of children. Most pregnancies are planned by parents, and parents are normally happy with one or two children – in the UK and the USA, certainly, it is rare to find parents who want more than four or five children. What determines family size, in most circumstances, is the number of children the parents want. With better nutrition and health care, parents do not need large numbers of children to ensure that some survive to adulthood, as used to be the case. So will beauty and family size go together?

The relationship between attractiveness and reproductive success has been tested by collecting information from women who grew up in a rural region of Poland.[23] Most had been wives of farmers, and it could be argued that the community from which they came may have made them less likely to use birth control than in other Western societies. Here, then, was a society in which good looks could, in principle, translate into increased number of offspring. The group of women studied were all over 40 (so their reproductive days were by then likely to be limited) and they were able to provide photographs of themselves at an early age (18–27), before they had had children; usually the images were wedding pictures. According to attractiveness theories, the *most* attractive of these Polish women when young should have been more fecund and produced more children than the *least* attractive women.

In this Polish sample, the attractive women tended to marry tall men. This is a step in the right direction, since large-scale studies have found a relationship between men's height and their reproductive success: tall men report more children than short men.[24] In fact, though, this study of rural Polish wives found no relationship between their attractiveness and how many children or grandchildren they had produced – there was no evidence that attractiveness is good in the long run. It is possible, however, that the study missed some relevant evidence because it focused on Polish *brides*, and not all women get married.

We can now turn to studies in Western urban societies, remembering, though, that we may not find links between attractiveness and offspring number because of contraception and the complexity and other opportunities that modern society brings. In the Berkeley, California, area, one group of people were studied intensively in their childhood, and were then followed for the rest of their lives by the Institute of Human Development. Almost fifty years after the studies had begun, the marriages and children of two hundred and twenty-nine of this cohort could be related to each individual's appearance in late adolescence.[25] All but ten individuals in the sample got married, and these ten were on average rated low in attractiveness compared to the rest of the sample group. In other, larger studies in the USA, high-school beauty has been found to be correlated with earlier marriage.[26] So attractiveness does relate to mate selection. How about the number of children produced? Twenty-nine of the Berkeley sample had no children; these twenty-nine were again rated low in attractiveness compared to the other two hundred individuals who *did* have children. Facial attractiveness and the production of kids were linked mainly because the attractive people got married and did so at a young age, whereas the less attractive people were less likely to get married or, if they did, to marry while young.

In all this, one wonders whether the findings from 50–70 years ago still apply. Society changes at an ever-accelerating pace, so what was true for our parents or grandparents is way out of date for today's young adults. There are also conflicting tendencies in different studies; currently, for instance, if attractive individuals stay on longer in education[27] they will not be the youngest to marry, and a delay in starting a family is unlikely to be associated with heightened reproductive output.

A study of Americans growing up in Wisconsin gives a more thorough answer to the question about attractiveness and progeny.[28] From high-school yearbooks, the photographs of 1200 women and 1000 men taken at age 18 were judged for attractiveness. When these individuals reported on their families fifty years later, it was clear that having an attractive face meant more biological children. Handsome men did have more descendents. The least attractive quarter of men had 11 per cent fewer children than other men. Women with above-average attractiveness had 11 per cent more children than those with below-average attractiveness. Interestingly, the most prolific women were only moderately attractive, scoring above average in the facial beauty stakes but not getting top marks. Attractive women were more likely to become parents and to have a second child than their less attractive counterparts, but the most attractive women were likely to stop there with a nuclear family of two children. Limiting the family in this way can mean that more care and resources are poured into fewer children: this may give the children a long-term advantage in ensuring that they prosper and have their own offspring. It's evident that producing more and more children does not necessarily mean that you will have more and more grandchildren. It will be interesting to see whether beauty still relates to number of descendents after further generations – given the pace of change, it would be against the odds.

This is a small but important part of the puzzle of how appearance affects human life. But much of it remains incomplete. Facial appearance seems critical in attracting a partner and marrying while still young. In an age where most families are small and children are planned with the aid of contraception and fertility treatments, the relationship between appearance and reproductive success is hard to study. So saying, the relationship is detectable in the last 50–70 years, and studies do show that attractive individuals are more likely to produce children than unattractive individuals. This may have been more obvious in our evolutionary past, but we can see the same things happening for people who rely on hunting or subsistence farming, and even for people living in the industrialized world.

So far we have seen hard evidence that beauty is partly responsible for many of the good things in life: high self-esteem, high income, good health, longevity, and a greater number of descendents. By these measures, the desire stirred up by an attractive face is not something fanciful; it's an urge that makes biological sense[29]. At the same time, other factors obviously pertain. Successful relationships are those in which partners are compatible in a variety of dimensions like personality, age, prior experience, and so on – all of which make attractiveness a personal matter that supersedes the unitary notion of beauty. We will explore them in the rest of the book.

Chapter 7
FIT FACE

How our health is reflected in our faces

If facial appearance can help us forecast prosperity, longevity, and the likelihood of having grandchildren, for example, can it tell us anything about health? A simple way to discover what looks healthy and what does not is to ask people to judge the health of individuals from face photos, and then to blend together the faces that score high and separately those that score low. Figure E (Plate II) shows the result when applied with collections of Scottish students.[1] The difference between the blended images made from the most healthy-looking and least healthy-looking students is subtle, but this distinction can be amplified (see Chapter 4). Now the unhealthy individuals look tired and somewhat glum, their faces are heavier, and they have a pasty complexion that might be consistent with poor diet, excess study, lack of exercise, and lack of sun (don't forget these are students in Scotland, where blue sky is a rare commodity). The healthy students are the opposite – they may not offer a picture of perfect health, but their demeanour and complexion looks significantly better. But does the way people look reflect reality? Somebody may *look* fit and healthy, but is this true? This chapter considers what cues might constitute a real certificate of health – or a health warning.

A healthy attraction

We should be able to tell whether someone is full of vim and vigour or that they are feeling sick as a dog, but can we make a longer-term forecast? Can we say, for example, judging only by appearance, 'This is someone who rarely gets sick'?

If so, that would surely be attractive – a partner needs to be healthy if the relationship is to prosper. Remarkably, there are deeply committed loving couples in which one partner cares for the other through years of chronic illness or disability, yet all partners would want each other fit and well. Health is important in so many ways. For a start, if a short-term or long-term partner has some form of sickness, he or she is likely to pass on that malady to you. At a basic level, it is difficult in an intimate moment to avoid a runny nose, and in fact not just cold germs but a whole spectrum of nasties can get shared. They may be minor irritations, such as head lice or, more intimately, crabs; they may be serious sexually transmitted diseases that could make you sterile and even mad (syphilis) or the variety of illnesses that can follow HIV infection; or they may be bacteria that invade your guts and cause relatively minor illnesses, such as dysentery, or fatal ones (especially if hygiene is poor), such as cholera.

Then there are the fringe benefits of good health. A healthy partner can give you healthy kids and should be able to help take the strain of the kids growing up. A healthy lifelong mate also represents a pension plan, both in terms of finance and in terms of companionship. Old age will be a lonelier place without a partner and a fine, fully fledged family. So when it comes to choosing a partner, we should all be just as picky about health as we are about other criteria.

In the short term, of course, we may be able to see clear signs of current illness, all unpleasant, but those need not necessarily be a turn-off – what we really want to know is whether the person will fare beyond this particular illness. Is this illness a one-off or is it characteristic of frequent poor health? If we knew the answer, we could include it in our cost/benefit analysis and work out whether that person is worth our commitment – for better for worse, in sickness or health.

In Chapters 4 and 5 we considered the facets of a face that make it pretty or handsome. If health is really such a make-or-break issue, then one might reasonably expect that the same attractive cues would also be telling us that a person is *healthy*. There's no point in choosing the most symmetrical, normal-looking, yet masculine man, if these same face characteristics are a health warning. Face symmetry, normality, and sex typicality, so important to allure, are likely to be characteristics of health[2] – not just health right now, but health for the years to come.

As you would expect, there have indeed been studies to find out whether or not this is the case. Given the importance of health and beauty, you might think that by now the answers would be clear, but linking faces to health and illness is hard – first the way to make the links must be discovered. Until recently, therefore, the picture has remained confused. One might blame the scientists for not yet doing their job well enough, but on this path there are many traps, mires, and diversions, so that it is only recently that the route has begun to clear.

One difficulty in assessing health is that there are different types of illness. Some can affect you for months or years; others, fortunately, are here today, gone tomorrow. Symmetry, averageness, and sexual dimorphism are all stable traits – someone's face won't suddenly pop into perfect alignment by morning. However a person's face looks when you go to bed is more or less how it will look in the morning. The underlying structure of a face reflects the person's overall quality and capacity to grow according to plan (see Chapter 4), and may indicate his or her long-term health. Life events such as catching a cold, getting a bruise, or developing some spots do produce facial changes that indicate current health, yet they leave averageness, symmetry, and masculinity unchanged. Before we consider what else affects our facial appearance and perceptions of health, let's see how health links to *these* aspects of face structure.

Even health

Many studies show that the more symmetrical a face is, the healthier it looks. Some of these measured actual symmetry, by comparing the size of the ear on the left with the one on the right, and so on. Other studies simply asked people 'How symmetrical do you think this face looks?' Further studies chopped the face vertically into two and then reflected each half to make up two chimeric faces: a left plus its mirror image, and separately a right plus its mirror image. If these two chimeras look similar, the original face must be pretty similar on both sides, so it must be symmetrical; if the chimeras look distinct, then the original face must be asymmetrical (see Figure 7.1). Yet other studies manipulated symmetry using computer graphics. All of these studies indicate that symmetry and looking healthy go together.[3] With so many different methods giving the same result, you would think you could be sure: symmetry equals health.

But no. The problem is that *looking* healthy is not good enough – we need our partner to *be* healthy, not just to look the part. The car salesman may have been very nice when he sold you the car and told you it had had 'only one careful owner', but that doesn't really ensure that the car is fit for purpose: you would want a year's warranty to give you time to find out whether you'd been had. Facial symmetry provides no clear guarantee of long-term good health. Two studies provide links between self-reported health and measured symmetry.[4] In contrast, a further study[5] found *no* link between symmetry and a person's lifetime health, as assessed from medical records. Which study should we believe?

Students at Michigan[6] were measured for facial symmetry and gave personal reports on a very extensive set of mental and physical ailments suffered over a four-week period. One can highlight some of the positive findings, as the authors did. For example, men who had asymmetrical faces reported more of the abnormal symptoms from an inventory of fifty-three items – items such as 'feeling lonely' and 'trouble staying asleep'.

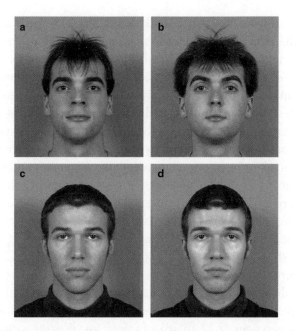

Figure 7.1 The scissors-and-mirror test of symmetry. Photos of individuals were cut vertically into two halves. Each half photo was then mirrored to create two face 'chimeras' (a left plus a reflected left, and a right plus a reflected right). *Upper row*: For asymmetrical individuals, the resulting pair of images look quite different. *Lower row*: For individuals with symmetrical faces, the resulting images look more similar.

I.S. Penton-Voak *et al.* (2001).

Asymmetrical women reported a greater tendency to 'cry or having an urge to cry'. The authors label these symptoms 'physiological', as if they were linked to health by strict biology, but one can see the problems as psychological. We also do not know what causes what – if asymmetry means that a face is not attractive, perhaps it is that which leads to frequent upsets. (That said, attractiveness by itself does not ensure happiness.)

While this study was large and pioneering, what it revealed was only a hint that asymmetry went with health problems, and the problems appeared to be more in the mind than in the body. A caveat for the study was that it included 918 'health' measures in an attempt to find a relationship between symmetry and health. You might think that such a large number indicates that the study was comprehensive and thorough, and you'd be right; the difficulty is that when conducting that many tests, one would expect to find a few apparent relationships just by chance. Actually, by chance alone, quite a few of the relationships will confirm the proposal that symmetry affects health, even if there is no causal link between the health symptom and symmetry. This is because science relies on statistics, and to use statistics properly scientists, like bookies at the racetrack, set odds – they try to estimate how often something might happen just by chance, and then sit up and pay attention if it actually happens more often than that. Thus, if no one knows anything about the horses – or, in this case, the factors at the start of the experiment – the odds for picking a winner are set at 20:1.[7] In the Michigan study, 54 results were highlighted as significant. Given the odds of 20:1, we could expect that out of 918 comparisons, 46 (one in twenty) might be highlighted just by chance. The actual number, 54, is greater than 46 but not much, so there really isn't much to write home about. Of course, it's easy to be critical in hindsight: this study was certainly on the right track, it was correct and pioneering to move on from asking about *impressions* of health from a face picture and to attempt instead to measure each person's *actual* health and ailments.

Another study, this time of 300 people from Berkeley, California, all of whom were born in the 1920s, tracked these people's lives against the detailed medical records kept by the physicians at the august Institute of Human Development.[8] Health in the teens was defined by annual assessments (between ages of 11 to 18) of infectious diseases such as measles, German measles, and respiratory diseases. Health in adult life was based mainly on a single examination by a physician. In this study one gets a little more concerned about reliability: does a single-shot health measure provide a broad enough perspective on health in an entire adult life? Perhaps we should not pay too much attention to this study's claim that facial symmetry had no relation to health.

And there are further reasons for caution. Firstly, of the faces in the photographs, most, we are told, were *neutral* in pose. That means that the others were smiling or frowning. It is hard enough to get people to smile pleasantly for a photograph, but it is even harder to get everyone to adopt a strictly *neutral* expression – many will break into a faint or open smile. A feature of smiling is that it often makes the face look asymmetrical. A natural smile is itself often asymmetrical – usually the lip is raised more on the left than right. As the scientists measured symmetry using points that included the left and right lip corners, we should treat these measurements with caution. Secondly, symmetry is hard to measure because people don't face the camera square on: they tend to turn so that just one eye is aimed at the photographer. The Berkeley faces were cropped from whole-body photographs and, given that the images were taken about fifty years previously, the precise details of the face may not have been completely clear. So again we have reason to treat the measurements of symmetry as somewhat suspect. As is generally the case, we do not place too much faith in any single study.

A 2006 study in New Mexico did find a relationship between symmetry and health.[9] It asked for reports of disease over the last three years, recording illness duration and frequency. Respiratory infection (flu) was more frequent and longer-lasting in asymmetrical individuals. This study included 400 individuals, so given the large sample size one might expect the results to be reliable. The fact is, the greater the number of people surveyed in any study, the more likely the study is to detect even small effects that may not in fact have great import. For example, the public is often warned about links between lifestyle and disease, and you probably know that smoking increases the chance of getting cancer, but what are the actual statistics? Of women who live to 90, 12 per cent will get breast cancer. For women who *smoke* and live to 90, 16 per cent will get breast cancer. If women smoke, therefore, they increase their risk of getting breast cancer by 33 per cent (from 12 per cent to 16 per cent).[10] This is a very important effect: clearly it's much wiser not to smoke. By contrast, asymmetry has only a small association with colds and flu: it accounted for 1 per cent of the variation in the number of infections, and 2 per cent of how long they lasted. What might this mean in terms of your catching an infection? In the study, participants on average had two infections every three years, each lasting nine days. Suppose we divide the world into symmetrical and asymmetrical people. If you fall within the asymmetrical group, your risk of getting a cold each year would be 1 per cent higher than your symmetrical brethren. Rounded up, that would mean one more cold in a lifetime. Likewise, your infection would last 2 per cent longer than the infections of symmetrical people – about four hours! So don't worry if one of your ears is bigger than the other: you may be a tad less healthy, but you aren't going to suffer that much more.

Unusual health

Among the Berkeley males, those who had fared worse in health assessments as children tended to look facially more unusual (that is, different from the 'average' or 'norm') by the time they were 17 years old, but their health from early teens through to mid-life was not related to how unusual their face looked at 17. For these males, it seems, growing up with illness may have made their faces slightly different from normal, but that had no bearing on the likelihood of their catching illnesses later in life. Of the 17-year-old Berkeley females, those who had average facial proportions reported better health at 17 than those who had unusual face shapes.

When the scientists buried themselves in the Berkeley data once more, it emerged that having an unusual face was associated with illness only if the face was *conspicuously* unusual. The medics' expression 'FLK syndrome' (funny-looking kid) might apply – this expression means that the face indicates that something is up, but the medic doesn't know what.[11] If all the Berkeley faces were arranged in a long line, from the most normal-looking to the most unusual, and the line were split in the middle, unusualness would be associated with illness only in the more unusual half of the population.[12] So averageness *is* a cue to health – but not a very robust cue, as it doesn't apply to 50 per cent of the population.

A feminine side to health

The New Mexico study reports a link between female facial femininity and reduced number and duration of chest infections a woman had experienced.[13] By contrast, analysis of the Californian faces could find no link between perceived femininity of women at age 17 and their medical history over the previous six years.[14] As mentioned earlier, in this study it seems that some of the individuals in the photos were smiling while most were not, and one wonders whether observers were distracted in their judgements of femininity by the smiling – smiling certainly does make faces more attractive. On balance, it is safest to argue that, from the available evidence, femininity in female faces does relate to actual health.

As an aside, smiling does affect the perception of health. Our research group found that having a healthy lifestyle (in terms of doing things such as taking exercise that make you live longer) made women's faces look healthier,[15] but this was apparent only when the women wore a neutral expression – the relationship disappeared when the same faces wore a smile. Smiling elevates attractiveness, and this can mask underlying problems that would otherwise be visible. 'Putting on a brave face' can cover up a malaise.

Sex hormones are responsible for the curvaceous feminine aspects of female bodies,[16] so rather than obtaining health reports from a doctor or self-reports from the subjects (of the number of runny noses per year, for example), we measured sex-hormone levels as a direct and tangible index of reproductive status.[17] For sexually active women with regular monthly cycles that are not being disturbed by hormonal contraceptives, the chance that they will get pregnant is related to how much oestrogen and progesterone their ovaries produce. Those who produce lots of oestrogen and progesterone are more fertile and more likely to conceive.[18]

Our group measured sex hormones excreted in the urine of 60 women who were not altering their reproductive physiology by using hormone contraceptives. We assessed hormones at several points across the menstrual cycle. During the peak of fertility, at the mid-point in their monthly cycles, the faces of women who had the highest oestrogen levels throughout their cycle were judged to be healthier and more feminine than the faces of women with lower oestrogen levels (see Figure F, Plate III). There are many different ways of assessing health and illness – hormones may seem to be an indirect measure of health, but they are a practical way of determining reproductive status and they help in diagnosing problems in fertility.

Tough, strong, and healthy men?

Studies agree that masculinity is healthy (which fits theories discussed in Chapters 5 and 6). If you measure the faces of males and females, you will find that men typically have more pronounced brows and more developed jawbones. Brow and jaw shape alone allows one to sort faces pretty accurately into men and women. The same information can be used to give a measure of masculinity – if the jaw and brow shapes suggest strongly that the face is male, then the face may be described as 'masculine', but if the shapes suggest maleness only weakly then the face may be described as 'feminine', even if its owner is actually a man. By this measure, men in New Mexico with manly shaped faces were healthier; they reported fewer and shorter chest infections and a lower use of antibiotics.[19] And of the Berkeley boys, those with masculine-looking faces at age 17 had better health in adolescence.[20]

Despite the links to health in these two studies, our group cannot find any clear link between facial masculinity and a man's perceived health.[21] The masculinity of a man's face shape clearly links to how *dominant* he looks,[22] but there is no consistent relationship to how *healthy* he looks. As we saw in Chapter 5, masculinity in face shape is not seen by all women as an attractive thing. It is therefore possible that attraction to particular male appearances is getting in the way of health judgements, much as smiling inhibited people from correctly evaluating healthy lifestyles in women. If judges are attracted to a guy, they will find it difficult to say that he looks a bit sickly!

Most of us are blinded by beauty – we tend to think that attractive people are healthy and unattractive people are unhealthy. If we can look *beyond* beauty, then we are quite good at judging health from face photos. One nice way of demonstrating this is to remove all the really attractive faces and all the really unattractive faces, thereby leaving just the 'normal-looking' people. For these faces, anyway, how healthy they *look* is a fairly accurate guide to how healthy they actually *are*.[23]

Weight-watching

One possible explanation for why researchers find so inconsistent a relationship between aspects of attractiveness and health could be that they have failed to take into account other aspects of a person's face shape besides symmetry, averageness, and masculinity or femininity. A person's overall weight, for example, influences the shape of the face, and there are clear links between weight and health: obesity is linked to a whole variety of health problems, including heart disease and diabetes; while eating disorders such as anorexia, which lead people to become severely underweight, also increase the risk of heart disease, kidney problems, and chest infections, and suppress the immune system. In Western societies, currently, the predominant problem is that people are overweight.

Our group found that it is straightforward to judge the body weight of men and women from their faces alone.[24] We studied students with a range of weights from slightly underweight to overweight. Very few in the sample would be classed as 'obese', according to medical definitions. Looking at just the face, judgements of the relative weights of different people were surprisingly accurate (see Figure G, Plate III).

As we put on weight, fat gets laid down under the surface of the skin (subcutaneous fat) and around the internal organs (visceral fat). When you pinch a fold of skin, the wider your fingers stay apart – even if you press hard – the more subcutaneous fat you have. In comparison with women, more of men's fat accumulates around the internal abdominal organs,[25] adding to their 'beer gut'. On this basis, then, it should be easier to estimate weight from women's faces than from men's, but in fact it is just as easy to estimate weight from either sex (see Figure G, Plate III).

The students in our study[26] whose faces suggested that they were overweight had worse chest infections and significantly higher blood pressure, and also took more antibiotics, a finding that confirms facial fatness to be an accurate cue to actual health. The relationship between blood pressure and weight is well known, but what was striking in our study was just how strong the relationship was. Apparent-weight judgements accounted for just under a quarter (23 per cent) of the variation in blood pressure across the sample. Weight judgements also explained an eighth (7 per cent) of the severity of illness that was reported. These percentages may seem quite modest in size, but they are much bigger than the link between symmetry and infections described earlier. Thus there are strong links from facial appearance through to a person's current physical health. While the study was of young adults, those with blood pressure in the high end of the normal range may be storing up problems for the future. Unfortunately weight tends to go up with age: a young person with a high weight and with blood pressure at the high end of the normal range is likely (without a change in lifestyle) to develop high blood pressure and attendant health problems later in life. The impressions of these young adults' health suggested by their faces, in the 'prime of their life', are therefore quite likely to be a good predictor of future health during middle age and even old age.

Interestingly, although women of perfectly normal weights were judged to be the healthiest, women towards the lower end of the normal range were judged to be the most attractive. This is both reassuring, in the sense that people apparently recognize that women with low or low normal weight are not the most healthy, but also cause for concern, in that the weight seen as the most attractive is lower than that seen as the healthiest. It seems that the fashion among Hollywood actresses and TV stars to reach 'size zero' may indeed have shifted public taste, so that thinness has become more attractive, even though people think it looks unhealthy.

The value put on thinness does depend on culture. People in rural areas in developing countries, for example, show a preference for higher body weight than do those in urban areas of the developed world.[27] In the former places, uncertainty in food supply and the prevalence of disease, often accompanied by severe weight loss, means that being heavy symbolizes both prosperity (with a guaranteed dinner) and longevity. Weight is an indicator of health for people the world over, but what counts as a healthy weight will vary as to whether in your circumstances a coronary or starvation is more likely to get you.

The level of fat is a fairly obvious and reliable cue to health; it is very apparent in the face. Indeed fatness may be the key to some of the other relationships between facial features and health. Earlier we saw that people with asymmetrical faces are (slightly) less healthy. It could be excess weight that is making faces asymmetrical and predisposing people to illness. Heavier people are certainly less symmetrical,[28] although it is difficult here to explain what causes what. It might be that asymmetrical individuals have a different metabolism or that they put on weight if they are unhappy (with their own appearance, for example, or with their love life). Alternatively, it could be that subcutaneous fat contributes to the asymmetries by stretching the skin unevenly. Similarly, subcutaneous fat can also change the impression of femininity; as weight goes up, women are seen as more masculine. Earlier it was argued that femininity in female faces means better actual health, but perhaps it is not femininity that is controlling health but weight – after all, an increase in fat levels both detracts from the woman's sex-typical looks and increases her risk of contracting a disease.

Skin deep

There are other potential signs of health in the face. Skin texture and colour are obvious candidates, so research has begun exploring these. Our group found that young men with attractive faces have skin that looked healthier.[29] This was an impressive finding, because skin health had been evaluated from an image of a small area of skin on the cheek, with no other facial cues available. As a follow-up, we manipulated facial skin colour and texture using computer graphics, keeping the face shape exactly the same but creating faces that were either high or low in skin health. In this way, we could test whether a person's skin influenced how attractive they looked, all other things being equal. Sure enough, faces with high skin health were judged to be more attractive than those with low skin health.

There are several aspects to the apparent health of skin: skin tone, evenness of colour, size of pores, and the presence of spots, fine lines, and wrinkles. In the skin of young adults, the evenness of skin pigmentation seems particularly important. The images in Figure H (Plate III) should make it obvious that one can judge how healthy skin looks. (Most people think the skin with uneven pigmentation looks less healthy.)

Our health is apparent to others in a variety of ways, whether from the tone of the voice, the natural smell of the body, or the shape of the naked body – healthy people signal 'good quality' in several ways. For example, symmetrical people look, sound, and smell sexier than asymmetrical people.[30] Since many good attributes are found in the same body, our group wondered whether or not skin health and face symmetry also go together.[31] Does a person with a lop-sided face, say, have worse skin than someone with an even-sided face? We therefore measured face shape from photos, and compared this with judgements made when we zoomed in on a region of cheek that was not obscured by beard. What we found was that men with a more symmetrical shape to their face did indeed have skin that was judged to be healthier in appearance. This is really quite surprising – it's like being able to tell by looking at a single piece of a jigsaw puzzle whether the entire picture when complete will be symmetrical and attractive.

Healthy gene pairs

An insight into health and appearance comes from genetic studies of men. For this purpose, their genetic make-up was considered in relation to just three genes: three genes that control aspects of immunity. The major histocompatibility (MHC[32]) genes provide a line of defence against a variety of pathogens.[33] They make it possible for the body to create proteins

Plate I

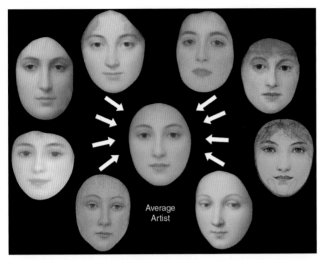

Figure A Who did the painting? The outer ring gives composite images blending the work of eight different painters. Can you guess which artist each of the eight faces typifies? To help, the eight artists are (in alphabetical order) Botticelli, Gérôme, Ingres, Klimt, Manet, Mucha, Raphael, and Renoir – but which is which? At the centre is a composite of all eight images; it could be termed an 'average' artist's portrait.

P. Grogan & D.I. Perrett (1996) Perception Lab.

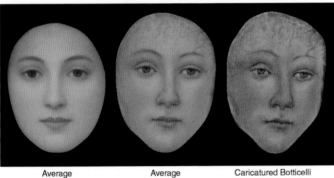

Average Artist   Average Botticelli   Caricatured Botticelli +75% shape & colour

Figure B Exaggerating style. *Left*: An average of eight artists' portraits with no particular style. *Centre*: The composite of Botticelli's portraits. *Right*: An image that caricatures the way in which Botticelli painted. The shape and colour differences between the central image (the average Botticelli) and the left image (the 'average' artist's portrait) have been amplified by 75 per cent. This exaggerates the tilt of the face, the thinness of the eyebrows, the slenderness of the nose, and the droopiness of the eyelids, as well as the sepia colour and the frizzy bleached hairstyle of the Renaissance era.

P. Grogan & D.I. Perrett (1996) Perception Lab.

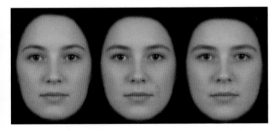

Figure C Feminine charm? *Centre*: This face represents the average face shape of a collection of young adult women at the University of St Andrews. *Right and left*: The shape has been subtly altered, moving the configuration (but not the skin tones) towards and away from that typical of men of an equivalent age. *Left*: The central image has been 'feminized' by moving it away from the male face shape. *Right*: The central image has been 'masculinized' by moving towards the male face shape.

Left and right: D.I. Perrett *et al.* (1998). *Centre*: D.I. Perrett *et al.*, Perception Lab.

Plate II

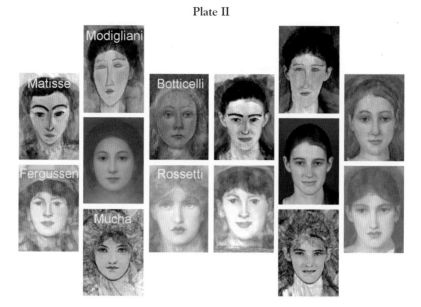

Figure D Computer art forgery. *Left-hand group*: Around the circumference are composite images of female faces, as painted by six different artists (Modigliani, Rossetti, Botticelli, Mucha, Matisse, and Fergussen; for an explanation, see Figure A). In the middle of the group lies a nondescript average of multiple artists (*centre left*); no one style should be recognizable. *Right-hand group*: The differences in shape and colour between the central average and particular artists' styles have been applied to the face of a real person, Rachel (*centre right*). The resultant images, arranged in a circle around Rachel's own image, should recapitulate the styles of the particular artists – and yet Rachel should still be recognizable to people who know her. If you would like to make a masterpiece with your own face image using face-transformation software, try www.Perceptionlab.com.

D.I. Perrett *et al.* (1998) Perception Lab.

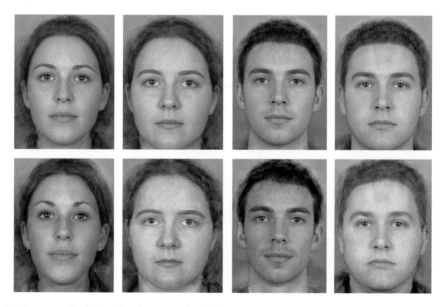

Figure E Apparent health under the magnifier. *Upper row*: Composite images combining the 20 per cent most healthy-looking (*left*) and the 20 per cent least healthy-looking (*centre left*) female students, and the equivalent images for male students (*centre right and right*). *Bottom row*: Images derived by amplifying the shape, colour, and texture differences between the healthy and unhealthy looks.

D.I. Perrett *et al.* (2001) Perception Lab.

Plate III

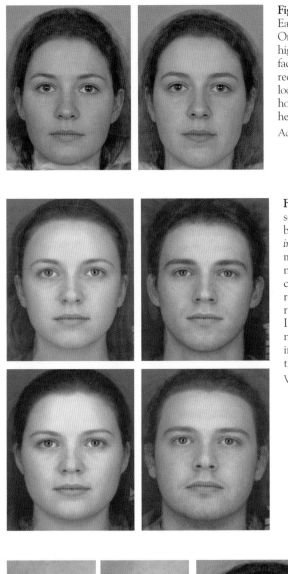

Figure F Sex hormones and facial appearance. Each image is a blend of the faces of ten people. One blends the faces of the ten women with the highest recorded oestrogen levels, and the other face blends the faces of the ten with the lowest recorded oestrogen levels. Which do you think looks healthier or more feminine? Higher sex-hormone levels were associated with feminine and healthy looks (left).

Adapted from: M.J. Law Smith *et al.* (2006).

Figure G Weighty matters. The faces of two sets of women and two sets of men have been averaged by blending them. *Top two images*: These blends represent women and men who have weights that place them in the normal range, once their height is taken into consideration. *Bottom two images*: These blends represent women and men who have a weight range that puts them in the overweight category. It should be apparent which face represents the normal and which the overweight group; more interesting is to estimate the relative health of the faces in each pair.

V. Coetzee (2008) Perception Lab.

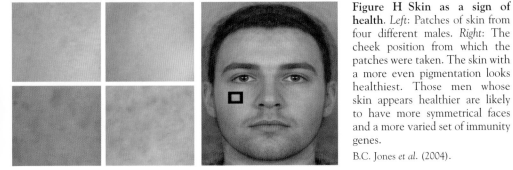

Figure H Skin as a sign of health. *Left*: Patches of skin from four different males. *Right*: The cheek position from which the patches were taken. The skin with a more even pigmentation looks healthiest. Those men whose skin appears healthier are likely to have more symmetrical faces and a more varied set of immunity genes.

B.C. Jones *et al.* (2004).

Plate IV

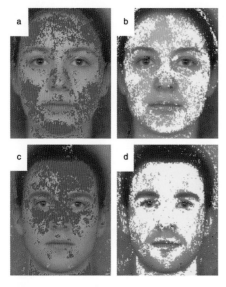

Figure I Scanning for colour cues to health in faces. *Upper row*: Composite images using 31 female faces. *Lower row*: Composite images using 42 male faces. *Left side (a, c)*: These images display points where a red or green colour tint to the skin is associated with looking healthy. *Right side (b, d)*: These images display points where a yellow or blue colour tint to the skin is associated with looking healthy. The images show that, for skin areas throughout the face, red and yellow skin tones were associated with looking healthy. (If colour–health correlations in faces were due simply to chance, with no real relationship between them, one-twentieth of the points that make up the total image would be either red or green, with those red and green points scattered evenly across the entire image.)

M. Stirrat *et al.* (2005) Perception Lab.

- Deoxygenated blood +

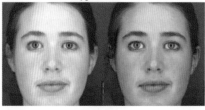

Figure J Pump up the blood. *Upper row*: The change in appearance with less (*left*) or more (*right*) 'stale' deoxygenated blood. *Lower row*: The change in appearance with less (*left*) or more (*right*) 'fresh' oxygenated blood.

I.D. Stephen *et al.* (2009).

- Oxygenated blood +

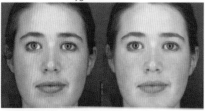

Figure K Shape and colour changes that accompany ageing in a face. *Upper left*: An original image (age 27). *Upper right*: The image reshaped with the shape changes typical of ageing thirty years. *Lower left and right*: The upper images with, in addition, the colour changes that typically accompany an age increase from the late twenties to early fifties.

D.M. Burt & D.I. Perrett (1995).

Plate V

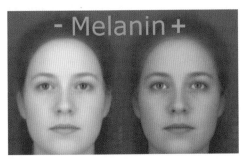

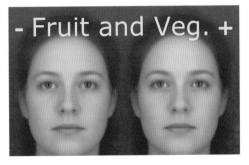

Figure L Suntan and apparent health. Suntan depends on increased levels of melanin, which make the skin darker and more yellow. Adding melanin to facial skin increases apparent health, but this change is related to the face becoming yellower rather than darker.

I.D. Stephen (2008) Perception Lab.

Figure M Fruit and vegetables alter skin colour and apparent health. Eating fruit and vegetables raises the levels of plant pigments in the skin, a change that makes the skin more yellow but does not make the skin darker. This colour change to facial skin increases apparent health.

I.D. Stephen (2008) Perception Lab.

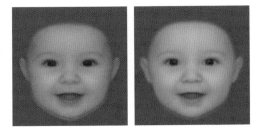

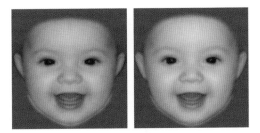

Figure N Pink or blue? These two images are composite faces of baby boys and baby girls, but which is which? Many people think it is impossible to tell, yet they nonetheless feel they can tell which infant looks more independent and which more sociable. (To find out which baby is which, see note[30] in Chapter 8.)

B. Wiffen (2007) Perception Lab.

Figure O Puppy dog tails. Baby boy faces were found to be more attractive when moved towards the shape of baby girl faces. The two images contrast feminization (*left*) and masculinization (*right*) by moving the images towards or away from a girl's face shape, respectively.

B. Wiffen (2007) Perception Lab.

Plate VI

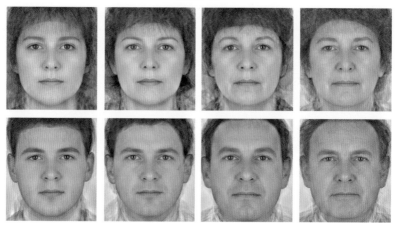

Figure P Signs of age. Composite images of Europeans in different decades of life, between their twenties and their fifties.

K.A. May *et al.* (1993–2001) Perception Lab.

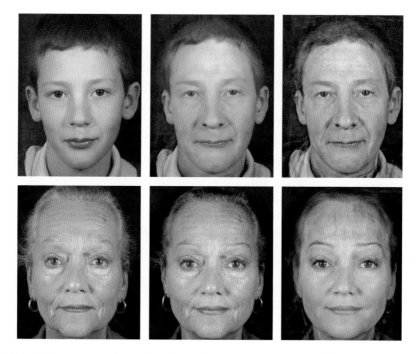

Figure Q Convincing age transformations depend on texture processing. *Upper row*: A 10-year-old boy undergoing a fifty-year age increase. *Lower row*: A 55-year-old woman undergoing a thirty-year age decrease. *Left column*: Original images. *Centre column*: Shape and colour transformations. *Right column*: Shape, colour, and texture transformations.

B.P. Tiddeman, Perception Lab; B.P. Tiddeman, *et al.* (2001).

Plate VII

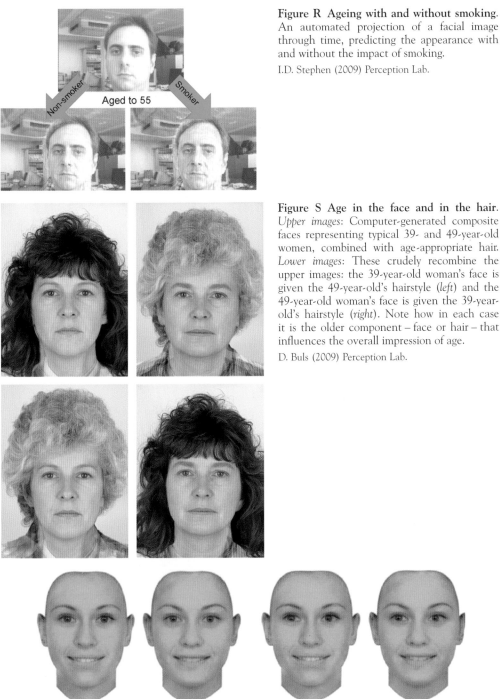

Figure R Ageing with and without smoking.
An automated projection of a facial image through time, predicting the appearance with and without the impact of smoking.

I.D. Stephen (2009) Perception Lab.

Non-smoker

Smoker

Aged to 55

Figure S Age in the face and in the hair.
Upper images: Computer-generated composite faces representing typical 39- and 49-year-old women, combined with age-appropriate hair. *Lower images*: These crudely recombine the upper images: the 39-year-old woman's face is given the 49-year-old's hairstyle (*left*) and the 49-year-old woman's face is given the 39-year-old's hairstyle (*right*). Note how in each case it is the older component – face or hair – that influences the overall impression of age.

D. Buls (2009) Perception Lab.

Figure T Effect of social interaction cues on attractiveness. Each pair of faces differs subtly in colour, such that the left image should look slightly more attractive. The difference in attractiveness between the left and right face in each pair seems more pronounced when the faces look and smile at us (as they do for the left pair) than when the faces look past us (as they do for the right pair) – we are attracted to beauty when a person engages with us positively.

B.C. Jones *et al.* (2006).

Plate VIII

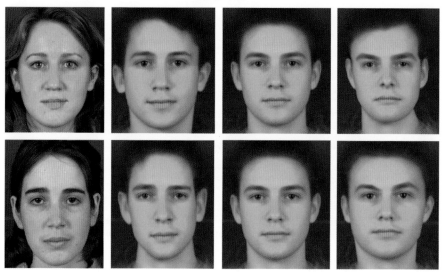

Figure U Creating look-alikes and opposites. *Column 1:* The faces of two females. *Column 2:* Male faces shaped to have proportions similar to those of the female face in column 1. *Column 3:* Male faces with average shape and colour. *Column 4:* Male faces constructed to have the opposite or complementary shape characteristics to those of the female in column 1. The female at the top left has thin eyebrows, positioned high in the face; her opposite male at the top right has thick eyebrows, positioned low in the face.

I.S. Penton-Voak *et al.* (1999).

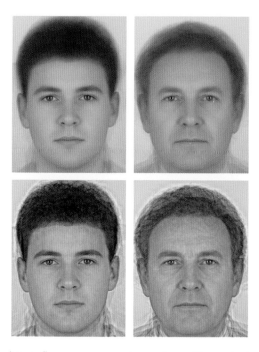

Figure V Parental age and its influence on attraction to faces. Composite images of fifteen males aged 20–24 and fifteen males aged 50–54. The upper pair look younger than the lower pair because in the lower images the skin texture has been enhanced. The presence of wrinkles and skin textures associated with age had no impact on the judgements of those born to older parents, whereas wrinkles were unattractive to those born to younger parents.

D.I. Perrett *et al.* (2002).

which spotlight small parts of infectious organisms; once the immune system has recognized these invaders, it can attack them.

Across different people there are many different versions of these MHC genes. This is good because there are many different infectious microbes, each with a distinctive protein coat. One can think of the microbes and our immune system as invaders and defenders. We and the microbes are in an arms race, continually trying to outwit each other. Some microbe will invent a changed protein coat which cloaks it from our eagle-eyed defending soldiers: if the change enables the microbe to get past the defences, that microbe will then spread rapidly through the individual, and from this individual host to other humans. Within a short time, that particular microbe will become pretty common. In turn some fortunate human will be born with a mutation, a new form of MHC gene that can recognize and bind to the new cloak of the changed microbe. Once that happens, the balance tips the other way – the individual now has the edge, being able to outwit the microbe's stealth and to neutralize any new attack from that variety. This individual is more likely to leave descendants with the same prize immunity.

It is good to have variants of the MHC genes that can build proteins to recognize the protein stealth cloaks of a variety of microbes. Since humans get one set of genes from mum and a second set from dad, our chances of combating disease will be greater if our maternal and paternal genes are different. If they are identical, which can happen after long periods of inbreeding,[34] then the chances of fighting off diseases will be reduced. So in principle it would be good when sizing up a potential partner to be able to spot whether or not he had different MHC genes. Clearly that's not possible ... or is it? Remarkably, men with *different* MHC genes from mum and dad are also men who are judged to be more attractive than those who had the *same* genes from mum and dad.[35] This finding seems incredible – how could genes against infections possibly be linked to facial attractiveness? Well, one way in which MHC genes might contribute to attractiveness is through their impact on the state of the skin. Men with a good immunity might not get so many skin infections, spots, or scars, and they might have less clumping of melanin pigment at the battle sites of past infections. And sure enough, the men whose genes give them better defences had better-looking skin than those with more restricted defences.

In this chapter we have been hunting for relationships between facial attractiveness and health. At the time of writing, no one has yet shown that men with a gene profile conferring more varied immunity or men with great skin get fewer infections. Nevertheless, there is a smoking gun.[36] The state of the skin influences whether or not someone's face looks healthy and beautiful. Now we find that the state of the skin also reflects the variability of the genes that control our ability to fight disease. Skin condition, beauty, and health are intimately linked. This makes a lot of sense because many of the things we do that cause us to age prematurely have their effects, first and foremost, on the appearance of our skin. If our skin looks old or just old for our age, then perhaps our bodies too have aged, and our skin is an indication that we may have less time to live than others with young-looking skin. We will return to ageing in Chapter 8.

Smoking your skin

Take smoking, for example. We know how bad this is for our health, but it's also bad for the skin. It leads to what has been dubbed 'smoker's face'[37] – characteristic lines and wrinkles, especially around the mouth and eyes (all that puckering up to inhale, and squinting to avoid getting smoke in your eyes), a slightly gaunt appearance, leathery skin, and an unusually grey skin colour.

The chemicals in smoke destroy Vitamin C,[38] which is essential in producing collagen. This is something of a problem, as approximately 80 per cent of our skin is made from collagen. Along with two other proteins, keratin (of which your hair, finger nails, and toenails are made) and elastin, collagen gives skin its resilience, its flexibility, and its elasticity. A reduction in collagen is the main reason why smokers get more wrinkles than non-smokers.

Smoking has further effects on the face, too. It constricts the blood vessels in the top layers of the skin, thereby reducing the supply of blood; and the carbon monoxide inhaled in the smoke reduces the amount of oxygen carried by the blood. Poor circulation and a lack of oxygen together make it difficult for the skin to renew itself, and this can give smokers an unhealthy skin complexion (for reasons we shall see below).

Scanning the face for health

These days no case in a TV medical drama is complete without an expensive x-ray or MRI scan of the head or body. The scan results are shown to the TV viewer with the mundane anatomy in black and white and the cause of the ailment – the tumour or whatever – coloured in as a red-hot area on the same image. Colour is used to make obvious which bit of the scan is important.

In a similar way, though without the big expensive scanning machine, our group have developed our own 'face scans' to identify the cues related to looking healthy. To do this, we take (say) fifty faces and ask people to sort them into those that look healthy and those that do not. After bringing all the faces into alignment (see Figure I, Plate IV), we then work out whether the colour at a given point relates to how healthy the faces looked – for example, most of the faces that look healthy might have a good skin colour at this point, whereas most of the unhealthy faces might have pale skin at the same point. You may recall from Figure E, Plate II that one of the differences between healthy-looking and unhealthy-looking students was the complexion: faces deemed hale and hearty have a richer colour, whereas those deemed to be less than 100 per cent fit show the colour drained from the skin.

Figure I, Plate IV shows the face scans in which we tested how skin colour relates to a healthy appearance.[39] First we computed 'What colour looks healthy?', and second we computed 'Where does the colour matter?' For example, it might be that having rosy-red cheeks is a sign of health, but that having red skin elsewhere on the face suggests that something is wrong. If this were true, then Figure I would show red on each cheek but no red elsewhere.

What we found instead was that healthy-looking faces were more red (and less green) than sickly looking faces, and that these colour differences were located just about *everywhere* in the face.[40] In other words, healthy-looking individuals did not just have redder cheeks and redder lips than unhealthy-looking faces: their skin was in fact redder all over. At the same time, and to our surprise, looking healthy was associated with having skin that was more yellow (and less blue); having yellow skin throughout the face was important for a healthy appearance. These same colour cues to health were found both in men's and in women's faces. In clean-shaven men, the colour relationships were not detected on skin where the beard would grow, perhaps because of the variable presence of stubble and skin rash associated with shaving.

One thing that the scans do not tell us is *why* the colours red and yellow look healthy. Presumably this has something to do with the pigments that are the actual source of colour in the skin, but which pigments are these and why are they a sign of health?

In the pink

The face scans reveal that people with *more* red in their face look healthier than people who have *less* red in their face. This raises questions, such as 'How red should a face be to look optimal in terms of health?' One can guess that the red colour is due to blood in the skin; one can therefore suppose that too much blood might look unwholesome. And what about the precise colour of the blood – does that matter?

To answer these questions our group assessed how the blood supply to the skin (the blood perfusion) influenced impressions of a person's health.[41] To do this, we measured the colour of skin that was flushed with 'fresh' blood (oxygenated) or full of 'stale' blood (deoxygenated).

You should be able to see these colour differences in your own skin. Try this: raise one hand above your head, and lower the other towards the ground. Stay like that for thirty seconds or so. Now bring both your hands together and look carefully at their colour – the one that was lowered towards the ground should look redder. This is because in the lowered hand blood will have accumulated under gravity, whereas it will have drained away from the raised hand. If you leave your hand lowered for some time, the blood that gathers in the skin will be largely deoxygenated – in the prolonged time the blood has been away from the lungs, the oxygen in it will have been used up. We used this technique to measure the change in skin colour due to the presence of increased levels of deoxygenated blood.[42]

You will no doubt have noticed that when you spend too long in a hot shower, when you start to sweat with exertion, or when you get warmed up after being very cold, you turn a little red in the face. This red skin colour indicates the presence of oxygenated blood – your raised temperature has caused the blood vessels in the skin to dilate, and now the heart can more easily push the fresh blood into the small blood vessels (capillaries) in the skin. Flushing of the skin and sweating help you to cool off – literally. We used this hot-skin state to measure the colour of oxygenated blood. We simply measured the colour change that occurred in people's hands before and after they had put them into hot water.[43]

With these colour measurements, we know how to *mimic* the effects of fresh (oxygenated) or stale (deoxygenated) blood in the skin. With all other factors held constant, we can now test the role of blood colour in contributing to a person's looks. As you can imagine, someone might look neither comfortable nor healthy when tilted upside-down or when hot and bothered; now, instead, we could take photos of relaxed faces and adjust their skin colour (mimicking blood-flow changes) without anyone needing to move a muscle (Figure J, Plate IV).

We asked evaluators to adjust the amount of blood colour in a face image so as to make it look as healthy as possible. They adjusted the colour to represent differing levels of oxygenated blood, which is bright red in colour, and deoxygenated blood, which is slightly more bluish-purple in colour. They could add more colour to the skin, in effect making the person look more hot-blooded, or they could reduce the colour levels, in effect draining the blood out of the skin. So what would evaluators do?

Would they go for more of the 'hot stuff', or would they like a 'cool and collected' appearance?

The evaluators went for the hot stuff. Astonishingly, we could improve the appearance of just about everybody by making just a slight change in their colour. Infusing just a little blood colour into their faces made people look healthier than their natural state. Those that started out pale (that is, those who lacked redness in their face) required quite a lot of extra blood colour to get them looking healthy. Virtually all of the faces (98 per cent) appeared better with extra oxygenated blood colour, but only 66 per cent of faces looked healthier after adding deoxygenated blood colour. Faces that were pale to start with looked better with either sort of extra blood in them – stale or fresh. Those who were red in the face already looked better when the stale stuff in their face was reduced.

Next we gave evaluators the opportunity to adjust both oxygenated and deoxygenated blood simultaneously. This time they could raise the amount of blood in the skin *and* they could alter the type of blood (that is, whether it was oxygenated or deoxygenated). In this situation, evaluators made a small increase in the *amount* of blood in the skin, but a big change to the *mix* of the blood. They increased the levels of fresh blood in faces, and decreased the levels of stale blood. In other words, in their eyes a healthy appearance depends on having a good blood supply to the skin and also on this supply containing oxygenated blood. Skin looks sickly either if it is drained of blood or if it is full of stagnant deoxygenated blood. It seems that very subtle differences in blood status are visible to the naked eye. Note that the evaluators didn't go overboard with blood colour, not even with the good stuff. They raised the levels just a little – enough to make the faces healthy and attractive. Raising the levels too much makes the face look unhealthy and even aggressive.[44]

Our work on blood colour so far had been on pale-skinned Europeans. Supposing that blood changes might be more difficult to detect in darker skin, we now repeated the work with a range of skin types. We found that faces of East Asians, South Asians, Africans, and people of mixed ethnicity *all* looked healthier if more red was added to their skin. This was true irre-spective of whether the people evaluating the faces were white Australians, white Britons, or black Africans: the cues to health from blood appear to be independent of the evaluators' ethnic origin and culture.

These effects of blood colouration fit with what we know about the effects on the skin of smoking. Smoking removes the oxygen from the blood, making it bluer; this gives the smoker a less healthy colour. Giving up smoking isn't only good for health – it'll do wonders for appearance, too! Being physically fit and active tends to increase blood flow in the skin;[45] by contrast many kinds of illness, including diabetes and heart problems, are associated with reduced oxygen in the blood and with blue-tinted skin.[46] There are also ways in which blood flow can indicate other healthy qualities, such as fertility. In women,[47] higher sex-hormone levels are associated with a better blood supply to the skin[48] and a greater tendency for the skin to flush.[49] Returning to Figure F, Plate III, colour might be a contributory factor in the healthy appearance of women with high oestrogen levels.

Our surprising sensitivity to skin colour allows us to detect health differences that result from a range of lifestyle influences and illnesses. We can detect how much blood is getting to the skin, and whether that blood is full or starved of oxygen. The colour of the skin sends out warning signals when someone is suffering in the short term and is about to faint; it also signals longer-term complaints such as anaemia or possible heart problems. And, of course, skin colour also tells us whether or not they are full of life and reproductively fit.

A healthy tan?

Sun damage ages the skin (see Chapter 8), but wrinkles and age spots are the least of our worries – much more important is that excess sun exposure can cause skin cancer. Sunlight includes ultra-violet (UV) radiation, which damages our DNA – and the DNA contains the instructions needed to repair and maintain skin cells. Damaged DNA can lead to cells multiplying out of control, forming cancerous tumours on the skin.

One of the ways we have evolved to protect ourselves from the damaging effects of sunlight is by producing melanin, the pigment that causes tanning and which also acts as a natural sunscreen. Melanin darkens the skin; in so doing, it helps to filter out the cancer-causing UV rays.[50] Melanin is also needed to prevent vitamin B9 (folic acid) from being destroyed by UV.[51] Having too little folic acid slows DNA production, hindering the production of new cells and tissue in the body. This is why women who hope to get pregnant are advised to bump up their intake of folic acid: growing a whole new human being requires the manufacture of a lot of DNA and a shortage of folic acid can lead to birth defects. This raises an interesting and obvious question: given that melanin is so important for the integrity of DNA, why aren't we all as darkly pigmented as people from Africa?

The variation we see in skin colour is graded with latitude – people whose ethnic family origins were near the Equator are darker-skinned than those whose antecedents lived at northern and southern latitudes. This reflects variation in the amount of UV radiation received at the Earth's surface, with more arriving at the Equator and less toward the Poles. Dark-skinned humans like Africans have proportionately more melanin in their skin, which acts as a protectant given the greater exposure to UV. Light-skinned people like Europeans have proportionately less melanin; although sun exposure triggers an increase in the melanin in the skin, this is not enough to cope with the intense sun exposure at the Equator. The lighter skins of Europe and central Asia offer a natural sun protection factor (SPF) of around only 2.5, whereas the darker skins of Africans give a natural SPF of 10–15. Lighter-skinned and darker-skinned people both tan when they spend time in the sun; for those with darker skins, the combined effect of the innately high melanin and the extra melanin produced in response to sun exposure means that they are well protected against intense UV and the consequent risk of skin cancer.

The lower melanin content of light-skinned people does give them an advantage in another area: the production of vitamin D, also known as the 'sunshine vitamin'. Humans can manufacture vitamin D in their skin when it is exposed to UV light from the sun.[52] Vitamin D is essential for the absorption of calcium into the body, and ensures healthy bones and teeth; conversely, a lack of vitamin D in childhood leads to weak calcium-deficient bones which can become deformed. High levels of melanin in the skin slow the production of vitamin D. Although that isn't a big problem for dark-skinned people who are living close to the Equator where there is plenty of intense sunshine, it becomes more of a problem away from the Equator; in less sunny conditions a paler skin is beneficial, so that the filtering effects of melanin will not impede vitamin D production.

The darkness of human skin represents a trade-off between not having *enough* melanin, and thus suffering folic-acid depletion and DNA damage, and having *too much* melanin, and thus being less able to produce vitamin D. When modern humans first migrated out of Africa, they were dark-skinned. As our species migrated across the globe, natural selection adjusted our skin colour as sun protection was balanced against vitamin D production. Among the populations that moved north, individuals who happened to have lighter skin would have produced more vitamin D and absorbed more calcium, and this would have allowed them to survive and reproduce more successfully in northern latitudes than those with darker skins. It is therefore health considerations that account for geographic differences in the relative amounts of skin melanin.

Colour, culture, and sex

On top of differences in skin colour that relate to ethnicity, there are differences that relate to gender. Women's skin tends to be lighter than men's, regardless of the overall level of pigmentation in a population.[53]

The difference could be explained by the need for vitamin D. When women are pregnant, the calcium stored in their bones is used to help build the bones of the unborn child, and these stores then need to be replenished. If the woman has insufficient vitamin D, she cannot absorb calcium from the diet and both she and her baby suffer. It is therefore possible that natural selection has ensured that women have lighter skin than men, so that they can produce more vitamin D. If they were too light-skinned, on the other hand, this would leave them prone to skin cancer and folic-acid deficiencies, so the difference in skin colour between men and women is small: it's just enough to give women the edge in vitamin D production, and no more.[54]

In many cases, preference for high or low levels of melanin and tan reflect cultural influences. In Europe during the nineteenth century, for example, well-heeled young women remained pale in order to indicate that they didn't need to labour in the open, whereas today, of course, a deep tan in northern Europe may indicate that the owner has sufficient wealth to afford holidays in the sun.[55] European colonization and the experience of slavery have also left lingering impacts on definitions of beauty. In multi-ethnic societies, light skin may be seen as attractive because of associations with wealth and access to health care.[56]

The variability in preferences for dark or light skin shown across different populations and cultures also highlights how seemingly nonsensical people's attitudes and behaviour can be. While natural selection has provided us with a beautifully calibrated skin-protection system, we live in a world in which people with light skins may collectively spend a fortune acquiring deep tans, which they consider attractive and desirable but which do nothing but deplete their folic-acid stores and damage their DNA; while people with dark skins collectively spend large amounts of money on skin-lightening agents and creams that inhibit melanin production, thereby increasing their vulnerability to sun damage, and expose themselves to chemicals such as hydroquinone that eventually damage the skin, leaving it rough and blotchy. Our efforts to appear attractive and healthy can be remarkably counter-productive, sometimes serving to damage our health rather than to improve it, and ultimately to diminish our looks sooner than would have happened in the natural ageing process.

Does a tan look healthy?

As is evident from the discussion above, melanin and health are intricately related through melanin's role in protecting DNA and folic acid and in impeding vitamin D manufacture, as well as its historical association with social status. There is a further way in which melanin is related to health.

Throughout much of the animal kingdom, the cells that make melanin also have a role in defending against bacterial infections.[57] These cells swallow bacteria whole, and the melanin-producing organs within the cells then help to break down and digest the trapped bacteria. The melanin-producing cells in human skin could also perform this shielding role if the skin gets infected.

Raised levels of melanin might look healthy for some of these reasons; equally, lowered levels of melanin might look healthy for the other reasons. It's time to find out what people actually think – how do they perceive faces with subtly altered melanin levels?

Predicting how melanin affects health perception is tricky, but it is straightforward to define the colour changes associated with melanin: one can simply compare the colour in regions of the body that are habitually covered up with the colour of neighbouring skin regions that are normally exposed to the sun. With this colour information, our group allowed British evaluators to subtract or add melanin colour to the skin of white European faces in images (see Figure L, Plate V). Our evaluators chose to increase the melanin (tan) level of all faces to make them look healthier. Perhaps it is no surprise that in Scotland a tan was seen as healthy, especially given the association between getting a tan and sunny holidays.

While it was clear that British evaluators thought tanned faces looked healthy, certain details suggested that something else was going on as well. It didn't seem that the tan was being increased just to make the faces look darker – if it had been, then the evaluators would have added most tan to faces that were initially the lightest, yet they did not; instead they put the highest tan levels in faces that lacked *yellow* in the skin colour,[58] and that's puzzling.

In separate studies, we asked our evaluators to change just the lightness of the skin. With this manipulation, we found that British evaluators actually *increased* the lightness of skin in most European faces to make them look healthy.[59] This was particularly true for women's faces – to look their best, the fairer sex were made even fairer.[60] African evaluators also lightened the skin of a variety of African, Asian, and European faces, even more than British evaluators had done. If British and African evaluators were asked to make faces look healthier and could control only the level of yellowness in the skin, they made the faces more yellow. So a tan makes the face darker and more yellow; yet skin colour looks healthier when it is lighter and has more yellow in it. Why is this?

Five-a-day

Another effect of smoking is that it destroys vitamin A, which helps the skin to function as a barrier to bacteria and viruses; smokers are thus more vulnerable to infection. Vitamin A found in animal products is absorbed in the form of retinol. You may have heard this name, as retinol is used as a treatment for acne – retinol helps to detach excess skin cells from the base of hair follicles, where they can otherwise block the follicle and lead to the formation of pus-filled pimples. Retinol also helps to stimulate collagen production, and is sometimes used to combat sun damage to the skin and as an anti-ageing treatment for wrinkles. (The downside is the effects last only as long as you use the retinol; if you stop, the wrinkles come back with time. The return of wrinkles creates a continuing demand for retinol, to the benefit of cosmetic companies' profits.)

Vitamin A can be obtained from fruit and vegetables, including carrots, peppers, kale, and tomatoes. These contain coloured substances called carotenoids[61] which the body can convert into vitamin A. Carotenoids are yellow-red pigment molecules that are important to health in their own right. They help to protect against infection and UV damage from sunlight by absorbing molecules known as 'free radicals', which are produced when UV rays interact with skin cells.[62] Free radicals are destructive chemicals: they harden cell membranes, trash DNA, ruin enzymes, and cause the metabolic power-plants of the cells to break down. When our immune cells chop up a bacterium, masses of these reactive free radicals pour out from the ruptured bacterial carcass, and carotenoids are needed to mop them up.[63] If they aren't mopped up, the free radicals cause their mayhem and contribute to the general degradation of cells, which is happening anyway as part of ageing. While carotenoids can come to the rescue, the process of neutralizing free radicals burns them up,[64] so during an infection carotenoid levels in the blood fall. The only thing that can help is to replenish the stocks of carotenoids through diet – by eating more fruit and vegetables.

Carotenoids are colourful pigments, and eating large quantities can colour an animal's skin or feathers.[65] Flamingos, for example, are pink because the shrimp they eat are rich in carotenoids; if you see a *white* flamingo, it's not a different kind of bird but a standard flamingo whose diet is lacking in these pigments. Similarly, people who consume vast quantities of carrots, tangerines, or carotenoid supplements may sometimes find that their skin turns orange.

It's not just flamingos whose coat is coloured by carotenoid pigments; many other species of fish and birds also get the bright colour of their ornaments from the plant pigments that they eat. Our group wondered whether variation in a person's natural diet and intake of carotenoid plant pigments might affect the skin colour,[66] and also whether fruit and vegetable pigments make people's skin look healthy.

The first thing to establish was whether a person's natural diet could lead to detectable changes in the colour of their skin. We asked some European students to record how frequently they ate foods of different types, and we measured the colour of their skin. Sure enough, we found that the more fruit and vegetables a student ate, the more yellow his or her skin became. The specific way in which the skin reflected light of different wavelengths allowed us to determine that the change in yellowness was indeed due to people's consumption of the colourful carotenoid plant pigments.

The next step was to find out whether people could *see* these colour differences, and whether faces with raised carotenoid colour were considered healthier than other faces. Using similar methods to the blood-colour study, we showed students faces that varied in the amount of colour from fruit and vegetables, and asked them to adjust each face until it looked its healthiest (see Figure M, Plate V). All the faces became healthier-looking when the amount of plant-pigment colour was increased. The evaluators did not go to excess and turn the faces into a tangerine colour – that did not look healthy – but they did raise the level of fruit and vegetable pigmentation for an optimal appearance.

Putting this information together, we see improvement to the apparent health of faces when we add either suntan or dietary pigment colour. Plant pigments increase the yellowness of skin but maintain its lightness, whereas suntan darkens the skin as well as making it more yellow. Both the dietary pigment and the suntan improvements in appearance depended on how yellow the face was before the colour was adjusted; the faces that initially lacked yellow benefited most from additional tan or dietary colour. The health benefits from tan or from dietary colour did not depend on how fair or dark the faces were to start with. All these facts suggest that the melanin added to a face by evaluators was added mainly to make it more *yellow*, rather than to make it *darker*. This could explain, at least partly, why people perceive tanned skin to be healthy – the increased production of melanin that goes with a tan mimics the effect of dietary pigments in making the skin more yellow, and it is this yellowing, not the darkening of the skin specifically, that is seen as more healthy. More conclusive to this interpretation was the finding that, when given the choice of altering both, the evaluators preferred to alter dietary pigment colour rather than suntan. (Here it should be noted that from their point of view, evaluators were simply altering face colour – they were not told anything about the pigment basis of the colour change, and had no idea that the colour was related to diet or to UV protection.)

The effect of dietary pigment colour is evident across different cultures: Asian and African faces are adjusted for yellow colour in the same way as

European Caucasian faces, and this doesn't depend on the nationality and skin colour of the people making the evaluation. Across all the cultures we've tested, people raise the amount of yellow in the face in order to maximize apparent health.

Colour me beautiful

For many creatures, carotenoid colour is central to attractiveness. The red plumage of the northern cardinal bird, the yellow eye-margin of penguins, the red colour of guppies, and of stickleback fish are all based on carotenoid colours and are all important in getting selected as a mate. In birds it is usually the males who wear the bright colours, the females tending to have drab colours so that they can hide away on a nest while rearing the chicks. The brightly coloured male ornaments signal quality, and give females an easily visible way of selecting the best mate.[67] The colour of the ornaments depends both on diet and on the health of the immune system. Carotenoids used in ornaments cannot be used to fight off disease, which means that the males with the brightest colours must have extra-good immune systems.[68] Females who choose the males with the brightest-coloured plumage are choosing themselves a male who isn't sick and isn't likely to get sick, and also one who is able to get sufficient high-quality food.

Plant-pigment colour in human skin may function in a similar way; by preferring more yellow facial skin colouring and finding this more attractive, one would be more likely to secure a healthier mate. Carotenoids laid down in the skin, like those incorporated into bird feathers, are unavailable thereafter for any other function such as helping with defence against illnesses. Further, the skin surface continually renews itself; the outer layers are cast off and replaced by the lower layers. When carotenoid intake is low for any length of time, therefore, or when blood supplies are depleted by diseases,[69] fewer carotenoids will be laid down in the skin, and this will eventually show in a person's complexion.

Although the mechanisms are not clear, carotenoids are important for reproduction, and normal levels appear necessary for success in fertility treatment; raised levels may even benefit fertility.[70] So skin that is richly coloured with ingested plant pigments can indicate a currently disease-free status, a healthy immune system, and a healthy reproductive system.

Since it contributes to apparent health, skin colour in humans is likely to have a role in sexual selection similar to those of facial shape and body shape. Throughout our history, individuals with healthy-looking faces, healthy-looking bodies, and a healthy skin colour would have been preferred as mates, and the same is true today. By choosing your mate on the basis of the healthiness of his or her skin complexion, you are favouring those individuals who are most capable of acquiring and maintaining healthy food resources and who are best able to resist disease – and people who are so good at both of these that they can afford to lavish some of the nutrient benefits from their diets just on skin colouration.

Health education

Given that health in faces is attractive, it would seem that appealing to people's vanity might pay dividends in Government campaigns to promote a healthy diet. What is particularly salient in any dietary survey is how little fruit and how few vegetables people actually eat in comparison with Government guidelines. Our own survey was of relatively wealthy and well-educated, and, one might assume, healthy students, yet even among these, the average intake of fruit and vegetables was three portions a day – substantially less than the minimum of five portions a day recommended by UK health services. Note that in setting such targets, organizations working with the UK Government may have been cautious, not wanting to create unrealistic goals; other countries urge people to eat even higher amounts – France recommends ten portions of fruit and vegetables a day, for example, and the USA recommends up to thirteen portions, depending on calorie intake.[71] What is clear is that no one in our sample was eating too many fruit and vegetables; the majority were eating too few. The implication is that increasing the intake of fruit and vegetables would change skin colour favourably, reduce long-term health risks, and increase current well-being.

Governments of Western countries conclude from large-scale studies of cancer and cardiovascular disease that the intake of fruit and vegetables is extremely important to health. It is a major concern that our children are just not eating the right foods. Could our lab's finding – that eating the right kind of food makes skin colour more attractive – be the extra persuasion people need to change their diet and reap the benefits in health?

Is health always attractive?

The ability to detect health by looking at faces is valuable in biological terms because it increases our own chances of staying fit and healthy. Our group found that pregnant women and women in the second two weeks of their menstrual cycle all showed a greater preference for healthy-looking faces, in both males and females, than women who were in neither of these conditions.[72] One suggestion is that women prefer healthier-looking faces when pregnant because being only with healthy people reduces the risk of their contracting an infection. Illness can severely disrupt foetal development and may even lead to birth defects or miscarriages, so keeping away from sick people is crucial and the ability to detect health from facial appearance at a distance would be highly advantageous. The preference for healthy faces seems to be linked to the hormone progesterone, which is high in the groups of women who expressed this preference; high levels of progesterone are needed to maintain pregnancy and to prevent miscarriage, and women in the latter part of their cycle are producing more progesterone to prepare their body in case of pregnancy.

Preference for health is linked to aspects of our personality, and this too may influence our risk of contracting disease. In an intriguing study we found that anxiety levels had a large impact on health preferences.[73] Low- and high-anxiety individuals were shown video clips that portrayed people either turning their heads towards the viewer and smiling (as if showing pleasant interest in the viewer) or turning their heads away from the viewer and smiling (as if showing interest directed away from the viewer). The faces in the video clips had been manipulated so that some appeared to be very healthy and some appeared to be unhealthy. Low-anxiety individuals liked the healthy faces who showed social interest in them, but not the unhealthy ones. High-anxiety individuals, on the other hand, liked *anyone* smiling at them, whether healthy or unhealthy. The desire of the anxious for positive social engagement evidently took precedence over any health cues. Perhaps the well-established relationship between high anxiety and frequent illness arises not only because anxiety and stress depress the immune system, but also because anxious people expose themselves more to the risk of infection – perhaps they are so focused on social reward that they interact without regard to health or sickness in others. A lack of prejudice against sickness may be desirable from a social perspective, but, as those working in the medical profession know, kindness can still be accompanied by hygiene and self-care.

This last section reinforces the theme emphasized throughout the book in relation to facial attractiveness. People differ in the extent to which they find a given trait personally attractive. Health is important for everyone, certainly, and signs of health are attractive. But the personal set of priorities that guide our search for a partner differs for each one of us, and may change over time. In some people's eyes health is not as attractive as smiling; for others health wins every time. Once again, encouragingly, we see that no single set of facial characteristics makes us attractive – or unattractive – to everyone.

Chapter 8
WITHER THE FACE

On the cuteness of babies and the effects of time

'Age cannot wither her ...' says a character about Cleopatra, in Shakespeare's *Antony and Cleopatra*. Age certainly withers the rest of us, and some more so than others. Western society has learned to associate beauty with youth and to set great store by appearances, and there are many reminders of this harsh reality: 'Keep young and beautiful / If you want to be loved', wrote Al Dubin in the lyrics of a 1933 song.

Despite this advice, the fact is that we *cannot* 'Keep young and beautiful' – we can't avoid or escape the ageing process entirely, no matter what cosmetic surgeons or the blurb on our moisturizing lotion may tell us; life leaves its marks on our faces in ways that become increasingly hard to eradicate as we get older. We live in a youth-obsessed culture, perhaps more so now than at any other time in human history, and seemingly we all accept that 'youth is beauty' (some more grudgingly than others, perhaps), but – given the prevalence of Botox, chemical peels, breast implants, and the like – we should be less inclined to accept that 'beauty is truth'.[1] In consequence, we tend to think of 'age' as synonymous with 'old age', and to associate this stage in our lives with the loss not only of our youth but also our looks. Yet we actually begin ageing from the moment we're born, so how does our attractiveness change over our lifespan?

You looked better as a baby

Sadly, perhaps, the news is that we start to become less attractive almost as soon as we complete our first year of life. Thanks to the 'infant schema' shown by the young of many animals[2] including humans, babies are generally considered more attractive to look at than older children. The large foreheads, large eyes, small noses, and small chins that characterize baby faces bring out a nurturing response in adults. This urge can be so powerful that it crosses species – we know that humans go gooey at the sight of puppies and kittens, but there are also records of a gorilla[3] and an orang-utan[4] caring for kittens; and if you think that's improbable, there's even a case of a lioness in the wild *adopting* infant antelopes instead of eating them![5] Perhaps that exemplifies the biblical prophesy (Isaiah 11:6) of predators and prey living in harmony;[6] unfortunately, however, other lions were more true to form and *ate* the foster kids, so the prophecy has not yet come entirely to pass.

Infant facial features are highly attractive but relatively short-lived, and attractiveness continues to decline as we lose our distinctive baby-faced characteristics in early childhood. 'Attractiveness' is defined here in terms of *the enjoyment of looking at a face*.[7] Attraction does not imply sexual interest, although a subset of attractive adult faces may indeed be sexually alluring. (In this sense, then, a heterosexual may find the face of a same-sex adult attractive, just as a homosexual may enjoy looking at an adult of the other sex.)

Adults, and especially young women, prefer looking at photographs of baby faces to looking at photographs of older children and adults.[8] It's not just that looking at baby faces is enjoyable; infant faces seem to be 'wired in' to provoke a reaction – we find it difficult to ignore them. A photo of a human baby holds our attention to a much greater extent than a photo of an adult face, and this holds good for both men and women.[9] Remarkably, this attention-grabbing effect is greater for the *left* side of our vision. This curious fact ties in with another observation: that humans also show a bias to cradling babies using their left arms,[10] a pattern seen across all cultures – paintings throughout our history depict the same bias in showing women carrying infants on their left side. This may reflect a desire by mothers to see (and hear) their babies from the left: this would bias the communicative signals from the baby to the right side of the brain, the side more strongly involved in face perception (see Figures 2.1–2.3).[11]

While just about all infants are attractive, some are even more attractive than others. Their lives are fortunate. Their good looks persuade adults to act with increased care and warmth, and to hold better beliefs about the infant's abilities. Attractive babies are looked at for longer and receive more enjoyable social attention from adults. A more positive personality is attributed to them by the adults in their lives, and they are thought to be easier to care for, more sociable, more active, and more competent.[12] These favourable adult attitudes will encourage the infants to develop in reality the character that the adults expected of them. In short, attractiveness helps to create self-fulfilling prophecies. Adults assume sociability, and the attractive infants come to manifest this heightened social competence. (This is discussed further in Chapter 9.)

Mothers, like everyone else, succumb to the charm of their baby's looks. Mothers of more attractive babies spend more time holding their babies close, suggesting that they find the interactions more rewarding and fulfilling, and they maintain more eye contact and kiss their babies more.[13] One of the strongest and most affectionate bonds is that between a mother and her own child and, as you might expect, pictures of a mother's own children at 1–6 years old produce more activity in the 'reward' regions of the brain than images of other familiar children of the same age.[14] Even when looking at unrelated toddlers, a mother's brain will show at least some activation in the same 'pleasure centres',[15] which shows that there are two types of evaluation taking place. One is a general response to *all* infants, all of whom are attractive and rewarding to look at, and the other is a more marked response to her *own* infant, whom she finds even more rewarding to look at.[16] The infant's emotional expression can boost the same reward system still further, and the strongest activation in these parts of the brain occurs when a mum sees her own infant smiling.

Cute or what?

The reaction to baby faces isn't limited only to women who are already mothers. Young women are more accurate at selecting the cuter of two composite baby-face images (Figure 8.1) than men.[17] This doesn't mean that men don't find babies cute: they do. Rather it means that men are unable to distinguish between babies whose faces differ only slightly in terms of cuteness.

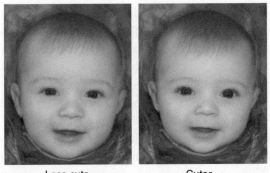

Less cute   Cuter

Figure 8.1 Cuteness in face shape. Facial composites of baby girls, altered in shape to decrease and increase cuteness. The cuter shape has a smaller chin and in general looks younger than the less-cute shape.

J.S. Lobmaier (2008) Perception Lab.

You may be thinking that such a sex difference could simply reflect upbringing – perhaps women learned to see subtle differences in cuteness when they were playing with baby dolls and cuddly toys during childhood; and although there is no sex difference in the ability to spot subtle differences between adult faces, perhaps men are worse at distinguishing adorable infant faces simply because in childhood they spent all their time kicking a football (or each other). The toy industry is well aware of what sells to children, and many toys aimed at girls are designed to maximize cuteness (think, for example, of 'My Little Pony' and 'Cabbage Patch Kids'). Such toys, having large eyes, a bulbous forehead, and a small chin, perfectly illustrate the infant schema.

In fact, our studies find that the ability to detect cuteness is linked to sex-hormone levels more than to experience. Older women who haven't yet gone through the menopause are much better at spotting the cuter of two babies than women, matched in age, who have. Amongst young women, those using hormonal contraceptive pills are more sensitive to cuteness than those who are not. As both pre-menopausal women and those on the pill have higher circulating levels of natural or synthetic oestrogens and progestogens than post-menopausal women and non-pill takers, it is likely that the female sex hormones establish a greater ability to spot cuteness. If so, this could relate to the way women see the world – hormonally charged women may have better visual skills when it comes to infant faces – or it could reflect a difference in emotional response. The hormones may mean that infant faces generate a stronger emotional response, and it may be this that gives a better ability to detect cute babies.

By now you may be thinking that this research is confirming undesirable sex-role stereotypes – that men are just hopeless and insensitive when it comes to anything to do with infants! Instead, when we change the task and ask people to judge which of two infants is *younger* or *happier*, the sex difference seen for cuteness judgements disappears and men perform at the same level as women.[18] Taken together, the two results are illuminating: the photos of the cutest infants are precisely those that are judged to be both younger and happier, which means that there *isn't* in fact any difference between men's and women's ability to spot subtle differences in infant faces. What this implies is that there must be something specific about cuteness to which women respond more readily than men. This may well reflect the biological differences between men and women, whereby women have been under stronger evolutionary pressure to respond in a nurturing fashion to babies, and even now it is primarily women who care for babies, and who have the equipment to feed them milk.

When do these hormonal effects begin to have their effect? One might suppose that this happens when women reach puberty and begin producing high levels of oestrogen and progesterone each month. Hormones also act during foetal development, and biases may be introduced then. In the developing male baby, while still inside the womb, there is a surge of testosterone which not only organizes the shape of his genitals but also creates particular connections in his brain, laying down future behavioural biases. In effect, testosterone masculinizes the brain and body; in the absence of the effects of testosterone, the systems default to a feminine mode.[19] Later in life, as puberty approaches, there is a sustained elevation of sex hormones that then lasts through our reproductive life. Hormones at puberty interact with the biases already established in life and help to activate sex-typical behaviour. And we're not just talking about wanting to sit with a beer and watch football with your mates – there is a whole gamut of interests that men develop, including getting aroused by the opposite sex.[20] Same-sex preferences may intensify at this time, too, though their origins are less clear.[21]

The development of a spectrum of sex-typical behaviour is apparent in our primate cousins. What do you think happens when young monkeys are given the chance to play with either a teddy bear or a toy with wheels? Yes, it's true; the females go for the teddy, while the males go for cars![22] We might have expected from Chapter 2 that adolescent monkey males would develop an interest in female monkey porn,[23] but cars for the boy monkeys and fluffy toys for girl monkeys – that's a surprise. And we can't blame TV advertising and the media for spreading sex-role stereotypes, or accuse the monkeys' parents of creating biases about which toys are appropriate for which sex[24] – it just seems that monkey males and females are predisposed to find one toy more appealing than the other. The juvenile males' interest was towards automobiles (which basically meant trying everything in their power to break them), whereas the juvenile female monkeys were biased toward cuteness, and were prone to cradle the teddy bear in the way that adult females carry their infants.

It is likely that female sex hormones in adults help to reinforce the connections that link the 'cute infant' face schema to the brain's reward centres. Women who may have spent a lifetime attending to toy infants and real infants don't suddenly lose this experience when they pass through menopause, yet their response does diminish. They won't have forgotten everything about infants in just a few years, but the drop in sex hormones that accompanies the menopause may stop the infant schema from driving reward centres and attention-grabbing brain circuits in the way it once did. Conversely, pre-menopausal women who take hormone pills may reinforce the connections that link visual cuteness with emotional reactions.

Hormones, then, have a profound impact on attraction to infants' facial characteristics. In males, some impact may occur during foetal development, when testosterone impresses mannish manners into brain circuits and curtails future infant interest. In females, a separate effect from female sex hormones during reproductive life amplifies the adult feelings of affection that are aroused by infant faces. Together, the hormones establish greater sensitivity in the sex and age group best equipped to give breast-feeding care.

Toddlers win Bonnie Baby contest

My mother was once given the task of judging who should win the 'Bonnie Baby' contest at the local village fête. A tricky choice: pick a baby, any baby – and win the wrath of the mothers of all the other contestants; who says women aren't competitive? As a nurse, she was qualified to choose the healthiest, but the term 'bonnie' implies being not only *healthy* but also *adorable*. How then to decide, given the babies' range in ages? Fortunately, the infant face schema can provide a yardstick for such now outmoded contests.[25]

Consideration of infant care suggests that the youngest babies should look the cutest, because they need to attract most support and nursing, but oddly it's *not* the youngest who look the bonniest: by general agreement, infant cuteness rises with age from birth, peaks around the age of 9–11 months, and then declines again.[26] Perhaps the youngest babies don't need the most care because they stay put if left on their own; babies approaching their first birthday are getting mobile, and may need more attention to keep them out of trouble.

It turns out that cuteness is determined not by the specific needs of the infant following birth, but rather by head shape and the dangers of childbirth. The size of the head of a foetus is limited by the size of its mother's pelvis – if the head grew any larger before birth, the baby could not be squeezed out into the world. Most of human brain growth (85 per cent) is completed outside the womb in the first year of life. During this time the skull increases in size to accommodate an expanding brain; this also produces a larger forehead and a lowering in position of the eyes, nose, and mouth.[27] This means that as the baby develops over its first year, the face conforms more and more to the infant face schema. After that, though, the rest of the face grows faster than the brain, and the face gets less cute in its proportions. No wonder, then, that it is the youngest toddlers who win the baby contests.

Cuteness – or the lack of it – is not without more serious consequences. The attractiveness of babies of any age varies from individual to individual; such differences influence the adults around the babies. Troublingly, research reveals that even in an intensive care unit, more attractive, cuter premature babies thrive better than less attractive babies, both gaining more weight and experiencing a shorter stay. This may possibly indicate that nurses provide greater nurturing and care to the more attractive infants.[28] You may be dismayed by this idea of differential treatment, or willing to accept it as part of human nature; whatever your opinion, demonstration of the existence of such biases towards cuteness is the first step in overcoming them.

Regardless of age, the cutest babies of any age group are always those who show the strongest infant schema – whether they are three months old or thirteen months old, babies assessed as 'cute' have large eyes, small noses and mouths, and large foreheads. In comparison with less attractive babies, cute babies' faces tend to be narrow below the eyes. Some of the features associated with cuteness in babies' faces are the same as those associated with femininity in adult faces,[29] which raises the possibility that differences between male and female babies could affect adult male and female perceptions of their cuteness. Since male babies are likely to look less feminine than female babies (thanks to the action of testosterone in the womb), they may also be judged to be less attractive. Many observers feel that they cannot tell the sex of infants; nonetheless, the same observers have little reticence in making judgements about how independent or sociable a baby is, and remarkably they give the baby boys and baby girls attributions that are stereotypically male or female. In tests, most people thought that the baby boy's face in Figure N (Plate V) would be likely to be seen as older and showing more independence and less sociability than the baby girl's face.[30] When forced to guess, it seems, adults aren't that bad at assigning sex, even if they believe otherwise.

When mistakes are made, those mistakes are interesting: regardless of whether the babies are actually female or male, people tend to think that cuter infants are female.[31] Even more convincingly, if people are able to manipulate an image of a baby face by turning the levels of femininity and masculinity up or down until the baby 'looks its best', most people tend to make male baby faces look more feminine (see Figure O, Plate V).[32]

Cuteness, though related to femininity, is evidently not quite the same thing, as our studies have not found that feminizing the shape of baby girls' faces benefits their appearance. At the time of writing, relatively little work has been done on the *characteristics* of cuteness in human infants. While we do now know some of the defining characteristics, this issue is likely to be as complex as adult facial attractiveness.

Baby faces control aggression

As well as evoking nurturing and care, the infant schema reduces aggression towards young animals. Among baboons, for example, the babyish facial appearance of youngsters, along with the fluffy black coat[33] they have until three months old, allows them to get up to all sorts of tricks with impunity. They clamber over adult males, hang onto ears, swing from tails or other appendages, and are generally irritating. In contrast, older juveniles who annoy older animals (including their mothers) may be hit, bitten, and dragged along screaming by an arm or a leg.

The infant schema undoubtedly acts in a similar way with human children, who keep their babyish features much longer than other creatures, and against whom aggression is rare but regrettably not entirely absent.[34] While physical child abuse is a complex phenomenon, one of the many factors that plays a role in it is the child's face. Baby-faced looks give the impression of naiveté and innocence; mature-faced children, by contrast, are likely to be seen as more skilled and grown-up than they really are. Parents who abuse their children often have unrealistic expectations of them,[35] and in vulnerable households mature looks in a child may present an extra risk factor as these may be more likely to precipitate punishment when the child fails to meet inappropriate expectations. Abused children tend to have smaller foreheads than other children,[36] and so lack the cuter, more baby-shaped proportions that might offer greater protection.

When people are shown line drawings of two-year-olds, those with younger forehead proportions are seen as needing greater nurturing, whereas those with older-looking face proportions are seen as being more in need of discipline. And this is despite the fact that the judges are told beforehand that all the drawings show children of exactly the same age.[37] Similarly, when parents of 11-year-old children are asked to look at images of 11-year-olds with large and small foreheads and to assign appropriate chores, those with more mature features are assigned the difficult tasks (those which only a 15-year-old could manage), whereas baby-faced 11-year-olds are assigned the easier tasks (those which a 7-year-old could do).[38] Even parents with first-hand experience of pre-teen capabilities still modify their expectations according to the child's facial appearance. The potential impact of face shape on adults' beliefs about children's abilities should not be underestimated; teachers' expectations, for example, are known to have a profound influence on educational success.[39]

Beautiful babies = beautiful adults?

How stable are these differences in cuteness and how long do they persist beyond babyhood? Do attractive babies grow into attractive children and then attractive adults? The answer is that they do, but things are different for boys and girls.

Our group compared photos of students that were taken when they were 6 months old, 6 years old, and 20 years old.[40] For females, both femininity and attractiveness were stable across development – a girl's attractiveness as an infant is a good predictor of how attractive she will be as a 6-year-old child and as a 20-year-old adult (see Figure 8.2).

| 6 months | 6 years | 20 years |

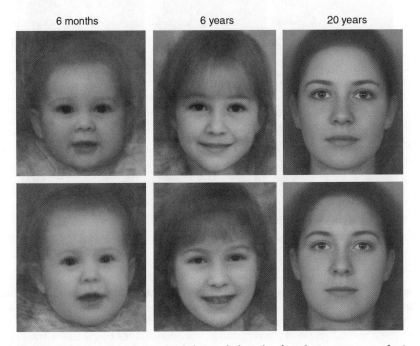

Figure 8.2 Sugar and spice: stability of female facial appearance during development. Composite images of babies at 6 months, children aged 6, and adults aged 20. One group of fifteen individuals contributes to the top trio of images; a second group of fifteen individuals contributes to the lower trio. The two groups of fifteen females were divided according to their attractiveness as children aged 6 years. The images of the infants therefore look *back* in time, and the images of the adults look *forward* in time. Attractiveness was consistent across the whole period.
D. Buls & R.E. Cornwell (2008) Perception Lab.

For males, the situation was more complex: although facial masculinity tends to be stable from babyhood into adulthood (see Figure 8.3), facial attractiveness isn't. Boys who are considered to be attractive as babies are not necessarily considered to be attractive as adults, and vice versa. The relationship between facial masculinity and attractiveness varies across time: masculinity is unattractive in babies, as we've seen above, but this relationship diminishes in childhood and by age 21 the reverse is true, so that men with more masculine faces are considered to be more attractive (with the caveats noted in Chapter 5). As boys grow into men, masculinity in facial structure can denote power and dominance, which some women find attractive.

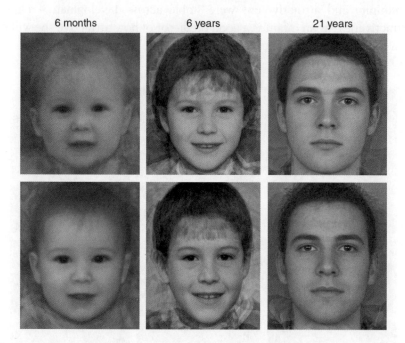

Figure 8.3 Ugly ducklings to swans: stability of male facial appearance during development. Composite images of babies at 6 months, children aged 6, and adults aged 21. One group of thirteen individuals contributes to the top trio of images; a second group of thirteen individuals contributes to the lower trio. The two groups of thirteen males were divided according to their facial masculinity as children aged 6 years. The group of masculine-looking boys turned into masculine-looking men; they were also perceived as masculine-looking babies. Conversely, the group of more feminine-looking boys turned into more feminine-looking men, and were seen as more feminine-looking babies. Masculinity detracted from the facial attractiveness of babies, but not from their facial attractiveness as men.
D. Buls & R.E. Cornwell (2008) Perception Lab.

So facial characteristics are steady over a large portion of life, but it is important to remember that even the most attractive children may go through an ugly stage. When milk teeth fall out, the gaps and growing teeth do not look good. Teenage acne, too, detracts from the beauty of those unfortunate enough to suffer it, so we're talking here about an overall pattern of consistency of looks, not necessarily month to month, or even year to year. There does appear to be stability in how we look over the first twenty years of life: masculine boys grow into masculine men, attractive girls grow into attractive women. It's true that 20 is still young, of course, and it's possible that face attributions change more radically over the rest of the lifespan, but since parents at 50 years of age share many facial characteristics with their offspring[41] (see Chapter 6), it's more likely that looking good is a durable trait. Indeed, it's amazing to think that facial traits can be so durable that already by 6 months of age one can tell so much about appearance way into adult life.

Like sand through the hourglass

Even quite young people can differ widely in how old they appear. When people were asked to estimate the age of university students, all of whom were aged between 21 and 23 years, the estimated age varied from 19 to 27. What is remarkable is that all these individuals had reached adulthood, yet some seemed to be living in the fast lane – they looked 33 per cent older than others who looked as though they were still shaking off puberty.[42]

To illustrate the differences in ageing quickly or slowly, one can blend together the faces of people who look young for their age and, separately, the faces of people who look older than their age. The average real age of each group is the same, yet facially there are clearly observable differences between them, as Figure 8.4 reveals. Although all the images show the faces of 22-year-olds, the faces on the left appear to be ageing slowly, while those on the right appear to be ageing quickly. As yet, it is not clear whether the entire ageing process is accelerated in the latter group or decelerated in the former.

While there are many environmental and genetic factors that affect ageing and fertility, women who start their periods early are likely to hit the menopause early too,[43] so it may be that those who look old for their age will live at a faster rate and die younger.[44] Figure 8.4 gives us some clues as to why this might be. Among women in their twenties, appearing old is associated with unhealthy looks. Later in life, looking young for your age can predict that you have more years left to live,[45] so perhaps slow facial ageing reflects a more robust and healthy constitution all round, which in turn may reflect a favourable environment or a 'lucky' genetic make-up.[46]

In the science of ageing, it is becoming increasingly clear that the best predictor of survival and longevity is not how many birthdays someone has clocked up but how old their body tissues are, in biological terms. Some animals have a fast heartbeat and a fast life-cycle, and reach old age in just a few years; others, like bowhead whales, may live for more than two centuries.[47] In humans, we can get a measure of biological age by combining measures of arthritis in bones (which increases with age) with bone-density measurements (which decline with age).[48] The estimate given by

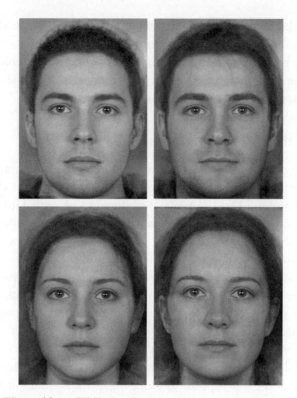

Figure 8.4 'How old am I?' For each image, can you estimate how old the face is? The answers may surprise you (see text).

M.L. Smith (2004) Perception Lab.

'true' biological age, calculated from a person's bones, is a much better predictor of how long that person will live than their chronological age. The rate of biological ageing appears partly genetic;[49] some people are just born to age at a faster rate.

One genetic disease, progeria, causes humans to age prematurely; life expectancy is a mere thirteen years.[50] A single gene mutation causes cells to divide much more quickly than normal, inducing baldness, wrinkles, and age-related diseases such as strokes at an age before that at which typically developing children have entered puberty. Fortunately, this tragic disease is extremely rare, affecting only 1 in 40 million people, but it serves to illustrate the point: different humans age at different rates.

One way of exploring any underlying biological differences that affect rates of ageing is by comparing identical twins (who developed from a single egg, and therefore have 100 per cent of their genes in common) and same-sex fraternal twins (who developed from separate eggs and sperm from the same parents, and who therefore share on average 50 per cent of their genes). Careful comparisons across these different sets of twins make it possible to detect which elements of ageing are determined by environmental and lifestyle factors, and which reflect a genetic predisposition. If identical twins are more alike than fraternal twins with respect to a given trait, this must reflect the influence of their shared genes.

Signs of ageing in the skin, such as wrinkles or pigmented spots, are found to be influenced by both genetic and environmental factors. Although some of us are lucky enough to inherit skin that is more naturally resistant to wrinkles, the rate at which our skin ages shows the strong effect of the kinds of environmental influences to which we are exposed; even the most wrinkle-resistant skin will age more rapidly if we choose to spend our lives as deep-sea fishermen, continually exposed to extremes of sun and wind. The impact of this environmental exposure is evident to different degrees at different stages in our lives. As children, the effects of sun damage are not very apparent, but by our late forties sun damage has begun to catch up, and time spent in the sun explains three-quarters of the variability in skin's age appearance between people of the same chronological age. Eventually all skin will show signs of ageing and, late in life, genetic factors will predominate in determining how old the skin looks.[51]

In contrast to the skin, greying hair and hair loss are influenced more strongly by inherited genetic factors, with identical twins showing more similarity than same-sex fraternal twins.[52] If your parents go grey, therefore, the chances are good (or bad, from most people's perspectives) that you too will develop grey hair, no matter what kind of lifestyle you have. Likewise, there is a strong genetic determination for male baldness:[53] if you're male and your dad or granddad went bald prematurely, then you too can expect an increasing need to wear something to keep your head warm.

Another biological factor that affects apparent age is gender. In studies in which we asked judges to guess the ages of faces, male students tended to look older than females, even when they were exactly the same age.[54] When the differences between male and female faces are enhanced, the effect alters how old the faces are judged to be. Making faces look more masculine *increases* perceived age, while feminization *decreases* the perceived age.[55] In Figure 8.4, the link between masculinity and older looks is quite striking.

Perhaps this association between maleness and older looks[56] should not be surprising – after all, men have a lower life expectancy than women. To some extent, this reflects the fact that men are more likely to engage in risky activities than women; many men do not die of natural causes, but

tead die in accidents resulting from activities like speeding. Even when
ch risky behaviour is taken into consideration, men still die younger
than women, which suggests that, biologically speaking, they may live
faster,[57] and so age faster, than women.

Ageing gracefully?

Our desire to be younger or older changes through life. To many children it seems unfair not to be allowed to do what their elder siblings
do, whether this is staying up late or getting to play the latest computer
game – more explicit in sex and violence than the last. In these circumstances, a younger sibling's strong desire is to be older and even to look
grown-up. Soon after adolescence, the reverse desire kicks in: everyone
dreads the appearance of grey hairs. We become jealous of peers whose
looks remain more youthful than our own.

At puberty, hormones surge and we see the development of sex differences typical of adults. These are as evident in the face as anywhere.
Metamorphosing almost as rapidly as a caterpillar into butterfly – though
without the resultant grace – a boy's face changes from the ages of 9 to 15,
as the bone structure forces his chin to broaden and elongate and his brow
ridge to thicken. Along with the structural transformation comes facial
hair, which begins to whisker out from between teenage spots, although a
full beard may not be in place until his late twenties. Androgens cause an
increase in growth of the hair follicles on the face, but paradoxically they
can slow growth on the scalp. There is extra hair on the face, but eventually there is less apparent on top.

Post-puberty, it's not that long before maturity turns to senescence. No
matter how healthy our lifestyle or how much we try to resist the ageing
process, we must all accept that eventually our faces will give away our
age through a variety of cues. Greying and the loss of hair are perhaps
the most obvious signs of ageing. During childhood and as young adults,
our hair cells contain melanin pigments which give our hair a range of
colours. The exact hue depends on the amount and type of melanin; one
version of melanin gives a reddish tinge, typical of the carrot-haired Scot,
a high concentration of another type produces the black colour typical
of Asian populations. In lower concentrations, this same type of melanin
produces the range of browns found across European populations, from
the dark browns of the southern Mediterranean countries to the natural
blonde of the Scandinavian countries. The melanin-producing cells derive
from stem cells at the base of each hair, and as we age the stem cells die
and the amount of melanin incorporated into our hair declines. The hair

turns grey and, when the pigment level drops to zero, white. The hair on different parts of our faces and bodies loses pigment at different rates, but if we live long enough the whole lot will eventually turn white.

Hair also changes shape as we age; we can easily see the difference by comparing successive generations, and not simply because older folk have got stuck on a hairstyle that has gone out of fashion. There are two types of biological change, with contrasting results. Melanin controls hair growth; with less melanin, individual hairs can grow thicker, more wiry, and less manageable. Hair thins, quite literally; each strand of hair becomes thinner, and growth is slower. A dwindling blood supply to the scalp brings less nourishment to the hair follicles, so their numbers decline and our hair also becomes less dense. This is most obvious in men, where the characteristic pattern of baldness follows the initially receding hairline.

Not only our hair changes colour and shape with age: so does our skin. The supply of blood to the lips declines as we age, with the result that the lips change from the bright red of youth to a pale pinkish colour, which may border on grey as we get really old. The changes in skin melanin across the lifespan are complex and depend a little on ethnicity. Among European adults our group found that between the ages of 20 and 55 the skin becomes more yellow and more dull (see Figure P, Plate VI). This suggests an increase in the levels of melanin as we age, but it might also reflect the fact that those in our older age group could afford more holidays in the sun.[58] In old age, melanin production in the skin declines in the same way as with our hair, so we can become much paler than youngsters. On the other hand, as our blood circulation becomes less efficient with age, our arteries can get clogged with cholesterol and this raises our blood pressure. Under some conditions this may increase the redness of the face.[59]

The hair changes; the skin changes; and so in time does the face itself. There is an inexorable change to the shape of the face and its features. Despite the fact that we may have put on weight elsewhere, ageing is associated with the loss of subcutaneous fat from our faces. The smoothness of young skin comes about not only from high levels of collagen and elastin, proteins that make up the skin's supporting structures, but also because the skin is plumped up with fat. As we lose this fat and elasticity from our skin, the skin hangs lower on our faces. Unlike the large eyes that are so characteristic of young children's faces, the eyes of an older person seem to shrink as they become partly covered by sagging skin above our upper eyelids. The jowls hang lower on the chin, and our lips become thinner, again because of the loss of underlying subcutaneous fat.

And that's not all. Another factor that gives away our age is the size of our ears and our noses. The cartilage in the nose and ears continues to grow throughout life, so ears get larger and noses get longer. Halloween masks reflect this; any self-respecting wizened witch or warlock must have a long pointy nose, possibly sprouting a few untameable hairs.

All of these visual changes in shape and colour can be captured in the way faces age on average (see Figure P, Plate VI). The changes can then be applied to an individual's current face image to project that person's face into the future – in this way our software can show people what they're likely to look like when they reach a particular age (see Figure K, Plate IV).

Wrinkles and age spots

By far the biggest changes as we age are those that take place in the texture of our skin, both in terms of the pigment distribution and in the three-dimensional surface structure. Many years of exposure to the UV component of sunlight causes the melanin pigment cells to clump, creating small areas of high melanin concentration within areas of less dense pigmentation. It is this uneven distribution that produces the 'liver spots' or 'age spots' so characteristic of older skin.

The reduction of skin elasticity with increasing years means that the skin we wear becomes stretched and, like an oversized garment, it hangs loose and puckers up. The creases, fine lines, and wrinkles induced by the expressions we make no longer disappear when our faces relax, and our predominant moods get etched into our face. As a kid you were probably warned not to pull a face in case the wind changed and your face got stuck. There is some truth in this warning; the wind shifts many times in a life, and those who frown frequently are likely to see furrows develop between their eyebrows, whereas those who smile often will have more 'smile lines' to look forward to.

Both the wrinkling and the unevenness of skin pigmentation can be captured in computer graphics in terms of local 'texture'.[60] For each place on the face, the average increase in lines, wrinkles, and age spots that occurs naturally with ageing can be defined as a specific kind of textural change. These changes can then be added to, or subtracted from, the appropriate face region. Figure 8.5 uses computer graphics to show how the texture of the skin may become modified locally. In these images, the skin around the eyes has been processed to show how this area would appear if the skin were subjected to more or less sun damage over time – perhaps seeing such images might motivate people to use more sun protection.

The average textural changes that occur with ageing can be combined with the shape and colour changes to produce a more accurate simulation of how the march of time affects a face (Figure Q, top row: Plate VI).

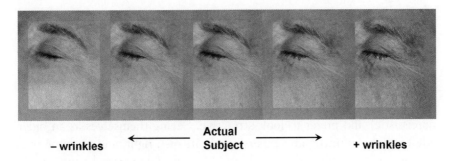

– wrinkles   **Actual Subject**   **+ wrinkles**

Figure 8.5 Sun-damage to the skin. *Centre*: The person's actual appearance. *Left*: How her skin might have looked had she kept out of the sun or used sun blocks to prevent UV damage. *Right*: Simulated images of the ageing process or high levels of sun damage.

S.S. Hawkins *et al.* (2002).

Alternatively, the age-related local textures can be removed to rejuvenate a complexion (Figure Q, bottom row). These texture cues are perhaps the most important cues to age, as just simulating colour and shape changes with age is not wholly convincing. When we attempt to age the image of a 10-year-old boy (Figure Q, top left) fifty years by adding the appropriate colour and shape changes (top middle), his face still looks unnaturally young for a 60-year-old. It is only when the additional skin wrinkles are included in the simulation that his face looks old enough (top right). Similarly, when the face of a 55-year-old woman (bottom left) is transformed in overall shape and colour to reconstruct her appearance thirty years earlier (bottom middle), she looks almost unchanged in age. It is only when the skin texture is reset to that typical of a woman thirty years younger (bottom right) that you can believe she is a younger woman.

The perils of smoking

Exposure to sunlight causes skin to age at an accelerated rate: so does exposure to smoke.[61] Indeed a life spent smoking produces an acceleration of the ageing process by about 15 per cent. The UK government has taken quite drastic action to discourage smoking. First, each packet contains a warning that could not be more frank than the Grim Reaper puffing away or a skull with crossed cigarettes: the warning message reads simply 'Smoking Kills', without the subtext that it also makes money for tobacco companies. Next the government has banned smoking in public places. Whatever the message, though, the campaign isn't going well; more Scottish teenagers are taking up the habit than in previous years, and now about one in three of them smoke.[62] One avenue of persuasion that can be followed is to appeal not to reason but to vanity. With our software we can show young people how they will appear in early adulthood, should they keep to the straight and narrow 'healthy lifestyle' of avoiding the nicotine habit, and then we can show them the likely results of a lifestyle that includes smoke. We assume that individuals are self-interested (even if not narcissistic) and prefer to look attractive. Seeing themselves as an older adult may be an intriguing experience in its own right, and we hope that seeing the extra ageing that would result from smoking may be sufficiently off-putting to change their attitudes and behaviour (Figure R, Plate VII).

Cosmetic surgery

These days, collagen fillers injected directly into the skin can be used to plump up one's face and to fill out the lines and wrinkles. This has the effect of moving the face at the base of Figure Q (Plate VI) from the centre to the right. The increased use of collagen fillers by cosmetic surgeons is a smart move, as this effectively mimics the natural state of affairs in women who are ageing well. The more traditional approach, the face-lift, stretches the skin more tightly over the face; it removes wrinkles but doesn't replenish the loss of subcutaneous fat. Check out Hollywood and TV stars to see this for yourself – no-one these days has the 'wind-tunnel' look of the classic face-lift. Instead, their faces look pushed out, thanks to all the artificial 'fat' injected into them.

Collagen fillers can also be injected into the lips, to make them fuller. Again this is a way to combat the signs of age, but it must be done very carefully in order to avoid the dreaded 'trout pout' – too much collagen filler can over-inflate the lips and lead to a bloated, rather fish-like appearance (see Figure 8.6; and this result is also reminiscent of the hagfish in Figure 1.1). This is due to the distortion of the lips' natural proportions. Our lower lip is generally around 1.5 times bigger than our upper lip, whereas over-enthusiastic collagen injections can inflate the upper lip to the same size as the lower one, distorting the shape of the cupid's bow so that the upper lip lacks its natural contours. While this can smooth out any fine lines around the lips, the overall effect, if overdone, is disturbing rather than attractive.

You're as young as your oldest part

So, which of the signs of ageing is the most telling? What is it that gives our age away without fail? As with judgements about the sex of a face,[63] judgements of age can be made from just about any face region: the eyes,

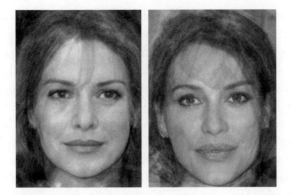

Figure 8.6 'Trout pout' This figure displays the effects of collagen implants to plump up the lips. *Left*: A composite of the faces of models. *Right*: A composite of models' faces after suspected collagen implants. If too much collagen is injected into the upper lip, it becomes disturbingly large and thus more fish-like.

D.I. Perrett (2008) Perception Lab.

the mouth, the cheeks, or the hair. When we look at a face to work out how old someone is, we could do some mental maths and take the average age of all the indicators, like this: 'Face shape looks 50, skin ... pretty good condition, say 40, hair ... hmm ... more like 60; all told I guess 50.' In fact we don't do this; when it comes to weighing up evidence from different cues, what we do is much less complicated: we simply focus on the oldest-looking part of the face!

One way to show this is to compare how people's perception of age varies when we transform images so that we have a younger woman's face combined with an older woman's hair, and vice versa (Figure S, Plate VII). Putting young hair on an older face did not shift the person's perceived age downward: the perceived age was maintained more or less unchanged from that of the original face with its age-appropriate hair. The offensive expression 'mutton dressed as lamb' seems pertinent; the young hairdo did not rejuvenate the overall impression of the older woman. Conversely, an old hairdo made even young women look old. The general rule emerging from our research is that in working out the age of a person, we are most swayed by the cue that gives the oldest estimate. For the face to look young, therefore, *all* of the facial cues must suggest youth. If any one part looks older than the rest, we pick up on this and ignore the parts that are wearing well.

Postscript

There is no magic formula that provides a foolproof means to ageing well. Many solutions to the ageing 'problem' have obvious pitfalls, one being the aberrations of cosmetic-surgery accidents. As we have seen, the speed of ageing is partly determined by our genes. There are some tips that really will help you age well, such as staying out of the sun, keeping healthy, and not smoking. Ideally, you should choose to be the child of parents who haven't gone grey and are fairly wrinkle-resistant, and of course you should lead a stress-free life, but sadly these are tall orders. Given what has been covered in this chapter, it may seem that there is little to look forward to in old age. There is one small consolation, perhaps – our sweat glands don't work as well as we get older, so we don't sweat as much, and as a result our body odour is better than that of younger adults.

The trick, though, is to grow old gracefully. Instead of spending vast amounts on surgery or cosmetics, trying to preserve what has gone and would now look out of place anyway, we can remember that what matters most may not be facial features but our personality and character. Maybe we can't 'keep young and beautiful', as the song advised us, but we can still be loved for who we are. And how our character relates to our face is the subject of the next chapter.

Chapter 9

FACES WITH ATTITUDE

How the personality we seek in a partner guides our face tastes

As we move from infancy to adulthood, we develop a sense of *self*. This is easy to say, of course, but what does it really mean? If asked, we'd probably answer that it had something to do with what we are like as a person: our likes and dislikes, and whether we are calm or anxious, cheerful or grumpy, a party animal or the quiet type. Interestingly, we only rarely attribute our sense of self to our physical appearance. We tend to think of our 'self' as what we are on the *inside*, not the outside. Yet this is an oversight: in reality, our sense of self is strongly linked to our physical body, and in particular to our face. 'The face is the soul of the body', is a quote attributed to Ludwig Wittgenstein,[1] and certainly the face is the means by which we connect to and communicate with other people, so how we 'see' ourselves is often a reflection of how others see and respond to us. Our facial appearance and our expressions offer others clues about how we are feeling and how we are likely to act – and we use their faces in the same way.

A basic connection to other people is made via facial expressions. In his book *About Face*,[2] the neurologist Jonathan Cole talks to people who, in one way or another, have suffered some kind of facial loss – an inability to make expressions, an inability to recognize the expressions of others, or the loss of a normal facial appearance. He explores what this means for their sense of self, and reveals the importance of the control of the face both to the social and to the emotional aspects of our being. Cole was first drawn to the subject by a neurological patient, Mary, who had gradually lost the ability to speak or to form facial expressions. Her story of how she had come to feel diminished – 'as a person, as a being, as *her*' – because she could no longer relate to people through and with her face is both moving and eye-opening. As Cole says (page 2), 'She brought into question for me the relation between a person's face and his or her personality and self, a relationship so fundamental and 'given' that I had never previously doubted it or even thought about it'. If you *do* think about it, you recognize the truth of what Mary's condition reveals about us, and how we 'live' by means of our faces and the faces of other people.

If this is true, then, does it mean that it's possible to tell what a person is like just by looking at their face? Is our character and personality somehow etched into our appearance in ways that are visible to others? Our behaviour suggests that we believe this to be so. If you're lost, you need to decide who to approach for directions; if you're at a party where everyone is a stranger to you, you need to decide who to talk to; when you get onto a bus or a subway train, you need to decide who to sit next to. How do you choose? We all use physical appearance as a guide to other people's personalities and their likely behaviour, and while clothes and hairstyles undoubtedly contribute to this assessment, our decisions about whether someone looks trustworthy or shifty, kind or unfriendly, rests in large part on what we see in their faces.

The problem here is that we have no way of knowing whether our assessments are *accurate* – someone who looks haughty or aloof may in fact be the friendliest, most helpful person one could hope to meet. If we avoid talking to such a person because of a snap judgement based on their face, we may never find this out. And we won't just miss out on getting to know that particular person: mistaking our own faulty assessment of what the person is like for a correct insight into their true nature, we will prob-ably perpetuate our error in future, similarly misjudging others who share the same characteristics. Consensus won't help, either; even if a whole bunch of people agree on what kind of face goes with a particular per-sonality trait, that level of agreement still isn't evidence that face-reading works – *all* of those judgements could be wrong.

So there are two issues that are interesting to explore. First, how accu-rate are the assessments of personality that we make on the basis of facial appearance – can we really identify personality traits from appearance alone? Secondly, regardless of how accurate our judgements are, what exactly is it about a person's face that leads us to think she or he is kind, or outgoing, or generous? What cues are we picking up on, and why those? And even before we address those two questions, we must first define what we mean by 'personality'.

What is personality?

At the heart of personality research is a thorny issue: do people express themselves consistently no matter what happens, or do they behave in different ways according to the situation? Some people have argued that very little of our behaviour (about 10 per cent only) can be predicted by tests of *personality*,[3] and that to foresee how a person will behave one needs also to consider the *situation*. You may be irritable in a traffic jam, for example, yet patient with the children at home. On this view, we act like chameleons: we change our colours to blend in with different people and different circumstances.

Perhaps any inconsistency between tests and actual behaviour reflects a failure to measure the relevant personality trait. People may differ in how much they seek social approval, and therefore they may also differ in how much they attempt to adapt to situations – if so, people who continually try to fit in will show variable behaviour across events and will appear to have inconsistent personalities. Despite this, the very *desire to fit in* could itself be a stable trait.

While personality may not explain why a person behaves in a particular way in a one-off situation, it does predict how a person will respond *on average*. If you are an optimistic person, for example, this stable aspect of your personality will make it possible to predict quite accurately how happy you are likely to be *in general* over the next year or so, even though it will not be possible to predict very accurately how happy you will be today. (Maybe your cat was sick over your shoes, you broke your favourite coffee mug, and you missed your bus – even the most optimistic person might feel a bit down after all that.)

If we accept that personality is 'real', another pressing question arises: how can we measure it? Francis Galton, a cousin of Charles Darwin, suggested that we could look to our everyday language for clues. Specifically, he suggested that the most obvious differences between people in their actions and demeanour would gradually become incorporated into language: if we examined *how* we speak about others, we should be able to pick out descriptions that represent stable personality traits.[4] Following Galton's insight, both early and modern personality tests often consist of simple lists of adjectives used to label dispositions and behaviour. People are asked to rate themselves on how strongly each adjective applies to them. In their answers one finds clusters of related adjectives describing similar traits. For example, if a person says that she is 'warm', she is likely also to describe herself as 'sociable' and 'friendly', but she might give herself a low score when it came to adjectives such as 'quiet', 'reserved', and 'unemotional'. This particular combination of responses epitomizes one trait: extroversion.[5]

From such tests the so-called 'Big Five' model was developed,[6] whereby the differences between people are distilled into five personality dimensions. These are *extroversion* (which includes descriptions such as 'sociable', 'outgoing', and 'energetic'), *emotional stability* (which includes descriptions such as 'secure' and 'relaxed'), *agreeableness* ('cooperative', 'sympathetic', 'kind', 'warm-hearted'), *conscientiousness* ('organized', 'careful', 'self-disciplined') and *openness to experience* ('arty', 'imaginative', 'curious', 'adventurous'). The different dimensions are independent, so scoring high or low on one dimension says nothing about one's score on the other four dimensions – an extrovert, for example, might be emotionally stable and relaxed or the opposite, emotionally unstable and anxious.

The same Big Five personality dimensions tend to emerge irrespective of culture and language, and there is good agreement about a person's traits, whether assessed by themselves or from the judgements of others who know the person well, so this particular personality assessment has some street credibility.[7] The private side of people, such as their sense of humour, is not captured by the Big Five, but as what we're interested in is the extent to which personality is evident in *faces*, the Big Five's emphasis on the public aspects of personality fits our need.

A brief history of face-reading

This idea that a person's personality and character can be read from their facial features has its origins among the Ancient Greeks, and the practice of reading faces is known as 'physiognomy'. Aristotle is usually credited as the author of a lengthy work on physiognomy, in which he pointed out, among other things, that men with large ears that stuck out were given to chattering, while those with narrow foreheads were fickle. In many cases, comparisons were made with other animals: 'persons with hooked noses are ferocious; witness hawks'. As often as not, though, the traits attributed to the animals had themselves derived originally from comparisons with humans and were now being projected back onto them again. A haughty-looking camel looking down its nose, for example, was probably first described in that way because the camel reminded someone of a haughty human looking down his or her nose. Standing tall with an uplifted face seems to be an innate expression of pride at winning conflicts – an expression that may extend across the animal kingdom.[8]

In Europe during the Middle Ages, physiognomy was considered to be an art possessed by a skilled few. It was accepted as a perfectly valid means of assessing character, and it was even taught at university, along with palm-reading, until it was banned by Henry VIII. Despite this royal seal of disapproval, physiognomy did not die and reached a new high point toward the end of the eighteenth century, due largely to a substantial work[9] called *Essays on Physiognomy* by Johann Lavater, a Swiss pastor, in which he attempted to describe systematically in no fewer than four volumes the correspondences between facial features and personality traits. His system was highly judgemental, seeing perfection in a facial feature as indicating perfection in the related quality of character. Similarly, a flawed face indicated an equally flawed character. These writings became so popular and influential that it is said that people went about the streets wearing masks, so fearful were they of having their faces appraised by others. In the early nineteenth century, Alexander Walker, a Scottish lecturer in anatomy and physiology, extended Lavater's work by explaining why certain features should be linked to certain traits.[10] Lips, for example, were sensitive to touch and were linked to the tongue, so they could be seen as indicators of a person's tastes and desires – thin lips meant little taste and fewer desires, while full lips meant the opposite.

During the 1860s, novelists began using these physiognomic conventions to describe the characters in their books, particularly the heroines. Because the conventional associations were by now well known, authors could *hint* at a certain raciness in their female characters (full lips, a large mouth) without needing to be so vulgar as to spell out details; and by giving their heroines irregular, imperfect features, they could reshape gentle, innocent, truthful, idealized female characters into more realistic human beings who were understood to engage in more unconventional conduct.[11] The interest and popularity of physiognomy among the reading public ensured that authors could rely on their readers to decode the meaning of a strong chin or an aquiline nose (hooked like an eagle's beak, and therefore usually indicating a strong will and independence). Charlotte Brontë, in particular, makes full use of physiognomic conventions to portray her unconventional heroines, including Jane Eyre. Jane says of herself: 'I sometimes wished to have rosy cheeks, a straight nose and small cherry mouth; I desired to be tall, stately, and finely developed in figure; I felt it a misfortune that I was so little, so pale, and had features so irregular and so marked.' Brontë also uses physiognomy to good effect when describing less sympathetic characters, such as Mr Mason: 'he repelled me exceedingly: there was no power in that smooth-skinned face of a full oval shape: no firmness in that aquiline nose and small cherry mouth; there was no thought on the low, even forehead; no command in that blank, brown eye'.

The increased interest in physiognomy that occurred during the 1860s was itself a consequence of the invention of the camera around ten years earlier. Having now a reliable method of recording people's faces accurately, and thus a means of making finely detailed comparisons between them, practitioners of physiognomy began to consider their art to be a truly scientific endeavour. One area of particular interest was in trying to identify whether various kinds of anti-social behaviour could be predicted from facial appearance. Francis Galton was very interested in this question and developed an innovative and ingenious method of composite photography to test it.[12] In face-perception research today our group and others still use essentially the same method, albeit in a rather more sophisticated form that befits the more sophisticated computer-based technology we now have at our disposal.

To try to identify features associated with felonious behaviour, Galton would take a series of photographs of individual faces and then expose each of them in turn onto a second photographic plate. The overlapping of all the faces on a single plate resulted in a 'blended' image, in which the common characteristics possessed by most of the faces were brought out, and the highly idiosyncratic features of individual faces tended to vanish. In effect, Galton was attempting to construct facial 'prototypes' of different kinds of criminals, often focusing on a highly specific kind of criminality. Figure 9.1, for example, shows Galton's composite of four individuals who had engaged in theft without violence.

Figure 9.1 Galton's composite photographs. Each photograph combined between four and eight criminal faces.
F. Galton (1883).

Galton found that as the number of images of different individuals was increased, so his composite portrait tended to become more 'average'-looking – and, indeed, more attractive. As Figure 9.1 shows, while four components result in quite a mean and shifty-looking portrait, with seven components we see a blandly average, not unpleasant face. This was true for all the different kinds of criminality Galton compared, which made it impossible to identify any particular facial feature that could be associated with any particular crime. While the averageness that Galton identified had implications for theories of facial attractiveness (see Chapter 4), his method was of no use at all in identifying criminals. This is probably because criminality isn't a consistent personality trait; people can end up becoming criminals for a variety of reasons – and this was probably even truer in Galton's time, when the absence of any kind of welfare state led many people to engage in theft just to hold body and soul together. There is no reason, therefore, to believe that particular facial features should be associated with particular kinds of crime, although our own recent research does link robustness in men's faces to a tendency to exploit the trust of others for personal gain.[13]

This more or less sums up the problem with physiognomy: no one had a good theory to explain why the size of people's noses, the shape of their eyebrows, or the fullness of their lips should indicate how energetic and determined they were. The reasoning was simply based on intuitions that the size of one's forehead must reflect something about one's brain and intelligence, but without any scientific evidence to show whether this was in fact the case.

Physiognomy's reputation wasn't helped by the fact that many of those who practised it were charlatans and fraudsters, motivated only by a commercial interest in relieving the gullible of their cash. Ever more outlandish pronouncements about what faces could reveal were the order of the day – puffy cheeks, for example, were thought to show the trait of 'aquasorbitiveness', a 'love for water'. Even more damning, from a scientific perspective, was that when people did begin to investigate the links between the specific shape of facial features and their owner's personality, they found very little evidence that facial features mapped onto personality traits.

By the early 1920s, one study was forced to conclude that 'the physical factors purporting to measure the same trait do not present even a suspicion of agreement ... the correlation between ratings of casual observers and physical measurements is best represented by 0.000'.[14] In other words, no two facial features that were supposed to indicate the same personality trait could be consistently related to one another or to the opinion of observers. To be even more blunt, classic physiognomic claims simply didn't hold water. Having by now acquired a reputation for being nothing more than pseudoscience, physiognomy fell out of fashion.

Why physiognomy won't fade away

Despite this history, the idea that a person's looks can indeed reveal something about his or her personality persists. When asked whether it is possible to know an individual's true personality from his or her face, up to 75 per cent of people say 'yes'.[15]

In rejecting the discredited art of physiognomy, we may have thrown the baby out with the bathwater. Consider a parallel: the medieval 'doctrine of signatures' contended that one could recognize a plant's suitability for treating a particular ailment by noting the similarity in looks between the plant and the organ to be treated – hence the names given to liverwort, toothwort, bloodroot, and lungwort. Even if we now reject this early herbalist theory of God-given signatures, we must still acknowledge that plants do contain powerful medicines, even though the medicinal plants and the organs they are useful in treating may be unrelated in form. Similarly, the theory and claims of physiognomy may be wrong, yet there might still be cues to personality in the face. A 1920s study disproving the validity of physiognomists' assertions[16] nevertheless showed substantial agreement between observers in their judgements about what an individual's personality was like, given his or her appearance, and between their ratings and the ratings of close acquaintances of the people being rated. As the observers were not personally known to the subjects they could not have witnessed the individuals' behaviour, so their accurate ratings must have been based on *some* visible features, even if those weren't the ones highlighted by the physiognomists.

In modern times, judgements of competence made from politicians' faces have accurately predicted US congressional election outcomes. In about 70 per cent of the Senate races in 2004, the candidate who won was the person judged to look most 'competent'.[17] As interesting as this seems, it's also inconclusive: the problem here is that although we may all vote for someone who *looks* competent, that doesn't mean that the person actually *is* competent (as is painfully obvious from monitoring certain politicians' careers) – it's possible that widespread agreement about who looks competent simply reflects widespread but still mistaken impressions of how faces relate to personality. More convincing evidence appeared when people were asked to make judgements about the faces of male chief executives (CEOs):[18] those CEOs who were rated as more competent, more dominant, and more mature also proved more likely to run successful companies with higher profits, suggesting that observers really can pick up some aspect of true competence. Even here, though, it is possible to question the interpretation: it might just be that the more successful companies can afford better photographers who are more effective at capturing in their portraits the dominant appearances of the CEOs. Alternatively, it could be that, when all other skills are equal, wealthier companies are able to outbid other companies for those who look the part.

Even so, there are now a number of studies that demonstrate the accuracy of our perceptions of others at 'zero-acquaintance'. For example, when people are asked to assess the personalities of strangers from photographs, video clips, or short face-to-face interactions in groups, the observers' assessments agree with the self-assessments made by the individuals.[19] Agreement is seen even when the study asks observers to compare across quite disparate cultures: Americans judging Chinese people's faces attribute the same personality traits to those faces as do other Chinese people, and the same is true when Chinese people judge American faces.[20]

In many such studies, cues other than the face can also be used to infer personality – an extrovert may be more likely than an introvert to wear flamboyant clothes or an attention-grabbing hairstyle, and she or he may speak more loudly and more often. So can we trust our observations and inferences from faces or not?

A kernel of truth?

It seems that there may be something to physiognomy after all, if we look at it in the right way. Although it is clear that particular features, like a big nose or thin lips, do not map directly and neatly onto specific personality traits, it does seem possible that we learn to associate certain kinds of looks with certain kinds of behaviour. Via self-fulfilling prophecies and our expectations, we may have amplified some of these associations in the first place.

There are many sources of information to give clues to our tendencies. A glance at our bedroom – how tidy it is and what we leave around – accurately spells out our personality along many dimensions.[21] This raises the question of whether the face alone, in the absence of other features such as clothes and hairstyles that influence our assessments of one another, is sufficient to provide cues to personality.

It seems that the answer to this question is a tentative yes. For both men's and women's faces, people can tell the difference between composite, blended images of extroverts and of introverts. See whether you can do this yourself – which of the faces in Figure 9.2 would you say belonged to an extrovert and which to an introvert? (The answers are given in the notes.[22]) If you found it hard to distinguish these, this may reflect well on your own personality (see later). How warm and generous a person is can also be detected from facial cues alone, and there is evidence that other personality dimensions, such as how emotionally stable or how anxious and neurotic a person is, can be read from the face too.

When all the idiosyncrasies have been blended away by the composite process, there do seem to be some common cues in a face that allow us to detect whether someone is more likely to enjoy dancing on a table-top or staying at home quietly watching a video.[23] If people are asked to judge photographs of real individual faces rather than composite blends, the same kinds of effects are found.

Other intriguing behavioural dispositions can be picked up from faces. One interesting finding is that facial appearance gives away cues to our sex life – or at least cues to our *attitude* toward sexual relations.[24] From the face alone, others can make a good guess at whether we prefer sexual relations only in the context of long-term loving relationships or whether

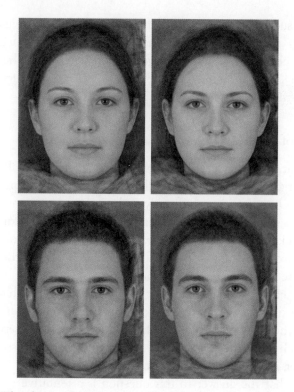

Figure 9.2 The faces of introverts and extroverts. Two introverts and two extroverts – but which is which?
I.S. Penton-Voak *et al.* (2006).

we are open to short-term sexual encounters without the necessity of love. For shorthand, we can label these two groups as 'devoted lovers' and 'no-strings people'. Photographs of people who had already self-rated themselves as a devoted lover or a no-strings person were shown to strangers who were asked to identify which sexual practice each person was likely to follow. Generally speaking, people could identify the two types of men and women both from real faces and from composite face images (Figure 9.3), although women were better at doing this than men. Women were particularly good at identifying the sexual practice of other women (although it is not obvious why women should benefit more than men from awareness of their rivals' sexual reputation).

Personality giveaways

So – how's it done? What *are* the cues in our faces that give away personality? One possibility is that we use the *overall attractiveness* of a face as a

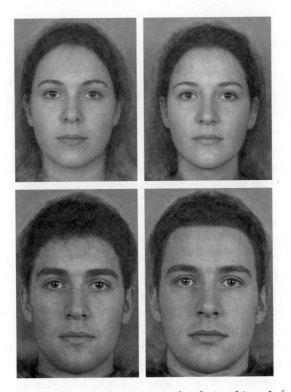

Figure 9.3 Faces reveal attitudes to sexual relationships. *Left*: Composite faces of people who contemplate sex only in the context of long-term loving relationships ('devoted lovers'). *Right*: Composite faces of people who are more likely to contemplate short-term sexual relationships ('no-strings people').

L.G. Boothroyd *et al.* (2008).

cue to certain socially desirable personality traits; this would be the same kind of 'halo effect' that causes us to think that good-looking people are smart. Socially, some personality traits are favoured over others: in general there is a preference for people who are extrovert, conscientious, open to experience, agreeable, and emotionally stable.[25] We tested the association between such personality traits and facial attractiveness and sure enough, the association existed – the faces of individuals who had these traits were judged to be more attractive than those who were lower on these traits.[26] It therefore seems likely that when we are drawn to someone's appearance, we use a simple stereotype – 'Whatever is beautiful is good' – to infer that the person *has* these desirable traits. And, as the faces that were judged more attractive belonged to individuals who actually *did* display these personality traits, it seems that such a stereotype does indeed provide a serviceable rule of thumb. Note that the relationship is only approximate – plenty of people who are not judged attractive are known for their extroversion, and many attractive people are shy. What is even more interesting is that people can still recognize who is more agreeable or more extrovert when confronted with images of people who are equally attractive or equally unattractive.[27] This ability shows that when we judge personality we're picking on something more than a face's simple aesthetic appeal – but what this is remains to be determined.

Another possible cue to particular personality traits is facial masculinity. In women, high levels of facial masculinity are associated with emotional stability. In men, facial masculinity is associated with traits such as dominance and assertiveness. Male faces that are low on masculinity, by contrast, are seen as more 'warm, kind and agreeable'.[28]

Along the same lines, recognition of a person's sexual strategy seems to be based on a cue of attractiveness as well: the faces of 'no-strings' women were judged to be more attractive than those of 'devoted' women, suggesting that their openness to short-term sexual relationships might stem from their having had more admirers and experienced more sexual opportunities, experiences that may have led them to develop more of a 'no-strings' outlook on relationships. Men preferred the looks of 'no-strings' women, not only as potential long-term partners but also in the short term. By contrast, women showed a marked preference for the facial characteristics of 'devoted' men as potential partners in long-term relationships. Interestingly, male 'no-strings' faces were often judged to be more masculine than those of 'devoted' lovers,[29] which fits with the findings (described in Chapter 5) that more mature-faced, masculine-looking males become sexually active at a younger age and report more sexual partners. (There are other possible explanations for why masculine men might have more sexual partners – see Chapter 5.)

Small kernel of truth

One shouldn't get too carried away with these results. While people's accuracy at judging personality from faces is better than chance, it is very far from perfect. The average accuracy in identifying extroverts' faces is only around 60 per cent – one would expect 50 per cent correct by chance alone – and not all of the so-called Big Five personality traits can be detected in faces. The kernel of truth is a very small one: there really is no need for us to go about wearing masks for fear that our faces will betray us.

There are also differences in how well people can detect personality in faces. Some people are excellent at reading faces, getting over 90 per cent correct when shown a series of extrovert–introvert pairs, while other people do no better than chance. Interestingly, extroverts are good judges of the same trait in others. This isn't so surprising, perhaps, as outgoing social types are likely to have had a lot of social experience and therefore plenty of opportunities to associate particular kinds of looks with particular kinds of behaviour. More surprisingly, warm-hearted and generous people are very poor judges of personality in faces – the best judges are those who report themselves to be somewhat cold-hearted and callous. One might have expected that warm-hearted people, who are generally more empathic and socially sensitive, would show greater accuracy, but perhaps their greater compassion means that they treat all people alike and it doesn't occur to them to assess whether people deserve such generosity. It seems that it's the more Machiavellian types who have honed their face-reading skills, perhaps because in order to exploit others they have learned to detect those of whom they can take advantage – namely, the warm-hearted and generous. Alternatively, a harsh environment may have taught them to be savvy to protect themselves from being exploited by others.

Agreement between self-reports and personality judgements by others could reflect a 'self-fulfilling prophecy'. One reason why people might assess themselves as extroverts is that that is how other people have always treated them – if people have always bounded up to them, friendly and enthusiastic, responding to the fact that they *look* approachable, friendly, and fun, they themselves may have learned to respond in kind, and so developed the characteristics of an extrovert in consequence. Whoever we are, other people's responses to our faces will certainly shape how our personalities grow.

Developing personalities

When do our personalities first begin to reveal themselves? And how could a self-fulfilling prophecy begin its influence? The answer to the first question seems to be almost as soon as we're born. Babies tested at four months of age for their response to colourful new toys showed distinct patterns of behaviour. Some babies didn't like the toys and leaned away from them, seemingly nervous and afraid. Other babies responded calmly and were interested in exploring the toys. In long-term studies those babies who didn't like the toys tended to grow into eleven-year-olds who were shy with interviewers, whereas babies who remained calm when presented new toys were more likely to be composed and sociable in their pre-teens.[30] The fact that patterns like these are so stable across childhood suggests that our temperament or personality may have a genetic component.

In line with this identical twins, who share all of their genes in common, are much more likely to share personality traits than non-identical twins. It's important to note that not *all* babies who were frightened by novel toys grew up to be shy, nor did those who were calm *always* grow up to be sociable; by most estimates from twin studies, genes account for about 50 per cent of personality, which implies that experience plays an equal role.[31] It is guesswork, but quite plausible, to suppose that the changes that occurred during development occurred because children learned from their parents' attitudes: it's likely that some anxious babies had parents who managed to keep them calm and to help them overcome their aversion to new things, while some bolder babies had parents whose over-protective responses encouraged the baby to feel that new things were to be avoided.

In interpreting infant behaviour, it's important to be aware of parents' expectations. Some adults were shown a video of a baby being surprised by a jack-in-a-box toy and bursting into tears, and they were then asked how the baby felt.[32] Some subjects were told that the baby was a boy, and some that the baby was a girl. Those told that the baby was a boy were more likely to say that he was 'angry', whereas those told the baby was a girl were more likely to say that she was 'afraid': the adults' expectations about how boys and girls would (or should) behave shaped their interpretations of the baby's behaviour. Even if we avoid the most obvious stereotyping – dressing our daughters in pink and giving them dolls to play with, while dressing our sons in blue and giving them toy trucks to play with – we may still unwittingly encourage our children to behave in gender-specific ways. This raises the very interesting question of whether *our looks alone* might influence the development of our personalities along gender-specific lines. A bit far-fetched? Well, read on ....

Let's consider masculinity in faces as an example. Masculinity is visible in our faces from the first year of life, and babies who look more masculine are perceived as less attractive and also as needing less care (Chapter 8). Masculinity in faces remains stable over time, so a masculine-looking baby boy grows into a masculine-looking seven-year-old, who then grows into a masculine-looking man (Chapter 8).

Now, imagine a baby boy whose genes predispose him to produce high levels of testosterone or who is unusually sensitive to the effects of testosterone. During the sixth month of his mother's pregnancy, this baby, like all baby boys, will produce a surge of testosterone, but in his case it will have a greater effect, including its effect on his face. When he is born, he will look both less cute and a little older than his age. The responses he gets from Mum, Dad, family, and friends are likely in consequence to be slightly less warm and friendly than they would be towards a baby whose appearance was more engaging, and they won't feel the same urge to pick him up and cuddle him as frequently as they might have felt if they had thought he was a real cutie-pie. They may not indulge in as much 'baby talk', either, as his looks will encourage people to treat him as though he were more mature. In these circumstances, archetypically masculine traits, such as independ-ence and self-reliance, are now being encouraged without anyone noticing that that's what's happening. So masculine-looking babies may evoke adult reactions that are likely to lead to mannish behaviour and a mannish per-sonality in the future.

Our ability to deduce aspects of people's personalities from their facial characteristics no longer seems quite so surprising: from the earliest weeks and months of life, the way in which we treat others ensures that they tend to develop precisely those traits that seem to match their faces!

Other ways to get the face you deserve

Self-fulfilling prophecies, in which behaviour comes to fit the face, needn't be the whole story. It is likely that the reverse is true as well: some aspects of our personalities may become reflected in our faces over time because of the expressions we habitually pull. People who are irritable most of the time, for example, tend to tense up their facial muscles in a way that produces distinctive skin creases. By the time we reach old age, our pre-dominant expressions will have been permanently etched with the pattern of lines and wrinkles acquired over a lifetime. As George Orwell said, 'at 50 everyone has the face he deserves',[33] and it is true, for instance, that older people with a history of hostility may look angry even when they try to maintain a neutral expression.[34]

Another possibility is that there is a common biological link between certain personality traits and certain facial characteristics. High testoster-one is associated with domineering and assertive behaviour, and is known to produce masculine-looking facial features (such as prominent eye brow ridges – see Chapter 5). Work on differences in face shape in males and females has revealed that people are very ready to ascribe a swathe of unpleasant personality traits to masculine faces, including coldness and dishonesty.[35] Given links like this, it becomes a simple matter to learn the associations between certain kinds of looks and certain kinds of behaviour, which we can then use to make predictions about someone's personality.

Looking smart

The potential problem in making predictions based on associations between facial characteristics and personality is that such associations will never be perfectly reliable. Not everyone who looks masculine, whether male or female, is domineering. Sometimes we may over-generalize, mistakenly attributing certain personality traits to individuals because of their looks, when our associations do not accurately reflect reality.

Most of us show just this over-generalization when it comes to intelligence. As noted before, there is a tendency to assume that attractive people are brighter than they are and that unattractive people are not so smart.[36] There are several developmental disorders that are likely to reduce intelligence and do indeed have an effect on facial appearance; foetal alcohol syndrome and Down's syndrome, for example, both tend to produce widely spaced eyes and a flattened bridge to the nose.[37] These unusual facial features are, in general, found less attractive (largely because they are out of the ordinary;[38] the 'shock of the new', see Chapter 4). From this type of association there can be a tendency to surmise that anyone with the same unusual features face has low intelligence. While it is true that there is a limited relationship between unattractive looks and low IQ, presumptions may go way beyond the actual evidence. We would be quite wrong to suppose that anyone whose face we find unattractive is unintelligent, just as we would be wrong to suppose that anyone we personally find attractive is smart. For people of average or better-than-average looks, there is no relationship between how *attractive* a person is and how *brainy* he or she is[39] – our preconceptions may simply give attractive people a rather unfair advantage.

There are other factors at play in how people rate intelligence. In one study, our lab found that certain facial characteristics caused female students to be perceived as intelligent both in Japan and in the UK. In this case, the cue to ascribing intelligence seemed to be based on the associations people make between intellect and alertness: girls who looked sleepy in their photographs were thought to be unintelligent, whereas those who looked alert and attentive were thought to be smart.[40] Such an association does make sense: if someone who is supposed to be listening to you glazes over (or, worse still, starts snoring), then there is little chance that she or he will have caught what you said and be able to make an insightful comment, and you are likely to judge the person accordingly. In doing so you would simply be linking the capacity for insight to the continuum running from alertness to coma. There is a danger, of course, that we may over-generalize this association, mistakenly underestimating the capabilities of anyone with 'sleepy' or droopy eyelids.

There is an allure to intelligent looks, over and above that caused by attractive facial features. Faces can be compared that are of equal attractiveness but of differing apparent intelligence.[41] When people are asked to choose between these faces, women, but not men, prefer the more intelligent-looking face.

This could reflect differences in what men and women want from a long-term partner.[42] Across different cultures, women are more concerned than men about a potential partner's earning capacity and access to resources,[43] and looking for brains may provide a good cue in identifying a man with good skills – which, these days, could mean job prospects and a healthy bank balance. Men's apparent lack of interest in intelligence may reflect a different sort of bias. By and large, smarter-looking women also appeared more masculine, and men may have been more concerned with femininity than with intelligence. It seems unlikely that men aren't interested in intelligence at all (although it does appear that many men actively do *not* want a partner who is as clever as, or more clever than, they are themselves), but as long as the woman isn't a complete bubblehead, intelligence for its own sake may lie lower on the typical man's list of priorities.

Baby-faced adults

Over-generalization extends to many facial domains. In Chapter 8 we noted how the large eyes, large foreheads, small chins, and small noses of babies (the 'infant schema') triggers a caring response. Since adults have a range of face shapes, those with a large forehead and a small chin will look a little more baby-faced than the others. We tend to over-generalize our knowledge of infants and easily assume that baby-faced adults are less alert, less intelligent, and less strong. We see such people as more naïve, more submissive, and in general less threatening and more lovable than mature-faced people.

What's more alarming, perhaps, is that baby-faced looks affect the way individuals fare in court cases.[44] Specifically, if your crime is one that involves a certain degree of nefarious intent – actively falsifying records to embezzle funds, say – then you're more likely to be acquitted or get a lighter sentence if you have a baby face, perhaps because baby-faced people are generally perceived to be more honest and trustworthy than mature-faced individuals.[45] If on the other hand your crime involves unintentional negligence – forgetting to inform a customer that a product may have hazardous side-effects, for instance – then baby-faced individuals are *more* likely to be convicted than mature-faced defendants. Apparently we think that a baby-faced individual is unlikely to do wrong deliberately, but is quite likely to do wrong by accident.

What is good is beautiful?

The link between beauty and a positive personality may reflect the reality that attractiveness makes it easy to become good-natured. If because you are physically attractive everyone is keen to know you, everyone rushes to serve you in a shop, everyone asks your opinion, and everyone assumes you're smart and lots of fun, you won't find it hard to be a little ray of sunshine. This doesn't seem to be the whole explanation, however: as we get to know people and appreciate their personalities, the way we see them changes, quite literally – they really do appear more physically pleasing to us.

When people are asked to rate the attractiveness of those with whom they were at high school, for example, it turns out that the people they liked or admired most are judged as having been more attractive. When *strangers* rate the same individuals using photographs from the high-school yearbook, their more objective aesthetic ratings bear no resemblance to those made by the people who had actually known them.[46] Similarly, the ratings that people give each other at the beginning of a team exercise – being part of a rowing team, for instance, or taking part in an archaeological dig – compared with the ratings that they give at the end show the same effects: by the end of such endeavours, people have changed their assessments of another person's *physical* attractiveness according to their perception of how helpful, co-operative, and hard-working this other person has been. The changes in attraction are more marked for women than men. Women's assessments of physical appearances strongly reflect what they have found out about personalities and deeds. Men's judgements of attractiveness are more resilient; although swayed by deeds, they continue to a large extent to reflect actual physical appearance. In this respect men, it seems, are a little more 'shallow'.

So, despite being clichéd, it really does seem that inner beauty is what matters most. What the cliché fails to convey is that our consideration of another person's inner beauty, as expressed through their personality, actually translates into an assessment of their outward *physical* beauty. An excellent beauty tip, therefore, is that you should aim to be a valuable social partner – and unlike the claims made for many allegedly beautifying creams and lotions, this one really *has* been 'scientifically proven' to work.

Faces that fit

Most research work on facial attractiveness focuses on *structure* (such as symmetry and sex typicality), yet *personality* is crucial when it comes to choosing a partner.[47] While some personality characteristics, such as generosity, are uniformly admired, not everyone will place the same emphasis on a given trait.

If people differ in the traits they want, and if personality shines through in a face, then it follows that different faces will be attractive to different people. We already know that people look at faces and draw inferences about personality. These inferences will affect attractiveness as the inferences drawn may make a given face desirable to one person but undesirable to another – we would expect that individuals who want an extrovert partner would be attracted to the faces of those who appear extrovert, for instance. These effects of *apparent* personality could exist even if the link between *real* personality and appearance is not 100 per cent sure, in the same way that we may buy a product because advertisements make us believe that the product has a property we desire, whether or not it actually does have that property.

To check this out, our lab showed men and women a set of facial photographs of female and male models taken from magazines, and then asked them to rate each photograph for attractiveness.[48] Finally, each person filled in a questionnaire in which they were asked to say how much they desired ten particular personality traits in a partner: warmth, assertiveness, sexiness, competitiveness, easy-going nature, extroversion, maturity, relaxed nature, scatter-brained nature, and responsibility. Using the attractiveness ratings and the partner-personality hit-lists, we could consider each personality trait in turn and identify which faces were rated as most attractive by people who desired that trait in a partner, and which faces were rated as most attractive by people who *didn't* want that trait in a partner. The two sets of faces were then made into two composite images and the process repeated for each of the ten traits. The results are shown in Figure 9.4 for two example traits.

Figure 9.4 Constructing the face of an ideal partner. Which female face looks the more easy-going, A or B? And which male face looks more assertive, C or D? (See the text for an explanation.)

A.C. Little *et al.* (2006).

Which female face looks more easy-going, do you think? And which male face looks more assertive? If you chose B for the female face and D for the male, then you chose the composite of the faces that were most preferred by men who wanted an easy-going partner, as well as the composite of the faces most preferred by women who wanted an assertive partner.

Let's pause to consider the implications. First, you probably found it easy to make personality inferences – 90 per cent of folk asked about the assertiveness of the images C and D in Figure 9.4 answered in the way we predicted. You should recall that the original judges were simply identifying the faces they found most attractive – we did not ask them to consider personality. When choosing the best-looking models, they were not asked to think about assertiveness, yet personality clearly did influence their aesthetic judgements.

Another point to notice is that although all of the faces that went into the composites were considered attractive, they were attractive to different people. It is true that some traits are desired by everyone – no one likes hostility, for example – yet the extent to which people give priority to warmth, for instance, varies across the range of individuals. Some will prize warmth above all else; others will think it important, but not as important as (say) sexiness. People differ in the kinds of personality traits they would like in a partner. This is fortunate for all of us – for one thing, we would otherwise all be fighting over the same mate; for another, the fact that out there are people with a range of desires means that there is more chance that someone will find *us* appealing.

The same process of relating personality to appearance can be applied the other way round, too. One can ask someone what personality traits she or he is most keen to find in a partner, and then generate a face to fit just those requirements: the face of someone who exudes those traits, in just the right proportion and priority – the 'perfect match'. Ah, if only it were as easy to find just such a person in real life, confirm his or her actual credentials, and then convert the perfect match into the perfect catch ... !

So far, then, we've seen that what people desire in a partner in terms of personality shapes what they find attractive in a face. Further, what we desire in a partner's personality is strongly related to our own personality: if we are conscientious, warm, and open to experience, then this is what we want also in our ideal partner.[49] Given this finding, it now seems that we should expect couples to share both personality characteristics and facial appearance! Indeed, we might even expect partners' *looks* to be more similar than their actual *behaviour* – as we've seen, it's possible for a person's looks to influence our beliefs about that person, and this might override any evidence from his or her actions!

Of dogs and men

Work in the Perception Lab has indeed investigated the links between couples' looks and their personalities – although bizarrely the original impetus for this work came via a request from a journalist who, in conjunction with the BBC science programme *Tomorrow's World*, wanted us to find out whether or not people looked like their dogs! We advertised for dog owners to send in passport-type photographs of themselves (and their partners, if appropriate), along with similar images of their pooches. Some relationships did emerge – little old ladies tended to own little dogs, for instance, though this is hardly surprising; few such elderly ladies would have the energy or inclination to cope with a large and bouncy dog. One surprise we got was that women who owned a big dog also tended to have a big partner. Size obviously *does* matter!

Although the project did not produce spectacular similarities – it would have been entertaining to find greyhound owners with sleek faces or bulldog owners with large jaws – this help from the media incidentally gave us access to a substantial collection of images of couples. When we asked people who did not know the dog owners to rate images of each half of the couple separately, we found that observers did tend to ascribe similar traits to married partners along several personality dimensions, and that this effect was independent of any similarity or dissimilarity in the attractiveness or age of the couples.[50]

We can use composite faces to check for similarity. By making two composite faces, one from the husbands of women judged to be extrovert, and one from the husbands of women judged to be introvert, we can check whether or not the men follow their wives in apparent personality (Figure 9.5). If there is *no* similarity between the apparent personalities of husbands and wives, then the two different husband images should look the same – if extrovert-looking women are just as likely to be married either to introvert-looking or to extrovert-looking men, then the different types of men will cancel each other out, resulting in two neutral images. What do you think – do the men in Figure 9.5 look to you as though they have the same temperament? If not, which one would you say represented the men married to extrovert-looking women? If you picked the relaxed face on the right, you'd be correct. It seems, therefore, that in terms of apparent personality there *is* a high degree of facial similarity between partners.

Indeed, when comparing looks within couples, while there seems to be very little evidence at all for the maxim 'opposites attract', there are some amusing complementary traits in partners.[51] Domineering women tend to have 'hen-pecked' husbands; technically speaking, men who were rated as looking 'quiet' were likely to be partnered by women who were rated

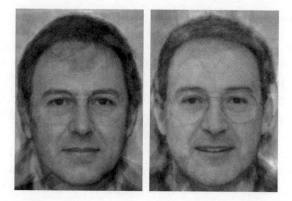

Figure 9.5 Similarity between partners. Composite images of two types of married men: one blends the husbands of women judged to be extrovert-looking, the other the husbands of women judged to be introvert-looking – can you judge which is which?

J. Engelmann & D.I. Perrett (2001) Perception Lab.

as looking 'ruthless'. Another amusing finding was that men whose faces were rated as lacking 'self-discipline' tended to be partnered to women who looked 'insecure' – could it be that unreliable men literally drive their wives to distraction? At present, of course, we have no idea whether the personality traits that are apparent in people's faces do map onto their actual behaviour within a partnership, but given that we have some evidence that people's personality is partly reflected in their faces, it does seems plausible that couples do tend to have matching or complementary personalities and behaviour.

Obviously, the behaviour of partners contributes to the dynamics and the stability of relationships. While the observations above may be amusing, there are more intriguing findings that personality traits, as reflected in looks, relate to relationship stability. People who have been married longer aren't more similar in obvious traits like physique (such as height and weight), attractiveness, masculinity, or distinctiveness: nevertheless, they *do* look more similar in terms of the particular personality traits that can be detected in their faces. There are two ways in which we can explain increased similarity in partners' looks over time. One is that couples may grow more alike in both actual and perceived personality the longer they remain together as a result of shared experiences – the joys and sorrows of life will become etched into both of partners' faces in a similar manner.[52] The other is the possibility that people who look more similar to begin with tend to have better-quality relationships and to stay married longer. The exact profile of personalities leading to marital harmony is not clear, but some studies have shown that, in comparison with dissimilar partners, couples with a similar physical and psychological make-up are more likely to have a high sense of well-being and to remain together.[53]

These studies, which looked at the physical similarity of *actual* couples in terms of *perceived* personality, have therefore brought us full circle. We have established that at least some aspects of personality are reflected in our faces, and that other people can detect these traits, with a moderate degree of accuracy, just by looking at our faces. Our desire for a partner with particular personality traits leads us to find attractive the faces that display those traits, and our preferences often reflect various aspects of our own personality. Studies of actual couples have revealed that such desires translate into real-life partnership choices, and that similarity in personality traits, as revealed by similarity in looks, relates to the durability of relationships.

This chapter has also argued that our personality traits can often be the result of self-fulfilling prophecies dictated by our looks. While the real driver for partnerships is likely to be actual behaviour, we should not overlook the dual role played by our faces – in making us into the people that we are, and in influencing the kinds of relationships that we form.

Chapter 10
ALL IN THE FAMILY

How parents and peers shape our attraction to faces

If you are single, who would be your perfect match? It would have to be someone with impeccable taste, obviously – someone who understands your sense of humour, who shares your general outlook on the world … In fact, why not someone just *like* you? Your clone, perhaps? Of course, if you're straight, the 'clone' would have to be a person of the opposite sex. Still, who could be a better person to hook up with than a carbon copy of you, identical in every respect except your sex?

But would such a person really be ideal? Very occasionally, fraternal twins – twins who grew from different eggs, and do not have identical genes – have been separated at birth, adopted into different households, and brought up without knowing of one another's existence. A man and a woman with just this upbringing met, fell in love, and married, quite unaware of their parentage. In January 2008, once it had been discovered that they were in fact brother and sister, the UK High Court annulled their marriage.[1] One would imagine that any siblings meeting for the first time might feel some bond of affection.

The perfect match for us?

Meeting an unknown twin is a highly unusual event, obviously, but in the lab one can make the extraordinary happen. Our lab constructed images to look like the twin brothers of some female students.[2] The purpose of these graphics was to find out whether or not seeing male twins for the first time would 'inspire desire' – would women like their twins' faces more than unrelated faces?

Figure U (Plate VIII) shows this construction for two such students. The woman at the top left has relatively thin, arched eyebrows, and a wide face and neck; the one at the bottom left has by contrast thicker eyebrows, but a thinner face and neck. For each woman shown, we made a man with a face that was similar but not identical in shape (Figure U, column 2).

Each man in column 2 shows corresponding facial characteristics to the woman to the left, so the man at the top of column 2 has thin arched eyebrows and a wide face and neck like his 'sister', whereas the man at the bottom of column 2 has thicker eyebrows and a thin face, just like *his* 'sister'.

What we found was quite exciting: the more similar a man's face was to the woman's face, the higher she ranked his face in attractiveness. This result seems to show that people fancied their own facial features when worn by others. Is this like twins meeting and falling in love? No – another explanation seems more likely. As discussed in Chapter 4, we don't much like unusual faces. We don't get to see unusual faces very often and when we do we find their strangeness unattractive. The thing about unusual faces is precisely that they are *unusual*; they are not really like anybody we know. The majority of people will find any particularly unusual face unappealing. In our research we had constructed some pretty unusual male faces,[3] and when we showed these constructed faces to all of the women, *nobody* liked them – their mothers might have loved them, but their 'twin sisters' did not. Each of the women concerned was no more attracted to her own look-alike 'male' face than other women were.[4] A dislike of unusualness is thus enough to explain the apparent attraction to self-similar men:[5] the women may have been attracted to men who looked similar to themselves because, far from looking unusual and weird, those men looked reassuringly familiar – just like someone they saw in the mirror, in fact.

Although these computer graphic studies show that *women* aren't actually drawn to their own characteristics in the faces of the opposite sex,[6] *men* might be. And indeed men *are* attracted to a little of their own face blended into the face of a woman. This isn't simply due to the narcissism that tends to go with being male; if it were, men would show a similar bias towards their own face blended into the face of another man, which they don't.[7] Although men like the self-similarity, they are ready to drop this interest and pay more attention to absolute beauty, given half a chance. Faced with two women of moderate attractiveness, a man will pick the one with a face more like his own – but if he's then shown a third woman who is more attractive, both of the first two will lose hands down.

When dirty laundry smells sexy

It could be that women are 'programmed' to avoid incestuous inbreeding because of the increased chance that genetic disorders such as cystic fibrosis might appear in their children. If so, they would not be attracted to self-similar faces, but would instead be attracted to someone with opposite or complementary features. Several investigations have shown that women will choose a guy who has a complementary immune make-up.[8] This type of complementarity means that any kids coming from the partnership get a greater variety of immune genes, which will help them deal with the various bugs in the environment.

Part of our immune system has genes[9] that enable us to create sticky proteins on the outside of cells which bind only to particular bugs. These provide a first line of defence to combat viruses, bacteria, and other microscopic parasites that lurk in the environment. It would be great if we had the right arsenal of sticky proteins to combat *all* the disease-causing micro-organisms that we might encounter during our life. The trouble is that we only have genes to make a limited number of these proteins, and – worse – diseases are changing all the time: we never really have enough proteins to be sure of being trouble-free. As we know from the news in recent years, flu viruses keep mutating and the new strains of bird flu or swine flu can be lethal if we lack the proteins to recognize these new variants. As noted above, therefore, we and our offspring need the appropriate genes that will allow us to make as many of these proteins as possible, and the best way to ensure this is to shop around for a mate who has genes different from our own, so that the kids get two sets of immunity genes – with two sets of genes, our kids can knock out twice as many bugs or give any one bug a double whammy.

A varied immune profile may be desirable, but you might wonder how you could choose such a profile in a potential husband or wife – after all, it's not something you can find in the personal ads: 'Male aged 35 with immune profile MHC-B*0801, A*68011 … would like to meet …' (And even if it were, the personal ad would be less engaging than descriptions of character, such as 'good sense of humour'.) Surprisingly, though, there *is* a way of assessing the compatibility of a person's immune system: it's through our sense of smell. It really is possible to shop around for the right genes, because the immune proteins made using them are later broken down and released from our skin (and in our urine), and some of the resulting fragments waft through the air for others to smell. Because the distinct variants of genes create proteins that have unique odours, you really can *smell* a person's immune profile.

Ingenious researchers have performed 'sweaty T-shirt' experiments. First, participants are asked to cleanse their bodies from artificial odours for a couple of days – to stop wearing perfumes or deodorants, to avoid smoking, not to eat garlic, curries, or anything else strongly spiced, and to wash with unperfumed soap. The odour-'detoxed' individuals are then asked to wear a standard-issue cotton T-shirt overnight and to return it to the lab to be sealed up and stored cold, to keep their aroma 'fresh'. The interesting part of such experiments is when the T-shirts are lined up and new participants go along the line, rating the odour of each T-shirt. The distinctive smells certainly are important: the judges who do the sniffing prefer the T-shirts worn by individuals who have a complementary immunogenetic make-up. Each participant finds the T-shirt odour of people with a *similar* immune profile unpleasant, and each finds the T-shirt odours of people with *different* immune profiles correspondingly pleasant. So it's clear: because of our sense of smell, we're attracted to individuals with an immunity that is complementary to our own.[10]

Do opposites attract?

Hearing about these smell experiments, in which women fancied the sweaty smell of guys with immune profiles that were complementary to their own, the Perception Lab wondered whether our female study participants would similarly be drawn to a *face* that was complementary in nature to their own. If a woman has a long nose and a wide face, would she be impressed by a man with a short nose and a narrow face? We returned to our computer graphics, but with a different aim: this time we created a wide range of face shapes. For each woman in our study, we made a continuum, starting with a guy whose face was *similar* in appearance to hers (see Figure U, column 2, Plate VIII) and ending with a guy *opposite* in shape in every way to hers (Figure U, column 4). Her thin lips would translate to his thicker lips, her small chin translates to his large chin, and so on. Now, we asked each woman for whom we had made a continuum: 'From the range available, please select the face shape that is most attractive to you.'

The results were uneventful. We found no particular focus of attraction – neither to faces that were similar, nor to those that were opposite in shape. We had nice computer graphics and a potentially interesting story, but nothing really showed up. This did not stop incorrect reports of the results appearing – there were stories that people fell in love with their own image when this was portrayed in the opposite sex. Although that had been our *initial* result, we had later discounted it! Admittedly the data and explanations were difficult to follow, but scientific findings must never be discarded in favour of an interesting story.

The experiments with dirty laundry indicated a preference among women for the odour of men with complementary immune genes. We repeated the design of this research, but this time we gave the women a chance to cast votes for the guys' *faces* rather than for their T-shirts' *smell*. The women were asked to consider unadulterated photographs of guys' faces in two contexts: a short-term situation (a brief affair) and a long-term situation (a partnership). This time, rather than fancying a complementary person, each female was attracted to the faces of guys whose immune profiles were *similar* to hers, particularly when she was considering someone with whom to settle down in a serious relationship.[11] Smell and vision seem to be taking people in opposite ways: by smell we choose someone who is complementary; by sight we are drawn to genetic similarity in real faces.

It is not clear what dimensions of facial similarity are important, or why the computer-graphic experiments were unable to evoke attraction to similarity in faces. Furthermore, the experiment does not tell us how the immune system and face characteristics are linked together – they must be linked somehow, since face choice was not random but was systematically related to the gene profile for those sticky immune proteins, yet *how* they are linked remains a mystery. One possibility is that if two people have similar immunity genes they may have many other genes in common too. The more genes that two people share, the more closely they are related: perhaps this may be an indication that relatedness contributes to facial attraction.

Family business

A line of thought running through all these experiments was that we might all like faces similar to our own because they remind us of our family, so we should turn now to whether or not there is a family influence in attraction.

As mentioned in Chapter 3, when chicks hatch they follow the first thing they see moving, be it a mother hen or a human. It's a simple start, but any young animal, including human infants, needs to learn quickly the particular characteristics of individuals who provide succour. In many species families live cheek by jowl, and it is no simple matter for mum and junior to find one another – think of a field full of bleating lambs or a vast colony of nesting birds. If the infant mistakes its parents, it may be rejected or attacked, and parents, conversely, run the risk of becoming surrogates in a foster family. Among humans, there have been cases in which infants were accidentally swapped at birth. A notable instance occurred in the Czech town of Trebic. The distressing mistake was discovered when one of the fathers had a DNA paternity test after being teased that he looked nothing like 'his' baby – he and his partner were both dark-haired and brown-eyed, yet they had a blonde-haired, blue-eyed baby. Accused of cheating, the mother too had a DNA test, and this showed that she wasn't the mother, either![12]

The early learning of parents' characteristics is termed 'imprinting' because it is as if the parent's characteristics get stamped onto the mind of the offspring. The process is mutual: the young will imprint on their mother, and the mother will imprint on her young. Given the importance of recognition, imprinting needs to be precise about the details of both parents and offspring.

Early imprinting affects not only attraction to the mother during childhood but also the sex lives of the offspring many years later. Take the example, described in Chapter 3, of the foster mothers' characteristics becoming imprinted on the male sheep and goats to an extent that later determined the characteristics sought in a sexual partner.[13] Sexually mature billy goats and rams approached females of their foster mothers' species, not their own. The *female* sheep and goats showed no particular sexual preference at maturity, perhaps because cross-fostering was arranged with a foster mother but not with a foster father, so there was no particular male model for the female sheep and goats to imprint on. It is likely, though not proven, that both male and female mammals show sexual imprinting.

It is clear that throughout the animal kingdom early learning has a profound influence on preferences for sex partners later in life. Given that imprinting allows accurate recognition of family traits, we can expect to see sexual preferences for the same family traits on maturation. A young animal learns from its parents not only about its species, but also about sub-species, local populations, and particular nuances of kin, and all of these may come to the fore in desires at puberty.

Could this apply to humans too? Might our parents influence our sex lives? Through centuries of speculation, there was very little basis for deciding what was true and what was just a fanciful story. Within the last few years, though, critical measures from faces have indicated that parents do have some influence.

Parent age

If humans show imprinting on parents, then people are likely to choose sexual partners based on a predilection for parental traits assimilated early in life. A problem for researchers, therefore, is to determine how someone's parents looked twenty years ago in order to check whether or not their appearance then could predict that person's preferences right now.

When our lab looked at particular characteristics of parents' faces, one thing we could be certain about was parental age – how old mum and dad were when the child was born. So the question we asked was: 'Are individuals born to older parents more attracted to older partners?' The answer was a clear yes. We studied students in Liverpool and in St Andrews. At each location we showed faces of a whole range of ages and asked participants to rate the attractiveness of the faces. Not surprisingly, students were most attracted to peers – to members of their own age group – and the attractiveness of faces declined steeply with the age of those faces. What was critical was that students born to parents who were relatively old (30 years old or more at the time of each student's birth) were not so enamoured of youth: they were much more attracted to the older faces. In contrast those born to younger parents (29 or less at the time of the student's birth) prized youth and were harsh in judging older age groups.[14]

When it came to details such as the skin textures associated with age – all those lines and wrinkles – students born to older parents simply paid no attention. By contrast, whether looking at faces in their early 20s or early 50s, students born to younger parents were particularly keen on smooth young skin (see Figure V, Plate VIII).

We found indications that both men and women were influenced by their parents' facial characteristics. The appearance of their mum was more influential on men's attraction to female faces than the appearance of their dad. Individuals are likely to see their parents often throughout childhood and early adulthood, so it's not clear that the bias toward the mother's characteristics comes just from early learning. It sounds wrong, but it could be that a male student returning home at Christmas (or to get his washing done) *relearns* facial characteristics that will bias his desires. It seems inappropriate … but then the mature Anne Bancroft (as Mrs Robinson) did manage a convincing seduction of the naïve Dustin Hoffman in *The Graduate*. What would seem more plausible is if the imprinting occurred during early life only, so that the characteristics learned then, which would later bias the man's sex life, were by that later stage age-appropriate. Thus when mum gives birth, she must be of a reproductive age: if the baby imprints on his mum's characteristics *at that time*, this model will be apt in due course in guiding his choice of a partner for a prosperous reproductive career.

The parental influences picked up by our studies affected choices for a soul mate rather than general aesthetics. Their mum's age affected men's attraction to women's faces and had no impact on their attraction to men's faces. Indeed, for the male participants, *only* their mum's age affected facial preferences – their dad's age had no effect on attraction to either sex. The effects of their mum's influence, however, did not extend to men's attraction to female faces in the context of a short-term relationship; Mrs Robinson may never have been a serious long-term proposition! Men prefer young women as partners, but may be less choosy about short-term arrangements. This, then, was our initial evidence that sexual imprinting could affect facial preferences as an adult.

Hair and eye colour

Many personal ads mention the colour of the advertiser's eyes and hair. Why are blue eyes or dark brown eyes something to boast about? Given the severe limits on the number of words that can be included, wouldn't you think that people would spend the space on other details, such as describing their personality more fully? But no, hair and eye colour are seen as important. Some of us are drawn to bright blue eyes, others are captivated by dark eyes. We inherit our own eye and hair colours from our parents, but our parents also affect us more subtly: we may get addicted to *their* eye and hair colours and seek similar characteristics in our partners.

Like parental age, parental eye and hair colour are relatively easy to define. The Perception Lab set up a large-scale survey and recruited 300 men and 400 women, all of whom currently had heterosexual partners and all of whom had had a two-parent upbringing.[15] We then asked them to classify their own hair and eye colour, and those of their mum and dad and their partner. From this information we found first that partners look alike – the participants and their partners tended to have similar hair colour and similar eye colour. This could be because individuals demonstrate a self-similar preference or narcissism, we thought, so we looked deeper into the data to work out what might be the most important influence on the choice of partner's eye and hair colour.

The single best predictor for partners' eye colour was the eye colour of the parent of the opposite sex. Thus, if a woman's mother had blue eyes and if her father had brown eyes, she would be most likely to be partnered to a guy with brown eyes, just like her father. Likewise, if a man's mum had blue eyes and his dad had brown eyes, then *his* partner was likely to have blue eyes, just like his mum. Similarly, the mother's hair colour was the single best predictor of a male partner's hair colour. These results indicate that individuals choose partners who resemble their opposite-sex parent both in eye and in hair colour.

The lifelong effects of parent–child bonds

A study in Poland measured the faces of women's fathers and the male faces that those women fancied.[16] The results showed a clear relation between the two. The male face shapes to which a given woman was attracted bore a geometric similarity to the face shape of her father. What was really interesting was that this was found to be true only for daughters who had had a good relationship with their fathers during early childhood: when a woman got on well with her father, she was drawn to men who looked like him. The relationship quality depended on the leisure time the dad spent with his daughter, how actively involved he was in her upbringing, and the emotional investment she had received from him. The *quality* of contact was evidently more important than its quantity, since it did not seem to matter if dad was away from home for short or for long periods of time. Here, then, the imprinting of a daughter on her father's face shape depends on a positive emotional bond between the two.

The attraction of a woman to father-similar faces doesn't occur only for women who are looking at photographs: it may also translate into real-life marriages. This emerges from a number of studies of faces in the extended families of young people at the University of Pécs in Hungary.[17] As might be expected, there are six critical members in these families: the young couple in the long-term relationship and both sets of parents.

Photographs were taken of the young couple, and photos of their parents during their own early adulthood were collected. These photos showed several things. First, each young couple had faces that were similar. The face similarity between spouses was evident to the naked eye; observers could spot the matches between the true spouse pairs and could detect false pairings.[18] Part of the perceived similarity related to equivalence in attractiveness, as you might expect (see Chapter 4); part related to similarities in face shape – whether the faces were round or thin, for instance, or whether the noses were long or short.

Of more importance, though, is the similarity between a young guy's partner and his mother.[19] This resemblance, too, is evident to the naked eye; again observers could spot the matches between the true spouse–mother pairs and could detect false pairings. Reciprocally, in a separate study it was found that a young woman's father was facially similar to the man she chose as a long-term partner.[20] These results show clearly that young adults form partnerships with individuals who resemble their opposite-sex parents. The guy marries a woman whose face looks like his mum's, and the gal marries a man whose face looks like her dad's.

Among these young couples there was no obvious relationship between the faces of the partners and faces of the same-sex parents – observers could not match the guy's father to the guy's spouse more accurately than one would expect purely by chance.[21] This last result is interesting; it means that we do not like particular faces just because they resemble familiar family members – if familiarity were important in that way, then our spouse would resemble *both* our parents.

Adopted children

Parents' characteristics evidently have a strong effect on what offspring find attractive, in terms of age, eye, hair colour, and face shape. It's probable, therefore, that the effects of the parental imprinting extend to other domains, too, and personality, masculinity, and health, which we have already seen (in earlier chapters) to be important in facial attraction, are likely candidates. It seems that in childhood each *male* child is learning about his *mother's* appearance and each *female* child is learning about her *father's* appearance. This learning guides the children as they grow up and start to look for lovers.

Something else could be going on. Perhaps there is an element of inheritance, not just learning. It could be that what mum likes in men is specified at a genetic level; if so, this might be passed on to her daughters. Likewise, dad's predilection for particular face features, were this controlled in part by his genetic make-up, could be handed down to his sons. Parents and same-sex offspring might have similar tastes in whom they find attractive even *without* any learning – this is an area yet to be explored. (There is further discussion of inherited preferences in Chapter 6.)

One way to show characteristics that are definitely the effect of learning rather than genetics is to study *adopted* individuals.[22] A remarkable study collected photographs from twenty-six families into which daughters had been adopted and in which they had grown up; the daughters later married.[23] Pictures were obtained of the adoptive father and mother as they looked when the daughter was a child between 2 and 8 years old. Photos of the daughters' husbands were also collected.

If *imprinting* is important, rather than or as well as *genetics*, then the image of the girl's husband should match the appearance of her adoptive father during her childhood. In contrast, if genes are the only influence, then the adopting father and the daughter's husband should look dissimilar, shouldn't they? In practice, observers were able to spot the facial similarity between the husband and the adoptive father. (You can try this for yourself, using Figure 10.1: which of the four men on the right is the son-in-law of the adoptive father on the left?) This seems conclusive for sexual imprinting rather than a purely genetic transfer of preference: daughters learned the appearance of their dad, and later, when hunting husbands, they used this unconsciously as the image for which they sought.

Although it seems unlikely that inherited preferences could play any part in the adopted daughter's attraction to faces that resemble her adoptive father's, there *is* still some room for genetic effects. It is possible that the adopting father is more likely to grow close to his adopted daughter if she bears a visual resemblance to him, but could they also share some genes? They could. Although we assume, correctly, that adopted children are unrelated to their adopting parents, they may still share *some* genes – we all share some genes with other members of our species, though we share far more if we are closely related. Studies using sweaty T-shirts show that a woman can detect with her nose when strangers share a genetic profile with her family.[25] Genetic relatedness is also detectable in faces. We may end

Figure 10.1 Adoptive sons-in-law. *Left*: An adoptive father when the daughter was between 2 and 8 years old. *Right*: Four men, one of whom is the daughter's later husband – which one do you think he is? (For the answer, see note[24].)
T. Bereczkei *et al.* (2004).

up liking individuals who share genes, odours, and facial features with key members in our family. For the adoptive father, this may lead to stronger bonding with his daughter, and this in turn means that he will have more influence on his daughter's future choice of partner. It is quite likely that parents also can detect some aspects of the gene profile of adoptive children and prospective sons or daughters-in-law. All forms of bonding in the family may be enhanced by similarity in terms of odour and faces.

The arguments have got quite involved here, so let's step back and see what rules are emerging. First, learning is a strong component in attractiveness. It is from looking at our parents that we learn what features of a face are attractive. More specifically, heterosexual individuals are learning from their opposite-sex parent. Loosely speaking, women generally like men with faces that 'remind them of dad', while men generally like women with faces that 'remind them of mum'. Note that the similarity of desired partners to parents is not conscious:[26] no one is deliberately trying to find a duplicate of their parent, yet subtle similarities with parents in age, hair, eye colour, and face shape are unconsciously attractive.

The extent to which this holds true depends on the quality of the emotional bond between parent and offspring. Without a strong bond, offspring may learn about parental appearance but not be attracted to parental characteristics in others. If the daughter felt that her adoptive parents showed emotional warmth 'with words and gestures', then her husband was more similar to her adoptive father. Similarly, when a son felt his biological mother had rejected him, the woman he married bore no similarity to his mother.[27] Where family members felt attached, then mums and son's wives showed facial similarities.

Incest and inbreeding

People are attracted to the faces of others on the basis of facial similarity to their parents. If we are heterosexual, we find a facial resemblance to someone in our own family particularly attractive when the face resembles our opposite-sex parent. Here is a paradox. A theme throughout this book is that we are attracted to faces that offer advantages for reproduction: unconsciously, we are looking for a face that will help us produce children and grandchildren. Yet if we are attracted to those who bear a family resemblance, this is likely to lead to inbreeding: to reproducing with a relative.

Adults do not literally want to reproduce with their opposite-sex parent; no, we are simply attracted to someone who *resembles* the key parent. We may love family members, but that is not the same as feeling sexual attraction. Nonetheless, in a small population it is likely that people who share a resemblance will be related, and attraction between similar individuals will therefore enhance inbreeding.

In the West we frown on marriages between relatives. From the mid-fourteenth century onwards, the Roman Catholic Church banned marriage to first cousins. (Some say that this was not to prevent inbreeding but to stop wealth and property accumulating in families.) It is illegal in many US states to marry a cousin, but consanguineous marriages (marriages between relatives) are neither illegal nor discouraged in all cultures.

From a biological perspective, marriage to relatives is regarded as bad because the inbreeding results in an increased number of genetic disorders. In Asia and Africa such marriages are common, making up a fifth to a half of all marriages, but such unions do not result in fewer children. Marriages to relatives tend to occur at a younger age and so the mother is younger at her first birth: this early start to reproduction can mean that the increased number of pregnancies makes up for the increased chance that some of the offspring will die from genetic problems associated with inbreeding,[28] so in these cultures marriage to relatives does not in practice result in fewer grandchildren than marriage to non-relatives. There may even be some advantages to avoiding marriage to individuals who are very dissimilar. If so, there could be an optimal relatedness for a partnership: someone who is neither too close genetically (a sibling or a parent) nor totally unrelated.[29]

Parental guidance

A survey of marriage records of individuals in Hawaii attempted to relate the composition of interracial marriages to the reported ethnicity of the parents of the bride and groom:[30] Was there any association between parents and their offspring's choices of partner? The records showed that spouse's ethnicity corresponded to the father's ethnicity for 60 per cent of brides and for 40 per cent of grooms. This relationship was reversed for mothers – the mother's and spouse's ethnicity corresponded for 40 per cent of brides and 60 per cent of grooms. These results again indicate that offspring marry individuals who resemble their opposite-sex parent; this time the similarity is in ethnicity.

Imprinting may not be the only explanation, of course – marriage reflects more than just personal preferences; social factors undoubtedly come into play. Parents may encourage offspring to enter marital relationships similar to their own, believing that what's good enough for mum and dad should be good enough for their children, too. When the marriage needs to be negotiated, it is critical to get parental endorsement. In some populations, it is the custom for parents to choose a possible husband for a daughter: the daughter may be able to assent to or to veto her parents' choice. Even in modern Western society, meeting the boyfriend's or girlfriend's parents remains daunting because it is so important to get their approval. If things go well, there could be free future babysitting and even some inheritance; if things go badly, there might be a lifetime of hostility – a lot hangs in the balance. It is inevitable that parents will exert pressure on offspring to make the right choice and that they will voice their opinion as to who is a good or a poor match. My wife remembers getting on well with my mother, but hearing her voice hostility towards a former girlfriend. Parents can be so outspoken (or just plain rude). As an aside, we might note that similarity between spouse and parent can be encouraged by parents' approval, because the attraction of the parents to the prospective son- or daughter-in-law may depend on that person sharing key facial features with existing family members. In hunter-gatherer societies, it is customary for male parents to control whom their daughter marries,[31] and dad may well be choosing a man in his own image.

Parental choice in matchmaking can be seen in other guises, too. In a remote region of south-east Peru, in virtual isolation from the rest of the world, people were tested for their preferences for male faces that varied in masculinity. The young women selected the feminine male faces, but their mothers selected the masculine male faces. The mothers were selecting sons-in-law who would be tough and strong, while the daughters were selecting kinder, more pliable partners.[32]

The legacy of Freud

On the basis of a story in Greek mythology in which Oedipus unknowingly kills his father and marries his mother, Sigmund Freud invented the term 'Oedipal complex'. Freud argued that a child growing up has a sexual desire for the opposite-sex parent and wants the same-sex parent to die. According to Freud's theory, these desires are present only at a very young age.

Freud's writings may be entertaining, but they were based on opinion rather than evidence. Whatever we think of Freud's ideas, his work was important in drawing attention to the significance of early childhood and to the influence of the opposite-sex parent. According to Freud, such early complexes later resolve in the majority of people. Nevertheless, we can see from psychological studies of faces that our parents really do exert lifelong influences on who we're attracted to.

Peer pressure

Parents are one guide to our love life, even if we would prefer them not to be. Peers are another matter; with our friends we are far more likely to swap secrets about our dreams and conquests. We have so little time on the planet to evaluate the character and behaviour of each potential partner; we have to take shortcuts. If we ask for opinions and listen to the gossip then we can use reputations as a guide to who to chat up and who to chase away. Alternatively, we don't need to listen to what's said about someone: we can just check out who else is interested in her or him. If a person is good enough for people we admire, the same person should be good enough for us, too. How shallow, you might think, to be swayed by the crowd – yet it happens.

But wait – should we trust just anyone as a guide for our romantic life? Surely it would be wiser to pay attention to those around us whom we think are well-informed,[33] and to take heed of those who are more experienced than ourselves? Well, attractive individuals get more offers of dates, so they should be worth attending to. And sure enough, in one study women's ratings of a man's facial attractiveness rose when that man's face was paired with a pretty female, 'his supposed partner'.[34] Even being *told* that a woman depicted in a photo is popular is enough to increase the power of her influence over the perceived attractiveness of her partner. Reciprocally, a woman's face is rated as more attractive if she is 'accompanied' in an adjacent photo by a masculine man. Attractive people control our love life, it seems, even when we believe they are out of our league in terms of attractiveness.

Simple manipulations, such as saying how old a woman is, can affect how contagious is her apparent taste in men. For youthful and impressionable heterosexual female students, the age of a woman pictured accompanying a man influences how attractive they themselves find the man. An older woman (who is presumably more experienced and therefore wiser) has more effect on the students' perception of the man's attractiveness than a woman who is marked down as being younger (who is presumably more naïve). So popularity and opportunity for experience are badges that help us identify whom to copy in choosing our own mate.

If age is respected because of the experience it brings, then we should acquire more and more respect for our own experience as we move through life, with some love gained and some lost. In that case, the tendency to copy the mate choices of others should diminish with age, and this is indeed what seems to happen. Older women are less swayed by the age and experience of their would-be guides.[35]

Finally, we should not presume that all is well in a relationship – just because a man is married doesn't guarantee that the marriage is a bed of roses – so expression, too, can be persuasive. If a woman smiles slightly (presumably because he's kind and buys her flowers) then she will be more effective in swaying observers' opinions about the man than next to her in a photo than a woman who is looking a little glum.[36]

This situation need not look very lifelike; it can be demonstrated simply by the juxtaposition of photographs. In Figure 10.2, for example, the attractiveness of the male face on the left benefits in the bottom row from the presence of the smiling female face pointing towards him. Similarly, the male face on the right loses out: even though this face lies next to the same smiling female, she is pointed away from him. The apparently positive evaluation of one woman enhances a man's value or attractiveness in the eyes of other women. It is amusing in this context that the reverse happens for male evaluators: for them, a woman smiling at a man makes him *less* attractive. It's not hard to make men jealous!

These effects provide a path for cultural transmission of attractiveness. We learn from our peers who is attractive and who is not. This might

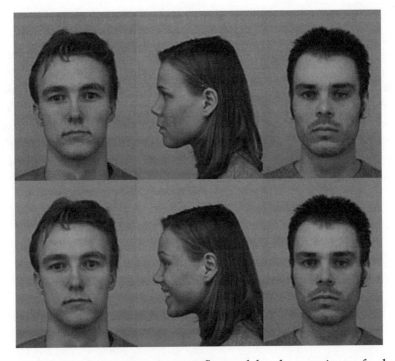

Figure 10.2 Facial attractiveness is influenced by the reactions of others. Female evaluators judge a man to be more attractive when they see another woman looking and smiling at him (as opposed to looking at him with neutral expression). For male evaluators, the same man becomes less attractive!
B.C. Jones *et al.* (2007).

well induce some common opinions about what is attractive, in which case everyone would be copying everyone else and ending up liking the same people. In fact, social learning through peers can induce *differences* in attraction. The particular mix of friends that we have is unique, just as each friend's opinion about others – whom they may admire and whom they may despise – is also unique. Far from introducing uniformity, opinions are going to diverge and this divergence will be propagated locally. One man may be revered within one circle of friends yet reviled by another.

The looks of Heroin Chic and of Goths are anything but healthy or universally admired. These are fashions – or as they may seem to the unfashionable, perversions – in facial appearance. Piercing, stretching, scarring, teeth-filing, skull-reshaping, and (for women) the tattooing of moustaches (see Chapter 4) all demonstrate membership of a particular group or fashion. They show that culture can evolve its own extremes. Within the larger population, sub-cultures prosper and can redefine the field of competition for mates. If we grow up within a community of Goth friends, for instance, we will grow to admire dark music and insipid facial complexions – even if we do not initially like such things, we will know that having these tastes is the only way to win the attentions of a Goth partner, and if such attentions are pleasant they may in turn nudge us into liking them.

In summary, attraction to faces depends on our experience; it depends on the people whom we see, and how they interact with us and with one another. Since our friends and our family are personal, we have a very personal set of influences on what face characteristics we find attractive. Because our learning experience is unique for each and every one of us, who we most fancy and who we end up marrying will also be unique.

Chapter 11
LOVE POTIONS

Transforming attraction to love

So far the focus of this book has been on the general and particular facial features that draw individuals together. It has not dealt with full-blown romantic love – that feeling of passionate affection for someone; that yearning to be in the presence of the beloved; those tender feelings evoked by a mere glimpse of his or her face. Can we understand the drive of love itself – why one individual's characteristics come to trigger such passion in us? What underlies the transition between interest and infatuation?

As yet the story is sketchy, at best. Measuring evaluators' attitudes to photos is easy: measuring why people get on during dates and enjoy being in bed together is much trickier.

Arousing emotional feelings

Emotional feelings are not created spontaneously: they are evoked by the behaviour and mood of others. What we end up feeling is bound up with our social environment, as we appraise the situation and catch from others the emotion appropriate to the moment.[1] This is evident from an experiment in which people were given a shot of adrenalin, though they were told it was just a vitamin, and then left in different waiting rooms with actors employed to create particular atmospheres. The adrenalin created all the well-known physiological effects that accompany high arousal, including a racing heart-beat and a jittery feeling, but the *mood* that people actually experienced depended on what was done by other people in the waiting rooms.

In one waiting room a 'Mr Angry' got impatient and complained volubly about the outrageous wait he was enduring. Those with the adrenalin high in this room ended up describing their mood as grim, more angry than happy. In another waiting room someone was frivolous enough to fly paper airplanes (reminiscent of school-day hilarity when the teacher's back was turned). In this light-hearted environment, the mood ratings of those with the adrenalin high tipped in favour of happiness.

People seemed to be interpreting their arousal as happiness or anger according to the mood and behaviour of others. When some of the people were told to expect a jittery feeling and racing heart as a side-effect of the 'vitamin' drug administered, then those people had a further way to account for their arousal – it was due to the drug and not to the waiting-room experiences. These 'guinea pigs', warned about the drug side-effects before going into the waiting rooms, did not catch the emotions of the other people in those rooms.

So arousal makes people emotional, but *which* emotion they experience depends on social cues. While this is a general theory that attempts to account for everyone's emotions, it may not apply evenly. People vary in the extent to which they are aware of their own emotions and the extent to which they catch the feelings of others. At the extreme is a condition called 'alexithymia', an inability to share the emotions of others. It is quite common, affecting perhaps as many as 8 per cent of the healthy population. Those who have this condition see themselves in terms of being either happy or unhappy and miss out on other emotions, such as anger, disgust, fear, or surprise. Their happiness is all-or-nothing, with no in-between states such as mild amusement. Such people are not unfriendly, but may be described as logical or unsentimental; they are emotionally detached and, not surprisingly, they connect less with others.

Such individuals would be unlikely to fall in line with the moods of the actors in the adrenalin experiment described. When people with alexithymia watch film clips of angry and fearful behaviour, many of the emotionally reactive systems in their brains remain unimpressed and not activated.[2] Yet for most of us our ability to respond to the emotions of others lies at the core of our social nature and is part of what makes it easy to form relationships, in which attraction may sometimes translate into love.

Arousal and attraction

What about attraction – is that subject to similar rules in turning adrenalin-based excitement into positive feelings for a particular person? This is an important issue, so we will spend a while considering the evidence.

One test was arranged in which college students took part in an experiment that was ostensibly about their sense of balance and their distractibility.[3] It just happened that the experimenter was of the opposite sex and quite attractive! Imagine yourself now as part of the study. You are blindfolded, and seated in a deep, motorized reclining chair. The chair activates and you begin to turn around slowly; meanwhile, soothing noises play overhead. After a number of rotations, the chair comes to rest and a loudspeaker above your head calmly asks you to point to where you last saw the experimenter. This procedure continues for a while; you relax into the comfort of the chair and are lulled by the slow swivelling movement. After a break, the experimenter explains that the chair will now be moved in all sorts of other ways. Nothing prepares you for the clamour of a heavy brass plate being dropped onto steel and the chair suddenly lurching backward. Your adrenalin levels rocket. Despite this, the experiment continues; you are again asked for directional judgements, but after all the commotion you are unlikely to be calm!

Not all of the study participants receive the shocks of sudden noise and unexpected movement. Others are spared these; for them the calm and gentle approach continues throughout. What happens next is interesting. The direction judgements were actually part of an elaborate ruse to find out how this process of arousal (experienced by some participants and not others) affects feelings towards the experimenter, who now helps the participant remove the blindfold and leads him or her away, explaining what has to be done in a final debriefing. In this, participants complete a confidential questionnaire to ensure that the experiment was a fair and 'pleasant' educational experience. Amongst the questions are some that evaluate the experimenter's competence. All of these stages disguise the lead-up to the really important measure of attraction: 'How much did you like the experimenter personally?' And the results? Men who had been through the arousing crash and the lurching chair gave higher ratings for their liking of the female experimenter than men who had had only the gentle chair swivels. Women, too, were more favourably impressed by the male experimenter if they had been startled.

Theories of emotion, and now theories of attraction, assert that arousal is interpreted within the social and physical context. In this experiment, participants attributed their excited state not solely to metal crashing on metal and the chair behaving like a rodeo horse, but in part to the experimenter; he or she must have caused the arousal. In the same circumstance, you too would be excited and aware of the attractive experimenter, and you too might assume that it is the experimenter who makes your heart race – in effect, you might think that you fancy the experimenter.

In this experiment, allegedly about balance, the exact social interplay will be crucial. The experimenter touches you when removing your blindfold; he or she also talks you through the debriefing. The conversation gives each aroused participant a unique experience: each person forms a personal sense of how considerate the experimenter can be, and each responds to the situation in his or her own way (for instance, a scared participant may share a joke to reduce the tension). We cannot know from reading the report exactly what gets said, nor can we know whether there are the reassuring smiles that are so important to attraction. What we *can* know is that interactions following this kind of excitement are different from the interactions that happen after mundane events, such as the calm version of the experiment.

In this chapter we are trying to evaluate what causes attraction.[4] The interpretation here is that arousal doesn't change the physical beauty of the experimenter's face, but shared exciting experiences set the scene by creating circumstances in which liking may develop, allowing protagonists to display humour and consideration. Who knows – the feelings may be mutual, with the experimenter feeling more attracted to participants who have endured the disturbing testing, perhaps because these participants become animated and because the experimenter feels some responsibility and even guilt.

This study started out with a pretty female experimenter and a handsome male experimenter: there was an edge to begin with. More recent studies show a comparable translation of arousal to attraction even with randomly chosen protagonists.[5] This does not mean that arousal *always* enhances attraction – if the experimenter is deliberately unpleasant, for instance, the arousal may enhance aversion rather than attraction.

Most social interaction will provoke some arousal; the physically closer the interaction, the greater the arousal. Excitement is more likely when we are interacting with someone whom we already think is interesting. Even if we are only vaguely attracted to them, when they do something unexpected, such as sitting close, this may generate a little flutter inside. The flutter will make us behave differently: the interaction will crank up a notch in liveliness and possible flirtation. At the next meeting our minds and bodies will remember that exhilaration and heightened interactions may continue. We will start to think that we are excited by this person and must be attracted to her or him.

A further study shows how arousal can begin to turn social contact into romance. This study asked men to walk out on a narrow rope-suspension bridge (high arousal) or a more solid bridge (low arousal) at the same scenic spot.[6] There they were confronted by an attractive female experimenter, who asked them to construct stories in response to picture cards. The men interviewed by the experimenter on the high-arousal bridge were more likely to make up sexually orientated stories than the men meeting the same researcher on the low-arousal bridge. Men who met the researcher in the scarier circumstance were also more likely to phone her later (ostensibly for a 'debriefing') than the men who met her in safer circumstances.

Here the experimental transformation of arousal to attraction carries over into real life and creates the potential for real romantic entanglements. Again, we must not think that excitement causes inevitable attraction, but rather that arousal makes people behave differently and allows situations to develop in more interesting ways. We do not know how the female experimenter reacted to stories that included sexual innuendo. The guys who found themselves being bold may have been more likely to check up to see how their 'advances' had gone down. A guy's follow-up may not have derived solely from a change in aesthetic evaluation of the experimenter; the rickety bridge created an opportunity to make a pass, and he took it. The whole character of the meeting changed as a result of excitement.

Bernard Tiddeman, the computing wizard behind the Perception Lab graphic tricks, decided on a practical test of the 'arousal aids attraction' theory. With characteristic planning he contrived a trip to Paris that included a full ascent of the Eiffel Tower with his girlfriend Meg (who was, he hoped, psychologically naïve at the time). Bernie insisted that they both walk out onto the highest parapet of the iconic structure, aiming to induce a state of near-vertigo with high arousal, which from psychological experiments he could assume Meg would attribute to attraction. He then proposed to her. She accepted; but that was undoubtedly independent of the vertigo. His choice of location was planned for other reasons, too, including her love of France and Paris, and a sense of drama for the occasion. In any case, no one can accuse science of taking the romance out of relationships!

Positive social attention

Arousal is one ingredient of budding attraction; positive social engagement is another. It's difficult to like someone who's totally disinterested in us, someone with whom conversation dies as soon as it's initiated.

Research work on brain activity triggered by eye contact and smiles has shown the importance of these social cues in allowing beautiful faces to fascinate us and reside in our pleasure centres.[7] Similarly, the role of flirtatious cues in upping attraction has been demonstrated in other situations.[8] If one starts with pairs of faces that have been retouched so that one of each pair has a nicer skin colour than the other, then it is no surprise that observers prefer the face with the healthier-looking skin colour (Chapter 7). What is more pertinent here is that these preferences are strongest when the faces look and smile at the observer. If the faces look away or worse *smile* while looking away (perhaps being pleasant to

someone else off-camera), then this detracts from the observer's preferences (see Figure T, Plate VII). Physical beauty is one thing, but what we
find really attractive is a beautiful person who is happy to be interacting
with *us*: if the beautiful person is attentive to somebody else and seems to
be getting on well with her or him, then the person's beauty diminishes in
our eyes. Body language, expression, and direction of attention tell us who
is interested in whom. Because we are all egotistical, we tend to suppose
that people who smile are smiling at us and that people who are angry are
angry at someone else.[9] We like attractive faces to be orientated towards
us, whereas we think that less attractive faces look their best when turned
away from us.[10] We are indeed self-centred in nature – someone's attraction to us is a turn-on; their attraction to someone else is a turn-off.

Sex, drugs and attraction

Human   beings   experience   instinctive   rewards   in   particular
circumstances – warmth when cold, water when thirsty, calories when
hungry, and orgasm when sexually aroused. These natural rewards liberate
a chemical, dopamine, from the middle of the brain. Dopamine courses
through the brain's 'reward circuits' and induces a euphoric sense of pleasure: it just feels great, and we definitely want more of it. The rest of the
brain helps us to learn to do the things that get us the dopamine again,
and the sense of pleasure that comes with it. We learn to snuggle up next
to a warm body, to raise our own body heat; we learn how to eat politely,
to get food from our family; and we discover the rules of romance and
foreplay, which may bring sexual contact.

There are plenty of chemicals manufactured by plants (or by chemists)
that have direct access to the brain's reward system: alcohol, caffeine,
nicotine, and opium are just a few. These chemicals cause our own drug
dopamine to rocket and this, as always, gives us pleasure. Then there are
the cues that we learn: cues that often occur just *before* we get the rewarding chemicals. The bitterness of beer and the dark fruit aroma that spells
out a good cabernet sauvignon become associated with the alcohol hit; the
burnt aromas that characterize roasted coffee beans or a lit cigarette remind
us of the pleasurable effects of caffeine and nicotine; and the smooth
texture of chocolate becomes linked to an expectation of the cocktail of
psychoactive compounds found in cocoa beans. In turn, these cues can
become associated with other, more abstract signals, so that the sound of
a cork being pulled or descriptions of the main course on the menu fore-
shadow the taste of good wine and the many sensations of fine dining. The
pop of a bottle opening and the glug of liquid pouring get us drooling, just as

the bell did for Pavlov's dogs. Our learning gets ever more sophisticated as with time we learn which coffee shop gives us the best hit of caffeine, and which wine labels are associated with the fewest side-effects from less pleasant ingredients that make the wine sour or that give us premature symptoms of a hangover.

Our romantic life has similar cues, with general and very personal connotations – a heartfelt hug, an affectionate tone, and eye contact with a knowing smile can each be associated with fondness or with sexual feelings. Indeed all sorts of what others may perceive as perversions or fetishes can relate to experiences that have become associated with sexual arousal for particular people who have had the appropriate – or inappropriate – experiences. So cues to memory and expectation become pleasurable in their own right; sometimes they may become even essential to enjoyment. It is easy, therefore, to see how someone's face, body, and hands can become associated with passion, and why simply looking at that person or calling her or him to mind becomes rewarding in itself because we remind our reward systems of past pleasures and begin to anticipate enjoyable possibilities.

Being besotted about one person is made possible by the brain cells we can dedicate to particular faces (see Chapter 2). When the sight of one familiar person's face becomes preferentially linked to our pleasure systems then we will find that person's visage particularly attractive. But do these descriptions of reward give us a full enough account of romantic love? They certainly tell us about the pleasures that can come from intimacy, from the thrill of physical contact. These are components of romantic love, certainly, yet they are not enough. A further ingredient is required: the component of faithfulness, which makes the company of the other so significant. While in principle many individuals could meet our romantic needs and even provide sexual gratification, in practice there may be one person only whom we wish to fulfil this role. Love includes commitment and exclusivity.[11] The commitment and the exclusivity may have bounds that do not precisely match wedding vows, but the craving for faithfulness is nonetheless real and couples may feel it deeply.

Sex and the brain's love potions

Direct scientific studies of humans and the basis of love are few. In purely biological terms, there are some studies of brain activity during erectile changes in the genitals and during orgasm. While these studies may be dramatic compared to other studies inside brain scanners, they tell us little about the basis of committed love. For insight into this mysterious and all-important aspect of love, we can turn to studies of brain hormones and their effects on bonding and faithfulness in other animals.

Let's look at two species of vole. One is a species that forms long-term bonds, in which the male dedicates himself to his partner and to bringing up the pups; the other is a species in which the male hangs around only long enough for sex and then disappears, leaving all the parental care to the female. The two species differ critically in the way their brain makes and responds to two 'love hormones': oxytocin and vasopressin. The faithful species produces more of both of these hormones. It also has more binding sites – places that respond to the hormones – in the brain areas that control commitment and care. If experimenters block these binding sites so that the hormones no longer have their effect, previously devoted males and females fail to form any kind of lasting relationship. Oxytocin and vasopressin are critical to the formation of partnership bonds: when levels are raised in the relevant brain regions, the faithful voles form an exclusive attachment – they become monogamous.

We are focusing here on the bond that underlies faithful partnerships, which is a manifestation of committed love that can be studied in any species. In voles, it's a simple pairing of odour and love hormones that does the trick. During sex, the love hormones are elevated and, in concert with the rewarding aspects of dopamine, they establish a bond between the consenting partners, in which the partner's odour becomes associated with the pleasure of sex. This odour then becomes pleasurable, something that the partners will work to stay in contact with.

In the voles, the two chemicals have different sex roles – oxytocin is critical to the female's pair-bonding, and vasopressin is critical to the male's pair-bonding. Often in biology a given chemical may serve different purposes, and in this case too the hormones have additional related roles in the body and the brain: in females, oxytocin makes the muscles in the nipple contract to help express milk, and also controls parental protectiveness; in males, vasopressin helps make the penis erect,[12] and also has a role in the marking of territory and in aggression.[13]

The same love hormones are also found in other species of voles and mice that *don't* form pair-bonds. These animals also enjoy sex and learn the odours that are around at the time of sex, and they too may learn to find the sex-associated odours arousing and motivating – the critical difference in relation to bonding seems to be in the number of the love-hormone *receptors*. In unfaithful species there are fewer receptors, and they are not so strongly linked to the reward centres in the brain. Scientists can alter the solitary or pair-bonding lifestyles of the two types of vole simply by changing the levels of the love hormones and their receptors.

So does all this apply to human love? We aren't voles or mice, of course, and therefore the rules of pair-bonding and love are going to differ. And yet, while the details of brain structure and function may be different between species, the same cocktail of hormones and the same brain systems are just as critical in explaining human love as they are in accounting for social and family bonds in other species.

Oxytocin and vasopressin undoubtedly have similar roles in humans, controlling both the bodily responses of erectile tissue (in the nipples and genitals) and psychological bonding. Although the work on rodents may seem far from human love and relationships, the era of the human genome brings it very close. It is now possible to read the genetic codes of large numbers of people and to look at the parts that give rise to the brain receptors for these love hormones.

Errors can occur in genes. Sometimes, for example, very small sections get repeated over and over again, and such repetition in the DNA code can alter the function of the gene. The repetitions can detract from the sense of the code, much like repeated letters in a mistyped word or a repeated word in a sentence. In Huntington's disease, for example, the more repetitions or 'stutters' of a particular section of a particular gene, the worse the disease and the quicker it develops.[14] This type of variation in the DNA code can diminish or amplify the effectiveness of hormone receptors, and in this way the changed code may exaggerate behavioural traits and sexual proclivities.

A recent study of 550 Swedish people in heterosexual partnerships found that the gene for vasopressin receptors related to the quality of relationships. Men with a longer stuttering DNA stretch inside the vasopressin gene had lower scores on commitment and relationship quality. If they had *two* copies of the longer gene[15] they were less likely to be married, and if they were married they were twice as likely to have had a marital crisis.[16] Commitment varies between men, as it does between voles – some are more like the committed fatherly vole, while others are more like the rakish unattached vole. Exactly where each human stands on the faithfulness spectrum varies within and between populations. We can see that part of this variation is attributable to genes such as that for vasopressin (though genetic status will count for naught in a divorce court), but although faithfulness is partly down to genes, life events too can amplify or diminish commitment in relationships and in parenting styles.

Mother love

As noted above, hormones tend to have multiple roles, and both oxytocin and vasopressin influence not only the bonds between parents but also the bonds between parents and offspring. For humans, as for all other mammals, the stretching of the cervix and vagina during birth stimulates high levels of the hormone oxytocin. For sheep, this stimulation is key to the mother learning the odour of the newborn lamb when she licks the lamb clean after birth.[17] If the ewe's cervix is stimulated within a few days of giving birth, she can be persuaded at that time to accept the odour of an unrelated lamb: she becomes bonded to this lamb and will defend and care for it as her own, while rejecting other lambs.

Oxytocin's role in pair-bonding has been known for only a relatively short time, whereas its role in maternal behaviour is well established. One of the most potent causes of oxytocin release is the stimulation of the nipple by the infant's efforts to obtain milk. In this context oxytocin has a role in the expression of milk: when oxytocin rises, milk is expressed more easily. The long periods of breast-feeding, accompanied as they are by high oxytocin, help form the maternal bond with the infant. It is known that in comparison with women who have had a Caesarean section, women who have experienced natural childbirth show greater activity in the brain areas involved in empathy and reward in response to the sound of their baby crying.[18] Perhaps it is the cervical stimulation during childbirth that is important in the imprinting process, or perhaps breast-feeding is easier for women following natural birth and leads to a closer bond with the baby.

What is interesting here is the commonality of the brain systems and hormones involved in the bonds between mother and infant and between pair-bonded adults. Both nipple and vaginal stimulation are potent releasers of oxytocin, and both have a role in the formation of maternal and romantic bonds. While these are basic biological triggers of oxytocin, the faces of infants and of lovers quickly get associated with the triggers and themselves become potent in activating the love hormones. When romantic partners gaze into each other's eyes, they activate many of the same brain regions that are stimulated by a mother looking at the face of her own child.[19] One's own offspring and lovers both produce a big hit of neural activity in the regions of the brain's reward system that are rich in oxytocin and vasopressin receptors (see also Chapter 2). The faces of unrelated children, and of adults who may be familiar friends but are not lovers, are much less effective in activating these systems.

In this section we have considered how loving bonds are formed. The key lies in the neural connections leading to the brain reward centres (such as those from the brain cells' face analysis, described in Chapter 2); these, coupled with the actions of love hormones, cause the characteristics of the partner or offspring to become pleasurable and motivating.

While the mechanisms are very general and equip adults with the ability to form a bond with *any* infant or adult, once set in motion they become very specific. The imprinted infant or partner will gain the power to trigger positive emotions, anxiety at separation, the willingness to be selfless in care – in short, all the intense feelings of parental and romantic love.

One must not see natural childbirth, breast-feeding, and oxytocin surges as a panacea that will lead always to perfect harmony between mother and baby. In humans, as in other mammals, there are cases where mothers fail to bond with their offspring. For humans there are many contributory causes, including postnatal depression.[20] Fortunately maternal bonding is the rule rather than the exception, otherwise there would be no human race.

Conversely, the labour of childbirth is *not* essential in evoking mother love. You might wonder about the care from a grandparent or an adoptive parent – such relationships clearly lack some of the primary biological stimulation that can cause oxytocin or vasopressin to be released and so facilitate parental bonding, yet strong loving bonds flourish here too. There are many other stimuli that are potent in releasing hormones in men and women, and the very acts involved in ongoing parental care probably trigger the release of oxytocin and vasopressin.

The care one gets is the care one gives

This kind of aphorism presumes an underlying reciprocity in human relations – that in general we receive in proportion to how much we give, and conversely that what we receive may influence what we are able to give. Life deals both equalities and inequalities, and this is true in relationships also. A recurrent theme in this book is that our experiences, particularly in early life, can affect *whom* we love in later life; if the studies of rodents are anything to go by, it may also change *how much* love we can give.

The likelihood of rats and mice giving maternal or paternal care to infants can be boosted or diminished according to the early experience of care that the individuals received when they themselves were infants. A caring nature can pass down generations just as surely as genetically inherited traits.[21] The care received by an infant rodent in the form of licking and fur-cleaning relaxes the individual receiving it and indirectly changes the levels of hormones in the brain. These changes in turn affect the packaging around the genes[22] in particular areas of the brain, making the genes easier to read. More loving care therefore indirectly causes increased production of the oxytocin receptor proteins from the relevant genes, and as the increased number of receptors is permanent, the result stays with that individual for life. This in turn can affect maternal care: if a mother rodent received a lot of attentive licking and cleaning when she herself was an infant, she will have more receptors and will thus be more responsive to oxytocin and more motivated to lick and clean her own infants. This attentiveness will pass in turn to her own daughters, and so on.

For humans too, early experience proves critical for later mood states such as anxiety, for the care given by the adult to her or his own infants, and quite probably for how close individuals get to partners and how likely they are to stay with them. As with rodents, early human experience affects the receptors for the love hormones, and these in turn affect a spectrum of social behaviour, from looking after the kids, through socializing with friends, to the dedication of a lover.

People show a range of 'attachment styles', which are first evident when parents leave their infant alone in a strange environment. One group, *securely attached* infants, frets but is easily comforted by the parents when they return. Another group, *anxiously attached* infants, shows the same upset at separation, but may be irreconcilable when the parents return or may become ambivalent towards their caregivers, resisting contact on their return. A further group, *avoidant* infants, shows no distress at separation and tends to avoid contact with caregivers more generally. Avoiding comfort on reunion may be a way of punishing the absentee parent or a form of self-protection from further upsetting partings.[23] These attachment styles between infants and parents are carried forward as later attachment styles between adults in romantic relationships,[24] and affect whether we can form close bonds to others or remain more distant, and whether we become a jealous type, anxious when our partner is with someone else. Thus the different styles of relationship and love we prefer to receive and are able to give depend on both our genes and on the style of parenting that we ourselves received.[25]

These differences and constraints, imposed by the realities of our lives, mean that not everyone will form durable, fulfilling relationships. Individuals may reiterate their parents' dysfunctional relationship, for instance; they may move from one unsatisfactory liaison to another. Alternatively, each liaison may be fulfilling but impermanent.

One thing to note about parental love is that it is naturally inclusive of multiple children, each bonded in the same way. This raises the delicate issue of how commitment relates to exclusivity in adult relationships, as through the means described above more than one face at a time could become personally attractive. Throughout much of Africa, Arabia, and

India, it is accepted that a man can have more than one wife. In Nepal or Tibet, one woman may be married to two or more brothers. In these places, exclusivity is not required by religion or law, and may not even be desired by one or all parties. In the animal kingdom, penguins are often held up as a model of devoted parents,[26] yet their commitment to one another is not necessarily exclusive within a breeding season or across breeding seasons.[27]

It would be daft to assume that human relationships that start out loving will remain stable and exclusive: the facts flatly deny this assumption, since in the USA the divorce rate is now half the marriage rate.[28] The focus in this book has been on how attraction increases in successful relationships, rather than on how it degrades in dissolving relationships, but we should not assume that the end of a relationship means the end of attraction – facial features that were passionately attractive at one time may turn up again in subsequent relationships, too, whether socially sanctioned or illicit.

More to love than sex

Earlier, the story of how sex led to partner formation was given in an abridged form, focusing on the raunchy details of how sex activates reward systems and triggers highs in the love hormones. This shortened story skipped over the fact that the female vole can form a strong partner bond with a male just by being in his company. Scientists can act like parental censors and intervene, separating the courting male and female before the act of consensual sex. Despite the scientists' intervention the separated virgin female may still have formed a commitment to the courting male. The male vole, too, may have formed a strong attachment to the female just by being in her presence, even though consummation of his desires has been curtailed. The brain mechanism involved in bonding, it seems, is essentially the same with or without the sex. Both of the hormones (oxytocin and vasopressin) *and* the partner's odour are needed if the bonding is to happen – the sex act, though, is not necessary.

This is good news! It means that love, attraction, and bonding can all flower before sexual intimacy. Such mechanisms do not deny the additional contribution of sex to the relationship or to infatuation: it's just that sex isn't actually essential. All that is needed is other triggers for dopamine and oxytocin release, and there are a myriad of such triggers (Figure 11.1) – it turns out that conversation with the loved one, being with the loved one, kissing the loved one, and caresses with the loved one are all quite sufficient to elevate oxytocin.

Figure 11.1 Rodin's sculpture of lovers kissing. The act of kissing liberates masses of oxytocin – a love potion, which bonds the couple. In the course of this bonding, each lover's face becomes personally attractive to the other. (This sculpture is a reproduction of the original sculpture and is held at the Ny Carlsberg Glyptotek in Copenhagen.)
Wikimedia.

There are other pleasure systems, too; being touched or hugged causes us to make our own opiate chemicals (similar to codeine and heroin).[29] These drugs that we ourselves produce float around in our brains and provide their own type of pleasure; they too have a role in bonding.[30] All these chemical pleasure responses act in concert with the high levels of oxytocin and lead to loving attachment between couples. As noted before, release of reward chemicals in our brain becomes trained, in the same way that we become trained to salivate when we see appetizing food; repeated enjoyable contact with a person means that the mere sight of that person makes us produce all of our pleasure chemicals.

There is a hidden edge to the potent symbol of erotic passion that is depicted between the characters in Rodin's sculpture (Figure 11.1). *The Kiss* illustrates Dante's tale of forbidden love, passion between a woman and her husband's handsome brother, whose infatuation was stimulated by reading the tale of Lancelot and Guinevere, who cheated on her husband,

King Arthur. The couple depicted by Dante are killed by the jealous, uncouth, and disfigured husband, and they are doomed to be punished in hell for adultery.[31] Notwithstanding the mortal sin in this case, a tender kiss will always have the same effects, whoever the participants: it will involve the same addiction, and the lovers' faces will thereafter be a continuing source of pleasure to one another.

This last chapter has been devoted to explaining how we come to be interested in others, how our attraction to them increases, and how this attraction may transform into love. We have also dealt with the love of offspring, which is no less intense than the adoration felt for an adult. In each case, love is specific to individuals; yet again our story says that facial attraction is profoundly personal, and here we see that it is idiosyncratic, bordering on idiotic.

There is a dissociation between beauty and attractiveness: the two words seem more distinct for women than men.[32] A clear majority of women surveyed informally thought that they could be attracted to someone who was not beautiful. A majority of men thought the words the same: they probably found all beautiful women personally attractive, but at least some men recognized that particular women are attractive though not necessarily beautiful.

Attractiveness reflects the personal desire to approach and be with someone. One can realize that people are 'plain', from the perspective of a classic beauty magazine, and yet still find them highly desirable, from a purely personal perspective. Their features aren't symmetrical; they aren't young; their nose is longer or shorter than the average ... we know all this, and yet we know also that we love them. Their features would not be more attractive if they were other – yes, they might be more beautiful, but, no, we would not feel greater affection for them. For us, theirs is the face of love.

EPILOGUE

The overriding message I hope every reader will take away from this book is that attraction to faces is personal. As I have tried to make clear, there is no contradiction between this message and the fact that people tend to agree on who looks beautiful, sexy or fit. Each of us comes with a unique set of genes and experiences; each of us is cared for by different adults and are likely to grow attracted to their facial features; each of us has a unique set of friends and idols who bias our tastes as we adopt some of their facial values; and each person has their own moments of ecstasy and despair in relationships with others. Such individual experiences ensure that what we come to find attractive in faces is intensely personal. Intimacy, or feelings of love or hatred release chemicals that can cement or corrode what we desire in faces.

Another point I hope will stick is that life teaches each one of us to be pragmatic. Some people so eclipse our own attractiveness that their disdain for us teaches us to shun their particular facial cues and place more emphasis on other cues – those that suggest compatibility in personality, family values, and humour. We learn to be attracted to the attainable.

Conceptions and misconceptions

Most people think they can tell character from a face. Chapter 9 looked at the evidence carefully and, yes, face-reading is alive and well and to a degree, legitimate. Many aspects of a character *are* written in the face (even if the clues we used to discern character have yet to be defined). Nonetheless, there needs to be a word of caution. Most of us are not very good at face-reading. We may do better than chance at guessing someone's temperament, which can help in social encounters, but we should not get carried away because our accuracy in assessing character from faces is low and the personality we presume that others have may contribute to the way they behave. Moreover, some aspects of life are simply not written in the face, despite popular belief. Sexual orientation and religious faith, for example, are indiscernible. Certainly, many people choose to display outwardly their persuasions or beliefs but others do not, and, without the display, 'gaydar' – and its equivalent for religion – do not work, at least from facial cues alone.

232

Future directions

One aspect of attraction that remains a mystery to scientists is the question of the origins of sexual preferences. The book has dealt with what is attractive in male and female faces but has not dealt with sexual preferences. Preferences are hugely powerful and are actuated by some biological switch so far concealed to science. Yes, there may be hints in early behaviour but nothing really predictive of adult preferences. Some have suggested a role for the pheromones discussed in Chapter 5 and there is likely to be something in this. Certainly putative pheromones are similar in structure to sex hormones and we have specialized smell recep-tors exclusively for them. Little is known about how naturally occurring levels of these substances affect attraction. There is a mystique about pheromones: they may influence behaviour without conscious awareness. Their role in attraction and how preferences develop through puberty more generally are important subjects of ongoing study.

A criticism of research on facial characteristics is that much of it involves artificial choices with observers marking scores on a scale of 1–7 to indicate how much they are attracted to a face. Little has been done to connect such ratings with real romances, and without a doubt, attraction researchers need to discover what goes on in life rather than in the labo-ratory. Of course, the real world is not made up of computer-generated images of faces, so researchers will have to be clever. The first steps in this direction are being taken with data from research on speed-dating.

Interpretations of attraction to male faces have assumed that mascu-linity symbolizes a healthy immune system, and that male attractiveness is defined by this health cue. It's a nice story but the evidence so far is not convincing. For a start there are myriad more obvious cues to health discussed in Chapter 7, and I am sure that there are even more cues to health waiting to be found in the structure of the face and in the texture of the skin. Chapter 5 painted a dark picture of aspects of masculinity, but future face research may redress the balance and show that masculinity is a boon for other admirable qualities such as leadership, decisiveness and heroism.

Technological advances that have made the systematic study of attractiveness possible continue apace, and we can look forward to emp-loying the techniques for creating life-like 'virtual' humans that have been developed for use in video games and cinema. We can look forward in the science of attraction to using these advances to study the role of emotion and personality in the faces of computer-generated actors who will 'react' to our questions, gestures and expressions. Indeed, it is easy to understand the growing preoccupation with life in virtual worlds where our own avatars – commonly idealized versions of ourselves – are attracted to those of others and we become enmeshed in cyber-romances. The rules of attraction in such imaginative worlds will be unconstrained by our mortal form. Digital and real worlds could blend and attraction in this future compound of virtual and actual worlds will be intriguing both for psychology and for the entertainment industry. Society will need to be prepared to deal with the social problems too, such as the kind of predatory behaviour that exists in the real world, that are likely to arise in interactions between avatars.

In this book we have explored what we know and don't know about beauty in the human face, but it is reasonable to wonder whether the techniques we have developed to do that can be applied to wider aesthetic judgements. Could we develop an empirical science of beauty in art, music or the natural world? Historically, beauty has been the domain of philosophers, poets, art critics and artists – and it might seem that a science of aesthetics is an oxymoron. The actual subject of enquiry, however, is identical: it is the evolving human mind which perceives and prefers. I see no reason why beauty found in phenomena other than faces cannot be studied with scientific methods. Perhaps one day we will learn that what we find attractive in nature and art reflects, in part, what we are attracted to in humans.

NOTES

Chapter 1

1 Ears are positioned on the front of the body too, but usually on the sides of the face. This lateral position allows us to detect the direction from which sounds originate – the ear at which the sound arrives first, or to which it sounds louder, will be the one nearer to the sound source.

2 Changizi, M.A., Zhang, Q. & Shimojo, S. (2006) Bare skin, blood and the evolution of primate colour vision. *Biology Letters* 2: 217–221.

3 Fleagle, J.G. (1999) *Primate Adaptation and Evolution*, 2nd edn. New York: Academic Press.
   Klein, R.G. (2009) *The Human Career: Human Biological and Cultural Origins*, 3rd edn. Chicago: University of Chicago Press.

4 Foley, R. (1987) *Another Unique Species: Patterns in Human Evolutionary Ecology*. Harlow: Longman Scientific & Technical.

5 Rilling, J.K. (2006) Human and nonhuman primate brains: are they allometrically scaled versions of the same design? *Evolutionary Anthropology* 15: 65–77.

6 The brain size of ancestral *Homo erectus* varied, with some of the largest specimens reaching 1200 cubic centimetres. Modern man or *Homo sapiens* has a brain size of about 1400 cubic centimetres.

7 Perrett, D.I., Lee, K., Penton-Voak, I., Burt, D.M., Rowland, D., Yoshikawa, S., Henzi, S.P., Castles, D. & Akamatsu, S. (1998) Sexual dimorphism and facial attractiveness. *Nature* 394: 884–886.

8 Daegling, D.J. (1993) Functional morphology of the human chin. *Evolutionary Anthropology* 1: 170–177.

9 Abbott, D.J., Baroody, F.M., Naureckas, E. & Naclerio, R.M. (2001) Elevation of nasal mucosal temperature increases the ability of the nose to warm and humidify air. *American Journal of Rhinology* 15: 41–45.

10 Morgan, E. (1997) *The Aquatic Ape Hypothesis*. London: Souvenir Press.

11 McNeill, D. (1998) *The Face: a Natural History*. New York: Little, Brown & Company.

12 Kobayashi, H. & Kohshima, S. (2001) Unique morphology of the human eye and its adaptive meaning: comparative studies on external morphology of the primate eye. *J. Human Evolution* 40: 419–435.

13 Baron-Cohen, S. (1994) How to build a baby that can read minds: cognitive mechanisms in mindreading. *Cahiers de Psychologie Cognitive* [*Current Psychology of Cognition*] 13: 513–552.
   Perrett, D.I. & Emery, N.J. (1994) Understanding the intentions of others from visual signals: neurophysiological evidence. *Cahiers de Psychologie Cognitive* [*Current Psychology of Cognition*] 13: 683–694.

14 Jellema, T., Baker, C.I., Wicker, B. & Perrett, D.I. (2000) Neural representation for the perception of the intentionality of hand actions. *Brain and Cognition* 44: 280–302.

15 Perrett, D.I. & Mistlin, A.J. (1990) Perception of facial attributes. In: Stebbins, W.C. & Berkley, M.A. (eds) *Comparative Perception, vol. II: Complex Signals*, pp. 187–215. New York: John Wiley.

16 Boesch, C. & Boesch-Achermann, H. (2000) *The Chimpanzees of the Taï Forest: Behavioural Ecology and Evolution*. New York: Oxford University Press.

17 Sadr, J., Jarudi, I. & Sinha, P. (2003) The role of eyebrows in face recognition. *Perception* 32: 285–293.

18 Surakka, V. & Hietanen, J.K. (1998) Facial and emotional reactions to Duchenne and non-Duchenne smiles. *International Journal of Psychophysiology* 29: 23–33.

19 Messinger, D. & Fogel, A. (2007). The interactive development of social smiling. In: Kail, R.V. (ed.) *Advances in Child Development and Behavior*, pp. 327–366. Amsterdam, NL: Elsevier.

20 Ekman, P. & Friesen, W.V. (1969) The repertoire of nonverbal behavior: categories, origins, usage, and coding. *Semiotica* 1: 49–98.

   Young, A., Perrett, D.I., Calder, A., Sprengelmeyer, R. & Ekman, P. (2002) *Facial Expressions of Emotion: Stimuli and Test (FEEST)*. Bury St Edmunds, Suffolk: Thames Valley Test Company.

   Cultural universality of expression recognition has been questioned recently, but the study is based on a small sample (12) of recent Chinese immigrants who were not tested in their native language.

   Jack, R., Blais, C., Scheepers, C., Schyns, P. & Caldara, R. (2009) Cultural confusions show that facial expressions are not universal. *Current Biology* 19: 1543–1548.

21 Tracy, J.L. & Matsumoto, D. (2008) The spontaneous expression of pride and shame: evidence for biologically innate nonverbal displays. *Proceedings of the National Academies of Sciences* 105: 11655–11660.

22 For discussion, see: de Waal, F. (2006) *Primates and Philosophers: How Morality Evolved*. Princeton, NJ: Princeton University Press.

23 Marler, P. & Evans, C.S. (1996). Bird calls: just emotional displays or something more? *Ibis* 138: 26–33.

24 Brosnan, S.F. & de Waal, F.B.M. (2002) Regulation of vocal output by chimpanzees finding food in the presence or absence of an audience. *Evolution of Communication* 4: 211–224.

25 Kunz, M., Mylius, V., Schepelmann, K. & Lautenbacher, S. (2004) On the relationship between self-report and facial expression of pain. *The Journal of Pain* 5: 368–376.

26 Rosenstein, D. & Oster, H. (1988) Differential facial responses to four basic tastes in newborns. *Child Development* 59: 1555–1568.

27 Burt, D.M., Payne, K.R. & Perrett, D.I. (2003) Perceptual judgements of others' tasting experiences: are they enjoying their food? *Perceptual and Motor Skills* 96: 444–454.

28 Bechara, A., Damasio, H., Tranel, D. & Damasio, A.R. (1997) Deciding advantageously before knowing the advantageous strategy. *Science* 275: 1293–1295.

29 Evans, C.E.Y., Kemish, K. & Turnbull, O.H. (2004) Paradoxical effects of education on the Iowa Gambling Task. *Brain and Cognition* 54: 240–244.

Chapter 2

1 Zeki, S.M., Watson, J.D.G., Lueck, C.J., Friston, K., Kennard, C. & Frackowiak, R.S.J. (1991). A direct demonstration of functional specialization in human visual cortex. *Journal of Neuroscience* 11: 641–649.

2 Downing, P., Jiang, Y., Shuman, M. & Kanwisher, N. (2001) A cortical area selective for visual processing of the human body. *Science* 293: 2470–2473.

Pinsk, M.A., Arcaro, M., Weiner, K.S., Kalkus, J.F., Inati, S.J., Gross, C. G. & Kastner, S. (2009) Neural representations of faces and body parts in macaque and human cortex: a comparative fMRI study. *Journal of Neurophysiology* 101: 2581–2600.

3 Burt, D.M. & Perrett, D.I. (1997) Perceptual asymmetries in judgements of facial attractiveness, age, gender, speech and expression. *Neuropsychologia* 35: 685–693.

4 Young, A.W., Hellawell, D.J., Van de Wal, C. & Johnson, M. (1986) Matching familiar and unfamiliar faces on identity and expression. *Psychological Research* 48: 63–682.

5 Nobre, A.C., Allison, T. & McCarthy, G. (1994) Word recognition in the human inferior temporal lobe. *Nature* 372: 260–263.

6 Kanwisher, N. & Yovel, G. (2006) The fusiform face area: a cortical region specialized for the perception of faces. *Philosophical Transactions of the Royal Society of London, B: Biological Sciences* 361: 2109–28.

7 Grill-Spector, K., Knouf, N. & Kanwisher, N. (2004) The fusiform face area subserves face perception, not generic within-category identification. *Nature Neuroscience* 7: 555–562.

8 Pinsk, M.A., Desimone, K., Moore, T., Gross, C.G. & Kastner, S. (2005) Representations of faces and body parts in macaque temporal cortex: a functional MRI study. *Proceedings of the National Academy of Sciences U.S.A.* 102: 6996–7001.

Pinsk, M.A., Arcaro, M., Weiner, K.S., Kalkus, J.F., Inati, S.J., Gross, C.G. & Kastner, S. (2009) Neural representations of faces and body parts in macaque and human cortex: a comparative fMRI study. *Journal of Neurophysiology* 101: 2581–2600.

Schwarzlose, R.F., Baker, C.I. & Kanwisher, N. (2005) Separate face and body selectivity on the fusiform gyrus. *Journal of Neuroscience* 25: 11055–11059.

9 Tsao, D.Y., Freiwald, W.A., Tootell, R.B.H. & Livingstone, M.S. (2006) A cortical region consisting entirely of face-selective cells. *Science* 311: 670–674.

10 Perrett, D.I., Oram, M.W., Hietanen, J.K. & Benson, P.J. (1994) Issues of representation in object vision. In: Farah, M. & Ratcliff, G. (eds) *The Neuropsychology of Higher Vision: Collated Tutorial Essays*, pp. 33–61. Hillsdale, NJ: Lawrence Erlbaum.

Harries, M.H., Perrett, D.I. & Lavender, A. (1991) Preferential inspection of views of 3-D model heads. *Perception* 20: 669–680.

Perrett, D.I., Hietanen, J.K., Oram, M.W. & Benson, P.J. (1992) Organization and functions of cells responsive to faces in the temporal cortex. *Philosophical Transactions of the Royal Society of London* 335: 23–30.

11 Perrett, D.I., Oram, M.W. & Wachsmuth, E. (1998) Evidence accumulation in cell populations responsive to faces: an account of generalisation of recognition without mental transformations. *Cognition* 67: 111–145.

12 There are in fact additional views (e.g. half-profile) represented in the brain as the head rotates, but the copies of the plans for the principal views (front, side, and back) are more numerous.

13 Perrett, D.I., Oram, M.W. & Wachsmuth, E. (1998) Evidence accumulation in cell populations responsive to faces: an account of generalisation of recognition without mental transformations. *Cognition* 67: 111–145.

14 Thompson. P. (1980) Margaret Thatcher: a new illusion. *Perception* 9: 483–484. (The same can be done with anybody's face, not just Lady Thatcher's.)

15 Leopold, D.A., Bondar, I.V. & Giese, M.A. (2006) Norm-based face encoding by single neurons in the monkey inferotemporal cortex. *Nature* 442: 572–575.

   Young, M.P. & Yamane, S. (1992) Sparse population coding of faces in the inferotemporal cortex. *Science* 256: 1327–1331.

   Kendrick, K.M. & Baldwin, B.A. (1987) Cells in temporal cortex of conscious sheep can respond to the sight of faces. *Science* 236: 448–450.

   Perrett, D.I., Smith, P.A., Potter, D.D., Mistlin, A.J., Head, A.S., Milner, A.D. & Jeeves, M.A. (1984) Neurones responsive to faces in the temporal cortex: studies of functional organization, sensitivity to identity and relation to perception. *Human Neurobiology* 3: 197–208.

16 Quiroga, R.Q., Reddy, L., Kreiman, G., Koch, C. & Fried, I. (2005) Invariant visual representation by single neurons in the human brain. *Nature* 435: 1102–1107.

   Bowers, J.S. (2009) On the biological plausibility of grandmother cells: implications for neural network theories in psychology and neuroscience. *Psychological Review* 116: 220–251.

17 Interestingly, although the 'Jennifer Aniston' neurone responded consistently to pictures of her in many different poses and light conditions, it did *not* respond to images of her in which she was shown with her former husband, the actor Brad Pitt.

18 Fried, F. (2007) From percept to memory: single neuron recordings in the human temporal lobe. Paper presented to the International Symposium on Cognitive Neurosurgery, 17–20 March 2007. Germany: Castle of Weitenburg.

   Quiroga, R.Q., Mukamel, R., Isham, E., Malach, R. & Fried, I. (2008) Human single neuron responses at the threshold of conscious recognition. *Proceedings of the National Academy of Sciences U.S.A.* 105: 3599–3604.

   Földiák, P. (2009) Neural coding: non-local but explicit and conceptual. *Current Biology* 19: R904–R906.

   See also an interview: Horgan, J. (2005) Can a single brain cell think? *Discover* 6/05. Available online at http://cbcl.mit.edu/news/files/kreiman-hogan-5-05.htm [accessed: 5/11/09].

19 The issue of how many cells are necessary is hotly debated. Experiments show that brain cells signal a particular person or a given object in an obvious manner; scientists listening from the outside can work out just who is visible from tuning in to the activity of only a few brain cells! If scientists can do this from the outside, the rest of the brain can, too. Our brains can tell who or what we are seeing from the activity of just a few cells in our memory system. Although we have countless billions of brain cells, it takes only one or two to know who we are looking at. But even if one were sufficient, importance demands lots of spares. In the same way, it takes one sperm to fertilize an egg, but men ejaculate 100 million at a time to make sure.

   Bowers, J.S. (2009) On the biological plausibility of grandmother cells: implications for neural network theories in psychology and neuroscience. *Psychological Review* 116: 220–251.

20 Quiroga, R.Q., Kraskov, A., Koch, C. & Fried, I. (2009) Explicit encoding of multimodal percepts by single neurons in the human brain. *Current Biology* [available online: 23/7/09].

21 Sacks, O. (1985) *The Man Who Mistook His Wife for A Hat and Other Clinical Tales*. London: Duckworth.

22 Behrmann, M., Avidan, G., Marotta, J.J. & Kimchi, R. (2005). Detailed exploration of face-related processing in congenital prosopagnosia: 1. Behavioral findings. *Journal of Cognitive Neuroscience* 17: 1130–1149.

23 For example, http://www.faceblind.org/ [accessed: 5/11/09].

24 Kennerknecht, I., Plümpe, N., Edwards, S. & Raman, R. (2007) Hereditary prosopagnosia (HPA): the first report outside the Caucasian population. *Journal of Human Genetics* 52: 230–236.

25 Bauer, R. (1984). Autonomic recognition of names and faces: a neuropsychological application of the Guilty Knowledge Test. *Neuropsychologia* 22: 457–469.

26 Milders, M.V. & Perrett, D.I. (1993) Recent developments in the neuropsychology and physiology of face processing. In: Kennard, C. (ed.) *Baillière's Clinical Neurology: Visual Perceptual Defects*, vol. 2, pp. 361–388. London: Baillière Tindall.

Wallace, M.A. & Farah, M.J. (1992) Savings in relearning face–name associations as evidence for 'covert recognition' in prosopagnosia. *Journal of Cognitive Neuroscience* 4: 150–154.

27 Butler, P.V. (2000). Diurnal variation in Cotard's syndrome (co-present with Capgras delusion) following traumatic brain injury. *Australian and New Zealand Journal of Psychiatry* 34: 684–687.

28 Hirstein, W. & Ramachandran, V.S. (1997) Capgras syndrome: a novel probe for understanding the neural representation of identity and familiarity of persons. *Proceedings of the Royal Society B* 264: 437–444.

29 Rolls, E.T., Perrett, D.I., Caan, W. & Wilson, F. (1982) Neuronal responses related to visual recognition. *Brain* 105: 611–646.

30 Ellis, H.D., Young, A.W., Quayle, A.H. & De Pauw, K.W. (1997) Reduced autonomic responses to faces in Capgras delusion. *Proceedings of the Royal Society B* 264: 1085–1092.

31 The brain wiring is crossed, so the left side of the world is processed initially by the right side of the brain. Right-sided brain damage can therefore result in a reduction of attention towards (neglect) of left space. Although left-side neglect and size distortion are commonly associated, they can occur separately.

32 Intriguingly, even were the person concerned to employ a tape measure to check that the left and right sides of an object were the same, this would still not reveal the distortion, as the tape itself might appear shrunk on the left.

33 Young, A.W., Edward, H.F., de Haan, E.H.F., Newcombe, F. & Hay, D.C. (1990) Facial neglect. *Neuropsychologia* 28: 391–415.

34 Trojano, L., Conson, M., Salzano, S., Manzo V. & Grossi, D. (2009) Unilateral left prosopometamorphopsia: a neuropsychological case study. *Neuropsychologia* 47: 942–948.

35 Assal, G. (1991) Disorders of face recognition. Paper presented to the Parisian Neuropsychological Club. Paris: Hôpital de la Salpêtrière.

36 Bauer, R.M. (1982) Visual hypoemotionality as a symptom of visual-limbic disconnection in man. *Archives of Neurology* 39: 702–708.

Sadr, J., Duchaine, B.C. & Nakayama, K. (2004) The perception of facial attractiveness in prosopagnosia. *Journal of Vision* 4: 914.

Some patients with prosopagnosia can sort faces on the basis of attractiveness: they even may produce a rank order from least to most attractive that parallels the rankings of normal people. It is difficult to know what these patients use as a basis for judging attractiveness. Faces may be sorted for symmetry, smiling expression, sex typicality, youth, and complexion, perhaps: such dimensions can still be judged, even after damage to face-processing systems sufficient to stop a patient identifying individual people. All the attributes listed contribute to beauty, as is discussed in Chapters 4, 7, and 9, but working out such face qualities is only one step in finding the face rewarding to gaze at.

37 Bauer, R.M. (1984) Autonomic recognition of names and faces in prosop-agnosia: a neuropsychological application of the Guilty Knowledge Test. *Neuropsychologia* 22: 457–469.

38 Jones, B.T., Jones, B.C., Thomas, A.P. & Piper, J. (2003) Alcohol consumption increases attractiveness ratings of opposite-sex faces: a third route to risky sex. *Addiction* 98: 1069–1075.

Lyvers, M., Cholakians, E., Puorro, M. & Sundram, S. (2010) Beer goggles: blood alcohol concentration in relation to attractiveness ratings for unfamiliar opposite sex faces in naturalistic settings. *Journal of Social Psychology*: in press.

Regular hazardous levels of drinking may prevent the effects from occurring, and may even produce long-term problems in making facial-attractiveness judgements.

Neave, N., Tsang, C. & Heather, N. (2008) Effects of alcohol and alcohol expectancy on perceptions of opposite-sex facial attractiveness in university students. *Addiction Research & Theory* 16: 359–368.

Oinonen, K.A. & Sterniczuk, R. (2008) An inverse relationship between typical alcohol consumption and facial symmetry detection ability in young women. *Journal of Psychopharmacology* 21: 507–518.

Parker, L.L.C., Penton-Voak, I.S., Attwood, A.S. & Munafò, M.R. (2008) Effects of acute alcohol consumption on ratings of attractiveness of facial stimuli: evidence of long-term encoding. *Alcohol and Alcoholism* 43: 636–640.

39 Friedman, R.S., McCarthy, D.M., Förster, J. & Denzler, M. (2005) Automatic effects of alcohol cues on sexual attraction. *Addiction* 100: 672–681.

40 Aharon, I., Etcoff, N., Ariely, D., Chabris, C.F., O'Connor, E. & Breiter, H. (2001) Beautiful faces have variable reward value: fMRI and behavioral evidence. *Neuron* 32: 537–551.

Like humans, male monkeys will work to see beautiful females. Indeed, male monkeys are so keen on viewing female monkeys that they are willing to forgo liq-uid refreshment in exchange for viewing such pictures, particularly smutty pictures of females. Unlike humans, they will also work to see images of dominant rivals.

Deaner, R.O., Khera, A.V. & Platt, M.P. (2005) Monkeys pay per view: adaptive valuation of social images by rhesus macaques. *Current Biology* 15: 543–548.

41 Levy, B., Ariely, D., Mazar, N., Chi, W., Lukas, S. & Elman, I. (2008) Gender differences in the motivational processing of facial beauty. *Learning and Motivation* 39: 136–145.

42 Schlaepfer, T.E., Cohen, M.X., Frick, C., Kosel, M., Brodesser, D., Axmacher, N., Joe, A.Y., Kreft, M., Lenartz, D. & Sturm, V. (2008) Deep brain stimula-tion to reward circuitry alleviates anhedonia in refractory major depression. *Neuropsychopharmacology* 33: 368–377.

43 Male sexual arousal from visual pornographic material is greater than female sexual arousal from pornographic material. Heterosexual men get much more aroused by seeing sexual images of women than by seeing sexual images of men. Heterosexual women get mildly aroused by both!

Chivers, M.L., Rieger, G., Latty, E. & Bailey, J.M. (2004) A sex difference in the specificity of sexual arousal. *Psychological Science* 15: 736–744.

44 Aharon, I., Etcoff, N., Ariely, D., Chabris, C.F., O'Connor, E. & Breiter, H. (2001) Beautiful faces have variable reward value: fMRI and behavioral evidence. *Neuron* 32: 537–551.

45 Kranz, F. & Ishai, A. (2006) Face perception is modulated by sexual preference. *Current Biology* 16: 63–68.

Ishai, A. (2007) Sex, beauty and the orbitofrontal cortex. *International Journal of Psychophysiology* 63: 181–185.

46 Chivers, M.L., Rieger, G., Latty, E. & Bailey, J.M. (2004) A sex difference in the specificity of sexual arousal. *Psychological Science* 15: 736–744.

47 Berridge, K.C. & Robinson, T.E. (2003) Parsing reward. *Trends in Neurosciences* 26: 507–513.

48 With age may come Alzheimer's disease, in which key proteins clump together into large masses, causing nerve cells to become damaged and tangled up such that they do not connect properly. We think of dementia in Alzheimer's disease as a general decline in mental abilities, and in the advanced stages it is: when the disease first strikes, however, it can affect just one place in the brain, so at first disorders may be quite selective.

49 Platek, S. (2009) Self-face recognition is affected by schizotypal personality traits. *Schizophrenia Research* 57: 81–85.

Traub, A.C. & Orbach, J. (1964) Psychophysical studies of body-image, I: The adjustable body-distorting mirror. *Archives of General Psychiatry* 11: 53–66.

Orbach, J., Traub, A.C. & Olson, R. (1966). Psychological studies of body-image, II: Normative data on the adjustable body-distorting mirror. *Archives of General Psychiatry* 14: 41–47.

50 Psychologists use reactions to mirrors as an indication of self-awareness. One may play a trick on a young chimp by painting some hair colour on the top of its head (without the chimp feeling it). If the chimpanzee notices the 'strange' hair colour on seeing itself in a mirror, and if it reacts (by adjusting its head posture to see the coloured hair more clearly, say, or by using the reflection to guide a hand to the coloured patch), then that chimp is said to be 'self-aware' – the chimp realizes that the image in the mirror is an extension of itself. This understanding of mirrors is a sophisticated ability and takes months of learning. Human infants under 15 months of age treat their own reflection as if it were another infant; only later do they show self-awareness.

51 Allison, T., Puce, A. & McCarthy, G. (2000) Social perception from visual cues: role of the STS region. *Trends in Cognitive Science* 4: 267–278.

Perrett, D.I., Harries, M.H., Mistlin, A.J., Hietanen, J., Benson, P.J., Bevan, R., Thomas, S., Ortega, J., Oram, M. & Brierly, K. (1990) Social signals analysed at the single cell level: someone's looking at me, something touched me, something moved. *International Journal of Comparative Psychology* 4: 25–50.

Chapter 3

1 Goren, C., Sarty, M. & Wu, P. (1975) Visual following and pattern discrimination of face-like stimuli by newborn infants. *Pediatrics* 56: 544–549.

Johnson, M.H., Dziurawiec, S., Ellis, H. & Morton, J. (1991) Newborns' preferential tracking of face-like stimuli and its subsequent decline. *Cognition* 40: 1–19.

2 Farroni, T., Csibra, G., Simion, F. & Johnson, M.H. (2002) Eye contact detection in humans from birth. *Proceedings of the National Academy of Sciences USA* 99: 9602–9605.

3 Hüppi, P.S., Warfield, S., Kikinis, R., Barnes, P.D., Zientara, G.P., Jolesz, F.A., Tsuji, M.K. & Volpe, J.J. (1998) Quantitative magnetic resonance imaging of brain development in premature and mature newborns. *Annals of Neurology* 43: 224–235.

   Johnson, M.H. (2005) Subcortical face processing. *Nature Reviews Neuroscience* 6: 766–774.

4 Simion, F., Valenza, E., Macchi Cassia, V., Turati, C. & Umiltà, C. (2002) Newborns' preference for up-down asymmetrical configurations. *Developmental Science* 5: 427–434.

5 Farroni, T., Johnson, M.H., Menon, E., Zulian, L., Faraguna, D. & Csibra, G. (2005) Newborns' preference for face-relevant stimuli: effects of contrast polarity. *Proceedings of the National Academy Sciences USA* 102: 17245–17250.

6 In a frontal view of a face while making eye contact, little of the whites of human eyes is visible.

7 Myowa-Yamakoshia, M. & Tomonagaa, M. (2001) Development of face recognition in an infant gibbon (*Hylobates agilis*). *Infant Behavior & Development* 24: 215–227.

8 Bard, K.A., Platzman, K.A., Lester, B.M. & Suomi, S.J. (1992) Orientation to social and nonsocial stimuli in neonatal chimpanzees and humans. *Infant Behavior & Development* 15: 43–56.

9 Mendelson, M.J. (1982) Clinical examination of visual and social responses in infant rhesus monkeys. *Developmental Psychology* 18: 658–662.

10 Scaife, M. (1976) The response to eye-like shapes by birds, II. The importance of staring, pairedness and shape. *Animal Behaviour* 24: 200–206.

11 Marx, G. & Kanfer, S. (2000) *The Essential Groucho: Writings By, For and About Groucho Marx*. Vintage.

12 Warland, D.K., Huberman, A.D. & Chalupa, L.M. (2006) Dynamics of spontaneous activity in the fetal macaque retina during development of retinogeniculate pathways. *Journal of Neuroscience* 26: 5190–5197.

   Huberman, A.D., Wang, G.Y., Liets, L.C., Collins, O.A., Chapman, B., Chalupa, L.M. (2003) Eye-specific retinogeniculate segregation independent of normal neuronal activity. *Science* 300: 994–998.

13 One may speculate that, if waves in the eye or from the ancient parts of the brain start out from a particular point just above the centre of vision, this kind of training might just give rise to babies' sensitivity to top-heavy patterns.

   Bednar, J.A. & Miikkulainen, R. (2003) Learning innate face preferences. *Neural Computation* 15: 1525–1557.

14 Bushnell, I.W.R., Sai, F. & Mullin, J.T. (1989) Neonatal recognition of the mother's face. *British Journal of Developmental Psychology* 7: 3–15.

   Pascalis, O., De Schonen, S., Morton, J., Deruelle, C. & Febre-Grenet, M. (1995) Mother's face recognition by neonates: a replication and an extension. *Infant Behavior & Development* 18: 79–85.

   Bushnell, I.W.R. (2001) Mother's face recognition in newborn infants: learning and memory. *Infant and Child Development* 10: 67–74.

15 Sai, F.Z. (2005) The role of the mother's voice in developing mother's face preference: evidence for intermodal perception at birth. *Infant and Child Development* 14: 29–50.

Kisilevsky, B.S., Hains, S.M.J., Lee, K., Xie, X., Huang, H., Ye, H.H., Zhang, K. & Wang, Z. (2003) Effects of experience on fetal voice recognition. *Psychological Science* 14: 220–224.

16 Ellis, H.D., Shepherd, J.W. & Davies, G.M. (1979) Identification of familiar and unfamiliar faces from internal and external features: some implications for theories of face recognition. *Perception* 8: 431–439.

Bushnell, I.W.R. (2003) Newborn face recognition. In: Pascalis, O. & Slater, A. (eds) *The Development of Face Processing in Infancy and Early Childhood*, pp. 41–53. New York: Nova Science Publishers.

17 Farroni, T., Csibra, G., Simion, F. & Johnson, M.H. (2002) Eye contact detection in humans from birth. *Proceedings of the National Academy of Sciences USA* 99: 9602–9605.

18 Elsabbagh, M., Volein, A., Csibra, G., Holmboe, K., Garwood, H., Tucker, L., Krljes, S., Baron-Cohen, S., Bolton, P., Charman, T., Baird, G. & Johnson, M.H. (2009) Neural correlates of eye gaze processing in the infant broader autism phenotype. *Biological Psychiatry* 65: 31–38.

Williams, J.H.G., Waiter, G.D., Perra, O., Perrett, D.I. & Whiten, A. (2005) An fMRI study of joint attention experience. *Neuroimage* 25: 133–140.

Waiter, G.D., Williams, J.H.G., Murray, A.D., Gilchrist, A., Perrett, D.I. & Whiten, A. (2005) Structural white matter deficits in high-functioning individuals with autistic spectrum disorder: a voxel-based investigation. *Neuroimage* 24: 455–461.

19 Baron-Cohen, S., Allen, J. & Gillberg, C. (1992) Can autism be detected at 18 months? The needle, the haystack, and the CHAT. *The British Journal of Psychiatry* 161: 839–843.

20 Grossman, T., Johnson, M.H., Lloyd-Fox, S., Blasi, A., Deligianni, F., Elwell, C. & Csibra, G. (2008) Early cortical specialization for face-to-face communication in human infants. *Proceedings of the Royal Society of London B* 275: 2803–2811.

21 Coss, R.G. (1978) Perceptual determinants of gaze aversion by the lesser mouse lemur (*Microcebus murinus*). *Behaviour* LXIV: 3–4.

22 Gómez, J.C. (2004) *Apes, Monkeys, Children, and the Growth of Mind*. Cambridge, MA: Harvard University Press.

23 de Waal, F.B.M. & van Roosmalen, A. (1979) Reconciliation and consolation among chimpanzees. *Behavioral Ecology and Sociobiology* 5: 55–66.

24 Doherty-Sneddon, G., Bruce, V., Bonner, L., Longbotham, S. & Doyle, C. (2002) Development of gaze aversion as disengagement from visual information. *Developmental Psychology* 38: 438–445.

25 There could well be cultural differences in these interactions.

26 Pascalis, O., de Haan, M. & Nelson, C.A. (2002) Is face processing species-specific during the first year of life? *Science* 296: 1321–1323.

27 Pascalis, O., Scott, L.S., Kelly, D.J., Shannon, R.W., Nicholson, E., Coleman, M. & Nelson, C.A. (2005) Plasticity of face processing in infancy. *Proceedings of the National Academy of Science*, 102: 5297–5300.

28 It's not clear whether it is the interest or the ability to pick up on subtle feature differences that is lost. It might be that we can no longer *see* how monkeys differ, or it might be that we no longer *care* how they differ.

29 Kuhl, P.K., Williams, K.A., Lacerda, F. & Stevens, K.N. (1992) Linguistic experience alters phonetic perception in infants by 6 months of age. *Science* 255: 606–608.

30 More precisely, the phonetic segments /l/ and /r/.

   Goto, H. (1971) Auditory perception by normal Japanese adults of the sounds 'l' and 'r'. *Neuropsychologia* 9: 317–323.

   Pallier, C., Bosch, L. & Sebastián-Gallés, N. (1997) A limit on behavioral plasticity in speech perception. *Cognition* 64: B9–B17.

31 English speakers use up to thirteen monophthongs (simple vowel sounds) depending on dialect and an additional seven diphthongs.

32 Sugita, Y. (2008) Face perception in monkeys reared with no exposure to faces. *Proceedings of the National Academy of Sciences USA* 105: 394–398.

33 Utt, A.C., Harvey, N.C., Hayes, W.K. & Carter, R.L. (2008) The effects of rearing method on social behaviors of mentored, captive-reared juvenile California condors. *Zoo Biology* 27: 1–18.

34 Kendrick, K.M., Hinton, M.R., Atkins, K., Haupt, M.A. & Skinner, J.D. (1998) Mothers determine male sexual preferences. *Nature* 395: 229–230.

35 Immelmann, K. (1975) Ecological significance of imprinting and early learning. *Annual Review of Ecology and Systematics* 6: 15–37.

36 Kendrick, K.M., Hinton, M.R., Atkins, K., Haupt, M.A. & Skinner, J.D. (1998) Mothers determine male sexual preferences. *Nature* 395: 229–230.

37 Meltzoff, A.N. & Moore, M.K. (1977) Imitation of facial and manual gestures by human neonates. *Science* 198: 75–78.

   Field, T.M., Woodson, R., Greenberg, R. & Cohen, D. (1982) Discrimination and imitation of facial expressions by neonates. *Science* 218: 179–181.

38 Anisfeld, M., Turkewitz, G., Rose, S.A., Rosenberg, F.R., Sheiber, F.J., Couturier-Fagan, D.A., Ger, J.S. & Sommer, I. (2001) No compelling evidence that newborns imitate oral gestures. *Infancy* 2: 111–122.

   Meltzoff, A.N. & Moore, M.K. (1983) Newborn infants imitate adult facial gestures. *Child Development* 54: 702–709.

   Myowa-Yamakoshi, M., Tomonaga, M., Tanaka, M. & Matsuzawa, T. (2004) Imitation in neonatal chimpanzees (*Pan troglodytes*). *Developmental Science* 7: 437–442.

   Bard, K.A. & Russell, C.L. (1999) Evolutionary foundations of imitation: social cognitive and developmental aspects of imitative processes in non-human primates. In: Nadel, J. & Butterworth, G. (eds) *Imitation in Infancy*, pp. 89–123. Cambridge: Cambridge University Press.

39 Dresser, N. (8/11/97) *Los Angeles Times*: http://articles.latimes.com/1997/nov/08/local/me-51420 [accessed: 9/09].

40 Jacobson, S.W. (1979) Matching behavior in the young infant. *Child Development* 50: 425–430.

   Jones, S.S. (1996) Imitation or exploration? Young infants' matching of adults' oral gestures. *Child Development* 67: 1952–1969.

   Neonatal imitation may be more specific during the first month of life.

41 Tomalski, P., Johnson, M.H. & Csibra, G. (2009) Temporal-nasal asymmetry of rapid orienting to face-like stimuli. *NeuroReport*: 20: 1309–1312.

42 Johnson, M.H. (2005) Subcortical face processing. *Nature Reviews Neuroscience* 6: 766–774.

43 Gilchrist, I.D. & Proske, H. (2006) Anti-saccades away from faces: evidence for an influence of high-level visual processes on saccade programming. *Experimental Brain Research* 173: 708–712.

44 Tomalski, P. (2008) Personal communication. Centre for Brain and Cognitive Development, School of Psychology, Birkbeck College, London.

45 Snowdon, C.T. (2003) Expression of emotion in nonhuman animals. In: Davidson, R.J., Scherer, K.R. & Goldsmith, H.H. (eds) *Handbook of Affective Sciences*, pp. 457–480.
    Chevalier-Skolnikoff, S. (1974) Male-female, female-female, and male-male sexual behavior in the stumptail monkey, with special attention to the female orgasm. *Journal Archives of Sexual Behavior* 3: 1573–2800.
    The connection between licking and courtship is much older. Reptiles lick the air to get odours on their tongue which are then carried to receptors on the roof of their mouth. In many species, from reptiles onward, the system is the route by which sex-hormone odours (pheromones) produce their reaction. Stallions, stags, and bulls, for example, lick the female or the air near her to taste her sexual status. This behaviour can also be seen in monkeys.

46 Ferrari, P.F., Visalberghi, E., Paukner, A., Fogassi, L., Ruggiero, A. & Suomi, S.J. (2006) Neonatal imitation in rhesus macaques. *Public Library of Science Biology* 4: 1501–1508.

47 Fontaine, R. (1984) Imitative skills between birth and six months. *Infant Behavior and Development* 7: 323–333.

48 Williams, J.H.G., Whiten, A., Suddendorf, T. & Perrett, D.I. (2001) Imitation, mirror neurons and autism. *Neuroscience and Behavioural Reviews* 25: 287–295.

49 Kelly, D.J., Quinn, P.C., Slater, A.M., Lee, K., Ge, L. & Pascalis, O. (2007) The other-race effect develops during infancy: evidence of perceptual narrowing. *Psychological Science* 18: 1084–1089.

50 Kelly, D.J., Liu, S., Lee, K., Quinn, P.C., Pascalis, O., Slater, A.M. & Ge, L. (2009) Development of the other-race effect during infancy: evidence toward universality? *Journal of Experimental Child Psychology* 104: 105–114.

51 In these experiments, experience is found to alter attraction of the young infant to faces. It is not clear how experience will affect attraction in later life (though see Chapter 10); early multicultural experience could well have a positive effect on social integration of different ethnic groups.

52 Kelly, D.J., Quinn, P.C., Slater, A.M., Lee, K., Gibson, A., Smith, M., Ge, L. & Pascalis, O. (2005) Three-month-olds, but not newborns, prefer own-race faces. *Developmental Science* 8: F31–F36.

53 Quinn, P.C., Yahr, J., Kuhn, A., Slater, A.M. & Pascalis, O. (2002) Representation of the gender of human faces by infants: a preference for female. *Perception* 31: 1109–1121.

54 Van Duuren, M., Kendell-Scott, L. & Stark, N. (2003) Early aesthetic choices: infant preference for attractive premature infant faces. *International Journal of Behavioral Development* 27: 212–219.
    Rubenstein, A.J., Kalakanis, L. & Langlois, J.H. (1999) Infant preferences for attractive faces: a cognitive explanation. *Developmental Psychology* 35: 848–855.
    Langlois, J.H., Ritter, J.M., Roggman, L.A. & Vaughn, L.S. (1991) Facial diversity and infant preference for attractive faces. *Developmental Psychology* 27: 79–84.
    Langlois, J.H., Roggman, L.A., Casey, R.J., Ritter, J.M., Rieser-Danner, L.A. & Jenkins, V.Y. (1987) Infant preferences for attractive faces: rudiments of a stereotype. *Developmental Psychology* 23: 363–369.

55 Slater, A., von der Schulenburg, C., Brown, E., Badenoch, M., Butterworth, G., Parsons, S. & Samuels, C. (1998) Newborn infants prefer attractive faces. *Infant Behavior and Development* 21: 345–354.

56 Slater, A.M., Bremner, G., Johnson, S.P., Sherwood, P., Hayes, R. & Brown, E. (2000) Newborn infants' preference for attractive faces: the role of internal and external facial features. *Infancy* 1: 265–274.
57 Quinn, P.C., Kelly, D.J., Lee, K., Pascalis, O. & Slater, A.M. (2007) Preference for attractive faces in human infants extends beyond conspecifics. *Developmental Science* 11: 76–83.
58 Tiger, tiger, burning bright
    In the forests of the night,
    What immortal hand or eye
    Dare frame thy fearful symmetry?
           William Blake (1757–1827)
59 A word of caution is needed, however: in some situations longer looking times may be indicative of novelty rather than aesthetics.
    Rhodes, G., Geddes, K., Jeffery, L., Dziurawiec, S. & Clark, A. (2002) Are average and symmetric faces attractive to infants? Discrimination and looking preferences. *Perception* 31: 315–321.
60 Walton, G.E. & Bower, T.G.R. (1993) Newborns form 'prototypes' in less than 1 minute. *Psychological Science* 4: 203–205.
    de Haan, M., Johnson, M.H., Maurer, D. & Perrett, D.I. (2001) Recognition of individual faces and average face prototypes by 1- and 3-month-old infants. *Cognitive Development* 16: 659–678.

Chapter 4

 1 http://www.flickr.com/photos/24443965@N08/3553333048/in/set-72157607060944155/ [accessed: 20/9/09].
    Poisson, B.A. (2002) *The Ainu of Japan*. Minneapolis: Lerner Publications.
 2 Burriss, R.P., Rowland, H.M. & Little, A.C. (2009) Facial scarring enhances men's attractiveness for short-term relationships. *Personality and Individual Differences* 46: 213–217.
    Lizot, J. (1985) *Tales of the Yanomami: Daily Life in the Venezuelan Forest*. Cambridge: Cambridge University Press.
 3 Jones, A. (2001) Dental anthropology: dental transfigurements in Borneo. *British Dental Journal* 191. 98–102.
 4 Frank, H.A. (1926) *East of Siam: Ramblings in the Five Divisions of French Indo-China*. New York: Century.
 5 Wolf, N. (1991) *The Beauty Myth: How Images of Beauty Are Used Against Women*. Garden City, N.Y.: Anchor Books.
 6 Perrett, D.I., May, K.A. & Yoshikawa, S. (1994) Facial shape and judgements of female attractiveness. *Nature* 257: 128–131.
    To know just how general agreement is, one should examine remote cultures where Western media has had little influence. In these cultures, opinion about many aspects of facial beauty (including those discussed in this chapter) is consistent with that in the West, although there are differences in opinion over the level of body weight that is considered attractive.
    Tovée, M.J., Swami, V., Furnham, A. & Mangalparsad, R. (2006) Changing perceptions of attractiveness as observers are exposed to a different culture. *Evolution and Human Behavior* 27: 443–456.
 7 Langlois, J.H., Kalakanis, L., Rubenstein, A.J., Larson, A., Hallam, M. & Smoot, M. (2000) Maxims or myths of beauty? A meta-analytic and theoretical review. *Psychological Bulletin* 126: 390–423.

8 Bate, B. & Cleese, J. (2001) *The Human Face*. New York, N.Y.: DK Publishing. See also: http://www.beautyanalysis.com/ [accessed: 20/9/09].

9 The ratio 8/5 (1.6) is an approximation to the golden ratio $(1+\sqrt{5})/2$ or 1.618.

10 Markowsky, G. (1992) Misconceptions about the golden ratio. *The College Mathematics Journal* 23: 2–19.

  Falbo, C. (2005) The golden ratio – a contrary viewpoint. *College Mathematics Journal* 36: 123–134.

11 Technically these random asymmetries are referred to as 'fluctuating asymmetries'. Across the population, some have a larger left side, while others have a larger right side. On average, there is no consistent asymmetry – the degree of asymmetry 'fluctuates' from individual to individual – but for each individual, the degree of asymmetry is fixed: it does not wax and wane like the moon.

12 Møller, A.P. (1993) Female preference for apparently symmetrical male sexual ornaments in the barn swallow *Hirundo rustica*. *Behavioral Ecology and Sociobiology* 32: 371–376.

13 Blount, B.C., Mack, M.M., Wehr, C.M., MacGregor, J.T., Hiatt R.A., Wang, G., Wickramasinghe, S.N., Everson, R.B. & Ames, B.N. (1997) Folate deficiency causes uracil misincorporation into human DNA and chromosome breakage: implications for cancer and neuronal damage. *Proceedings of the National Academy of Sciences U.S.A.* 94: 3290–3295.

14 Deviations from perfect bilateral symmetry were measured in traits including ear size and nostril width. Symmetrical subjects had lower best 800- and 1500-metre times than asymmetrical subjects.

  Manning, J.T & Pickup, L.J. (1998) Symmetry and performance in middle distance runners. *International Journal of Sports Medicine* 19: 205–209.

15 Brown, W.M., Cronk, L., Grochow, K., Jacobson, A., Liu, C.K., Popovi, Z. & Trivers, R. (2005) Dance reveals symmetry especially in young men. *Nature* 438: 1148–1150.

16 Brown, W. (2009) Paper presented at *The Science of Attraction*. British Science Festival: 5–10/9/09. Guildford: University of Surrey.

17 Martin, S.M., Manning, J.T. & Dowrick, C.F. (1999) Fluctuating asymmetry, relative digit length, and depression in men. *Evolution and Human Behavior* 20: 203–214.

  Thornhill, R. & Gangestad, S.W. (1999) The scent of symmetry: a human pheromone that signals fitness? *Evolution and Human Behavior* 20: 175–201.

  Hughes, S.M., Harrison, M.A. & Gallup, G.G. (2002) The sound of symmetry: voice as a marker of developmental instability. *Evolution and Human Behavior* 23: 173–180.

  Manning, J.T., Scutt, D. & Lewis-Jones, D.I. (1998) Developmental stability, ejaculate size, and sperm quality in men. *Evolution and Human Behavior* 19: 273–282.

18 Thornhill, R., Gangestad, S.W. & Comer, R. (1995) Human female orgasm and mate fluctuating asymmetry. *Animal Behavior* 50: 1601–1615.

  Shackelford, T.K., Weekes-Shackelford, V.A., LeBlanc, G.J., Bleske, A.L., Euler, H.A. & Hoier, S. (2000) Female coital orgasm and male attractiveness. *Human Nature* 11: 299–306.

19 Emmanuele Jannini at the University of L'Aquila claims that anatomical differences mean that some women have the elusive G-spot (and vaginal orgasms) and some don't.

Gravina, G.L., Brandetti, F., Martini, P., Carosa, E., Di Stasi, S.M., Morano, S., Lenzi, A. & Jannini, E.A. (2008) Measurement of the thickness of the urethrovaginal space in women with or without vaginal orgasm. *Journal of Sexual Medicine* 5: 610–618.

20 Valentine, T. (1991) A unified account of the effects of distinctiveness, inversion and race in face recognition. *Quarterly Journal of Experimental Psychology* 43A: 161–204.

21 Graves, R., Goodglass, H. & Landis, T. (1982) Mouth asymmetry during spontaneous speech. *Neuropsychologia* 20: 371–381.

Graves, R. & Landis, T. (1990) Asymmetry in mouth opening during different speech tasks. *International Journal of Psychology* 25: 179–189.

Wolf, M.E. & Goodale, M.A. (1987) Oral asymmetries during verbal and non-verbal movements of the mouth. *Neuropsychologia* 25: 375–396.

22 Kowner, R. (1996) Facial asymmetry and attractiveness judgement in developmental perspective. *Journal of Experimental Psychology: Human Perception and Performance* 22: 662–675.

Samuels, C.A., Butterworth, G., Roberts, T., Graupner, L. & Hoyle, G. (1994) Facial aesthetics: babies prefer attractiveness to symmetry. *Perception* 23: 823–831.

Langlois, J.H., Roggman, L.A. & Musselman, L. (1994) What is average and what is not average about attractive faces. *Psychological Science* 5: 214–220.

23 Perrett, D.I., Burt, D.M., Penton-Voak, I.S., Lee, K.J., Rowland, D.A. & Edwards, R. (1999) Symmetry and human facial attractiveness. *Evolution and Human Behavior* 20: 295–307.

24 It is possible that asymmetry was preferred in some other studies because *skin texture* looked worse in the symmetric faces. Blending a whole face with its entire mirror image actually *increases* the number of apparent blemishes. For example, a face with a dark spot on the left cheek combined with its mirror image would generate a face with two spots at symmetrical positions on the left and right cheeks. Although this face would look symmetrical, the increased spottiness might look unhealthy.

Swaddle, J.P. & Cuthill, I.C. (1995) Asymmetry and human facial attractiveness: symmetry may not always be beautiful. *Proceedings of the Royal Society B* 261: 111–116.

25 Perrett, D.I., Burt, D.M., Penton-Voak, I.S., Lee, K.J., Rowland, D.A. & Edwards, R. (1999) Symmetry and human facial attractiveness. *Evolution and Human Behavior* 20: 295–307.

26 The outline shape of a face feature can be symmetrical even though the skin pattern is asymmetrical.

27 Perrett, D.I., Burt, D.M., Penton-Voak, I.S., Lee, K.J., Rowland, D.A. & Edwards, R. (1999) Symmetry and human facial attractiveness. *Evolution and Human Behavior* 20: 295–307.

28 Dunning, D., Meyerowitz, J.A. & Holzberg, A.D. (1989) Ambiguity and self-evaluation: the role of idiosyncratic trait definitions in self-serving assessments of ability. *Journal of Personality and Social Psychology* 57: 1082–1090.

Pahl, S. & Eiser, J.R. (2005) Valence, comparison focus, and self-positivity biases: does it matter whether people judge positive or negative traits? *Experimental Psychology* 52: 303–310.

Lobmaier, J.S., Tiddeman, B.P. & Perrett, D.I. (2008) Emotional expression modulates perceived gaze direction. *Emotion* 8: 573–577.

29 Little, A.C., Burt, D.M., Penton-Voak, I.S. & Perrett, D.I. (2001) Self-perceived attractiveness influences human female preferences for sexual dimorphism and symmetry in male faces. *Proceedings of the Royal Society B* 268: 39–44.

30 Even starting with a universally admired trait like symmetry, we soon find that the *degree of attraction* to symmetry varies between people. This can level the playing field and give everyone a chance of finding a mate.

31 Langlois, J. & Roggman, L.A. (1990) Attractive faces are only average. *Psychological Science* 1: 115–121.

32 Penton-Voak, I.S. & Perrett, D.I. (2001) Male facial attractiveness: perceived personality and shifting female preferences for male traits across the menstrual cycle. *Advances in Animal Behaviour* 30: 219–259.

Little, A.C. & Hancock, P.J. (2002) The role of masculinity and distinctiveness on the perception of attractiveness in human male faces. *British Journal of Psychology* 93: 451–464.

33 Benson, P.J. & Perrett, D.I. (1992) Face-to-face with computer transformations. *New Scientist* 133 (1809): 32–35.

Penton-Voak, I.S. & Perrett, D.I. (2001) Male facial attractiveness: perceived personality and shifting female preferences for male traits across the menstrual cycle. *Advances in Animal Behaviour* 30: 219–259.

34 Being far from average *may* be stigmatized because of the potential association with genetic abnormalities. The limitations of such a generalization are discussed in Chapter 9.

35 Halberstadt, J. & Rhodes, G. (2000) The attractiveness of nonface averages: implications for an evolutionary explanation of the attractiveness of average faces. *Psychological Science* 11: 285–289.

36 Actual order, clockwise from 12 o'clock: Klimt, Manet, Mucha, Raphael, Botticelli, Renoir, Gérôme, and Ingres.

37 Grogan, P. (1996) *Recognition of Prototypes and Caricatures of Famous Artists' Portraits*. University of St Andrews: BSc Psychology project.

This project tested style recognition by art history students and staff at the university. Participants were shown the faces in eight original portraits by each of the painters in Figure 4.7, plus one computer composite for that painter (combining the eight different originals by that artist). The pictures were shown one at a time and participants asked which of the eight named artists had painted the face. Background cues were carefully removed so that recognition depended on the faces alone.

38 One can treat the face image as if it were a sheet of rubber – pull at one feature landmark on the sheet and the neighbouring face parts will stretch with it.

39 Brennan, S.E. (1985) The caricature generator. *Leonardo* 18: 170–178.

Benson, P.J. & Perrett, D.I. (1991) Synthesising continuous-tone caricatures. *Image and Vision Computing* 9: 123–129.

Benson, P.J. & Perrett, D.I. (1991) Perception and recognition of photographic quality facial caricatures: implications for the recognition of natural images. *European Journal of Psychology* 3: 105–135.

40 Lee, K.J. & Perrett, D.I. (2000) Manipulation of colour and shape information and its consequences upon recognition and best-likeness judgements. *Perception* 29: 1291–1312.

41 In work with Emma O'Loghlen, we found that 21 out of 26 different artists' styles were recognized at an above-chance rate by St Andrews art history students.

O'Loghlen, E. (1998) *The Use of Computerized Transforms to Investigate Differential Recognition of Artistic Styles*. University of St Andrews: BSc Psychology project.

42 Carbon, C.C. & Leder, H. (2006) The *Mona Lisa* effect: is 'our' Lisa fame or fake? *Perception* 35: 411–414. http://www.perceptionweb.com/misc/p5452/ [accessed: 14/12/09].

43 Rhodes, G., Jeffery, L., Watson, T.L., Clifford, C.W.G. & Nakayama, K. (2003). Fitting the mind to the world: face adaptation and attractiveness aftereffects. *Psychological Science* 14: 558–566.

44 Exactly how durable effects are has not yet been resolved. They can certainly last a day, and probably a lot longer, depending on test circumstances.

Carbon, C.C., Strobach, T., Langton, S.R., Harsányi, G., Leder, H. & Kovács, G. (2007) Adaptation effects of highly familiar faces: immediate and long lasting. *Memory and Cognition* 35: 1966–1976.

Leopold, D.A., Rhodes, G., Müller, K.-M. & Jeffery, L. (2005) The dynamics of visual adaptation to faces. *Proceedings of the Royal Society B* 272: 897–904.

45 Bestelmeyer, P.E.G., Jones, B.C., DeBruine, L.M., Little, A.C., Perrett, D.I., Schneider, A., Welling, L.L.M. & Conway, C.A. (2008) Sex-contingent face aftereffects depend on perceptual category rather than structural encoding. *Cognition* 107: 353–365.

Little, A.C., DeBruine, L.M., Jones, B.C. & Waitt, C. (2007) Category contingent aftereffects for faces of different races, ages and species. *Cognition* 106: 1537–1547.

Little, A.C., DeBruine, L.M. & Jones, B.C. (2005) Sex-contingent face aftereffects suggest distinct neural populations code male and female faces. *Proceedings of the Royal Society B* 272: 2283–2287.

Webster, M.A., Kaping, D., Mizokami, Y. & Duhamel, P. (2004) Adaptation to natural facial categories. *Nature* 428: 557–561.

46 Perrett, D.I., May, K.A. & Yoshikawa, S. (1994) Facial shape and judgements of female attractiveness. *Nature* 368: 239–242.

The average of any random sample of people should be approximately the same as that for any other random sample, and should be the same as the average of the whole population. If beauty is just the central value of the population, then the average of unattractive individuals – who deviate a lot from the population centre, but in randomly different ways – should balance one another out, and their average should be the same as the average of everybody. Indeed, it should be the same as the average of attractive individuals (who should differ little from the population central value). The sum of small random deviations about a point should be the same as the sum of large random deviations about the same point. So the averageness hypothesis predicts that all three shapes will be the same. If beauty is systematically related to a feature like height, then predictions differ. The average of tall individuals will be taller than the average of all individuals, which in turn will be taller than the average of short individuals. In fact the High, Overall, and Low averages differ in attractiveness in just such an order.

DeBruine, L.M., Jones, B.C., Unger, L., Little, A.C. & Feinberg, D.R. (2007) Dissociating averageness and attractiveness: attractive faces are not always average. *Journal of Experimental Psychology: Human Perception and Performance* 33: 1420–1430.

47 Perrett, D.I., May, K.A. & Yoshikawa, S. (1994) Facial shape and judgements of female attractiveness. *Nature* 368: 239–242.

48 DeBruine, L.M., Jones, B.C., Unger, L., Little, A.C. & Feinberg, D.R. (2007) Dissociating averageness and attractiveness: attractive faces are not always average. *Journal of Experimental Psychology: Human Perception and Performance* 33: 1420–1430.

49 This logic has been suggested by several researchers. For example: Rubenstein, A.J., Langlois, J.H. & Roggman, L.A. (2002) What makes a face attractive and why: the role of averageness in defining facial beauty. In: Rhodes, G. & Zebrowitz, L. (eds), *Facial Attractiveness: Evolutionary, Cognitive, and Social Perspectives*, pp. 1–34. Westport, CT: Ablex Publishing.

50 Mackie, L.M. (1994) *The Effect of Shape and Colour Manipulations on the Visual Perception of Facial Attractiveness*. University of St Andrews: BSc Psychology project.

Chapter 5

1 Jones, D. (1995) Sexual selection, physical attractiveness and facial neoteny: cross-cultural evidence and implications. *Current Anthropology* 36: 723–748.

2 Jasienka, G., Ziomkiewicz, A., Ellison, P.T., Lipson, S.F. & Thune, I. (2004) Large breasts and narrow waists indicate high reproductive potential in women. *Proceedings of the Royal Society B* 271: 1213–1217.

3 Singh, D. (2002) Female mate value at a glance: relationship of waist-to-hip ratio to health, fecundity and attractiveness. *Neuroendocrinology Letters* 4: 81–91.

4 Andean Indians prefer less hourglass-shaped bodies than European and North American populations. Yu, D.W. & Shepard, G.H. (1998) Is beauty in the eye of the beholder? *Nature* 396: 321–322.

5 Conard, N.J. (2009) A female figurine from the basal Aurignacian of Hohle Fels Cave in southwestern Germany. *Nature* 459: 248–252.

6 Weston, E.M., Friday, A.E. & Lio, P. (2007) Biometric evidence that sexual selection has shaped the hominin face. *Public Library of Science ONE* 2: 1–8.

7 Singh, D. (1993) Body shape and women's attractiveness – the critical role of waist-to-hip ratio. *Human Nature* 4: 297–321.

8 The images presented for testing had the hair, ears, and neck masked from view, as hairstyles can affect viewers' judgements.

9 Perrett, D.I., Lee, K., Penton-Voak, I., Burt, D.M., Rowland, D., Yoshikawa, S., Henzi, S.P., Castles, D. & Akamatsu, S. (1998) Sexual dimorphism and facial attractiveness. *Nature* 394: 884–886.

10 Lee, K. (1997) *Computer Caricatures and Recognition of Facial Characteristics*. University of St Andrews: PhD thesis.
     See Chapter 8, 'Attractiveness and effects of manipulating sexual differences', pp. 137–199.

11 Jamaican women also prefer higher degrees of masculinity in male faces than British women.
     Penton-Voak, I.S., Jacobson, A. & Trivers, R. (2004) Populational differences in attractiveness judgements of male and female faces: comparing British and Jamaican samples. *Evolution and Human Behavior* 25: 355–370.

12 It could be that, for the rural Jamaican evaluator, masculinization makes the faces look heavier, with the implication of greater fat reserves that would support pregnancy and breast-feeding and aid in surviving food shortages. In rural areas, heavier bodies too are more admired.

Tovée, M.J., Swami, V., Furnham, A. & Mangalparsad, R. (2006) Changing perceptions of attractiveness as observers are exposed to a different culture. *Evolution and Human Behavior* 27: 443–456.

13 Thornhill, R. & Gangestad, S.W. (1999) Facial attractiveness. *Trends in Cognitive Science* 3: 452–460.

Fink, B. & Penton-Voak, I. (2002) Evolutionary psychology of facial attractiveness. *Current Directions in Psychological Science* 11: 154–158.

14 Andersson, M. (1994) *Sexual Selection*. Princeton, N.J.: Princeton University Press.

Folstad, I. & Karter, A.J. (1992) Parasites, bright males, and the immunocompetence handicap. *American Naturalist* 139: 603–622.

15 Kleven, O., Jacobsen, F., Izadnegahdar, R., Robertson, R.J. & Lifjeld, J.T. (2006) Male tail streamer length predicts fertilization success in the North American barn swallow (*Hirundo rustica erythrogaster*). *Behavioral Ecology and Sociobiology* 59: 412–418.

16 Boothroyd, L.G., Jones, B.C., Burt, D.M. & Perrett, D.I. (2007) Partner characteristics associated with masculinity, health and maturity in male faces. *Personality and Individual Differences* 43: 1161–1173.

Boothroyd, L.G., Jones, B.C., Burt, D.M., Cornwell, R.E., Little, A.C., Tiddeman, B.P. & Perrett, D.I. (2005) Facial masculinity is related to perceived age but not perceived health. *Evolution and Human Behaviour* 26: 417–431.

The relationship between masculinity and long-term health is discussed in Chapter 7. Structural cues to masculinity could relate resistance to disease, even if not to current health.

17 Perrett, D.I., Lee, K., Penton-Voak, I., Burt, D.M., Rowland, D., Yoshikawa, S., Henzi, S.P., Castles, D. & Akamatsu, S. (1998) Sexual dimorphism and facial attractiveness. *Nature* 394: 884–886.

18 Carré, J.M. & McCormick, C.M. (2008) In your face: facial metrics predict aggressive behaviour in the laboratory and in varsity and professional hockey players. *Proceedings of the Royal Society B* 275: 2651–2656.

19 Penton-Voak, I.S. & Chen, J.Y. (2004) High salivary testosterone is linked to masculine male facial appearance in humans. *Evolution and Human Behavior* 25: 229–241.

Pound, N., Penton-Voak, I.S. & Surridge, A.K. (2009) Testosterone responses to competition in men are related to facial masculinity. *Proceedings of the Royal Society B* 276: 153–159.

20 A study of 4,000 men who had served in the US armed forces showed that men with high testosterone levels were less likely to marry than men with low testosterone. Once married, men with high testosterone were more likely to suffer troubled relationships, and this group also demonstrated increased incidence of domestic violence and sex outside the confines of a committed relationship.

Booth, A. & Dabbs, J. (1993) Testosterone and men's marriages. *Social Forces* 72: 463–477.

21 Swaddle, J.P. & Reierson, G.W. (2002) Testosterone increases perceived dominance but not attractiveness in human males. *Proceedings of the Royal Society B* 269: 2285–2289.

22 Fink, B., Neave, N. & Seydel, H. (2007) Male facial appearance signals physical strength to women. *American Journal of Human Biology* 19: 82–87.

See also: Sell, A., Cosmides, L., Tooby, J., Sznycer, D., von Rueden, C. & Gurven, M. (2009) Human adaptations for the visual assessment of strength and fighting ability from the body and face. *Proceedings of the Royal Society B* 276: 575–584.

23 Rhodes, G. (2006) The evolutionary psychology of facial beauty. *Annual Review of Psychology* 57: 199–226.

DeBruine, L.M., Jones, B.C., Smith, F.G. & Little, A.C. (in press) Are attractive men's faces masculine or feminine? The importance of controlling confounds in face stimuli. *Journal of Experimental Psychology: Human Perception and Performance.*

24 Wilcox, A.J., Weinberg, C.R. & Baird, D.D. (1995) Timing of sexual intercourse in relation to ovulation. Effects on the probability of conception, survival of the pregnancy, and sex of the baby. *New England Journal of Medicine* 333: 1517–1521.

25 The developing egg also produces testosterone, which is as important as oestrogen in influencing sexual behaviour and attraction to others. Testosterone levels are highest at peak fertility.

26 Details included how many days it was since their last period, and how long and how regular their cycles usually were.

27 Penton-Voak, I.S., Perrett, D.I., Castles, D.L., Kobayashi, T., Burt, D.M., Murray, L.K. & Minamisawa, R. (1999) Menstrual cycle alters face preference. *Nature* 399: 741–742.

Penton-Voak, I.S. & Perrett, D.I. (2000) Female preference for male faces changes cyclically; further evidence. *Evolution and Human Behavior* 21: 39–48.

Johnston, V.S., Hagel, R., Franklin, M., Fink, B. & Grammer, K. (2001) Male facial attractiveness: evidence for a hormone-mediated adaptive design. *Evolution and Human Behavior* 22: 251–267.

28 Puts, D.A. (2005) Mating context and menstrual phase affect women's preferences for male voice pitch. *Evolution and Human Behavior* 26: 388–397.

Feinberg, D.R., Jones, B.C., Law-Smith, M.J., Moore, F.R., DeBruine, L.M., Cornwell, R.E., Hillier, S.G. & Perrett, D.I. (2006) Menstrual cycle, trait estrogen level, and masculinity preferences in the human voice. *Hormones and Behavior* 49: 215–222.

Gangestad, S.W., Simpson, J.A., Cousins, A.J., Garver-Apgar, C.E. & Christensen, N.P. (2004) Women's preferences for male behavioral displays change across the menstrual cycle. *Psychological Science* 15: 203–207.

29 Little, A.C., Jones, B.C. & Burriss, R.P. (2007) Preferences for masculinity in male bodies change across the menstrual cycle. *Hormones and Behavior* 51: 633–639.

30 Note that there is no necessity for the woman to be thinking conciously about a man's genetic quality.

31 Little, A.C., Jones, B.C., Penton-Voak, I.S., Burt, D.M. & Perrett, D.I. (2002) Partnership status and the temporal context of relationships influence human female preferences for sexual dimorphism in male face shape. *Proceedings of the Royal Society B* 269: 1095–1103.

32 Peritz, E. & Rust, P.F. (1972) Estimation of nonpaternity rate using more than one blood-group system. *American Journal of Human Genetics* 24: 46–53.

33 Jones, B.C., Little, A.C., Boothroyd, L.G., DeBruine, L.M., Feinberg, D.R., Law Smith, M.J., Cornwell, R.E., Moore, F.R. & Perrett, D.I. (2005)

Commitment to relationships and preferences for femininity and apparent health in faces are strongest on days of the menstrual cycle when progesterone level is high. *Hormones and Behavior* 48: 283–290.

34 Gangestad, S.W., Thornhill, R. & Garver, C.E. (2002) Changes in women's sexual interests and their partners' mate-retention tactics across the menstrual cycle: evidence for shifting conflicts of interest. *Proceedings of the Royal Society B* 269: 975–982.

Gangestad, S.W., Thornhill, R. & Garver, C.E. (2005) Women's sexual interests across the ovulatory cycle depend on primary partner developmental instability. *Proceedings of the Royal Society B* 272: 2023–2027.

Haselton, M.G. & Gangestad, S.W., (2006) Conditional expression of women's desires and men's mate guarding across the ovulatory cycle. *Hormones and Behavior* 4: 509–518.

35 The benefit is actually to the propagation of the woman's genes, rather than to the woman herself.

36 Roberts, S.C., Havlicek, J., Flegr, J., Hruskova, M., Little, A.C., Jones, B.C., Perrett, D.I. & Petrie, M. (2004) Female facial attractiveness increases during the fertile phase of the menstrual cycle. *Proceedings of the Royal Society B* 271: S270–S272.

Pipitone, R.N. & Gallup Jr, G.G. (2008) Women's voice attractiveness varies across the menstrual cycle. *Evolution and Human Behavior* 29: 268–274.

Singh, D. & Bronstad, P.M. (2001) Female body odour is a potential cue to ovulation. *Proceedings of the Royal Society B* 268: 797–801.

Kuukasjärvi, S., Eriksson, C.J.P., Koskela, E., Mappes, T., Nissinen, K. & Rantala, M.J. (2004) Attractiveness of women's body odors over the menstrual cycle: the role of oral contraceptives and receiver sex. *Behavioral Ecology* 15: 579–584.

Scutt, D. & Manning, J.T. (1996) Ovary and ovulation: symmetry and ovulation in women. *Human Reproduction* 11: 2477–2480.

Haselton, M.G., Mortezaie, M., Pillsworth, E.G., Bleske-Rechek, A. & Frederick, D.A. (2007) Ovulatory shifts in human female ornamentation: near ovulation, women dress to impress. *Hormones and Behavior* 51: 40–45.

Grammer, K., Renninger, L. & Fischer, B. (2005) Disco clothing, female sexual motivation, and relationship status. is she dressed to impress? *Journal of Sexual Research* 41: 66–74.

37 Burriss, R.P. & Little, A.C. (2006) Effects of partner conception risk phase on male perception of dominance in faces. *Evolution and Human Behaviour* 27: 297–305.

Haselton, M.G. & Gangestad, S.W. (2006) Conditional expression of women's desires and men's mate guarding across the ovulatory cycle. *Hormones and Behavior* 49: 509–518.

38 This discussion is not intended to suggest that women are consciously and strategically planning what is best for potential children – such calculations will not occur even in the minds of those who choose to be unfaithful. The phenomena we observe are not the result of awareness and deliberate thinking, but of unconscious shifts in behaviour that represent the legacy of evolutionary development. Such explanations can apply to insects, penguins, or people.

39 Welling, L.L.M., Jones, B.C., DeBruine, L.M., Smith, F.G., Feinberg, D.R., Little, A.C. & Al-Dujaili, E.A.S. (2008) Men report stronger attraction to

femininity in women's faces when their testosterone levels are high. *Hormones and Behavior* 54: 703–708.

40 Pawlowski, B. & Sorokowski, P. (2008) Men's attraction to women's bodies changes seasonally. *Perception* 37: 1079–85.

Pawlowski and Sorokowski attribute changing attitudes to the seasonal change in women's clothing – winter brings less revealing dress, so men are more admiring of women's naked breasts. My colleagues and I have seen increased winter attraction to feminine female faces (unpublished studies), a result more consistent with winter-elevated testosterone than with the seasonal covering of faces with balaclavas.

41 Booth, A., Shelley, G., Mazur, A., Tharp, G. & Kittok, R. (1989) Testosterone, and winning and losing in human competition. *Hormones & Behavior* 23: 556–571.

42 Bernhardt, P.C., Dabbs Jr, J.M., Fielden, J.A. & Lutter, C.D. (1998) Testosterone changes during vicarious experiences of winning and losing among fans at sporting events. *Physiology and Behavior* 65: 59–62.

Pound, N., Penton-Voak, I.S. & Surridge, A.K. (2009) Testosterone responses to competition in men are related to facial masculinity. *Proceedings of the Royal Society B* 276: 153–159.

43 Edwards, D.A., Wetzel, K. & Wyner, D.R. (2005) Intercollegiate soccer: saliva cortisol and testosterone are elevated during competition, and testosterone is related to status and social connectedness with teammates. *Physiology and Behavior* 87: 135–143.

Gonzalez-Bono, E., Salvador, A., Serrano, M.A. & Ricarte, J. (1999) Testosterone, cortisol, and mood in a sports team competition. *Hormones and Behavior* 35: 55–62.

44 Bateup, H.S., Booth, A., Shirtcliff, E.A. & Granger, D.A. (2002) Testosterone, cortisol, and women's competition. *Evolution and Human Behavior* 23: 181–192.

45 Draper, P. & Harpending, H. (1982) Father absence and reproductive strategy – an evolutionary perspective. *Journal of Anthropological Research* 38: 255–278.

Ellis, B.J. (2004) Timing of pubertal maturation in girls: an integrated life history approach. *Psychological Bulletin* 130: 920–958.

46 Ellis, B.J., Bates, J.E., Dodge, K.A., Fergussen, D.M., Horwood, L.J., Petit, G.S. & Woodward, L. (2003) Does father absence place daughters at special risk for early sexual activity and teenage pregnancy? *Child Development* 74: 801–821.

47 Boothroyd, L.G. & Perrett, D.I. (2008) Father absence, parent–daughter relationships and partner preferences. *Journal of Evolutionary Psychology* 6: 187–205.

48 Feinberg, D.R., Jones, B.C., Law-Smith, M.J., Moore, F.R., DeBruine, L.M., Cornwell, R.E., Hillier, S.G. & Perrett, D.I. (2006) Menstrual cycle, trait estrogen level, and masculinity preferences in the human voice. *Hormones and Behavior* 49: 215–222.

The report of Feinberg *et al.* focused on oestrogen level and the menstrual cycle shift. The same data revealed that cyclic shifts were most prevalent in women who wanted short-term relationships. Other studies have noted that the *size* of cyclic shifts varies across women, being smaller in women who score high on a masculinity index – a group who had higher self-esteem.

Johnston, V.S., Hagel, R., Franklin, M., Fink, B. & Grammer, K. (2001) Male facial attractiveness: evidence for a hormone-mediated adaptive design. *Evolution and Human Behavior* 22: 251–267.

49 Preliminary results indicate that this is so (Saxton, T. & Perrett, D.I. (2009) Unpublished studies).

Further unpublished studies show that around ovulation women increase their preference for faces that they like in general (Ben Jones: personal communication, 9/09).

50 Chase-Lansdale, P.L., Cherlin, A.J. & Kiernan, K.K. (1995) The long-term effects of parental divorce on the mental health of young adults: a developmental perspective. *Child Development* 66: 1614–1634.

Krein, S.F. & Beller, A.H. (1988) Educational attainment of children from single-parent families: differences by exposure, gender, and race. *Demography* 25: 221–34.

Zill, N., Ruane Morrison, D. & Coiro, M.J. (1993) Long-term effects of parental divorce on parent–child relationships, adjustment, and achievement in young adulthood: families in transition. *Journal of Family Psychology* 7: 91–103.

51 Holden, C.J., Sear, R. & Mace, R. (2003) Matriliny as daughter-biased investment. *Evolution and Human Behavior* 24: 99–112.

For similar reasons, Holden *et al.* argue that uncertainty about parenthood means that it is sensible for parents and grandparents to invest in daughters rather than in sons. Grandparents may have more confidence in being related to grandchildren on their daughter's side than on their son's side.

52 Little, A.C., Burt, D.M., Penton-Voak, I.S. & Perrett, D.I. (2001) Self-perceived attractiveness influences human female preferences for sexual dimorphism and symmetry in male faces. *Proceedings of the Royal Society B* 268: 39–44.

53 Penton-Voak, I.S., Little, A.C., Jones, B.C., Burt, D.M., Tiddeman, B.P. & Perrett, D.I. (2003) Measures of female condition influence preferences for sexual dimorphism in faces of male *Homo sapiens*. *Journal of Comparative Psychology* 117: 264–271.

54 'Hot or Not?': http://www.hotornot.com/ [accessed: 24/11/09].

55 Little, A.C. & Mannion, H.D. (2006) Viewing attractive or unattractive same-sex images affects preferences for sexual dimorphism in opposite-sex faces. *Animal Behaviour* 72: 981–987.

56 See also: Welling, L.L.M., Jones, B.C., DeBruine, L.M., Conway, C.A., Law Smith, M.J., Little, A.C., Feinberg, D.R., Sharp, M. & Al-Dujaili, E.A.S. (2007) Raised salivary testosterone in women is associated with increased attraction to masculine faces. *Hormones and Behavior* 52: 156–161.

57 Cornwell, R.E., Boothroyd, L., Burt, D.M., Feinberg, D.R., Jones, B.C., Little, A.C., Pitman, R., Whiten, S. & Perrett, D.I. (2004) Concordant preferences for opposite-sex signals? Human pheromones and facial characteristics. *Proceedings of the Royal Society B* 271: 635–640.

There are further links in preferences for masculine faces and masculine voices.

Feinberg, D.R., DeBruine, L.M., Jones, B.C. & Little, A.C. (2008). Correlated preferences for men's facial and vocal masculinity. *Evolution and Human Behavior* 29: 233–241.

58 Wyatt, T.D. (2003) *Pheromones and Animal Behaviour: Communication by Smell and Taste*. Cambridge: Cambridge University Press.

Whether any substance is truly a human pheromone is contested. Objections include firstly the fact that concentrations of odours used in many psychological studies are much higher than those that occur naturally, and secondly that humans do not have the Jacobson organ that is responsible for pheromone analysis in other species:

see Wyatt, T.D. (2009) Sexual selection and pheromones. Paper presented at *The Descent of Man, and Selection in Relation to Sex*, The Association for the Study of Animal Behaviour Summer Conference: 9/09. Oxford.

Nonetheless, humans do have smell receptors dedicated to androstenone.

Keller, A., Zhuang, H., Chi, Q., Vosshall, L.B. & Matsunami, H. (2007) Genetic variation in a human odorant receptor alters odour perception. *Nature* 449: 468–472.

59 Perrett, D.I., Law Smith, M., Jones, B.C., Feinberg, D., Lawson, J. & DeBruine, L.M. (2006) Hormonal influences on human perception and preferences for potential mates. Paper presented at the Society for Behavioural Neuroendocrinology: 6/06. Pittsburgh, USA.

60 Cornwell, R.E., Boothroyd, L., Burt, D.M., Feinberg, D.R., Jones, B.C., Little, A.C., Pitman, R., Whiten, S. & Perrett, D.I. (2004) Concordant preferences for opposite-sex signals? Human pheromones and facial characteristics. *Proceedings of the Royal Society B* 271: 635–640.

61 The expression 'helping' does not imply conscious strategy to aid one's own genes.

62 DeBruine, L.M., Jones, B.C. & Perrett, D.I. (2005) Women's attractiveness judgments of self-resembling faces change across the menstrual cycle. *Hormones and Behavior* 47: 379–383.

63 DeBruine, L.M., Jones, B.C., Little, A.C. & Perrett, D.I. (2008) Social perception of facial resemblance in humans. *Archives of Sexual Behavior* 37: 64–77.

Jones, B.C., DeBruine, L.M., Perrett, D.I., Little, A.C., Feinberg, D.R. & Law Smith, M. (2008) Effects of menstrual cycle phase on face preferences. *Archives of Sexual Behavior* 37: 78–84.

64 *People* magazine. 17/11/97 and 15/11/06.

65 Pitman, J. (2006) *Manipulation of Facial Posture in Response to Interpersonal Cues.* Liverpool University: MSc thesis in Evolutionary Psychology (unpublished).

66 Roney, J.R., Mahler, S.V. & Maestripieri, D. (2003) Behavioral and hormonal responses of men to brief interactions with women. *Evolution and Human Behavior* 24: 365–375.

Roney, J.R., Lukaszewski, A.W. & Simmons, Z.L. (2007) Rapid endocrine responses of young men to social interactions with young women. *Hormones and Behavior* 52: 326–333.

67 Roney, J.R., Hanson, K.N., Durante, K.M. & Maestripieri, D. (2006) Reading men's faces: women's mate attractiveness judgments track men's testosterone and interest in infants. *Proceedings of the Royal Society B* 273: 2169–2175.

68 Morrison, E., Gralewski, L., Campbell, N. & Penton-Voak, I. (2007) Facial movement varies by sex and is related to attractiveness. *Evolution and Human Behavior* 28: 186–92.

Roberts, S.C., Saxton, T.K., Murray, A., Burriss, R., Rowland, H. & Little, A.C. (2009) Static and dynamic facial images cue similar attractiveness judgements. *Ethology* 115: 588–595.

69 Bressler, E., Martin, R. & Balshine, S. (2006) Production and appreciation of humor as sexually selected traits. *Evolution & Human Behavior* 27: 21–130.

70 Clark, A.P., Morrison, E.R., Jack, V. & Penton-Voak, I.S. (2009) Attractiveness in flux: female preferences for male facial motion depend on mating context

and non-additive cues to prosociality and proceptivity. *Journal of Evolutionary Psychology* 7: 99–109.

    Penton-Voak, I.S. (2008) Social perception of moving faces: increasing the ecological validity of attractiveness research. Departmental seminar: School of Psychology, University of St Andrews.

71 Gray, P. (2002) Marriage and fatherhood are associated with lower testosterone in males. *Evolution and Human Behavior* 23: 193–201.

72 Roney, J.R., Hanson, K.N., Durante, K.M. & Maestripieri, D. (2006) Reading men's faces: women's mate attractiveness judgments track men's testosterone and interest in infants. *Proceedings of the Royal Society B* 273: 2169–2175.

    Not all research indicates accurate perception of child affinity, however: Penton-Voak, I., Cahill, S., Pound, N., Kempe, V., Schaeffler, S. & Schaeffler, F. (2007) Male facial attractiveness, perceived personality, and child-directed speech. *Evolution and Human Behavior* 28: 253–259.

73 Cornwell, R.E., Law Smith, M.J., Boothroyd, L.G., Moore, F.R., Davis, H.P., Stirrat, M., Tiddeman, B. & Perrett, D.I. (2006) Reproductive strategy, sexual development and attraction to facial characteristics. *Philosophical Transactions of the Royal Society B* 361: 2143–2154.

74 The same appears true for masculinity in men's voices: women with fast sexual maturation prefer more masculine voices. B. Jones (2009) Personal communication: 9/09.

75 In this study, the masculine faces shown to evaluators included texture cues, so they had more stubble as well as a more masculine face shape. Both attributes would add to their appearance of maturity, which might underlie their appeal to fast-developing women (see Figure 5.8).

76 Saxton, T.K., DeBruine, L.M., Jones, B.C., Little, A.C. & Roberts, S.C. (2009) Face and voice attractiveness judgments change during adolescence. *Evolution and Human Behavior* 30: 398–408.

Chapter 6

1 If offspring are the only measure of success, then homosexual attraction presents a paradox. One suggestion is that sisters and aunts of homosexual males have more offspring than sisters and aunts of heterosexual males. If this is the case, then in following generations the absence of direct descendents of a homosexual man may be offset by *indirect* descendents – in the next generation, there will be copies of the genes owned by a homosexual man.

    Camperio-Ciani, A., Corna, F. & Capiluppi, C. (2004) Evidence for maternally inherited factors favouring male homosexuality and promoting female fecundity. *Proceedings of the Royal Society B* 271: 2217–2221.

    King, M., Green, J., Osborn, D.P.J., Arkell, J., Hetherton, J. & Pereira, E. (2005) Family size in white gay and heterosexual men. *Archives of Sexual Behavior* 34: 117–122.

    Iemmola, F. & Camperio-Ciani, A. (2009) New evidence of genetic factors influencing sexual orientation in men: female fecundity increase in the maternal line. *Archives of Sexual Behavior* 38: 393–399.

    Such an effect is usually attributed to traits and genes expressed in the female relatives, but could also derive from the homosexual male's behaviour in contributing to the reproductive success of his sister or cousin by supporting her or her children.

Bobrow, D. & Bailey, J.M. (2001) Is male homosexuality maintained via kin selection? *Evolution and Human Behavior* 22: 361–368.

But see: Rahman, Q. & Hull, M.S. (2005) An empirical test of the kin selection hypothesis for male homosexuality. *Archives of Sexual Behavior* 34: 461–467.

2 Research amongst the pastoral farming people of Kenya, for example, has shown that women with wealthy husbands have more children:

Borgerhoff Mulder, M. (1987) On cultural and reproductive success: Kipsigis evidence. *American Anthropologist* 89: 617–634.

Cronk, L. (1991) Wealth, status, and reproductive success among the Mukogodo of Kenya. *American Anthropologist* 93: 345–360.

3 BBC Motion Gallery: http://www.bbcmotiongallery.com/ Search words: 'birds' and 'courtship' [accessed: 30/11/09].

BBC Motion Gallery: *Funny Courtship Dances of our Feathered Friends*. http://www.youtube.com/watch?v=lMbDjNDD4cM [accessed: 30/11/09].

BBC *Planet Earth: Birds of Paradise*: http://video.yahoo.com/watch/2354190 [accessed: 30/11/09].

4 Miller, G. (1998) How mate choice shaped human nature: a review of sexual selection and human evolution. In: Crawford, C.B. & Krebs, D. *Handbook of Evolutionary Psychology: Ideas, Issues, and Applications*, pp. 87–129. Mahwah, NJ: Lawrence Erlbaum.

5 Pryke, S.R., Andersson, S. & Lawes, M.J. (2001) Sexual selection of multiple handicaps in the red-collared widowbird: female choice of tail length but not carotenoid display. *Evolution* 55: 1452–1463.

6 Andersson, M. (1992) Female preference for long tails in lekking Jackson's widowbirds: experimental evidence. *Animal Behavior* 43: 379–388. (Lekking is an organized display by males in which they strut their stuff and females wander around choosing which male will get to mate. It's a bird thing – a bit like a rut, but without the aggro between males.)

7 Fisher, R.A. (1958) *The Genetical Theory of Natural Selection*, 2nd edn. New York: Dover.

8 Weatherhead, P.J. & Robertson, R.J. (1979) Offspring quality and the polygyny threshold: 'the sexy son hypothesis'. *American Naturalist* 113: 201–208.

9 Cornwell, R.E. & Perrett, D.I. (2008) Sexy sons and sexy daughters: the influence of parents' facial characteristics on offspring. *Animal Behaviour* 76: 1843–1853.

10 These blended images illustrate the results of a large study involving more than three hundred photos, including one hundred photos each of dads, mums, and daughters. For illustration, the large-scale study can be boiled down to the six images shown.

11 There has been no test of whether attraction to masculinity passes from mother to daughter. It *could* do so, either by enculturation or via genes. Transmission of attraction to masculinity is one condition that is necessary for sexual selection. Environments differ: if disease is prevalent and stability low, this may favour masculinity; if the environment is stable, this may favour a high level of parental cooperation and investment in offspring. These latter environments may favour lower levels of testosterone and masculinity. For populations to adapt quickly to changes in the environment, three features would be needed: (a) variation in the level of male masculinity; (b) transmission of masculinity from father to son; (c) transmission between mother and daughter of a preference for masculinity. Research has established (a) and (b), but not yet (c).

12 Henderson, J.J.A. & Anglin, J.M. (2003) Facial attractiveness predicts longevity. *Evolution and Human Behavior* 24: 351–356.

13 Judge, T.A., Hurst, C. & Simon, L.S. (2009) Does it pay to be smart, attractive, or confident (or all three)? Relationships among general mental ability, physical attractiveness, core self-evaluations, and income. *Journal of Applied Psychology* 94: 742–755.

14 Rhodes, G., Simmons, L.W. & Peters, M. (2005) Attractiveness and sexual behavior: does attractiveness enhance mating success? *Evolution and Human Behavior* 26: 186–201.

15 BBCNews:http://news.bbc.co.uk/1/hi/scotland/tayside_and_central/7471713. stm [accessed: 30/11/09].

16 Soler, C., Núñez, M., Gutiérrez, R., Núñez, J., Medina, P., Sancho, M., Álvarez, J. & Núñez, A. (2003) Facial attractiveness in men provides clues to semen quality. *Evolution and Human Behavior* 24: 199–207.

17 In an Australian sample, Marian Peters found no relationship between male sperm quality and facial characteristics.
    Peters, M., Rhodes, G. & Simmons, L.W. (2008) Does attractiveness in men provide clues to semen quality? *Journal of Evolutionary Biology* 21: 572–579.

18 Dubey, A., Dayal, M., Frankfurter, D., Balazy, P., Peak, D. & Gindoff, P. (2003) The influence of sperm morphology on preimplantation genetic diagnosis cycles outcome. *Fertility and Sterility* 89: 1665–1669.

19 Waynforth, D. (1998) Fluctuating asymmetry and human male life-history traits in rural Belize. *Proceedings of the Royal Society B* 265: 1497–1501.

20 Manning, J.T., Scutt, D. & Lewis-Jones, D.I. (1998) Developmental stability, ejaculate size and sperm quality in men. *Evolution and Human Behavior* 19: 273–282.

21 Johnson, W., Gangestad, S.W., Segal, N.L. & Bouchard, T.J. (2008) Heritability of fluctuating asymmetry in a human twin sample: the effect of trait aggregation. *American Journal of Human Biology* 20: 651–658.

22 Hill, K. & Hurtando, A.M. (1996) *Ache Life History: the Ecology and Demography of a Foraging People.* New York: Aldine de Gruyter.

23 Pawlowski, B., Boothroyd, L.G., Perrett, D.I. & Kluska, S. (2008) Is female attractiveness related to final reproductive success? *Collegium Antropolgicum* 32: 457–460.

24 Pawlowski, B., Dunbar, R.I.M. & Lipowicz, A. (2000) Evolutionary fitness – tall men have more reproductive success. *Nature* 403: 156–156.

25 Kalick, S.M., Zebrowitz, L.A., Langlois, J.H. & Johnson, R.M. (1998) Does human facial attractiveness honestly advertise health? Longitudinal data on an evolutionary question. *Psychological Science* 9: 8–13.

26 Jackson, L.A. (1992) *Physical Appearance and Gender: Sociobiological and Sociocultural Perspectives.* Albany, NY: State University of New York Press.
    Udry, J.R. & Eckland, B.K. (1984) Benefits of being attractive: differential payoffs for men and women. *Psychological Report* 54: 47–56.

27 Judge, T.A., Hurst, C. & Simon, L.S. (2009) Does it pay to be smart, attractive, or confident (or all three)? Relationships among general mental ability, physical attractiveness, core self-evaluations, and income. *Journal of Applied Psychology* 94: 742–755.

28 Jokela, M. (2009) Physical attractiveness and reproductive success in humans: evidence from the late 20th century United States. *Evolution and Human Behavior* 30: 342–350.

29 Even though the urge makes biological sense, biology is of course no defence for actions without due consideration of morals, laws, and religions.

Chapter 7

1 Perrett, D.I., Jones, B.C. & Little, A.C. (2001) Faces and health. Paper presented at the Conference of the European Health Psychology Society and BPS Division of Health Psychology, 09/01. St Andrews, Scotland.

Jones, B.C., Perrett, D.I., Little, A.C., Boothroyd, L.G., Cornwell, R.E., Feinberg, D.R., Tiddeman, B.P., Whiten, S., Pitman, R.M., Hillier, S.G., Burt, D.M., Stirrat, M.R., Law Smith, M.J. & Moore, F.R. (2005) Menstrual cycle, pregnancy and oral contraceptive use alter attraction to apparent health in faces. *Proceedings of the Royal Society B* 272: 347–354.

2 Such cues could be neutral to health, as explained in Chapter 6, but they could not be indicative of poor health. A species with individuals attracted to cues of illness would not have good prospects.

3 Grammer, K. & Thornhill, R. (1994) Human (*Homo sapiens*) facial attractiveness and sexual selection: the role of symmetry and averageness. *Journal of Comparative Psychology* 108: 233–242.

Rhodes, G., Zebrowitz, L., Clark, A., Kalick, S.M., Hightower, A. & McKay, R. (2001) Do facial averageness and symmetry signal health? *Evolution and Human Behavior* 22: 31–46.

Jones, B.C., Little, A.C., Penton-Voak, I.S., Tiddeman, B.P., Burt, D.M. & Perrett, D.I. (2001) Facial symmetry and judgements of apparent health: support for a 'good genes' explanation of the attractiveness–symmetry relationship. *Evolution and Human Behavior* 22: 417–429.

Jones, B.C., Little, A.C., Penton-Voak, I.S., Tiddeman, B.P., Burt, D.M. & Perrett, D.I. (2001) Measured facial asymmetry and perceptual judgements of attractiveness and health. *Evolution and Human Behavior* 22: 417–429.

Penton-Voak, I.S., Jones, B.C., Little, A.C., Baker, S.E., Tiddeman, B.P., Burt, D.M. & Perrett, D.I. (2001) Symmetry, sexual dimorphism in facial proportions, and male sexual attractiveness. *Proceedings of the Royal Society B* 268: 1617–1623.

Zaidel, D.W., Aarde, S.M. & Baig, K. (2005) Appearance of symmetry, beauty, and health in human faces. *Brain and Cognition* 57: 261–263.

Jones, B.C., Little, A.C., Feinberg, D.R., Tiddeman, B.P., Penton-Voak, I.S. & Perrett, D.I. (2004) The relationship between shape, symmetry, and visible skin condition in male facial attractiveness. *Evolution and Human Behavior* 25: 24–30.

Fink, B., Neave, N., Manning, J.T. & Grammer, K. (2006) Facial symmetry and judgements of attractiveness, health and personality. *Personality and Individual Differences* 41: 491–499.

4 Shackelford, T.K. & Larsen, R.J. (1997) Facial asymmetry as an indicator of psychological, emotional, and physiological distress. *Journal of Personality and Social Psychology* 72: 456–466.

Thornhill, R. & Gangestad, S. (2006) Facial sexual dimorphism, developmental stability, and susceptibility to disease in men and women. *Evolution and Human Behavior* 27: 131–144.

Other studies have linked symmetry measured from the face and the body to estimates of health:

Milne, B.J., Belsky, J., Poulton, R., Caspi, A., Kieser, J. & Thomson, W.M. (2003) Fluctuating asymmetry and physical health among young adults. *Evolution and Human Behavior* 24: 53–63.

Waynforth, D. (1998) Fluctuating asymmetry and human male life-history traits in rural Belize. *Proceedings of the Royal Society B* 265: 1497–1501.

5 Rhodes, G., Zebrowitz, L.A., Clark, A., Kalick, S.M., Hightower, A. & McKay, R. (2001) Do facial averageness and symmetry signal health? *Evolution and Human Behavior* 22: 31–46.

6 Shackelford, T.K. & Larsen, R.J. (1997) Facial asymmetry as an indicator of psychological, emotional, and physiological distress. *Journal of Personality and Social Psychology* 72: 456–466.

7 These odds may seem arbitrary, but they are adopted throughout science. For an event to be attributed to the hypothesis rather than to chance, the probability of a result or an event should be less than 1 in 20 (less than 5%).

8 Rhodes, G., Zebrowitz, L., Clark, A., Kalick, S.M., Hightower, A. & McKay, R. (2001) Do facial averageness and symmetry signal health? *Evolution and Human Behavior* 22: 31–46.

9 Thornhill, R. & Gangestad, S. (2006) Facial sexual dimorphism, developmental stability, and susceptibility to disease in men and women. *Evolution and Human Behavior* 27: 131–144.

For a further review of face symmetry, see: Rhodes, G. & Simmons, L.W. (2007) Symmetry attractiveness and sexual selection. In: Barrett, L. & Dunbar, R.I.M.D. (eds) *Oxford Handbook of Evolutionary Psychology*, pp. 334–364. Oxford: Oxford University Press.

10 http://www.breastcancer.org/risk/understanding.jsp [accessed: 28/11/09].

11 There is a whole branch of medicine, dysmorphology, which involves detecting unusual features that signify particular genetic disorders. Dysmorphology experts often recognize characteristic symptoms and syndromes from face and body appearance. This is the serious and distressing side of the 'funny-looking kid' syndrome.

12 Zebrowitz, L.A & Rhodes, G. (2004) Sensitivity to 'bad genes' and the anomalous face overgeneralization effect: cue validity, cue utilization, and accuracy in judging intelligence and health. *Journal of Non-verbal Behaviour* 28: 167–185.

13 Thornhill, R. & Gangestad, S. (2006) Facial sexual dimorphism, developmental stability, and susceptibility to disease in men and women. *Evolution and Human Behavior* 27: 131–144.

14 Rhodes, G., Chan, J., Zebrowitz, L.A. & Simmons, L.W. (2003) Does sexual dimorphism in human faces signal health? *Proceedings of the Royal Society B – Supplement: Biology Letters* S93–S95.

15 The Alameda County health measures attribute shortened life to seven factors: sleeping too little or too much (7–8 hours is recommended); skipping breakfast; snacking; too little exercise; smoking; excess alcohol; and too much or too little weight:

Wingard, D.L., Berkman, L.F. & Brand, R.J. (1982) A multivariate analysis of health-related practices: a nine-year mortality follow-up of the Alameda county study. *American Journal of Epidemiology* 116: 765–775.

We (Jones, B.J. & Perrett, D.I., unpublished studies) used a combined score from Alameda County health measures (apart from units of alcohol consumed, which may not be appropriate in assigning current health in a student population). In a sample of 70 female students, we found that this combined Alameda health-risk score predicted healthy appearance in photographs of faces posed with a neutral expression.

16 Jasienska, G., Ziomkiewicz, A., Ellison, P.T., Lipson, S.F. & Thune, I. (2004) Large breasts and narrow waist indicate high reproductive potential in women. *Proceedings of the Royal Society B* 271: 1213–1217.

17 Law Smith, M.J., Perrett, D.I., Jones, B.C., Cornwell, R.E., Moore, F.R., Feinberg, D.R., Boothroyd, L.G., Durrani, S.J., Stirrat, M.R., Whiten, S., Pitman, R.M. & Hillier, S.G. (2006) Facial appearance is a cue to oestrogen levels in women. *Proceedings of the Royal Society B* 273: 135–140.

18 Baird, D., Weinberg, C.R., Zhou, H., Kamel, F., McConnaughey, D.R., Kesner, J.S. & Wilcox, A.J. (1999) Preimplantation urinary hormone profiles and the probability of conception in healthy women. *Fertility and Sterility* 71: 40–49.

19 Thornhill, R. & Gangestad, S. (2006) Facial sexual dimorphism, developmental stability, and susceptibility to disease in men and women. *Evolution and Human Behavior* 27: 131–144.

20 Rhodes, G., Chan, J., Zebrowitz, L.A. & Simmons, L.W. (2003) Does sexual dimorphism in human faces signal health? *Proceedings of the Royal Society B – Supplement: Biology Letters* S93–S95.

21 Boothroyd, L.G., Jones, B.C., Burt, D.M. & Perrett, D.I. (2007) Partner characteristics associated with masculinity, health and maturity in male faces. *Personality and Individual Differences* 43: 1161–1173.
   Boothroyd, L.G., Jones, B.C., Burt, D.M., Cornwell, R.E., Little, A.C., Tiddeman, B.P. & Perrett, D.I. (2005) Facial masculinity is related to perceived age but not perceived health. *Evolution and Human Behaviour* 26: 417–431.

22 Swaddle, J.P. & Reierson, G.W. (2002) Testosterone increases perceived dominance but not attractiveness in human males. *Proceedings of the Royal Society B* 269: 2285–2289.

23 Kalick, S.M., Zebrowitz, L.A., Langlois, J.H. & Johnson, R.M. (1998) Does human facial attractiveness honestly advertise health? Longitudinal data on an evolutionary question. *Psychological Science* 9: 8–13.

24 Coetzee, V., Perrett, D.I. & Stephen, I.D. (2009) Facial adiposity: a cue to health? *Perception*. Perception advance online publication DOI: 10.1068/p6423.

25 Enzi, G., Gasparo, M., Biondetti, P.R., Fiore, D., Semisa, M. & Zurlo, F. (1986) Subcutaneous and visceral fat distribution according to sex, age, and overweight, evaluated by computed tomography. *American Journal of Clinical Nutrition* 44: 739–746.

26 Coetzee, V., Perrett, D.I. & Stephen, I.D. (2009) Facial adiposity: a cue to health? *Perception*. Perception advance online publication DOI: 10.1068/p6423.

27 Furnham, A. & Baguma, P. (1994). Cross-cultural differences in the evaluation of male and female body shapes. *International Journal of Eating Disorders* 15: 81–89.
   Tovée, M.J., Swami, V., Furnham, A. & Mangalparsad, R. (2006) Changing perceptions of attractiveness as observers are exposed to a different culture. *Evolution and Human Behavior* 27: 443–456.
   Swami, V. & Tovée, M.J. (2005) Female physical attractiveness in Britain and Malaysia: a cross-cultural study. *Body Image* 2: 115–128.
   Swami, V. & Tovée, M.J. (2005) Male physical attractiveness in Britain and Malaysia: a cross-cultural study. *Body Image* 2: 383–393.

28 Milne, B.J., Belsky, J., Poulton, R., Caspi, A., Kieser, J. & Thomson, W.M. (2003) Fluctuating asymmetry and physical health among young adults. *Evolution and Human Behavior* 24: 53–63.

Hume, D.K. & Montgomerie, R. (2001) Facial attractiveness signals different aspects of 'quality' in women and men. *Evolution and Human Behavior* 22: 93–112.

Thornhill, R. & Gangestad, S. (2006) Facial sexual dimorphism, developmental stability, and susceptibility to disease in men and women. *Evolution and Human Behavior* 27: 131–144.

29 Jones, B.C., Little, A.C., Burt, D.M. & Perrett, D.I. (2004) When facial attractiveness is only skin deep. *Perception* 33: 569–576.

30 Thornhill, R. & Gangestad, S.W. (1999) The scent of symmetry: a human pheromone that signals fitness? *Evolution and Human Behavior* 20: 175–201.

Hughes, S.M., Harrison, M.A. & Gallup, G.G. (2002) The sound of symmetry: voice as a marker of developmental instability. *Evolution and Human Behavior* 23: 173–180.

31 Jones, B.C., Little, A.C., Feinberg, D.R., Penton-Voak, I.S., Tiddeman, B.P. & Perrett, D.I. (2004) The relationship between shape symmetry and perceived skin condition in male facial attractiveness. *Evolution and Human Behavior* 25: 24–30.

32 See Chapter 10. In humans, major histocompatibility (MHC) genes are called human leukocyte antigen (HLA) genes.

33 There is a separate immune system that builds antibodies. Antibodies are tailor-made to particular pathogens and antibody production depends on contact with the pathogen. Once the antibodies have been made, and assuming that the individual survives the first infection by the pathogen, he or she may have acquired immunity to further infections by the same pathogen. The antibody immunity changes across an individual's lifespan, whereas the MHC system does not.

34 Inbreeding happens when a small population of individuals is unable to mix and breed with individuals from other populations. This can happen if the population is geographically or functionally isolated.

35 The role of parental MHC genes is discussed further in Chapter 10.

Roberts, S.C., Little, A.C., Gosling, L.M., Perrett, D.I, Jones, B.C., Carter, V., Penton-Voak, I.S. & Petrie, M. (2005) MHC-heterozygosity and human facial attractiveness. *Evolution and Human Behavior* 26: 213–226.

36 Another study implicated the MHC genes in the general state of health, although it did not find face attractiveness determined by the MHC gene profile:

Coetzee, V., Barrett, L., Greeff, J.M., Henzi, S.P., Perrett, D.I. & Wadee, A.A. (2007) Common HLA alleles associated with health, but not with facial attractiveness. *Public Library of Science ONE* 2: e640.

37 Model, D. (1985) Smoker's face: an underrated clinical sign? *British Medical Journal* 291: 1760–1762.

38 Jarvinen, R. & Knekt, P. (1997) Vitamin C, smoking and alcohol consumption. In: Packer, L. & Jürgen Fuchs, J. (eds) *Vitamin C in Health and Disease*, pp. 425–456. New York: Marcel Dekker.

39 Our scans were made in terms of red/green colour and separately in terms of blue/yellow colour because humans see colour using these two colour axes:

Smith, T. & Guild, J. (1931) The C.I.E. colorimetric standards and their use. *Transactions of the Optical Society* 33: 73–134.

40 One might expect every part of the skin to be red, rather than to have red speckles. The apparent speckling in the composite images is due to the small

number of faces tested. Analysis of greater numbers of faces shows redness at virtually all points in the skin.

41 Stephen, I.D., Coetzee, V., Law Smith, M. & Perrett, D.I. (2009) Skin blood perfusion and oxygenation colour affect perceived human health. *Public Library of Science ONE* 4: e5083.

42 We used a Batman trick to check whether colour changes are different in the hand and face by getting subjects to lie back on a tilted platform (not exactly hanging upside-down!). This showed us that when blood accumulates under gravity, the skin colours in the hand and in the upside-down face are in fact the same.

43 We asked people to step up and down, using a platform, until their heart rate reached 80 per cent of their maximum. We found that the colour of fresh blood in the hot, flushed hands was then similar to the colour in hot, flushed faces.

44 Stephen, I.D., Coetzee, V., Law Smith, M. & Perrett, D.I. (2009) Skin blood perfusion and oxygenation colour affect perceived human health. *Public Library of Science ONE* 4: e5083.
   Stephen, I.D., Oldham, F.H., Perrett, D.I. & Barton, R.A. (submitted) Redness enhances perceived aggression, dominance and attractiveness in men's faces.

45 Armstrong, N. & Welsman, J.R. (2001) Peak oxygen uptake in relation to growth and maturation in 11–17-year-old humans. *European Journal of Applied Physiology* 85: 546–551.
   Johnson, J.M. (1998) Physical training and the control of skin blood flow: adaptations and the control of blood flow with training. *Medicine and Science in Sports and Exercise* 30: 382–386.

46 Charkoudian, N. (2003) Skin blood flow in adult human thermoregulation: how it works, when it does not, and why. *Mayo Clinic Proceedings* 78: 603–612.
   Panza, J.A., Quyyimi, A.A., Brush, J.R. & Epstein, S.E. (1990) Abnormal endothelium dependent vascular relaxation in patients with essential hypertension. *New England Journal of Medicine* 323: 22–27.
   Ponsonby, A.-L., Dwyer, T. & Couper, D. (1997) Sleeping position, infant apnea, and cyanosis: a population-based study. *Pediatrics* 99: e3, 1.

47 The link between skin redness and sex hormones has not yet been shown in men, but is likely to exist, given that in monkeys high testosterone relates to increased skin redness.
   Rhodes, L., Argersinger, M.E., Gantert, L.T., Friscino, B.H., Hom, G., Pikounis, B., Hess, D.L. & Rhodes, W.L. (1997) Effects of administration of testosterone, dihydrotestosterone, oestrogen and fadrozole, an aromatase inhibitor, on sex skin colour in intact male rhesus macaques. *Journal of Reproduction and Fertility* 111: 51–57.
   Setchell, J.M. & Dixson, A.F. (2001) Changes in the secondary sexual adornments of male mandrills (*Mandrillus sphinx*) are associated with gain and loss of alpha status. *Hormones and Behaviour* 39: 177–184.

48 Thornton, M.J. (2002) The biological actions of oestrogens on skin. *Experimental Dermatology* 11: 487–502.

49 Charkoudian, N., Stephens, D.P., Pirkle, K.C., Kosiba, W.A. & Johnson, J.M. (1999) Influence of female reproductive hormones on local thermal control of skin blood flow. *Journal of Applied Physiology* 87: 1719–1723.

50 Robins, A.H. (1991) *Biological Perspectives on Human Pigmentation*. Cambridge: Cambridge University Press.

51 Branda, R.F. & Eaton, J.W. (1978) Skin colour and nutrient photolysis: an evolutionary hypothesis. *Science* 201: 625–626.

52 Murray, F.G. (1934) Pigmentation, sunlight and nutritional disease. *American Anthropologist* 36: 438–448.

53 Jablonski, N.J. & Chaplin, G. (2000) The evolution of human skin coloration. *Journal of Human Evolution* 39: 57–106.
   Frost, P. (2005). *Fair Women, Dark Men: the Forgotten Roots of Color Prejudice.* Christchurch, New Zealand: Cybereditions Corporation Limited.

54 Sexual selection may have played an additional role in certain populations. If slightly lighter-skinned women have an advantage in absorbing calcium, men who preferred lighter-skinned women would be able to raise a greater number of healthy offspring than men who preferred darker-skinned women.

55 These days artificial tans can be cheaper than holidays, so tans are less of a cue to wealth.

56 Jones, D. (2000) Physical attractiveness, race, and somatic prejudice in Bahia, Brazil. In: Cronk, L., Chagnon, N. & Irons, W. (eds) *Adaptation and Human Behaviour: an Anthropological Perspective*, pp. 133–152. Edison, NJ: Aldine Transactions.

57 Burkhart, C.G. & Burkhart, C.N. (2005) The mole theory: primary function of melanocytes and melanin may be antimicrobial defense and immunomodulation (not solar protection). *International Journal of Dermatology* 44: 340–342.

58 Stephen, I.D. (2009) *Skin Colour, Pigmentation and Apparent Health in Human Faces.* University of St Andrews: PhD thesis.
   Stephen, I.D. & Perrett, D.I. (2008) Skin pigment colouration signals health in human faces. Human Behavior and Evolution Society, 4–8/6/08. Kyoto, Japan. *Conference Proceedings* 20: 13.

59 Stephen, I.D., Law Smith, M.J., Stirrat, M.R. & Perrett, D.I. (2009) Facial skin coloration affects perceived health of human faces. *International Journal of Primatology* 30: 845–857.

60 Presumably this is because light skin is needed more by women for vitamin D synthesis and supporting foetal bone growth.

61 Polsinelli, M.L., Rock, C.L., Henderson, S.A. & Drewnowski, A. (1998) Plasma carotenoids as biomarkers of fruit and vegetable servings in women. *Journal of the American Dietetic Association* 98: 194–196.

62 Alaluf, S., Heinrich, U., Stahl, W., Tronnier, H. & Wiseman, S. (2002) Dietary carotenoids contribute to normal human skin colour and UV photosensitivity. *Journal of Nutrition* 132: 399–403.

63 Hughes, D.A. (2001) Dietary carotenoids and human immune function. *Nutrition* 17: 823–827.

64 von Schantz, T., Bensch, S., Grahn, M., Hasselquist, D. & Wittzell, H. (1999) Good genes, oxidative stress and condition-dependent sexual signals. *Proceedings of the Royal Society B* 266: 1–12.

65 Massaro, M., Davis, L.S. & Darby, J.T. (2003) Carotenoid-derived ornaments reflect parental quality in male and female yellow-eyed penguins (*Magadyptes antipodes*). *Behavioural Ecology and Sociobiology* 55: 169–175.

66 Alaluf, S., Heinrich, U., Stahl, W., Tronnier, H. & Wiseman, S. (2002) Dietary carotenoids contribute to normal human skin colour and UV photosensitivity. *Journal of Nutrition* 132: 399–403.
   Stahl, W., Heinrich, U., Jungmann, H., von Laar, J., Schietzel, M., Sies, H. & Tronnier, H. (1998) Increased dermal carotenoid levels assessed by

non-invasive reflection spectrophotometry correlate with serum levels in women ingesting Betatene. *Journal of Nutrition* 128: 903–907.

Stephen, I.D. & Perrett, D.I. (2008) Skin pigment colouration signals health in human faces. Human Behavior and Evolution Society, 4–8/6/08. Kyoto, Japan. *Conference Proceedings* 20: 13.

Stephen, I.D., Perrett, D.I. & Coetzee, V. (2008) Carotenoids, skin colour and health. Human Behavior and Evolution Society, 4–8/6/08. Kyoto, Japan. *Conference Proceedings* 20: 104.

67 Wolfenbarger, L.L. (1999) Red coloration of male northern cardinals correlates with mate quality and territory quality. *Behavioural Ecology* 10: 80–90.

68 von Schantz, T., Bensch, S., Grahn, M., Hasselquist, D. & Wittzell, H. (1999) Good genes, oxidative stress and condition-dependent sexual signals. *Proceedings of the Royal Society B* 266: 1–12.

Hughes, D.A. (2001) Dietary carotenoids and human immune function. *Nutrition* 17: 823–827.

Blount, J.D, Metcalfe, N.B., Birkhead, T.R. & Surai, P.F. (2003) Carotenoid modulation of immune function and sexual attractiveness in zebra finches. *Science* 300: 125–127.

69 Friis, H., Gomo, E., Koestel, P., Ndhlovu, P., Nyazema, N., Krarup, H. & Michaelsen, K.F. (2001) HIV and other predictors of serum β-carotene and retinol in pregnancy: a cross-sectional study in Zimbabwe. *American Journal of Clinical Nutrition* 73: 1058–1065.

70 Coffey, M.T. & Britt, J.H. (1993) Enhancement of sow reproductive performance by β-carotene or vitamin A. *Journal of Animal Science* 71: 1198–1202.

Schweigert, F.J., Steinhagen, B., Raila, J., Siemann, A., Peet, D. & Buscher, U. (2003) Concentrations of carotenoids, retinol and α-tocopherol in plasma and follicular fluid of women undergoing IVF. *Human Reproduction* 18: 1259–1264.

71 HHS and USDA (2005) *Dietary Guidelines for Americans*. http://www.health.gov/dietaryguidelines/dga2005/document/pdf/DGA2005.pdf [accessed: 28/11/09].

In *The Guardian*, Thursday, 25/5/06, Luke Waterson suggested that an even higher intake is recommended in Japan. http://www.guardian.co.uk/lifeandstyle/2006/may/25/healthandwellbeing.health [accessed: 28/11/09].

72 Jones, B.C., Perrett, D.I., Little, A.C., Boothroyd, L., Cornwell, R.E., Feinberg, D.R., Tiddeman, B.P., Whiten, S., Pitman, R.M., Hillier, S.G., Burt, D.M., Stirrat, M.R., Law Smith, M.J. & Moore, F.R. (2005) Menstrual cycle, pregnancy and oral contraceptive use alter attraction to apparent health in faces. *Proceedings of the Royal Society B* 272: 347–54.

73 Conway, C.A., Jones, B.C., DeBruine, L.M., Little, A.C., Hay, J., Welling, L.L.M., Perrett, D.I. & Feinberg, D.R. (2008) Integrating physical and social cues when forming face preferences: differences among low- and high-anxiety individuals. *Social Neuroscience* 3: 89–95.

Chapter 8

1 John Keats (1795–1821): 'Ode on a Grecian Urn'.
2 The term *'kindenschema'* was originally used by Konrad Lorenz, the Austrian pioneer of the study of natural animal behaviour: Lorenz, K. (1943) Die angeborenen formen möglicher arfahrung (Innate forms of possible experience). *Zeitschrift fur Tierpsychologie* 5: 233–409.

3 Patterson, F. (1987) *Koko's Kitten*. New York: Scholastic Press.

4 http://redapes.org/video-media/pet-cat-keeps-tonda-the-orangutan-alive/ [accessed: 01/12/09].

5 BBC News: http://news.bbc.co.uk/1/hi/world/africa/1905363.stm [accessed: 01/12/09].

6 Isaiah 11:6 (Authorized Version): 'The wolf also shall dwell with the lamb, and the leopard shall lie down with the kid; and the calf and the young lion and the fatling together; and a little child shall lead them.'

7 In Chapter 3, infant attraction to a face was defined as the infant's compulsion to look at a particular face in preference to other patterns or faces. We cannot know how rewarding seeing the face is for the infant.

8 Fullard, W. & Reiling, A.M. (1976) An investigation of Lorenz's 'Babyness'. *Child Development* 47: 1191–1193.

   Hildebrandt, K.A. & Fitzgerald, H.E. (1978) Adults' responses to infants varying in perceived cuteness. *Behavioural Processes* 3: 159–172.

   Goldberg, S., Blumberg, S.l. & Kriger, A. (1982) Menarche and interest in infants: biological and social influences. *Child Development* 53: 1544–1550.

9 Brosch, T., Sander, D. & Scherer, K.R. (2007) That baby caught my eye ... attention capture by infant faces. *Emotion* 7: 685–689.

10 Vauclair, J. & Donnot, J. (2005) Infant holding biases and their relations to hemispheric specializations for perceiving facial emotions. *Neuropsychologia* 43: 564–571.

   The bias is present in left- and right-handed individuals: Donnot, J. (2007) Lateralization of emotion predicts infant holding bias in left-handed students, but not in left-handed mothers. *Laterality: Asymmetries of Body, Brain, and Cognition* 12: 216–226.

11 Left-sided cradling may also allow the baby to be soothed by the sound of the mother's heartbeat, something the baby would have learned about in the safe environment of the womb.

12 Karraker, K.H. & Stern, M. (1990) Infant physical attractiveness and facial expression: effects on adult perceptions. *Basic and Applied Social Psychology* 11: 371–385.

   Hildebrandt, K.A. & Fitzgerald, H.E. (1979) Facial feature determinants of perceived infant attractiveness. *Infant Behavior and Development* 2: 329–339.

13 Jackson, L.A. & Fitzgerald, H.E. (1988) What is beautiful is good. The importance of physical attractiveness in infancy and childhood. *Child International* 2: 4–6.

14 Bartels, A. & Zeki, S. (2004) The neural correlates of maternal and romantic love. *Neuroimage* 21: 1155–1166.

15 Strathearn, L., Li, J., Fonagy, P. & Montague, P.R. (2008) What's in a smile? Maternal brain responses to infant facial cues. *Pediatrics* 122: 40–51.

16 Strathearn, L., Li, J., Fonagy, P. & Montague, P.R. (2008) What's in a smile? Maternal brain responses to infant facial cues. *Pediatrics* 122: 40–51.

17 Sprengelmeyer, R., Perrett, D.I., Fagan, E.C., Cornwell, R.E., Lobmaier, J.S., Sprengelmeyer, A., Aasheim, H.B., Black, I.M., Cameron, L.M., Crow, S., Milne, N., Rhodes, E.C. & Young, A.W. (2009) The cutest little baby face: a hormonal link to sensitivity to cuteness in infant faces. *Psychological Science* 20: 149–54.

   Here 'cuteness' was defined democratically according to both male and female opinions. It is also possible to define 'cuteness' objectively, using the terms defined by Konrad Lorenz (1943) – see note 2 above.

18 Lobmaier, J.S., Sprengelmeyer, R., Wiffen, B. & Perrett, D.I. (2009) Female and male responses to cuteness, age and emotion in infant faces. *Evolution and Human Behaviour*. Available online 5/8/09. doi:10.1016/j.evolhumbehav.2009.05.004.

19 When receptors in a genetically male individual fail to respond to testosterone (in what is known as androgen insensitivity syndrome), the individual takes on a female nature in body and soul.

20 Chivers, M.L., Rieger, G., Latty, E. & Bailey, J.M. (2004) A sex difference in the specificity of sexual arousal. *Psychological Science* 15: 736–744.

21 Bailey, M. (2009) Sexual orientation: expression, development, and causation. Nonverbal aspects of mate-choice and courtship. Fifth International Anthropological Congress of Aleš Hrdlička, 9/09. Prague.

22 Hassett, J.M., Siebert, E.R. & Wallen, K. (2008) Sex differences in rhesus monkey toy preferences parallel those of children. *Hormones and Behavior* 54: 359–364.

23 Chapter 2, note 44 (see above).

24 Nevertheless, it could be that experience does have a role. Young monkeys will see adult females nursing and suckling infants: if infant females are more disposed to learn from other females rather than from males, then they could be biased to attend to infants. This would simply put the question of what determines gender-related behaviour one step further back: why are infants biased to learn from same-sex adults?

25 The Minsterley Show, Shropshire, continues to judge the best-looking farm animals on parade, but not the babies: http://www.minsterleyshow.org.uk/ [accessed: 01/12/09].

26 Hildebrandt, K.A. & Fitzgerald, H.E. (1979) Adult perceptions of infant sex and cuteness. *Sex Roles* 5: 471–481.
    Hildebrandt, K.A. & Fitgerald, H.E. (1979) Facial feature determinants of perceived infant attractiveness. *Infant Behaviour and Development* 2: 329–339.

27 The same argument may explain why premature babies look less cute the more prematurely they are born. From 31 weeks to full term (40 weeks), a baby's face gets wider, the eyes get larger, and the forehead increases in size.

28 Badr, L.K. & Abdallah, B. (2001) Physical attractiveness of premature infants affects outcome at discharge from the NICU. *Infant Behaviour and Development* 24: 129–133.

29 Perrett, D.I., Lee, K., Penton-Voak, I., Burt, D.M., Rowland, D., Yoshikawa, S., Henzi, S.P., Castles, D. & Akamatsu, S. (1998) Sexual dimorphism and facial attractiveness. *Nature* 394: 884–886.
    For a more detailed discussion of the impact of masculinity on attractiveness of adults, see Chapter 5.

30 The left face in Figure N is composed of baby girls' faces and the right image is composed of baby boys' faces.
    Wiffen, B. (2007) *What Makes Babies Cute? Testing Preferences for Masculinity and Femininity in Baby Faces*. University of St Andrews: BSc thesis.

31 Hildebrandt, K.A. & Fitzgerald, H.E. (1979) Adult perceptions of infant sex and cuteness. *Sex Roles* 5: 471–481.

32 Wiffen, B. (2007) *What Makes Babies Cute? Testing Preferences for Masculinity and Femininity in Baby Faces*. British Psychology Society Scottish Branch Undergraduate Conference, 14/3/07. University of Edinburgh.

33 Many African monkeys have natal coats – fur that differs in colour from adults. Human hair colour and texture often change through infancy and childhood, something that is very noticeable in Caucasians. Such changes could augment the infant schema.

34 Daly, M. & Wilson, M. (1985) Child abuse and other risks of not living with both parents. *Ethology and Sociobiology* 6: 197–210.

35 Justice, B. & Justice, R. (1976) *The Abusing Family*. New York: Human Sciences Press.

36 McCabe, V. (1984) Abstract perceptual information for age level: a risk-factor for maltreatment? *Child Development* 55: 267–276.

37 McCabe, V. (1988) Facial proportions, perceived age and care-giving. In: Alley, T.R. (ed.) *Social and Applied Aspects of Perceiving Faces*, pp. 89–100. Hillsdale, N.J.: Lawrence Erlbaum.

38 Zebrowitz, L.A., Kendall-Tackett, K. & Fafel, J. (1991) The influence of children's facial maturity on parental expectations and punishment. *Journal of Experimental Child Psychology* 52: 221–238.

39 Rosenthal, R. & Jacobson, L. (1992) *Pygmalion in the Classroom: Teacher Expectation and Pupils' Intellectual Development* (expanded edition). New York: Irvington.

40 Cornwell, R.E. (2005) *Sexual Dimorphism in Faces Across Development through Early Adulthood: Perceptions, Attributions and Stability*. University of St Andrews: PhD thesis.

41 Cornwell, R.E. & Perrett, D.I. (2008) Sexy sons and sexy daughters: the influence of parents' facial characteristics on offspring. *Animal Behaviour* 76: 1843–1853.

42 Law Smith, M. (2006) *Human Face Characteristics in Relation to Age, Health and Hormones*. University of St Andrews: PhD thesis.

43 Thomas, F., Renaud, F., Benefice, E., de Meeus, T. & Guegan, J.-F. (2001) International variability of ages at menarche and menopause: patterns and main determinants. *Human Biology* 73: 271–290.

44 It should prove possible to test this conjecture by comparing photographs and records.

45 Kligman, A.M. & Graham, J.A. (1986) The psychology of appearance in the elderly. *Dermatologic Clinincs* 4: 501–507.
   Olde Rikkert, M.G.M. (1999) Visual estimation of biological age of elderly subjects: good interrater agreement. *Gerontology* 45: 165–167.

46 Alternatively, the individual who is ageing slowly may have lived in a more physically and emotionally benign environment than an individual who appears old for her or his age.

47 George, J., Bada, J., Zeh, J., Scott, L. & Brown, S. (1999) Age and growth estimates of bowhead whales (*Balaena mysticetus*) via aspartic acid racemization. *Canadian Journal of Zoology* 77: 571–580.

48 Kalichman, L., Livshits, G. & Kobyliansky, E. (2006) Association between morbidity and skeletal biomarkers of biological aging. *Human Biology* 78: 77–88.

49 Karasik, D., Demissie, S., Cupples, L.A. & Kiel, D.P. (2005) Disentangling the genetic determinants of human aging: biological age as an alternative to the use of survival measures. *The Journals of Gerontology, Series A: Biological Sciences and Medical Sciences* 60: 574–587.

50 De Sandre-Giovannoli, A., Bernard, R., Cau, P., Navarro, C., Amiel, J., Boccaccio, I., Lyonnet, S., Stewart, C.L., Munnich, A., Le Merrer, M. &

Lévy, N. (2003) Lamin A truncation in Hutchinson-Gilford progeria. *Science* 300: 2055.

51 Norman, R.A. (2007) *Diagnosis of Aging Skin Diseases.* New York: Springer.

52 Hayakawa, K., Shimizu, T., Ohba, Y., Tomioka, S., Takahasi, S., Amano, K., Yura, A., Yokoyama, Y. & Hayakata, Y. (1992) Intrapair differences of physical aging and longevity in identical twins. *Acta Geneticae Medicae et Gemellologiae (Roma)* 41: 177–185.

 Gunn, D.A., Rexbye, H., Griffiths, C.E.M., Murray, P.G., Fereday, A., Catt, S. D., Tomlin, C.C., Strongitharm, B.H., Perrett, D.I., Catt, M., Mayes, A. E., Messenger, A.G., Green, M.R., van der Ouderaa, F., Vaupel, J. W. & Christensen, K. (2009) Why some women look young for their age. *Public Library of Science ONE* 4: e8021.

53 Nyholt, D.R., Gillespie, N.A., Heath, A.C. & Martin, N.G. (2003) Genetic basis of male pattern baldness. *Journal of Investigative Dermatology* 121: 1561–1564.

54 See also: Bulpitt, C.J., Markowe, H.L.J. & Shipley, M.J. (2001) Why do some people look older than they should? *Postgraduate Medical Journal* 77: 578–581.

55 Perrett, D.I., Lee, K., Penton-Voak, I., Burt, D.M., Rowland, D., Yoshikawa, S., Henzi, S.P., Castles, D. & Akamatsu, S. (1998) Sexual dimorphism and facial attractiveness. *Nature* 394: 884–886.

 Boothroyd, L.G., Jones, B.C., Burt, D.M. & Perrett, D.I. (2007) Partner characteristics associated with masculinity, health and maturity in male faces. *Personality and Individual Differences* 43: 1161–1173.

 Boothroyd, L.G., Jones, B.C., Burt, D.M., Cornwell, R.E., Little, A.C., Tiddeman, B.P. & Perrett, D.I. (2005) Facial masculinity is related to perceived age but not perceived health. *Evolution and Human Behaviour* 26: 417–431.

56 Boothroyd, L.G., Jones, B.C., Burt, D.M., Cornwell, R.E., Little, A.C., Tiddeman, B.P. & Perrett, D.I. (2005) Facial masculinity is related to perceived age but not perceived health. *Evolution and Human Behaviour* 26: 417–431.

57 Mealey, L. (2000) *Sex Differences: Developmental and Evolutionary Strategies.* New York: Academic Press.

58 Burt, D.M. & Perrett, D.I. (1995) Perception of age in adult Caucasian male faces: computer graphic manipulation of shape and colour information. *Proceedings of the Royal Society B* 259: 137–143.

59 If the heart and lungs don't work as well as they should, then there is a reduction in the amount of oxygen carried in the blood. This can turn the blood more purple in colour, with the result that people's faces can take on a rather unhealthy-looking bluish caste (see Chapter 7).

60 Tiddeman, B.P., Perrett, D.I. & Burt, D.M. (2001) Prototyping and transforming facial textures for perception research. *IEEE Computer Graphics and Applications, Research* 21: 42–50.

 Tiddeman, B.P., Stirrat, M.R. & Perrett, D.I. (2005) Towards realism in facial image archetyping, results of a wavelet MRF method. *Proceedings of the Theory & Practice of Computer Graphics Conference* 103–111.

61 Dupati, A. & Helfrich, Y.R. (2009) Effect of cigarette smoking on skin aging. *Expert Review of Dermatology* 4: 371–378.

62 BBC News: http://news.bbc.co.uk/newsbeat/hi/health/newsid_7813000/7813903.stm [accessed: 01/12/09].

63 Brown, E. & Perrett, D.I. (1993) What gives a face its gender? *Perception* 22: 829–840.

Chapter 9

1 'The face is the soul of the body' and 'human body is the best picture of the human soul' are quotes attributed to Wittgenstein.
   For discussion, see: Richter, D. (2004) *Historical Dictionary of Wittgenstein's Philosophy*. Lanham, Maryland: Scarecrow Press, p.177.
2 Cole, J. (1998) *About Face*. Cambridge, Massachusetts: MIT Press.
3 Mischel, W. & Shoda, Y. (1995) A cognitive-affective system theory of personality: reconceptualizing situations, dispositions, dynamics, and invariance in personality structure. *Psychological Review* 102: 246–268.
4 Galton, F. (1884) Measurement of character. *Fortnightly Review* 36: 179–185.
5 The association between the different adjectives that people apply to themselves is approximate – many quiet people may also describe themselves as 'emotional' and 'friendly', but in general those people who are loud and gregarious are more likely to claim that the 'emotional' and 'friendly' labels apply strongly to themselves.
6 Tupes, E.C. & Christal, R.E. (1961) Recurrent personality factors based on trait ratings. *USAF ASD Technical Report* (No. 61–96). Reprinted in 2008: *Journal of Personality* 60: 225–251.
7 McCrae, R.R. & Costa, P.T. (1987) Validation of the five factor model of personality across instruments and observers. *Journal of Personality and Social Psychology* 52: 81–90.
8 Tracy, J.L. & Matsumoto, D. (2008) The spontaneous expression of pride and shame: evidence for biologically innate nonverbal displays. *Proceedings of the National Academies of Sciences* 105: 11655–11660.
9 Lavater, J.K. (1775–1778) *Physiognomische Fragmente zur Beförderung der Menschenkenntnis und Menschenliebe*. Leipzig.
10 Walker, A. (1834) *Physiognomy Founded on Physiology, and Applied to Various Countries, Professions, and Individuals: with an Appendix on the Bones at Hythe, the Sculls of the Ancient Inhabitants of Britain and its Invaders*. London: Smith, Elder & Co.
11 Fahnestock, J. (1981) The heroine of irregular features: physiognomy and conventions of heroine description. *Victorian Studies* 24: 325–350.
12 Galton, F. (1878) Composite portraits, made by combining those of many different persons into a single resultant figure. *Journal of the Anthropological Institute of Great Britain and Ireland* 8: 132–142.
13 Stirrat, M.R. & Perrett, D.I. (2010) Valid facial cues to cooperation and trust: male facial width and trustworthiness. *Psychological Science* 21: 349–354.
14 Cleeton, G.U. & Knight, F.B. (1924) The validity of character judgments based on external criteria. *Journal of Applied Psychology* 8: 215–231.
15 Hassin, R. & Trope, Y. (2000) Facing faces: studies on the cognitive aspects of physiognomy. *Journal of Personality and Social Psychology* 78: 837–852.
16 Cleeton, G.U. & Knight, F.B. (1924) The validity of character judgments based on external criteria. *Journal of Applied Psychology* 8: 215–231.
17 Todorov, A., Mandisodza, A.N., Goren, A. & Hall, C.C. (2005) Inferences of competence from faces predict election outcomes. *Science* 308: 1623–1626.

18 Rule, N.O. & Ambady, N. (2008) The face of success: inferences from Chief Executive Officers' appearance predict company profits. *Psychological Science* 19: 109–111.

19 Zebrowitz, L.A. (1997) *Reading Faces: Window to the Soul?* Boulder, Colorado: Westview Press.

20 Albright, L., Malloy, T.E., Dong, Q., Kenny, D.A., Fang, X., Winquist, L. & Yu, D. (1997) Cross-cultural consensus in personality judgments. *Journal of Personality and Social Psychology* 72: 558–69.

21 Gosling, S.D., Ko, S.J., Mannarelli, T. & Morris, M.E. (2002) A room with a cue: personality judgments based on offices and bedrooms. *Journal of Personality and Social Psychology* 82: 379–398.

22 The left-hand image of each pair is the more extrovert.

23 Penton-Voak, I.S., Pound, N., Little, A.C. & Perrett, D.I. (2006) Personality judgments from natural and composite face images: more evidence for a 'kernel of truth'. *Social Cognition* 24: 490–524.
    Little, A.C. & Perrett, D.I. (2007) Using composite images to assess accuracy in personality attribution to faces. *British Journal of Psychology* 98: 111–126.

24 Boothroyd, L.G., Jones, B.C., Burt, D.M., DeBruine, L.M. & Perrett, D.I. (2008) Facial correlates of sociosexuality. *Evolution & Human Behavior* 29: 211–218.

25 Of course, not everyone may agree that being 'extrovert, conscientious, open to experience, agreeable, and emotionally stable' represents a positive set of characteristics, and in any case there are limits to the level at which any characteristic remains admirable.

26 Penton-Voak, I.S., Pound, N., Little, A.C. & Perrett, D.I. (2006) Personality judgments from natural and composite face images: more evidence for a 'kernel of truth'. *Social Cognition* 24: 490–524.

27 Penton-Voak, I.S., Pound, N., Little, A.C. & Perrett, D.I. (2006) Personality judgments from natural and composite face images: more evidence for a 'kernel of truth'. *Social Cognition* 24: 490–524.

28 Little, A.C. & Perrett, D.I. (2007) Using composite images to assess accuracy in personality attribution to faces. *British Journal of Psychology* 98: 111–126.

29 Boothroyd, L.G., Jones, B.C., Burt, D.M., DeBruine, L.M. & Perrett, D.I. (2008) Facial correlates of sociosexuality. *Evolution & Human Behavior* 29: 211–218.

30 Kagan, J. & Snidman, N. (2004) *The Long Shadow of Temperament*. Cambridge, Massachusetts: Harvard University Press.

31 Jang. K.L., Livesley, W.J. & Vemon, P.A. (2006) Heritability of the Big Five personality dimensions and their facets: a twin study. *Journal of Personality* 64: 577–592.

32 Seavey, A.A., Katz, P.A. & Zalk, S.R. (1975) Baby X: the effects of gender labels on adult responses to infants. *Sex Roles* 1: 103–109.

33 Orwell, G. (1949) Last words written in his notebook. http://www.britanica.com [accessed: 12/8/09].

34 Malatesta, C.Z., Fiore, M.J. & Messina, J.J. (1987) Affect, personality and facial expression characteristics of older people. *Psychology and Aging* 2: 64–69.

35 Perrett, D.I., Lee, K., Penton-Voak, I., Burt, D.M., Rowland, D., Yoshikawa, S., Henzi, S.P., Castles, D. & Akamatsu, S. (1998) Sexual dimorphism and facial attractiveness. *Nature* 394: 884–886.

36 Zebrowitz, L., Hall, J.A., Murphy, N.A. & Rhodes, G. (2002) Looking smart and looking good: facial cues to intelligence and their origins. *Personality and Social Psychology Bulletin* 28: 238–249.

37 Facial appearance and IQ scores vary across any defined group of people, yet – despite notable exceptions – group differences *do* exist as general tendencies. While it is not necessarily undesirable to make the associations between facial appearance and behaviour or capability, it *is* undesirable to be discriminatory or to make negative judgements about appearances or capabilities.

38 Langlois, J. & Roggman, L.A. (1990) Attractive faces are only average. *Psychological Science* 1: 115–121. (See Chapter 4.)

39 Zebrowitz, L. & Rhodes, G. (2002) Sensitivity to 'bad genes' and the anomalous face overgeneralization effect: cue validity, cue utilization, and accuracy in judging intelligence and health. *Journal of Nonverbal Behavior* 28: 167–185.

40 Perrett, D.I. & Yoshikawa, S. Unpublished studies.

41 Moore, F.R., Filipou, D. & Perrett, D.I. Apparent intelligence and femininity in female faces. Unpublished studies.

42 Buss, D.M. & Schmitt, D.P. (1993) Sexual strategies theory: an evolutionary perspective on human mating. *Psychological Review* 100: 204–232.

43 Buss, D.M. & Schmitt, D.P. (1993) Sexual strategies theory: an evolutionary perspective on human mating. *Psychological Review* 100: 204–232.

44 Zebrowitz, L.A. & McDonald, S. (1991) The impact of litigants' baby-facedness and attractiveness on adjudications in small claims courts. *Law and Human Behaviour* 15: 603–623.

45 Keating, C.F., Randall, D. & Kendrick, T. (2002) Presidential physiognomies: altered images, altered perceptions. *Political Psychology* 20: 593–610.

46 Kniffin, K.M. & Wildon, D.S. (2004) The effect of nonphysical traits on the perception of physical attractiveness: three naturalistic studies. *Evolution and Human Behaviour* 25: 88–101.

47 Buss, D.M. (1989) Sex differences in human mate preferences: evolutionary hypotheses tested in 37 cultures. *Behavioural and Brain Sciences* 12: 1–49.

48 Little, A.C., Burt, D.M. & Perrett, D.I. (2006) What is good is beautiful: face preference reflects desired personality. *Personality and Individual Differences* 41: 1107–1118.

49 Zentner, M.R. (2005) Ideal mate personality concepts and compatibility in close relationships: a longitudinal analysis. *Journal of Personality and Social Psychology* 89: 242–256.

50 Little, A.C., Burt, D.M. & Perrett, D.I. (2006) Assortative mating for perceived personality in faces. *Personality and Individual Differences* 40: 973–984.

51 Little, A.C., Burt, D.M. & Perrett, D.I. (2006) Assortative mating for perceived personality in faces. *Personality and Individual Differences* 40: 973–984.

52 Zajonc, R.B., Adelmann, P.K., Murphy, S.T. & Niendenthal, P.M. (1987) Convergence in the physical appearance of spouses. *Motivation and Emotion* 11: 335–346.

53 Hill, C.T., Rubin, Z. & Peplau, L. A. (1976) Breakups before marriage: the end of 103 affairs. *Journal of Social Issues* 32: 147–168.

Arrindell, W.A. & Luteijn, F. (2000) Similarity between intimate partners for personality traits as related to individual levels of satisfaction with life. *Personality and Individual Differences* 28: 629–637.

Chapter 10

1 *The Guardian*: http://www.guardian.co.uk/uk/2008/jan/12/uknews4 mainsection2 [accessed 18/12/09].

2 Penton-Voak, I.S., Perrett, D.I. & Pierce, J. (1999) Computer graphic studies of facial similarity and judgements of attractiveness. *Current Psychology* 18: 104–118.

3 These were created from a few unusual-looking women.

4 This was true even if the women had very unusual face features and the twin shared the same unusual features.

5 As an aside, we could turn the argument around and explain the attractiveness of faces with average proportions (see Chapter 4) by reference to our yearning for a familiar self-like appearance. An 'average face' is one that is similar to most of us, and hence most of us might like it because it reminds us of ourselves.

6 DeBruine, L.M. (2005) Trustworthy but not lust-worthy: context-specific effects of facial resemblance. *Proceedings of the Royal Society B* 272: 919–922.

DeBruine, L.M. (2004) Facial resemblance increases the attractiveness of same-sex faces more than other-sex faces. *Proceedings of the Royal Society B* 271: 2085–2090.

There is now evidence that women can be attracted to self-similar men's faces, but only under particular circumstances – for example, if the man looks highly masculine and is being considered for a short-term relationship. The worries about masculine men in this context may be offset by the sense of familiarity and trust engendered by the family looks:

Saxton, T.K., Little, A.C., Rowland, H.M., Gao, T. & Roberts, S.C. (2009) Trade-offs between markers of absolute and relative quality in human facial preferences. *Behavioral Ecology* 20: 1113–1137.

Another suggestion is that attractive women like self-similarity in men's faces, but unattractive women do not:

Little, A.C. & Roberts, C. Unpublished studies.

7 Kocsor, F., Rezneki, R., Juhász, Sz. & Bereczkei, T. (2009) Preference for self-resemblance in human mate choice. Symposium on *Non-verbal Aspects of Mate-choice and Courtship*, Fifth International Anthropological Congress of Aleš Hrdlička. Prague, Czech Republic.

8 Spouses are more different from one another in their immune genes than would be expected by chance. This dissimilarity has been noted in relatively small populations that choose not to breed outside that population:

Ober, C., Weitkamp, L.R., Cox, N., Dylek, H., Kostyn, D. & Elias, S. (1997) HLA and mate choice in humans. *American Journal of Human Genetics* 61: 497–504.

Immune gene differences between married partners have *not* been found in studies of some other populations:

Hedrick, P.W. & Black, F.L. (1997) HLA and mate selection: no evidence in South Amerindians. *American Journal of Human Genetics* 61: 505–511.

Havlicek, J. & Roberts, S.C. (2009) MHC-correlated mate choice in humans: a review. *Psychoneuroendocrinology* 34: 497–512.

9 These genes are known as the human leukocyte antigen (HLA) or major histocompatibility (MHC) genes.

Knapp, L.A. (2005) The ABCs of MHC. *Evolutionary Anthropology* 14: 28–37.

10 Wedekind, C. & Furi, S. (1997) Body odour preferences in men and women: do they aim for specific MHC combinations or simply heterozygosity? *Proceedings of the Royal Society B* 264: 1471–1479.

Thornhill, R., Gangestad, S.W., Miller, R., Scheyd, G., McCullough, J.K. & Franklin, M. (2003) Major histocompatibility genes, symmetry and body scent attractiveness in men and women. *Behavioral Ecology* 14: 668–678.

Jacob, S., McClintock, M.K., Zelano, B. & Ober, C. (2002) Paternally inherited HLA alleles are associated with women's choice of male odor. *Nature Genetics* 30: 175–179.

11 Roberts, S.C., Little, A.C., Gosling, L.M., Jones, B.C., Perrett, D.I., Carter, V. & Petrie, M. (2005) MHC-assortative facial preferences in humans. *Biology Letters* 1: 400–403.

12 *The Telegraph*: http://www.telegraph.co.uk/news/worldnews/1565861/Birth-mix-up-mother-refuses-to-swap-babies.html [accessed: 14/12/09].

The Scotsman: http://news.scotsman.com/weirdoddandquirkystories/Parents-agree-to-swap-their.3467552.jp [accessed: 14/12/09].

13 Kendrick, K.M., Hinton, M.R., Atkins, K., Haupt, M.A. & Skinner, J.D. (1998) Mothers determine male sexual preferences. *Nature* 395: 229–230.

14 Perrett, D.I., Penton-Voak, I.S., Little, A.C., Tiddeman, B.P., Burt, D.M., Schmidt, N., Oxley, R. & Barrett, L. (2002) Facial attractiveness judgements reflect learning of parental age characteristics. *Proceedings of the Royal Society B* 269: 873–880.

15 Little, A.C., Penton-Voak, I.S., Burt, D.M. & Perrett, D.I. (2003) Investigating an imprinting-like phenomenon in humans: partners and opposite-sex parents have similar hair and eye colour. *Evolution and Human Behavior* 24: 43–51.

16 Wiszewska, A., Pawlowski, B. & Boothroyd, L.G. (2007) Father–daughter relationship as a moderator of sexual imprinting: a facialmetric study. *Evolution & Human Behavior* 28: 248–252.

17 Bereczkei, T., Gyuris, P., Koves, P. & Bernath, L. (2002) Homogamy, genetic similarity, and imprinting; parental influence on mate choice preferences. *Personality and Individual Differences* 33: 677–690.

Bereczkei, T., Gyuris, P. & Weisfeld, G.E. (2004) Sexual imprinting in human mate choice. *Proceedings of the Royal Society B* 271: 1129–1134.

Bereczkei, T., Hegedus, G. & Hajnal, G. (2009) Facialmetric similarities mediate mate choice: sexual imprinting on opposite-sex parents. *Proceedings of the Royal Society B* 276: 91–98.

This paper was subsequently retracted by the journal because of statistical errors affecting the similarity assessments of male subjects' mates and parents: *Proceedings Biological Sciences* 276: 1199. (2009) http://www.pubmedcentral. nih.gov/articlerender.fcgi?artid=2679089 [accessed: 8/12/09].

18 Bereczkei, T., Gyuris, P. & Weisfeld, G.E. (2004) Sexual imprinting in human mate choice. *Proceedings of the Royal Society B* 271: 1129–1134.

19 Bereczkei, T., Gyuris, P., Koves, P. & Bernath, L. (2002) Homogamy, genetic similarity, and imprinting; parental influence on mate choice preferences. *Personality and Individual Difference* 33: 677–690.

20 Gyuris, P. (2003) *Homogamy, Imprinting, Evolution: Mate Choice of Women and Men Rearing in Various Family Environments*. University of Pécs, Hungary: PhD thesis. [In Hungarian.]

Similar results have been described: Bereczkei, T., Hegedus, G. & Hajnal, G. (2009) Facialmetric similarities mediate mate choice: sexual imprinting on opposite-sex parents. *Proceedings of the Royal Society B* 276: 91–98. See the comment above (note 17) about the status of this paper.

21 This might seem surprising, as spouses are similar, but note that similarity can lie anywhere between a slight match and an exact match for an identical twin.

In the end, there might be a slight similarity between the same-sex parent and the spouse as well, but the studies to date show a greater similarity to the opposite-sex parent than to the same-sex parent.

22 Studies of adopted individuals do not rule out effects of inherited preferences: these could be additional to any learning or imprinting on parents' characteristics.

23 Bereczkei, T., Gyuris, P. & Weisfeld, G.E. (2004) Sexual imprinting in human mate choice. *Proceedings of the Royal Society B* 271: 1129–1134.

24 The appropriate match is bottom left.

25 Jacob, S., McClintock, M.K., Zelano, B. & Ober, C. (2002) Paternally inherited HLA alleles are associated with women's choice of male odor. *Nature Genetics* 30: 175–179.

26 Perrett, D.I., Penton-Voak, I.S., Little, A.C., Tiddeman, B.P., Burt, D.M., Schmidt, N., Oxley, R. & Barrett, L. (2002) Facial attractiveness judgements reflect learning of parental age characteristics. *Proceedings of the Royal Society B* 269: 873–880.

27 Bereczkei, T., Gyuris, P., Koves, P. & Bernath, L. (2002) Homogamy, genetic similarity, and imprinting; parental influence on mate choice preferences. *Personality and Individual Differences* 33: 677–690.

28 Bittles, A.H., Mason, W.M., Greene, J. & Rao, N.A. (1991) Reproductive behavior and health in consanguineous marriages. *Science* 252: 789–794.

29 Bateson, P. (1978) Sexual imprinting and optimal outbreeding. *Nature* 273: 659–660.
   Bateson, P. (1980) Optimal outbreeding and the development of sexual preferences in Japanese quail. *Zeitschrift für Tierpsychologie* 53: 231–244.

30 Jedlicka, D. (1980) A test of the psychoanalytic theory of mate selection. *Journal of Social Psychology* 112: 295–299.

31 Apostolou, M. (2007) Sexual selection under parental choice: the role of parents in the evolution of human mating. *Evolution and Human Behavior* 28: 403–409.

32 Yu, D.W., Proulx, S.M. & Shepard, G.H. (2008) Masculinity, marriage and the paradox of the lek. In: Swami, V. & Furmham, A. (eds) *The Body Beautiful*, pp. 88–107. New York: Palgrave Macmillan.

33 Little, A.C., Jones, B.C., DeBruine, L.M. & Caldwell, C.A. (2009) Social influences on facial attractiveness judgements. Symposium on *Non-verbal Aspects of Mate-choice and Courtship*: Fifth International Anthropological Congress of Aleš Hrdlička. Prague, Czech Republic.

34 Little, A.C., Burriss, R.P., Jones, B.C., DeBruine, L.M. & Caldwell, C.C. (2008) Social influence in human face preference: men and women are influenced for long-term but not short-term attractiveness decisions. *Evolution and Human Behavior* 29: 140–146.
   You might think that we should not presume that a woman pictured next to a man is actually his partner; she could be there by accident. Providing a label stating that she is the man's partner does mean that she has far more effect on observers' judgements of his attractiveness than a woman labelled a non-partner.

35 Little, A.C., Jones, B.C., DeBruine, L.M. & Caldwell, C.A. (2009) Social influences on facial attractiveness judgements. Symposium on *Non-verbal Aspects of Mate-choice and Courtship*: Fifth International Anthropological Congress of Aleš Hrdlička. Prague, Czech Republic.

36 Jones, B.C., DeBruine, L.M., Little, A.C., Burriss, R.P. & Feinberg, D.R. (2007) Social transmission of face preferences among humans. *Proceedings of the Royal Society B* 274: 899–903.

Chapter 11

1 Schachter, S. & Singer, J.E. (1962) Cognitive, social and physiological determinants of emotional state. *Psychological Review* 69: 379–99.
2 Grezes, J. (2008) Processing emotions in body expressions. First meeting of the Federation of the European Societies of Neuropsychology, 9/08. Edinburgh.
  Moriguchi, Y., Decety, J., Ohnishi, T., Maeda, M., Mori, T., Nemoto, K., Matsuda, H. & Komaki, G. (2007) Empathy and judging others' pain: an fMRI study of alexithymia. *Cerebral Cortex* 17: 2223–2234.
3 Dienstbier, R.A. (1979) Attraction increases and decreases as a function of emotion-attribution and appropriate social cues. *Motivation and Emotion* 3: 201–218.
4 The interpretation advanced in previous literature is that arousal is likely to cause attraction.
5 Lewandowski Jr, G.W. & Aron, A.R. (2004) Distinguishing arousal from novelty and challenge in initial romantic attraction between strangers. *Social Behavior and Personality* 32: 361–372.
6 Dutton, D.G. & Aron, A.P. (1974) Some evidence for heightened sexual attraction under conditions of high anxiety. *Journal of Personality and Social Psychology* 30: 510–517.
7 O'Doherty, J., Winston, J., Critchley, H., Perrett, D.I., Burt, D.M. & Dolan, R.J. (2003) Beauty in a smile: the role of medial orbitofrontal cortex in facial attractiveness. *Neuropsychologia* 41: 147–155.
  Kampe, K.K., Frith, C.D., Dolan, R.J. & Frith, U. (2001) Reward value of attractiveness and gaze. *Nature* 413: 589.
8 Conway, C.A., Jones, B.C., DeBruine, L.M. & Little, A.C. (2008) Evidence for adaptive design in human gaze preference. *Proceedings of the Royal Society B* 275: 63–69.
9 Lobmaier, J.S., Tiddeman, B.P. & Perrett, D.I. (2008) Emotional expression modulates perceived gaze direction. *Emotion* 8: 573–577.
  Lobmaier, J.S. & Perrett, D.I. (2010) The world smiles at me: self-referential positivity bias when interpreting direction of attention. Cognition and Emotion (In press.)
10 Mullins, C. (2009) *Are You Interested? Preferred Head Orientation Changes with Attractiveness.* University of St Andrews: MSc thesis.
11 Sternberg, R.J. (1986) A triangular theory of love. *Psychology Review* 93: 119–135.
12 Becker, A.J., Uckert, S., Ness, B.O., Stief, C.G., Scheller, F., Knapp, W.H. & Jonas, U. (2003) Oxytocin plasma levels in the systemic and cavernous blood of healthy males during different penile conditions. *World Journal of Urology* 31: 66–69.
  Segarra, G., Medina, P., Domenech, C., Vila, J.M., Martínez-León, J.B., Aldasoro, M. & Lluch, S. (1998) Role of vasopressin on adrenergic neurotransmission in human penile blood vessels. *Pharmacology* 286: 1315–1320.
13 In rats and mice, anyway, it is clear that the two hormone systems also affect social learning about friends, not just about lovers. Mice that have been genetically engineered to lack receptors for either chemical fail to

recognize neighbours, who should be familiar because they have met before. Supplements of the chemicals to the relevant brain systems can restore or enhance social learning.

See: Bielsky, I.F. & Young L.J. (2004) Oxytocin, vasopressin, and social recognition in mammals. *Peptides* 25: 1565–1574.

14 It is interesting that the same gene variation affects both the clinical symptoms of the disease and face perception. The more repetitions there are within the gene, the harder it is for people who carry Huntington's disease to recognize the facial emotion of disgust.

Gray, J.M., Young, A.W., Barker, W.A., Curtis, A. & Gibson, D. (1997) Impaired recognition of disgust in Huntington's disease gene carriers. *Brain* 120: 2029–2038.

15 The men might have one copy of the longer gene from one parent and one shorter gene from the other parent, or two of the longer genes (one from each parent), or two of the shorter genes.

16 Walum, H., Westberg, L., Henningsson, S., Neiderhiser, J.M., Reiss, D., Igl, W., Ganiban, J.M., Spotts, E.L., Pedersen, N.L., Eriksson, E. & Lichtenstein, P. (2008) Genetic variation in the vasopressin receptor 1a gene (AVPR1A) associates with pair-bonding behavior in humans. *Proceedings National Academy of Science U.S.A.* 105: 14153–14156.

17 Kendrick, K.M., Da Costa, A.P.C., Broad, K.D., Ohkura, S., Guevara, R., Lévy, F. & Keverne, E.B. (1997) Neural control of maternal behaviour and olfactory recognition of offspring. *Brain Research Bulletin* 44: 383–395.

Keverne, E.B., Levy, F., Poindron, P. & Lindsay, D.R. (1983) Vaginal stimulation: an important determinant of maternal bonding in sheep. *Science* 219: 81–83.

18 Swain, J.E., Tasgin, E., Mayes, L.C., Feldman, R., Constable, R.T. & Leckman, J.F. (2008) Maternal brain response to own baby-cry is affected by cesarean section delivery. *Journal of Child Psychology and Psychiatry* 49: 1042–1052.

19 Bartels, A. & Zeki, S. (2004) The neural correlates of maternal and romantic love. *NeuroImage* 21: 1155–1166.

20 Taylor, A., Atkins, R., Kumar, R., Adams, D. & Glover, V. (2005) A new mother-to-infant bonding scale: links with early maternal mood. *Journal Archives of Women's Mental Health* 8: 45–51.

21 Champagne, F.A. (2006) *The Role of Epigenetic Modification in Mediating Natural Variations in Reproductive Behavior*. Society for Behavioural Neuroendocrinology. Pittsburgh.

22 'Packaging' is a general term referring to the chemical environment that surrounds the DNA. This environment can hinder or facilitate the ease with which genes can be used to make hormone receptors. It's rather like the sales packaging around an appliance you buy: until you remove this, the appliance may be useless.

23 Ainsworth, M., Blehar, M., Waters, E. & Wall, S. (1978) *Patterns of Attachment.* Hillsdale, NJ: Lawrence Erlbaum.

24 Fraley, R.C. & Shaver, P.R. (2000) Adult romantic attachment: theoretical developments, emerging controversies, and unanswered questions. *Review of General Psychology* 4: 132–154.

25 Belsky, J., Steinberg, L. & Draper, P. (1991) Childhood experience, interpersonal development and reproductive strategy: an evolutionary theory of socialisation. *Child Development* 62: 647–670.

26 *March of the Penguins* (2005) Warner Independent Pictures (US) / Lionsgate Films (Canada).

27 Davis, L.S. & Speirs, E.A.H. (1990) Mate choice in penguins. In: Davis, L.S. & Darby, J.T. (eds) *Penguin Biology*, pp. 377–397. San Diego, California: Academic Press.

28 Webster, A. (2000) Divorce rates by length of marriage – summary of methods and results. Tenth Biennial Conference of the Australian Population Association, 11/00. Melbourne, Australia.

U.S. Department of Health and Human Services (2009). Births, marriages, divorces, and deaths: provisional data for 2008. *National Vital Statistics Reports* 57: 19 (2009).

29 Keverne, E.B., Martensz, N.D. & Tuite, B. (1989) Beta-endorphin concentrations in cerebrospinal fluid of monkeys are influenced by grooming relationships. *Psychoneuroendocrinology* 14: 155–161.

Natural opiates are also produced during physical exercise and sex:

Goldfarb, A.H. & Jamurtas, A.Z. (1997) Beta-endorphin response to exercise: an update. *Sports Medicine* 24: 8–16.

30 Kalina, N.H., Sheltona, S.E. & Lynna, D.E. (1995) Opiate systems in mother and infant primates coordinate intimate contact during reunion. *Psychoneuroendocrinology* 20: 735–742.

31 Higgins, D.H. (ed.) (1998) Dante: *The Divine Comedy*, transl. Sisson, C.H. from Alighieri, D. (1308–1321): *Commedia*. Oxford: Oxford University Press. Inferno Circle 2, canto 5.

Longfellow, H.W. (transl.): http://italian.about.com/library/anthology/dante/blinfernoindex.htm [accessed: 10/12/09].

32 This was a surprise result that emerged in a show-of-hands survey in a Café Scientific discussion of the basis of attraction, 2008. Photographers' Gallery, London.

INDEX

Key: **bold**=extended discussion or term highlighted in the text; f=figure; n=endnote.